THE IMPACT OF INTERNATIONAL LAW ON INTERNATIONAL COOPERATION

Theoretical Perspectives

The point of departure of this book is that the disciplines of international law and international relations are inexorably inter-linked. Neither can be understood properly in isolation. Like every legal system that operates in a specific societal system, international law functions in the international system. International law grows out of the international society: it reflects the particular character of this society, and it also affects the relationships among the actors in this system. At the same time, international law produces norms that influence, if not shape, the behavior of international actors.

This book aims at advancing our understanding of the influences international norms and international institutions have over the incentives of states to cooperate on issues such as environment and trade. The different contributions to this book adopt two different approaches in examining this question. One approach focuses on the constitutive elements of the international legal order, including customary international law, soft law and framework conventions, and on the types of incentives states have, such as domestic incentives and reputation. The other approach examines closely specific issues in the areas of international environment protection and international trade. The combined outcome of these two approaches is a more refined understanding of the forces that pull states toward closer cooperation or prevents them from doing so, and the impact of different types of international norms and diverse institutions on the motivation of states. The insights gained suggest ways for enhancing states' incentives to cooperate through the design of norms and institutions.

EYAL BENVENISTI is Director, Cegla Center for Interdisciplinary Research of the Law, Tel Aviv University, Israel.

MOSHE HIRSCH is Vice Dean of the Faculty of Law and Senior Lecturer in the Faculty of Law and Department of International Relations, Hebrew University of Jerusalem, Israel.

THE IMPACT OF INTERNATIONAL LAW ON INTERNATIONAL COOPERATION

Theoretical Perspectives

edited by

EYAL BENVENISTI

MOSHE HIRSCH

CAMBRIDGE
UNIVERSITY PRESS

CAMBRIDGE UNIVERSITY PRESS
Cambridge, New York, Melbourne, Madrid, Cape Town,
Singapore, São Paulo, Delhi, Tokyo, Mexico City

Cambridge University Press
The Edinburgh Building, Cambridge CB2 8RU, UK

Published in the United States of America by Cambridge University Press, New York

www.cambridge.org
Information on this title: www.cambridge.org/9780521173407

© Cambridge University Press 2004

This publication is in copyright. Subject to statutory exception
and to the provisions of relevant collective licensing agreements,
no reproduction of any part may take place without the written
permission of Cambridge University Press.

First published 2004
First paperback edition 2011

A catalogue record for this publication is available from the British Library

ISBN 978-0-521-83554-1 Hardback
ISBN 978-0-521-17340-7 Paperback

Cambridge University Press has no responsibility for the persistence or
accuracy of URLs for external or third-party internet websites referred to in
this publication, and does not guarantee that any content on such websites is,
or will remain, accurate or appropriate.

CONTENTS

List of contributors page vii
Acknowledgments xi
List of abbreviations xii

1 Introduction 1
  EYAL BENVENISTI AND MOSHE HIRSCH

2 International law and international relations theory: a prospectus 16
  ANNE-MARIE SLAUGHTER

3 Pathways to international cooperation 50
  KENNETH W. ABBOTT AND DUNCAN SNIDAL

4 Customary international law as a judicial tool for promoting efficiency 85
  EYAL BENVENISTI

5 Reputation, compliance and development 117
  GEORGE W. DOWNS AND MICHAEL A. JONES

6 Rethinking compliance with international law 134
  EDITH BROWN WEISS

7 Compliance with international norms in the age of globalization: two theoretical perspectives 166
  MOSHE HIRSCH

8 Compliance and non-compliance with international norms in territorial disputes: the Latin American record of arbitrations 194
  ARIE M. KACOWICZ

9   International trade and domestic politics: the domestic sources of international trade agreements and institutions   216
    HELEN V. MILNER, B. PETER ROSENDORFF AND EDWARD D. MANSFIELD

10 Human rights, developing countries and the WTO constraint: the very thing that makes you rich makes me poor?   244
    PETROS C. MAVROIDIS

11 Back to court after *Shrimp–Turtle*: India's challenge to labor and environmental linkages in the EC generalized system of preferences   261
    ROBERT HOWSE

    Index   299

CONTRIBUTORS

Kenneth W. Abbott is the Elizabeth Froehling Horner Professor of Law and Commerce at Northwestern University School of Law, and Director of the Northwestern Center for International and Comparative Studies. Professor Abbott teaches courses on international organizations and governance, international trade and business, and international public health and environmental protection. He was the first American legal scholar to apply modern international relations theory to legal problems, and his research brings an interdisciplinary perspective to a range of international issues. He has lectured and taught in numerous countries around the world.

Eyal Benvenisti is Professor of Law at Tel Aviv University Faculty of Law and Director of the Cegla Center for Interdisciplinary Research of the Law. Previously Hersch Lauterpacht Professor of International Law at the Hebrew University of Jerusalem, Faculty of Law, and Director of the Minerva Center for Human Rights at the Hebrew University. Studied law at the Hebrew University of Jerusalem, (LLB), and Yale Law School (LLM, 1988; JSD, 1990). Taught at Harvard Law School, Columbia Law School, University of Michigan School of Law and New York University School of Law. Founding co-editor, and current Editor-in-Chief, Theoretical Inquiries in Law. Areas of teaching and research include constitutional law, international law, human rights and administrative law.

Edith Brown Weiss is the Francis Cabell Brown Professor of International Law at Georgetown University Law Center. She is the author or editor of ten books and numerous scholarly articles. Her book received the Certificate of Merit from the American Society of International Law (ASIL) for the most outstanding contribution to the development of international law. Edith Brown Weiss is the recipient of many other awards. She served as the Associate General Counsel for International at the US Environmental Protection Agency, where she established a new division for international and comparative environmental law. She was President of the American Society of International Law, and has been a member of the highest bodies of the US National Research Council, including the Commission on Geosciences, Environment and Resources and the Water Science and Technology Board.

George W. Downs is Dean of Social Science and Professor, Department of Politics, New York University. Areas of specialization are international institutions and international cooperation. Current research projects include books on the effectiveness of multilateral environmental agreements and on the role of reputation in promoting compliance with international regulatory agreements. He has authored or co-authored four books including *Tacit Bargaining, Arms Races and Arms Control,* and *Optimal Imperfection? Domestic Uncertainty and Institutions in International Relations,* edited a book on collective security after the Cold War and written articles in various political science, statistics and law journals. He is a member of the editorial boards of *World Politics* and *International Organization.*

Moshe Hirsch, Arnold Brecht Chair in European Law, is Vice Dean of the Faculty of Law and Senior Lecturer in the Faculty of Law and the Department of International Relations at the Hebrew University of Jerusalem. He is a member of the Think-Tank on the Future Status of Jerusalem, the Jerusalem Institute for Israel Studies. He is the author of *The Responsibility of International Organizations Toward Third Parties* (1995) and *The Arbitration Mechanism of the International Center for the Settlement of Investment Disputes* (1993). A significant part of his publications on various issues of international law and international economic law involves interdisciplinary research that employs, inter alia, game theory, sociological theories, politicial economy and political science.

Robert Howse is a Professor of Law at the University of Michigan Law School. Previously he taught at the Faculty of Law at the University of Toronto. He received his BA in Philosophy and Political Science with high distinction, as well as an LLB, with honours, from the University of Toronto. He also holds an LLM from the Harvard Law School and has traveled and studied Russian in the former Soviet Union. He has been a visiting professor at Harvard Law School and taught in the Academy of European Law, European University Institute, Florence. Professor Howse is a frequent consultant or adviser to government agencies and international organizations such as the OECD, and has undertaken studies for, among others, the Ontario Law Reform Commission and the Law Commission of Canada. His research has concerned a wide range of issues in international law and legal and political philosophy, but his emphasis has been on international trade and related regulatory issues.

Michael A. Jones is an Associate Professor in the Department of Mathematical Sciences at Montclair State University, New Jersey, and a Visiting Scholar in the Department of Politics at New York University. He specializes in the mathematics of the social sciences, including political science, economics and psychology. He has written many articles in political science, game theory and law journals.

Arie M. Kacowicz is a Senior Lecturer in International Relations at the Hebrew University of Jerusalem. He is the 2002–2003 Visiting Goldman Israeli Professor at the Department of Government at Georgetown University. He is the author of *Peaceful Territorial Change* (1994), *Zones of Peace in the Third World: South America and West Africa in Comparative Perspective* (1998), and co-editor of *Stable Peace among Nations* (2000). He has recently completed a book manuscript on "The Impact of Norms in International Society: The Latin American Experience, 1881–2001."

Edward D. Mansfield is Hum Rosen Professor of Political Science and Director of the Christopher H. Browne Center for International Politics at the University of Pennsylvania. His research focuses on international security and international political economy. He is the author of *Power, Trade, and War* (Princeton University Press, 1994) and the co-author (with Jack Snyder) of *Democratization and War* (MIT Press, forthcoming).

Petros C. Mavroidis is Professor of Law at Columbia Law School and the University of Neuchatel, Switzerland. He was previously Chair for Competition Law at EUI, Florence and member of the Legal Affairs Division of the GATT. He is currently serving as Chief Co-reporter for the American Law Institute (ALI) project "Principles of WTO Law".

Helen V. Milner is James T. Shotwell Professor of International Relations, Columbia University. She holds a BA from Stanford University, 1980; MA, Harvard University, 1982; PhD, 1986. She was a Research Fellow, Brookings Institution, 1983–1984; Advanced Research Fellow in Foreign Policy Studies, Social Science Research Council, 1989–1991; and Fellow, American Academy of Arts and Sciences, 2000 to the present. She also held a position with the Center for Advanced Study in the Behavioral

Sciences, 2001–2002 and has been Assistant Professor to Professor, Columbia University, 1986 to the present. She was the Editor, *Review of International Political Economy*, from 1996–1999; and a Member, Council of the American Political Science Association, from 1994–1996. She has been a member of the editorial boards of *International Organization* from 1998 to the present and of *International Studies Quarterly*, from 1995 to the present.

Peter Rosendorff is Associate Professor of International Relations and Economics at the University of Southern California. He has published widely on the political economy of trade policy, and much of his work concerns the linkages between domestic politics and institutions and international economic policy. He is currently serving as co-editor of the Blackwell journal, *Economics and Politics*, and is a member of the editorial board of *International Organization*. He has held visiting positions at the University of California, Los Angeles and Georgetown University. His latest research concerns the links between democracy, accountability and transparency, and what these mean for the design of domestic and international institutions such as the judiciary, central banks and preferential trade agreements.

Anne-Marie Slaughter is Dean of the Woodrow Wilson School of Public and International Affairs at Princeton University. She is also President of the American Society of International Law. Prior to becoming Dean, she was the J. Sinclair Armstrong Professor of International, Foreign and Comparative Law and Director of Graduate and International Legal Studies at Harvard Law School. She is a Fellow of the American Academy of Arts and Sciences and a member of the Council on Foreign Relations. She has written over fifty articles and edited or written four books, on subjects such as the effectiveness of international courts and tribunals, the legal dimensions of the war on terrorism, building global democracy, international law and international relations theory, and compliance with international rules.

Duncan Snidal is Associate Professor of Political Science and Public Policy at the University of Chicago and Director of the Program on International Politics, Economics, and Security (PIPES). His past research has focused on theoretical issues of international cooperation. He is currently working on issues of international legalization and international institutional design.

ACKNOWLEDGMENTS

This book is the outcome of a conference that took place at the Hebrew University of Jerusalem Faculty of Law in June 2001. This is an opportunity for us to thank the many people whose assistance, cooperation and support made the conference and this book possible. Israel Gilead, then the Dean of the Faculty of Law, supported the project since its inception, and raised the necessary funds for it. Maly Lichtenstadt and Yael Wyant helped with the organization of the conference; Dahlia Shaham assisted with the editing process leading up to publication. Felice Kahan-Siskin was responsible for the sensitive and accurate editing work.

We thank the participants at the conference whose comments contributed to the final versions of the chapters presented in this book, among them Emmanuel Adler, Ruth Lapidoth, Oren Perez, Arie Reich and Joseph H.H. Weiler.

We are grateful to the Hebrew University of Jerusalem Faculty of Law, the Dr. Emilio von Hofmansthal fund, the Hersch Lauterpacht fund, the Louis Marshall fund and the Harry and Michael Sacher Institute for Legislative Research and Comparative Law for their generous support of this project.

ABBREVIATIONS

ABM	Anti-Ballistic Missile
AD	anti-dumping
ADACS	Assistance with the Development and Consolidation of Democratic Stability (Council of Europe)
APEC	Asia-Pacific Economic Cooperation
ASEAN	Association of Southeast Asian Nations
BOP	balance of payments
CACJ	Central American Court of Justice
CITES	Convention on International Trade in Endangered Species
CTB	Comprehensive Test Ban Treaty
CVD	countervailing duty
CWC	Convention on the Prohibition of the Development, Production, Stockpiling and Use of Chemical Weapons and their Destruction
DSB	Dispute Settlement Body (WTO)
DSU	Dispute Settlement Understanding (WTO)
EPU	European Payments Union
ERM	Exchange Rate Mechanism
FAO	Food and Agriculture Organization (UN)
FC	framework convention
FDI	foreign direct investment
GATT	General Agreement on Tariffs and Trade
GEF	Global Environmental Facility
GSP	Generalized System of Preferences
ICJ	International Court of Justice
IL	international law
ILA	International Law Association
ILO	International Labour Organization
IMF	International Monetary Fund
INF	Intermediate Nuclear Forces

IR	international relations
ITC	International Trade Commission
ITTA	International Tropical Timber Agreement
ITTO	International Tropical Timber Organization
LDC	least developed country
LRTAP	European Long-Range Transboundary Air Pollution Regime
MFN	Most Favored Nation
NMD	National Missile Defence
NPT	Nuclear Non-Proliferation Treaty
OECD	Organization for Economic Cooperation and Development
PCIJ	Permanent Court of International Justice
PD	Prisoner's Dilemma
PIC	prior informed consent
SALT	Strategic Arms Limitation Talks
SEATO	South East Asian Treaty Organization
SPS	Agreement on Sanitary and Phyto-Sanitary Measures
TBT	Agreement on Technical Barriers to Trade
TPRM	Trade Policy Review Mechanism
TRIPS	Agreement on Trade-Related Aspects of Intellectual Property
UNCTAD	United Nations Conference on Trade and Development
UNDP	United Nations Development Programme
UNEP	United Nations Environment Programme
VER	voluntary export restraint
WHO	World Health Organization
WIPO	World Intellectual Property Organization
WTO	World Trade Organization

1

Introduction

EYAL BENVENISTI AND MOSHE HIRSCH

This book aims at advancing our understanding of the influences international norms and international institutions have over the incentives of states to cooperate on issues such as environment and trade. The different contributions to this book adopt two different approaches in examining this question. One approach focuses on the constitutive elements of the international legal order, including customary international law, soft law and framework conventions, and on the types of incentives states have, such as domestic incentives and reputation. The other approach examines closely specific issues in the areas of international environment protection and international trade. The combined outcome of these two approaches is a more refined understanding of the forces that pull states toward closer cooperation or prevents them from doing so, and the impact of different types of international norms and diverse institutions on the motivation of states. The insights gained suggest ways for enhancing states' incentives to cooperate through the design of norms and institutions.

This introduction begins with an overview of contemporary international law (IL) – international relations (IR) scholarship, to be followed by a short description of the contributions to this book.

IL–IR scholarship

The point of departure of this book is that the disciplines of IL and IR are inexorably interlinked. Neither can be understood properly in isolation. Like every legal system that operates in a specific societal system, international law functions in the international system. International law grows out of the international society: it reflects the particular character of this society, and it also affects the relationships among the actors in this system. At the same time, international law produces norms that influence, if not shape, the behavior of international actors.

Yet IL–IR interdisciplinary scholarship is quite a new phenomenon. Kenneth Abbott's well-known article in 1989 on IR theories and IL[1] is widely considered the harbinger of a wave of cooperation between IL and IR scholars. Anne-Marie Slaughter followed and significantly extended this direction in her 1993 article discussing the historical evolution of the IL–IR relationship since World War II.[2] Her article recommends to IL and IR scholars potential pathways of interdisciplinary research in this field. Indeed, many IL scholars (including most of the IL contributors to this volume) have adopted these recommendations, and a growing number of articles and books that draw on the common ground of these disciplines have been published in recent years.[3] On the IR side, the "move to law" in world politics was particularly manifest in the special issue of *International Organization* in the summer of 2000 that was devoted to the subject "Legalization and World Politics."[4]

Employing IR theoretical tools is of particular importance for IL scholars. Analysis of specific features of the international system is valuable for a proper understanding of the content and role of IL in a given period. Likewise, ascertaining the nature of developments in the international system at large are of great importance for understanding changes in IL and international legal institutions.

Different IR theories offer several sets of factors that motivate the behaviors of states and other actors in the international community. These factors explain the evolution of IL and its specific norms. Consequently, studying IR theories may enable IL scholars to explore why a particular legal concept or rule emerged in a given period (and not earlier, or later) and why alternative legal concepts or rules were discarded. Such theories also explain legal pluralism among different regional legal systems.

IR research may also assist practitioners and judges of IL who apply this body of law to particular factual situations. Application of international rules often requires interpretation which, in turn, frequently necessitates reference to the aim of a particular rule, as well as the historical context

---

[1] Kenneth W. Abbott, "Modern International Relations Theory: A Prospectus for International Lawyers" (1989) 14 *Yale J. Int'l L.* 335.
[2] Anne-Marie Slaughter Burley, "International Law and International Relations Theory: A Dual Agenda" (1993) 87 *Am. J. Int'l L.* 205.
[3] See the many books and articles referred to in Anne-Marie Slaughter, Andrew S. Tulumello and Stepan Wood, "International Law and International Relations Theory: A New Generation of Interdisciplinary Scholarship" (1998) 92 *Am. J. Int'l L.* 367.
[4] (2000) 54 *International Organization* (No. 3, Summer).

of its enactment.⁵ IR studies may aid agencies of interpretation in ascertaining the factual and theoretical background of particular legal rules or comprehensive legal regimes.

IR theories may also assist IL scholars in anticipating what kind of legal rules are likely to prevail under various circumstances in the future (e.g., if inequality between states increases, or if a bilateral setting is transformed into a multilateral one). IR theories do not predict precisely which rules will be adopted in a given situation but they may well give scholars significant indications of the expected trends and patterns of legal concepts that are likely to emerge in particular settings. Empirical studies are used to study the validity of such IR hypotheses, which have considerable significance for IL scholars.

As noted above, existing international legal concepts reflect to a significant measure the current traits of the international system. This observation should not lead us to under-estimate the dynamic dimension of IL. International legal regimes generally do not aim to reflect accurately and to perpetuate the existing situation in a given community.⁶ On the contrary, a basic function of IL is to generate change in the conduct of its subjects and also, occasionally, to modify the relationships among them.⁷ IL is often used as an instrument to alter conduct in the international system that is undesirable (either immoral or inefficient). This is the case, for instance, with international treaties that aim to prohibit racial or gender discrimination, or treaties that require signatory states to eliminate various barriers to international trade.

IR theoretical tools may help IL scholars and policy-makers employ IL as a purposive instrument. IR theories often aim to identify the critical factors that explain a particular international conduct (whether desirable or undesirable). Identification of the factors that motivate states to adopt a particular course of action in the normative sphere may indicate to IL scholars what kinds of legal mechanisms are needed to affect states' behavior in a given area. Desirable legal mechanisms, in accordance with IR theories, may include either existing or innovative legal concepts. For instance, certain legal rules may enhance the prospects of international

---

⁵ See Articles 31–32 of the 1969 Vienna Convention on the Law of Treaties, 8 *International Legal Materials* 679.
⁶ Martti Koskenniemi, *From Apology to Utopia: The Structure of International Legal Argument* (Finish Lawyers' Publishing Company, Helsinki, 1989), pp. 2–5.
⁷ On the function of law as an instrument of social change, see Roger Cotterrell, *Sociology of Law* (2nd ed., Butterworths, London, 1992), pp. 44–70.

cooperation in the sphere of environmental protection, and particularly in settings that are susceptible to collective action failure.[8]

The capacity of IL to reshape conduct and relationships in the international system should not be over-estimated. IL, like any other societal institution, has its own limitations. Still, IR theoretical tools may be helpful here in pointing out where new legal rules or institutions are unlikely to generate the desired change.

Interdisciplinary IL–IR scholarship is also valuable for IR scholars.[9] IR scholars investigate the role of IL in international politics. With the rapid increase in international treaties, institutions and tribunals in recent decades, IR scholars attempt to analyze rigorously the impact of these developments on states' behavior, as well as the structural changes resulting from this trend for the international system at large. IR scholars have devoted particular research efforts to exploring the puzzle of compliance with IL.

The distinction between rational choice and sociological analyses constitutes one of the major dividing lines in social sciences scholarship.[10] These paradigms posit different assumptions regarding the motivation for social behavior at large, as well as with regard to the central factors that affect the decision-making processes. Naturally, this theoretical cleavage resurfaces also in IR theoretical literature. As Slaughter shows in the opening chapter, the major theoretical approaches in IR (realism, institutionalism and liberalism) are based on both constructivist and rationalist causal mechanisms. Still, numerous realist, institutionalist and liberal analyses incline to emphasize the rational aspects of these approaches. This trend is also mirrored in most chapters of this book that widely employ the rational theoretical tools. Notwithstanding this, some contributors discuss and highlight the sociological (or "constructivist") approaches in IR theory. This is the case with the chapters written by Anne-Marie Slaughter, Moshe Hirsch, Edith Brown Weiss and Arie Kacowicz.

---

[8] See, e.g., Eyal Benvenisti, "Collective Action in the Utilization of Shared Freshwater: The Challenges of International Water Resource Law" (1996) 90 *Am. J. Int'l L.* 384; Moshe Hirsch, "Game Theory, International Law, and Environmental Cooperation in the Middle East" (1999) 27 *Denver J. Int'l L. and Policy* 75.

[9] See, e.g., Robert Keohane, "International Relations and International Law: Two Optics" (1997) 38 *Harvard Int'l L. J.* 487.

[10] See, e.g., Shaun Hargreaves Heap *et al.*, *The Theory of Choice: A Critical Guide* (Blackwell, Oxford, 1992), pp. 62–72.

The contributions in this book

The different contributions to this book set out to examine in what ways, if at all, international norms and institutions shape the attitude of states towards international cooperation.

Anne-Marie Slaughter's contribution opens the book (see Chapter 2) with an overview of the principal theoretical approaches in IR literature and discussion on the interrelationships between international law and international politics. This chapter starts with a concise summary of the three central paradigms that are widely employed in contemporary American political science: realism, institutionalism and liberalism. The brief analysis of the central tenets of each paradigm is accompanied by a discussion on the particular relevance of each of these approaches to international law. These theories suggest various legal strategies as how to resolve particular policy problems (such as wars or trade conflicts).

The interrelationships between IL and IR theories is demonstrated, inter alia, with regard to the centrality of the territory in both traditional international law and the realist paradigm. The UN Charter is presented as an institutionalist response to the fact of state power. From this point of view, the Charter's norms, including sovereign equality and prohibition of use of force, seek to create a fictional world in which power is equalized and shape reality to approximate this fiction. The liberal approach in IR also exerts significant influence on IL. The liberal conception of IL does not consider states as the principal subjects but rather as the agents of individuals and interest groups that states are assumed to represent.

The constructivist approach is analyzed in this contribution and Slaughter emphasizes its distinctive features vis-à-vis the rational approach. The fundamental difference between these approaches is explained with the distinction made by James March and Herbert Simon between the "logic of consequences" (that involves instrumental calculation) and the "logic of appropriateness" (that involves socialization). Slaughter underlines that realism, institutionalism and liberalism rely on both constructivist and rationalist causal mechanisms (but most standard overviews of IR theories privilege the rationalist version of each of the paradigms). Many international lawyers are drawn to constructivism but they can find constructivist or rationalist variants within all three of the major IR paradigms.

Five basic propositions are developed by Slaughter in the second part of this contribution. These propositions are about the role of law in shaping international politics, the role of politics in shaping international law, the prospects for a new generation of international institutions and the fate of the state. The propositions highlight the significance of power analysis to international lawyers, the difference between legalized and non-legalized rules and institutions, the particular role of soft law in global governance, international regime design and the importance of domestic politics (as well as international politics) for international lawyers.

The contribution of **Kenneth Abbott and Duncan Snidal** to this volume (Chapter 3), the result of a joint project undertaken by these two scholars of IL and IR (respectively), focuses on the dynamics of cooperation and legalization. It analyzes three alternative pathways to promoting cooperation among states and other international actors: the Framework Convention Pathway, the Plurilateral Pathway and the Soft Law Pathway.

The Framework Convention Pathway directs the involved parties to begin with a legally binding agreement with broad participation but shallow substantive commitments, and to deepen the substantive content over time. This dynamic pattern is well known in the sphere of international environmental protection. Prominent examples are the 1985 Convention for the Protection of the Ozone Layer, the 1992 Convention on Climate Change and the 1979 Convention on Long-Range Transboundary Air Pollution.

The Plurilateral Pathway suggests the institution of cooperative regimes that gradually increase the number of participating parties. Here the recommendation is to begin with a legally binding agreement with deep substantive commitments but limited membership, and then to expand membership over time. The prerequisite to expansion is, of course, that the cooperative regime be beneficial to potential members; if this condition is met, the regime's very existence will enhance incentives to join. The well-known example for such a dynamic is the establishment and enlargement of the European Community.

Finally, the Soft Law Pathway focuses on increasing legalization of the cooperative regime, mainly in terms of strengthening the legally binding nature of the relevant obligations. This Pathway directs the parties to begin with an agreement containing significant substantive commitments with wide participation, but which is not legally binding, or is only weakly binding, and then gradually to strengthen the legal obligations over time. The development of the universal human rights legal regime (from the 1948 Universal Declaration to the 1966 Covenants and subsequent treaties) well illustrates this pathway.

Abbott and Snidal note that certain pathways are associated with particular IR theories and they discuss several such theoretical connections. Still, their conclusion on this point is that individual pathways are "not tightly tied" to a particular understanding of international cooperation. Finally, the authors explore some factors that lead international actors to follow one of the three pathways. These factors include the nature of the problem (e.g., various types of uncertainty), the relative power of the involved parties (e.g., governments or NGOs) and the institutional arena in which the efforts to further international cooperation are taken.

Eyal Benvenisti (Chapter 4) examines the role of international judges and arbitrators in pushing states towards more efficient norms. He argues that such judges and arbitrators enjoy a unique opportunity to guide states into adopting more cooperative courses of action, and that they often make use of that opportunity. According to Benvenisti, the opportunity is provided by the doctrine of customary international law. This doctrine has often served as a reliable proxy for determining the efficient behavior for all states to follow, enabling international tribunals and other actors to impose sanctions on free-riders or others seeking to deviate from the efficient norm. But the proxy fails when global or regional conditions lead states to pursue inefficient behavior. In such situations, international tribunals can push states toward new, more efficient Nash equilibria. Tribunals do so by inventing what they portray as custom. A judicial declaration of one equilibrium as legally binding is likely to lead all players to modify their activities to conform to the judicially-sanctioned equilibrium. This equilibrium will thus become the new practice, the new custom.

The argument developed in this chapter is that the judicial authority to nudge states toward efficient equilibria exists in international law, and is often used by tribunals. When state practice fails to follow efficient modes of behavior, international adjudicators inform themselves directly or indirectly on the best available science to attain efficient norms. Judges in international tribunals therefore have a unique role in the advancement of international law. They have the genuine opportunity to translate science into law, on the pretext of "finding" customary international norms. They have in fact an authority, grounded in customary international law, to invent new custom.

George Downs and Michael Jones (Chapter 5) explore the impact of reputational costs on states' incentives to cooperate and comply with international obligations. Reputation is positively related to compliance. Because developing states have relatively worse compliance records than developed states – due to their fewer administrative and financial resources, their instability and their susceptibility to external shocks – developing states are more susceptible to reputation costs than developed states. Downs and Jones argue that the worry that developing states will become increasingly marginalized from the benefits of multilateral agreements is not corroborated by the evidence, and they seek to explain this phenomenon.

Their quest leads them to develop a case for multiple reputations, rather than a singular one. States distinguish between defections according to their timing and the types of agreements involved. Just as states might have different levels of reliability in connection with treaties in different areas, they can also have a variable record for reliability in connection with different treaties in the same regulatory area if they contain different amounts of ambiguity, require widely differing levels of resources from states in order to carry out or are subject to different political and economic shocks. As a result, the reputational consequences of a state's non-compliance in connection with a given agreement tends to be bounded. Other states will revise their estimates of its reliability but only in connection with agreements that they believe (1) are affected by the same or similar sources of fluctuating costs, and (2) are valued the same or less by the defecting state. This explains why, despite the assumption in the traditional theory that states have a unitary reputation, it is virtually impossible to find in the literature examples of a state's defection from an agreement in one area (e.g., environment) jeopardizing its reputation in other areas (e.g., trade and security). The bounded or segmented nature of reputation also helps account for why states often have widely divergent reputations in different spheres.

Downs and Jones suggest that the existence of segmented or multiple reputations mitigates the reputational costs that the traditional theory predicts for developing states. Because states have learned to pay attention to the importance as well as the nature of the underlying stochastic shocks that caused the non-compliance, developing states can suffer a severe reputational loss in connection with a particular regional trade or security treaty and still preserve a good reputation in connection with others in the same area that they value more. The limited reach of reputational implications, however, also portends drawbacks for developing states. While it limits their liability, it also limits the protection they can count on reputation affording them from the opportunistic defection of developed states. This is especially bad in the case of treaties that regulate private or club goods. The fact that reputational consequences only extend to other partners that the defecting state is believed to value the same or less means that the developed state will suffer a reputational loss only among other developing states. Since this could be a very small penalty, it is unlikely that the hope will be realized of reputation leveling the playing field between rich and poor states more than institutionalized compliance mechanisms.

Edith Brown Weiss's contribution (Chapter 6) analyzes the empirical data of a comprehensive research project on compliance with international treaties and highlights various compliance strategies employed in different spheres of international law. The first section presents three paradigms that serve as starting points for analysis. The Classical Paradigm assumes that countries join an international treaty when doing so is expected to promote their interests. Consequently, countries generally comply with international agreements and if not, sanctions are the preferred strategy to induce compliance. The power in the Network Paradigm is organized non-hierarchically in networks that include many important participants in addition to states. Compliance in this paradigm is a dynamic process and it varies among agreements and countries. The individual is the key participant in the Individualist Paradigm and compliance in this paradigm focuses primarily on educating and mobilizing civil society and pressurizing governments (and other actors) to abide by their international obligations. Compliance strategies that concentrate on transparency and capacity-building help empower individuals, NGOs and other non-state actors to comply.

Following a discussion of several propositions regarding compliance with agreements, Brown Weiss analyzes the employment of three principal compliance strategies: (i) transparency (or sunshine) methods that include national reporting, on-site monitoring, etc; (ii) positive incentives that include special funds for financial and technical assistance; (iii) coercive measures that include sanctions and various penalties. Brown Weiss examines the employment of these strategies in accordance with the particular profile of the contracting parties. Two dimensions have particular importance in this respect: intention to comply and capacity to comply.

Analysis of data resulting from the above research leads the author to the following conclusions regarding the desirable mix between the three compliance strategies: (i) If states have both the intent and the capacity to comply, transparency methods are particularly effective to induce compliance. (ii) If states intend to comply but lack the capacity, positive incentives are especially important to enhance compliance (transparency methods may also be important for such states). (iii) If states do not intend to comply but have the capacity to comply, targeted coercive measures may be useful (transparency methods may also exert pressure to comply in this category). (iv) If countries are weak both in intent and capacity, all compliance strategies are relevant.

An examination of non-environmental treaties along these parameters reveals different trends of compliance strategies. The threat or occasional use of sanctions is the primary means to induce compliance in the GATT/WTO system. International agreements concerned with human rights and with labor are more associated with compliance strategies that focus on transparency methods. Arms control agreements widely utilize transparency methods.

Overall, states are increasingly focusing on the negotiation, design and implementation of measures to enhance compliance. Generally, states' use of all of the compliance strategies described above is increasing. In particular, there is a growing emphasis on transparency methods and positive incentives that build the capacity of states to comply. These changes are explained by the author as a result of the increasing number of states in the international system and growing number of developing states who often lack the capacity to comply with international treaties. Positive incentives assist these states to comply. In some cases, developing states do not accord high priority to compliance and positive incentives may also assist them to shift their priorities towards compliance. Finally, as the non-hierarchical Network Paradigm revealed, there is also a growing role for civil society in securing compliance with international agreements. Consequently, the increasing trend of transparency measures can be targeted to enhance civil society's capacity to promote compliance.

The contribution of **Moshe Hirsch** (Chapter 7) also deals with the subject of compliance but the focus here is on the likely repercussions of globalization upon compliance. The central question is whether globalization will enhance or lessen compliance with international norms? In order to address this question, the author first identifies the major factors that prompt states to observe or violate their international obligations. Two distinct social sciences paradigms provide two different answers to the question of what are the factors that motivate or hinder compliance with international norms. The rational choice model and the sociological approach posit different assumptions regarding the motivation for social behavior in general, and regarding the central factors that affect the decision-making process.

Many proponents of the rational choice model in IR theory consider numerous settings in the international system as "collective action" problems. Analysis of collective action models that reflect the most prevalent patterns of state behavior reveal that the main variables that affect the prospects of compliance are the iteration of interaction among the involved parties, capacity to operate retaliatory measures, availability of information regarding the behavior of other parties and the parties discount factor regarding future gains or losses.

The second paradigm employed in this chapter to analyze compliance is the sociological perspective and its strand in the IR theory, social constructivism. Under the constructivist approach, decision-makers are motivated by impersonal social factors such as values, norms and cultural practices, rather than a calculation of material interests. The proponents of this approach argue that decision-makers are routinely inclined to obey international norms, and norm conformity is the default option in the international system. Still, certain social factors explain why states may violate international norms. These factors include: vague norms (where the social message encoded in a particular norm is subject to different interpretations), conflict between national and international norms, social detachment towards the international community and inadequate socialization processes of national decision-makers.

The analyses undertaken along the above theoretical lines do not lead to a single conclusion. Assuming that the current trends of globalization will proceed, the results regarding the prospects of compliance in the course of globalization are rather mixed. The rational choice analysis reveals that the trends of growing iteration, expanding capacity of retaliation, increasing amounts of reliable information, and the process of growing rebounded externalities, indicate that the prospect of compliance is likely to be enhanced. The sociological analysis shows that the trend of increasing interconnectedness among societies is likely to reduce the prospects of conflict between national and international norms, thus increasing the prospects of compliance. Analysis of the growing socio-economic inequality among states and its impact upon the social attachment of poorer states with the international society, however, implies that this process is likely to decrease compliance with international norms.

Arie Kacowicz (Chapter 8) explores to what extent states comply with international norms related to territorial disputes, such as *pacta sunt servanda* and the peaceful settlement of international disputes, and offers his views as to why they do so. His focus is on the peculiar reality of the Latin American international society, and its unique record of recourse to international arbitration to settle international disputes over territory. More than any other regional grouping, the Latin American countries have turned to international arbitration to settle their territorial disputes (about twenty-two times in the last part of the nineteenth and throughout the twentieth centuries), and have complied on almost half of the occasions. In particular, Kacowicz examines two cases of non-compliance with arbitration awards that were eventually resolved by mediation and direct negotiations: the dispute between Peru and Ecuador (1941 to 1998) and the dispute between Argentina and Chile (1977 to 1984).

Kacowicz shows that in the Latin American context, the factors inducing compliance (or non-compliance) were similar to those factors that influence states in general to comply with international law. This, he notes, is the case despite the fact that the Latin American region was mostly composed of non-democratic regimes. Thus, Kacowicz argues, the Latin American region has proven that non-democratic states can share some, if not all, of the normative perspectives and institutional restraints that seem to characterize democracies.

Helen Milner, Peter Rosendorff and Edward Mansfield (Chapter 9) examine the domestic sources of cooperation in the area of international trade. Their chapter offers two central arguments, both relating international trade to domestic politics. The first is that domestic political reasons can provide an important motive for leaders to sign trade agreements and abide by international trade rules. The second is that the internal design of international trade agreements may depend in part on domestic politics, as domestic political reasons prompt leaders in choosing specific structures for international trade agreements. Milner shows that the inclusion of escape clause mechanisms in international trade agreements can result from domestic incentives, and argues that without such escape clauses political leaders could not afford to sign trade agreements because of domestic pressures. Their inclusion and character are important for such agreements, and depend upon the shape of domestic politics in the countries in question.

Milner *et al.*'s contribution explores, first, the domestic sources of trade agreements. Political leaders face two sets of domestic pressures in the trade realm. Special interest groups often want protection and leaders may feel great pressure to provide it to them. Political leaders, especially if motivated by rent-seeking, may therefore impose a variety of trade barriers. On the other hand, political leaders need to be re-elected, and this depends in part on the reactions of voters. If voters condition their approval of leaders on their economic situation, then leaders may be caught between the pressures of elections and those of special interest groups. Too much protection may negatively affect the economy, and lead voters to seek new leaders.

Hence, leaders may be in the sub-optimal position of having to give more protection to domestic interests than is desirable. Leaders want to provide only as much protection to special interests as they can without hurting their re-election prospects. When they have complete discretion over trade policy, leaders may be unable to resist the pressures of special interest groups in the short run, even though they would like to for electoral reasons. Leaders therefore seek to limit their own discretion through international trade agreements. Such agreements convey information to voters about the activities of leaders, and this information helps leaders retain office. Trade agreements are both a commitment to a less protectionist policy and a device to convey credibly to the voters that a less protectionist policy has been adopted. International cooperation can thus help leaders increase their chances of re-election, thereby providing a strong reason for them to pursue such agreements.

Milner *et al.*'s second argument is that the internal design of international trade agreements may also depend much on domestic politics. Almost all international trade agreements include some form of "safeguard" clause, which allows countries to escape the obligations agreed to in the negotiations. Escape clauses erode both the credibility and the trade liberalizing effect of international trade agreements, but they also increase the flexibility of the agreement by adding some discretion for national policy-makers. This increased flexibility may be ideal for leaders in view of their domestic constraints. Including escape clauses may also make initial agreements easier to reach. Their flexibility allows states to be reassured about how long-term gains from the agreement will be divided. Indeed, without escape clauses of some sort many trade agreements would never be politically viable for many countries. Finally, increased flexibility (necessary for dealing with the uncertainty of the future) lessens the distributional problems of bargaining that may plague an initial agreement.

Petros Mavroidis (Chapter 10) addresses the controversial question of whether the participation of developing states in the WTO involves a certain mandatory level of human rights protection. Noting that the status of a "developing country" entails several trade concessions in the WTO legal system, the article starts with an examination of how this status is determined. The practice in the WTO members shows that the underlying rule is the "self-selection" principle, in accordance with which a unilateral declaration of the relevant state defines that status. While there are some developments that seem to curtail the "self-characterization" principle, (particularly with regard to the Agreement on Intellectual Property Rights), the point of departure for such determination is still the declaration of the relevant state.

Addressing the question of whether WTO membership entails an obligation to comply with some human rights standards led the author to examine the general issue regarding the freedom of the WTO members to pursue certain environmental, health and social policies. Mavroidis observes that the WTO system is essentially about negative integration and, generally, its members are largely unconstrained by the WTO agreements' provisions when it comes to deciding their regulatory intervention in various spheres. Thus, the WTO law does not impose a certain human rights policy on its members and the latter are free to choose the manner in which to protect human rights. WTO members' policies are only constrained by human rights standards that are prescribed by peremptory norms of international law (*jus cogens*).

The chapter analyzes also the argument that participation in the WTO gives rise to "races to the bottom" in the field of human rights (including labor standards). The likelihood of a race to the bottom intuitively seems higher in the sphere of labor standards but there is a little empirical evidence to suggest that trade liberalization generates negative impacts on labor standards. Mavroidis concludes his chapter by stating that while participation in the WTO does not prejudge the level of human rights protection, developed states may promote human rights policies in developing countries by offering additional trade concessions to states that comply with certain labor rights standards.

This controversial debate is further explored by **Robert Howse** (see Chapter 11) who contextualizes it using an actual dispute between India and the European Communities. The question that this dispute raises is to what extent unilateral measures of developed countries that condition market access on policies adopted by exporting developing countries, such as in the spheres of labor standards or environment protection, are compatible with the GATT regime and subject to judicial review of WTO dispute settlement bodies. Whereas so far discussion has focused on the interpretation of Article XX of GATT, and the question to what extent the Most Favored Nation treatment may be withdrawn due to the policies adopted by the exporting country, Howse examines a different but related claim that trade preferences given by developed to developing countries are not purely discretionary but instead are subject to legal constraint and judicial scrutiny. India is making this claim against EC measures that provide an additional margin of preference or incentive to countries that implement, through legislation and effective enforcement, ILO-defined core labor rights as well as environment protection standards promulgated by the International Tropical Timber Organization (ITTO). Howse offers his interpretation of the law, and elaborates on the diverse ramifications of different possible outcomes of the adjudication.

Each of the contributions, and the book as a whole, offer scholars of international law and international relations new insights into the theoretical study of international law and its role in domestic and international politics. In an era of globalization, when decisions are no longer the province only of national legislatures, it is imperative that these links be analyzed. Understanding these interrelations is, we believe, crucial for designing procedures for collective decision-making concerning trade, environment and other matters.

2

International law and international relations theory: a prospectus

ANNE-MARIE SLAUGHTER

Scholars of international relations generate a wide range of theories to solve the problems and puzzles of state behavior. Each theory offers a causal account of a particular outcome or pattern of behavior in interstate relations in a form that isolates independent and dependent variables precisely enough to generate hypotheses (predictions) that can be empirically tested.[1] At a higher level of generality, these theories can be grouped into different families or approaches on the basis of their underlying analytical assumptions about the nature of states and the relative explanatory power of broad classes of causal factors, such as the distribution of power in the international system, international institutions, national ideology and domestic political structure.

This chapter will summarize the three main theoretical approaches used in contemporary American political science: Realism, Institutionalism

---

[1] The theories described are all "positivist" theories, in the sense that they proceed from the premise that "every theory, to be worthwhile, must have implications about the observations we expect to find if the theory is correct." See Gary King, Robert O. Keohane and Sidney Verba, *Designing Social Inquiry* (1994), p. 28; also Richard K. Ashley, "The Poverty of Neorealism" in R. Keohane, *Neorealism and its Critics* (2nd ed., 1986), p. 281 (summarizing four basic tenets of positivism as: (1) there are objective scientific causes of events; (2) science can produce technically useful knowledge that is (3) value neutral; and (4) the truth can be empirically tested). But see Donald P. Green and Ian Shapiro, *Pathologies of Rational Choice Theory* (Yale University Press, New Haven, 1994), p. 6 (rational choice theory has not delivered on its empirical promises; this failure of empiricism as it bears upon the study of political phenomena is "rooted in the aspiration of rational choice theorists to come up with universal theories of politics.").

The precise meaning of "positivism" as it is used in international legal discourse, however, is somewhat distinct from the social science formulation of the term. See e.g., Anthony Clark Arend, *Legal Rules and International Society* (Oxford University Press, New York, 1999), p. 89 (noting that "traditional positivists would define the very existence of a treaty as evidence of an authoritative rule.").

and Liberalism.[2] Political scientists are likely to find the versions presented here overly simplified and distilled. Yet each approach gives rise to a distinct mental map of the international system, specifying the principal actors within it, the forces driving or motivating those actors and the constraints imposed on those actors by the nature of the system itself. Anyone who thinks about foreign policy or international relations, from either a political or a legal standpoint, must have some such map to guide her thinking, whether consciously or subconsciously.

Beyond mental geography, however, the explicit role of theory differs for political scientists and lawyers. For political scientists, the purpose of uncovering this map and explicating its underlying assumptions is to test the positive validity of those assumptions. Do states in fact behave as they are assumed to? Does the mental map correspond to what observers actually see, or think they see? Does it permit accurate diagnosis of international problems and generate valid predictions and prescriptions for their resolution? Clarity about underlying premises is an indispensable foundation for accurate positive explanation.

For lawyers, the significance of underlying positive assumptions about the way the world works may be less immediately apparent, but no less important. Assume an instrumental view of international law, in which law-makers and commentators design legal rules to achieve specific ends based on positive reasoning about how those ends may be achieved. This is by no means the only or even the best perspective on the discipline and practice of international law; many might prefer a deontological quest for

---

[2] Many political scientists would protest this selection of theoretical paradigms, arguing that it is too narrow and excludes such important theories as world systems theory, dependence theory and structuration theory, to name only a few. The choice of these three approaches does not deny the existence of other bodies of theory or seek to discourage international lawyers from drawing on them. The approach here is intended to be illustrative rather than exhaustive.

For additional explications of these and other IR theories within political science, see generally Peter J. Katzenstein, Robert O. Keohane and Stephen D. Krasner (eds.), "International Organization at Fifty: Exploration and Contestation in the Study of World Politics" (1998) 52 *International Organization* 1; Benjamin J. Cohen and Charles Lipson, *Issues and Agents in International Political Economy* (1999); John Mearsheimer, "The False Promise of International Institutions" (1995) 19 *International Security* 5; Jeffrey W. Legro and Andrew Moravcsik, "Is Anybody Still a Realist?" (1999) 24 *International Security* 5. For earlier versions of ongoing debates discussed in these sources, see David A. Baldwin (ed.), *Neorealism and Neoliberalism: The Contemporary Debate* (1993); Charles W. Kegley, Jr. (ed.), *Controversies in International Relations Theory: Realism and the Neoliberal Challenge* (1995); Robert J. Beck, Anthony Clark Arend and Robert D. Vanderlugt, *International Rules: Approaches from International Law and International Relations* (1996).

norms of international justice.³ Even from this perspective, however, part of the international lawyer's task will be to determine how these norms can be most effectively implemented. Thus, at some stage, excavating and challenging assumptions about the nature and form of the international system emerges as an essential component of legal analysis, an effort to understand the realm of the possible and expand the realm of the probable.

To illustrate, imagine a set of agreed exogenous goals, such as peace, increasing international cooperation, resolving international conflict, preserving common resources or advancing global prosperity. Altering positive assumptions about who the principal actors are in the international system and about the motives that drive them gives rise to different causal statements about the source of particular problems – war, conflict or non-cooperation. These differing analyses will in turn suggest different political and legal strategies as to how to resolve those problems in the service of the posited affirmative goals.⁴

The most prominent example of this type of reasoning is the differential diagnosis of the sources of war: an imbalance of power in the international system, misinformation and uncertainty or inadequate representation of the individuals and groups most directly affected by war in the decision to go to war.⁵ The first diagnosis gives rise to legal norms seeking to restrict or constrain state use of power. The second would suggest the creation of international institutions to facilitate communication and confidence-building measures among potentially warring parties. And the third would generate both rules and possibly institutions designed to expand political representation at the domestic level.

An equally important example concerns competing diagnoses of trade conflicts.⁶ Here again, the problem can be identified as a fundamental and

---

[3] See e.g., Janna Thompson, *Justice and World Order: A Philosophical Inquiry* (1992).
[4] See Benedict Kingsbury, "The Concept of Compliance as a Function of Competing Conceptions of International Law" (1998) 19 *Michigan J. Int'l L.* 345, 369–72 (explaining that the process of the selection of strategies to effect the attainment of affirmative goals such as compliance with transnational regulatory institutions, dependent as it is upon differing assumptions regarding the important actors and causal processes in international relations, is difficult to investigate through normative methods alone).
[5] See e.g., Evan Luard, *Conflict and Peace in the Modern International System* (1988) (providing an exposition of the broad domain of theoretical explanations and analyses of the causes of war).
[6] See e.g, Klaus Stegemann, "Policy Rivalry Among Industrial States: What Can We Learn from Models of Strategic Trade Policy?" (1989) 41 *International Organization* 73 (illustrating the various explanations for international trade conflicts).

inevitable conflict between states competing to gain a relative advantage over one another; a problem of institutional design affecting the ability of states to coordinate and cooperate to reach an optimal solution; or the misrepresentation of underlying individual and group interests such that conflicting state positions reflect the capture of domestic political processes by special interests. Each of these diagnoses would give rise to different political strategies and corresponding legal regimes: the facilitation of trade alliances to neutralize competition; an international regime designed to overcome coordination and information problems (the GATT); or strategies allowing domestic litigants to invoke international rules against domestic interest groups in court. This last strategy does not exclude an international institutional framework, but it would be intermeshed with domestic politics and law.

Some international law (IL) lawyers might conclude that these differential diagnoses are the preliminary steps that must be taken to determine what category of law is appropriate to the solution of a particular policy problem – international or domestic. On this view, competing paradigms of international relations (IR) theory thus serve above all to delimit the boundaries of disciplinary jurisdiction. For present purposes, international lawyering is defined as seeking legal solutions to international problems, regardless of the labels attached to any particular body of law. From this perspective, international relations theory is an important part of any international lawyer's toolkit.

Others will argue that it is IR/IL scholars who are determined to attach political science labels to concepts and modes of analysis that international lawyers already engage in, but without fanfare. This claim has some merit, particularly with regard to the overlap between much of traditional international law and what political scientists call regime theory.[7] Even here, however, the political science account of the role that international rules and institutions play in international life yields valuable insights into the workings of current international institutions and suggests new possibilities for institutional design. More generally, explicating the connections between the two disciplines may make international lawyers more aware of the extent to which deeply entrenched international legal rules and principles reflect outmoded or discredited assumptions about the

---

[7] For a description of this overlap, see Kenneth W. Abbott, "Modern International Relations Theory: A Prospectus for International Lawyers" (1989) 14 *Yale J. Int'l L.* 335; Anne-Marie Slaughter Burley, "International Law and International Relations Theory: A Dual Agenda" (1993) 87 *Am. J. Int'l L.* 205, 208; Stephan Haggard and Beth A. Simmons, "Theories of International Regimes" (1987) 41 *International Organization* 491.

international system. Following the analytical course charted by different theories of international relations may encourage them to challenge these assumptions and formulate fresh solutions to old problems.

Principal paradigms in international relations theory

The "theories" of international relations presented here are not precise theories of war or peace or economic relations among nations. They are rather families of theories, which can also be thought of as conceptual frameworks or paradigms. More specific theories can be grouped within these paradigms in terms of the fundamental assumptions that they share about the nature of the principal actors in the international system and the principal factors that determine the outcomes of interactions among these actors. With a basic grasp of these different sets of assumptions, it is possible to identify virtually any more specific theory as either belonging to or containing elements from one or more of these paradigms. More useful for international lawyers, it is also possible to analyze any current problem in international relations from several competing perspectives and quickly to generate a number of potential solutions. In this sense, knowledge of these paradigms and an understanding of the basic mindset that animates the political scientists who work within them is a valuable technology. It is a technology that international lawyers can use to suit their many purposes in the different kinds of projects they undertake, provided, as with any technology, that they understand both its strengths and its limits.

Realism

The dominant approach in international relations theory for virtually the past two millennia, from Thucydides[8] to Machiavelli[9] to Morgenthau,[10] has been Realism, also known as Political Realism. Realists come in many stripes. Most notably, they divide between Classical Realists and Contemporary Structural Realists or Neorealists. Classical Realists, according to Professor Michael Smith, share the following assumptions:

---

[8] Thucydides, *History of the Peloponnesian War* (Rex Warner (trans.), 1986).
[9] Niccolo Machiavelli, *The Prince* (1946).
[10] See Hans Morgenthau, *Politics Among Nations: The Struggle for Power and Peace* (1948), p. 244.

(1) Human nature displays an "ineradicable tendency to evil."[11]
(2) The important unit of social life is the collectivity; in international politics the only really important collective actor is the state.
(3) Power and its pursuit by individuals and states is ubiquitous and inescapable. Thus the "important subjects for theoretical consideration are the permanent components of power."[12]
(4) International institutions, networks or norms are epiphenomenal.[13] They are reflections of the prevailing power relations among states, rather than independent factors determining state behavior.
(5) The "real issues of international politics can be understood by the rational analysis of competing interests defined in terms of power."[14]

These assumptions are linked. If human nature displays an ineradicable tendency toward evil, humans cannot live together without a powerful central authority to keep them in check. This is Hobbes' Leviathan, the domestic sovereign that must exercise absolute control within its territory.[15] When sovereigns encounter each other in the international system, they display the same characteristics that humans do in the state of nature. They seek power and dominion over one another, but can be held in check by countervailing power. In this context, rules and institutions can only endure to the extent that they reflect the interests of the most powerful states in the system.[16]

---

[11] See Michael Joseph Smith, *Realist Thought from Weber to Kissinger* (1986), p. 219; see also *ibid.* at p. 1 (contending that "[e]vil is inevitably part of all of us which no social arrangement can eradicate: men and women are not perfectible").

[12] *Ibid.* at pp. 219–20.

[13] F. S. Northedge, *The Use of Force in International Relations* (1974), pp. 213–13 (noting that for Morgenthau the relative distribution of state military power determined whether legal, rather than political, attempts to regulate the use of interstate force would trump the resort to self-help measures).

[14] Smith, *Realist Thought*, p. 221.

[15] Thomas Hobbes, *Leviathan* (1651), p. 107.

[16] Smith, *Realist Thought*, p. 13. See also W. Michael Reisman and Andrew R. Willard (eds.), *International Incidents: The Law That Counts in World Politics* 5 (1988) (indicating that for Realists who think that it is a form of law, international law is the law of the lowest common denominator as it operates horizontally rather than vertically, proceeds via coordination rather than through subordination and superordination, and binds powerful states only to the degree that it is in their interest to be bound). Some Realists will not even go this far. Michael Smith, for instance, suggests that for Classical Realists, states would not "peacefully consent to the creation of [rules and institutions], even if [they] could be shown to be workable." Smith, *Realist Thought*, p. 1.

In the 1970s, Kenneth Waltz reformulated these assumptions in an updated version of Realism that he called Structural Realism.[17] He insisted that a true theory of international relations must be formulated not in terms of human nature or the nature of national governments, but rather only in terms of factors operating at the level of the international system. John Mearsheimer summarizes the assumptions of this approach as follows:

(1) The international system is anarchic; it has no central authority.
(2) "[S]tates inherently possess some offensive military capability, which gives them the wherewithal to hurt and possibly destroy each other."[18]
(3) "States can never be certain about the intentions of other states."[19]
(4) The "most basic motive driving states is survival. States want to maintain their sovereignty."[20]
(5) [S]tates think strategically about how to survive in the international system.[21]

In this version, Realism is driven not by human nature but by the *structure* of the international system. The basic principle of anarchy means that states must protect themselves from other states. In a system in which all states possess the means to harm each other through offensive military capability and states can *never be certain* about what other states' intentions are, they must prepare for the worst. Their very survival is potentially at stake; assuring that survival must become the priority in all interactions with other states. Thus foreign policy becomes an exercise in figuring out how to amass and maintain sufficient power to defend against other states and conquer them if necessary. Instead of pursuing strategies of cooperation to secure common interests, states instead maximize their specific gains relative to other states.[22]

Differences in these variants of Realism can be important for specific applications of Realist theory. For present purposes, however, the various assumptions set forth above can be distilled into three. First, Realists believe that states are the primary actors in the international system, rational unitary actors who are functionally identical. Second, they assume that the organizing principle of the international system is anarchy, which cannot be mediated by international institutions. Without a central authority,

---

[17] Kenneth Waltz, *Theory of International Politics* (1979), p. 91.
[18] Mearsheimer, "False Promise," p. 11.
[19] *Ibid.* [20] *Ibid.* at p. 12. [21] *Ibid.* [22] *Ibid.* at p. 14.

power determines the outcomes of state interactions. Third, states can be treated as if their dominant preference was for power.

International lawyers assessing Realist theory must be careful to understand the internal logic of the Realist paradigm, if only to dispel any notion that Realists are somehow immoral or love power for its own sake. On the contrary, as the name suggests, Realists perceive that they are describing the realities of the international system, however unpleasant they may be. Stanley Hoffmann highlights the value that Realists place on prudence, leading them often to counsel against well-intentioned but potentially disastrous exercises of power that can erode the foundations of sovereignty and diminish the intellectual bases for the "protection of a society's individuals and groups from external control".[23]

Further, although Realism is probably best known among international lawyers for rejecting any causal role for international legal norms in the international system, much of both the structure and substance of traditional international law appears to be built on a Realist foundation.[24] Realists and traditional international lawyers overlap on all three core assumptions: concerning actors, preferences and the constraints imposed by the international system. They do ultimately diverge, with international lawyers seeking to blunt or alter the implications of a pure Realist analysis, but less than either camp might suspect.

The clearest overlap concerns the relevant criteria for identifying participants in the international system. Both Realists and traditional international lawyers agree that the primary actors are states, and define states as monolithic units identifiable only by the functional characteristics that constitute them as states. Neither would take account of domestic political ideology or structure, or of the multiplicity of sub-state actors that determine state policy at the domestic level. Both would assume that rules governing state behavior apply to all states *qua* states, without regard to their internal identity. The first-order international legal principles of sovereign equality and exclusive domestic jurisdiction are safeguards of the identity and opacity of the sovereign sphere. International legal rules governing recognition and state succession similarly ensure a complete divorce between governments and states.

---

[23] Stanley Hoffmann, "The Politics and Ethics of Military Intervention Survival" (1995–96) 37 *IISS Quarterly* 29, 33–34.
[24] Slaughter Burley, *International Law*, p. 207. See also Harold Hongju Koh, "Why Do Nations Obey International Law?" (1997) 106 *Yale L. J.* 2599, 2607–8 (underscoring the Realist, particularly the statist and sovereigntist, foundations of traditional international law).

For post-Westphalian international lawyers, then, states are both the source and the subject of rules governing international relations. What motivates and constrains these states in their relations with one another? As will be discussed below with regard to Institutionalism, most international lawyers assume that states have at least some common ends and that they can arrange to achieve them by means other than power. Nevertheless, many aspects of traditional international law tacitly acknowledge the extent to which international relations are power relations.

To take only one example, consider the centrality of the territoriality principle in both international law and politics. For Realists, territorial boundaries define the area from which resources necessary for military and economic power can be extracted, thereby circumscribing the extent of state power. It is this notion of territorially defined power that underpins Arnold Wolfers' classic Realist image of states as billiard balls: opaque, hard, clearly defined spheres interacting through collision with one another.[25] The circumference of each sphere is defined by territory. For international lawyers, control over a defined territory is the first criterion of statehood, an indispensable prerequisite for participation in the international system. It thus appears that the ante for participation in the international game is the capacity to wield power.

More generally, consider the many international lawyers who have sought to reconcile their discipline with the primacy of state power in the international system. The great positivists were all steeped in this tradition. Michael Reisman reminds us of Oppenheimer's realism, his uncompromising recognition of the limits set by the balance of power.[26] David Kennedy similarly depicts Hans Kelsen as the progenitor of a line of international law scholars who "hoped to remain realistic about state power without becoming political scientists," who embraced "formalism and respect for sovereignty" as a realistic recognition of the limits of law and the persistence of power.[27] More sweepingly, Martti Koskenniemi dichotomizes all of international legal argumentation into a debate between the apologists and the utopians – those who accept that international law reflects whatever states do and those who would have

---

[25] Arnold Wolfers, *Discord and Collaboration: Essays on International Politics* (1962), p. 19.
[26] W. Michael Reisman, "Lassa Oppenheim's Nine Lives" (1994) 19 *Yale J. Int'l L.* 255 (reviewing S.R. Jennings and S.A. Watts, *Oppenheim's International Law* (1992)).
[27] David Kennedy, "The International Style in Postwar Law and Policy" (1994) *Utah L. Rev.* 7, 36.

international law transcend and constrain state behavior.[28] The apologists are Realists.

Institutionalism

To the extent that Institutionalism reflects the belief that "rules, norms, principles and decision-making procedures" can mitigate the effects of anarchy and allow states to cooperate in the pursuit of common ends, all international lawyers are Institutionalists. "Rules, norms, principles and decision-making procedures" is the definition of an international "regime," the much-studied phenomenon that reintroduced international law to political scientists in the 1980s.[29] According to Robert Keohane's influential account in *After Hegemony*, international regimes:

> enhance the likelihood of cooperation by reducing the costs of making transactions that are consistent with the principles of the regime. They create the conditions for orderly multilateral negotiations, legitimate and delegitimate different types of state action, and facilitate linkages among issues within regimes and between regimes. They increase the symmetry and improve the quality of the information that governments receive.[30]

---

[28] Martti Koskenniemi, *From Apology to Utopia: The Structure of International Legal Argument* (1989), p. 5 (contending that, by refusing to incorporate sufficient normative aspects into their scholarship, Realists "lack critical distance" from state behaviors that most would "refuse to accept at the moment of application" and consequently cannot overcome the status of apologists for such behaviors).

[29] See Stephen D. Krasner (ed.), *International Regimes* (1983), p. 2 ("Regimes can be defined as sets of implicit or explicit principles, norms, rules, and decision-making procedures around which actors' expectations converge in a given area of international relations.").

[30] Robert O. Keohane, *After Hegemony: Cooperation and Discord in the World Political Economy* (1984), p. 244. See also Robert O. Keohane, *International Institutions and State Power* (1989). For slightly different versions of regimes and regime theories, see Oran Young, *International Cooperation: Building Regimes for Natural Resources and the Environment* (1989) (defining regimes as human artifacts whose distinguishing feature is the conjunction of "convergent expectations" and recognized patterns of behavior or practice in a given issue-area of social relations); John G. Ruggie, "International Responses to Technology: Concepts and Trends" (1975) 29 *International Organization* 557, 570 (defining regimes as sets of "mutual expectations, rules and regulations, plans, organizational energies and financial commitments, which have been accepted by a group of states"); Robert O. Keohane and Joseph S. Nye, Jr., *Power and Interdependence: World Politics in Transition* (1977), p. 19 (treating regimes as simply "governing arrangements that affect relationships of interdependence"); Volker Rittenberger (ed.), *Regime Theory and International Relations* (1993), pp. 3–11 (explaining the German research on regime theory and its conceptualization of international regimes as, alternatively, either "a form of institutionalized collaboration distinct from governments, treaties, or international organizations," a series of "routinized and institutionalized transactions between and among states," or "explicit

International regimes also enhance compliance with international agreements in a variety of ways, from reducing incentives to cheat and enhancing the value of reputation, to "establishing legitimate standards of behavior for states to follow" and facilitating monitoring, thereby creating "the basis for decentralized enforcement founded on the principle of reciprocity."[31] Moreover, regimes are important factors not only in international political economy but also in the security area.[32] As a group of international political economists and security scholars demonstrated in the 1980s, regime theory can be usefully applied to explaining cooperation under conditions of conflict.[33]

Primarily through the work of Keohane and many of his students, regime theory evolved into Institutionalism, an alternative paradigm to Realism.[34] The basic assumptions of Institutionalism are the following:

(1) The primary actors in the international system are states.
(2) Absent institutions, states engage in pursuit of power, but in many areas their underlying interests are not necessarily conflictual.

---

sets of rules which achieve prescriptive status in the sense that actors refer regularly to the rules both in characterizing their own behavior and in commenting on the behavior of others").

[31] Keohane, *After Hegemony*, p. 245.

[32] For elaboration on this point, see Friedrich Kratochwil, *Rules Norms, and Decisions* (1989), p. 187 (noting that Realism does not *ipso facto* exclude security as an issue-area susceptible to regime development, as norms underpin and structure collective security even if they are more opaque and less robust than the norms that under-gird other issue-areas); see also Robert Jervis, "Security Regimes" in Krasner, *International Regimes*, pp. 173–94 (insisting that security regimes, though theoretically possible even under conditions of anarchy, are more difficult to construct and maintain than regimes in other issue-areas for the following reasons: (1) security is more competitive than other issue-areas; (2) securing one's own interests harms or menaces other states; (3) stakes, which include survival, are higher in security than in other issue-areas; and (4) detection of the actions of other states is more difficult in security than in other issue-areas, which complicates evaluation of relative security relationships).

[33] See Jervis, *Security Regimes*, 173–94; see also Kenneth Oye (ed.), *Cooperation Under Anarchy* (1986); Robert Axelrod, *The Evolution of Cooperation* (1984).

[34] Keohane, *International Institutions*. This volume is a collection of Keohane's essays on institutions through the 1980s. For those seeking to find their way through the bewildering maze of theoretical labels, the introductory essay offers a useful overview of the distinctions between Neoliberal Institutionalism, Neorealism and Liberalism. However, Keohane's summation of the Liberal tradition differs considerably from the Liberal paradigm described in the second half of this chapter. On the contrary, Keohane's definition of Liberalism "as a set of guiding principles for contemporary social science" essentially equates it with Institutionalism. Thus, "Neoliberal institutionalists accept a version of liberal principles that . . . emphasizes the pervasive significance of international institutions without denigrating the role of state power." *Ibid.* at p. 11.

(3) Institutions can modify anarchy sufficiently to allow states to cooperate over the long term to achieve their common interests.
(4) In assessing the factors that determine international outcomes, institutions "are as fundamental as the distribution of capabilities among states."[35]

Here, then, is the divergence from Realism. Whereas Institutionalists would agree that states are the primary actors in the international system and that, absent institutions, states are engaged in the pursuit of power, they would contend that the presence of institutions modifies the organizing principle of anarchy. The uncertainty and ever-present possibility of conflict that lead states in a Realist world to expect and prepare for the worst is diffused by the information provided by and through institutions.[36] These institutions must thus be factored into systemic explanations of state behavior independently of structure. Further, having ameliorated the conditions of conflict that force states to concentrate on the quest for power, institutions can facilitate the achievement of common ends.

How do institutions accomplish this function? In a wide variety of ways. In Keohane's account, they decrease the transaction costs of interstate relations, increase information to reduce uncertainty and facilitate communication. In addition, institutions can promote learning, create conditions for orderly negotiations and facilitate linkages in complex negotiations. They can also legitimize or delegitimize different kinds of behavior. Finally, they can enhance the value of a state's reputation for honoring commitments, facilitate monitoring of state behavior and make decentralized enforcement possible by creating conditions under which reciprocity can operate. Other theorists, explored in greater detail below, emphasize the ways in which institutions can create a particular normative environment that helps shape both state identity and interests.

A key point here is that Institutionalism depends on the existence of common interests among states, which will not necessarily obtain among all states or in all issue areas. Where state interests do not converge, power politics is likely to continue to rule. Thus a prerequisite for Institutionalist analysis is the identification of underlying common interests, even in

---

[35] Ibid. at p. 8. See also Peter J. Katzenstein, Robert O. Keohane and Stephen D. Krasner (eds.), *Exploration and Contestation in the Study of World Politics* (1998), p. 23 (elaborating the basic assumptions of institutionalism).
[36] Keohane, *International Institutions*, p. 33 (describing how institutions reduce information costs and enhance incentives toward cooperation and the preclusion of conflict.

apparently conflictual situations. The "game" in game theory, for instance, first involves identifying which of a number of games best fits a particular pattern of state interactions, a step that requires figuring out whether states have an interest in coordinating their behavior or in cooperating more extensively in a variety of ways. To be more concrete, states may all have an interest simply in coordinating their behavior around one common standard, such as an agreement on navigational rules on the high seas. Alternatively, they may face a situation as in international trade, in which all have collective interest in reducing tariffs, but absent an institution that can prevent defection and solve free-rider problems, each state will have an interest in raising or maintaining tariffs.

In large degree, the debate between Realists and Institutionalists recapitulates the ancient debate between Hobbes and Grotius.[37] Not surprisingly, international lawyers typically side with Grotius. If they did not believe that international institutions (defined so broadly as to include all international legal rules and doctrines, as well as formal international organizations) could modify state behavior and in turn bring common goals within reach, they could not justify their own existence. In the process, however, they, like the Institutionalists, continue to accept a largely Realist foundation and framework as the point of departure for conceptualizing the international system.

To take one example, the UN Charter is an Institutionalist response to the fact of state power. Whereas Realists design political strategies to answer power with power, international lawyers search for rules to define and thus to restrain legitimate and illegitimate uses of power. Norms of sovereign identity and equality seek to create a fictional world in which power is equalized; prohibitions on the use of force seek to shape reality to approximate this fiction. The UN Charter neatly blends both political and legal approaches, combining an absolute prohibition on the use of force in Article 2(4) with a mechanism for the concentration of power by a designated group of powerful states against a transgressor against international peace.[38]

[37] See the account of these different strands in international relations theory in Hedley Bull, "Martin Wight and the Theory of International Relations" (1972) 2 *British J. Int'l Studies* 101, 104–5 (describing Wight's differentiation of Realists, "the blood and iron and immorality men" whose principal philosophical font was the work of Machiavelli and Hobbes, from Institutionalists, "the law and order and keep your word men" who took instruction from Grotius, from Revolutionists, "the subversion and liberation and missionary men" for whom Kant was inspiration).

[38] See Anne-Marie Slaughter, "The Liberal Agenda for Peace: International Relations Theory and the Future of the United Nations" (1994) 4 *Transnational Law and Contemporary Problems* 377.

Liberalism

The principal alternative to Realism and Institutionalism among international relations theorists is Liberalism.[39] As in the domestic realm, Liberal international relations theories have been repeatedly characterized as normative rather than positive theories.[40] The best-known Liberal theory in this category is Wilsonian "liberal internationalism," popularly understood as a program for world democracy. As used here, however, Liberalism denotes a family of positive theories about how states do behave rather than how they should behave.

A number of political scientists have sought to reduce Liberalism to a set of positive assumptions that can be stated as succinctly as the Realist counterparts.[41] I draw here primarily on one particular version developed by Andrew Moravcsik.[42] The fundamental premise of Moravcsik's account of Liberal theory is that "the relationship of states to the domestic and transnational social context in which they are embedded critically shapes state behavior by influencing the social purposes underlying state preferences."[43] He elaborates this premise in terms of three core assumptions:

(1) The primacy of societal actors: "The fundamental actors in international politics are individuals and private groups, who are on the average rational and risk-averse and who organize exchange and collective action to promote differentiated interests under constraints

---

[39] I use "Liberalism" here and throughout this chapter as a term of art to refer to Liberal international relations theory. As Andrew Moravcsik has argued, the elements of this theory do indeed flow out of the political theory and philosophy called "liberalism," in its broadest sense. But that link is not of concern here. See Andrew Moravcsik, "The Liberal Paradigm in International Relations Theory: A Scientific Assessment" in Colin and Miram Fendius Elman (eds.), *Progress in International Relations Theory: Appraising the Field* (MIT Press, Cambridge, MA, 2003). See also Michael Doyle, *Ways of War and Peace: Realism, Liberalism, and Socialism* (1997).

[40] See Andrew Moravcsik, "Taking Preferences Seriously: A Liberal Theory of International Politics" (1997) 51 *International Organization* 513, 514 ("its lack of paradigmatic status has permitted critics to caricature liberal theory as a normative ... ideology").

[41] See e.g., Doyle, *Ways of War and Peace*; David Fidler, "Caught Between Traditions: The Security Council in Philosophical Conundrum" (1996) 17 *Michigan J. Int'l L.* 411, 443–46 (parsing the nuances that distinguish the various strands of Liberalism); Thomas Risse-Kappen, "Ideas Do Not Float Freely: Transnational Coalitions, Domestic Structures, and the End of the Cold War" (1994) 48 *International Organization* 185; Robert O. Keohane, "International Liberalism Reconsidered" in J. Dunn (ed.), *The Economic Limits to Modern Politics* 155 (1990); Joseph S. Nye, "Neorealism and Neoliberalism" (1988) 40 *World Politics* 235.

[42] Moravcsik, "Taking Preferences Seriously," 516–21.   [43] *Ibid.* at 516.

imposed by material scarcity, conflicting values, and variations in societal influence."
(2) Representation and state preferences: "States (or other political institutions) represent some subset of domestic society, on the basis of whose interests state officials define state preferences and act purposively in world politics."
(3) Interdependence and the international system: the configuration of interdependent state preferences determines state behavior, e.g., "what states want is the primary determinant of what they do."

Thus specified, this theory, hereafter referred to as Liberal theory or Liberal international relations theory, offers a way of looking at the world that is radically different from the traditional assumptions underlying international law and international relations theory.

(1) It is a bottom-up view rather than a top-down view.
(2) It is an integrated view that does not separate the international and domestic spheres but rather assumes they are inextricably linked.
(3) It is a view that preserves an important role for states but deprives them of their traditional opacity by rendering state-society relations transparent. They bear no resemblance to billiard balls, but rather to atoms of varying composition, whose relations with one another, either cooperative or conflictual, depend on their internal structure.
(4) It is a view that transforms states into governments. By requiring us to focus on the precise interactions between individuals and "states," it leads us quickly to identify and differentiate between different government institutions, each with distinct functions and interests.

To dichotomize Realism and Liberalism in more concrete terms, where Realists look for concentrations of state power, Liberals focus on the ways in which interdependence encourages and allows individuals and groups to exert different pressures on national governments.[44] Where Realists assume "autonomous" national decision-makers, Liberals examine the nature of domestic representation as the decisive link between societal demands and state policy.[45] Where Realists model patterns of strategic

---

[44] *Ibid.* at 516–17. The phenomenon of "interdependence," defined as a situation in which two or more nations each depend on the other, whether symmetrically or not, by virtue of trade and investment patterns, population flows or even cultural and other social exchanges, can be analyzed from either a Realist or a Liberal perspective. Realists focus only on the impact of interdependence on the power differential between the nations concerned, whereas Liberals analyze it as an international social phenomenon.

[45] *Ibid.* at 518.

interaction based on fixed state preferences, Liberals seek first to establish the nature and strength of those preferences as a function of the interests and purposes of domestic and transnational actors.

An international legal system seeking to accomplish instrumental goals such as the reduction of conflict and the increase of cooperation through laws grounded on Liberal assumptions looks very different from traditional international law.[46] To begin with, it assumes that the primary source of conflict among states is not a clash or imbalance of power, but a conflict of state interests. Further, it assumes that these interests vary from state to state as a function of the individual preferences of individuals and groups operating in society; of the distribution of different preferences within a particular society; and of the degree to which a particular government is representative of individuals and groups in its own society and in transnational society. Based on these assumptions, the best way to resolve conflict and to promote cooperation in the service of common ends is to find ways to align these underlying state interests, either by changing individual and group preferences or by ensuring that they are accurately represented. In the military context, prescriptive Liberal international relations theories thus seek to ensure that all sectors of a given society who are likely to be directly affected by a war are represented in the decision to go to war. In the economic context, Liberal international relations theorists seek to avoid trade wars by ensuring that special interest groups with trading interests that are not representative of the population as a whole do not capture the decision-making process.

Second, a Liberal conception of international law focuses on states as the agents of individual and group interests. This means that the law designed to achieve specific international outcomes does not have states as its subjects, but rather the individuals and groups that states are assumed to represent.[47] It does not mean, however, that international legal rules and institutions would no longer have states as subjects. Traditional international law, after all, imposes a duty of domestic implementation, requiring states to make whatever domestic legal changes are necessary to conform

---

[46] For further elaboration of this point, see Anne-Marie Slaughter, "Liberal Theory of International Law" (2000) 240 *Proceedings of the 94th Annual Meeting of the American Society of International Law*, April 5–8, 2000.

[47] Note that the concept of state representation of individual and group interests need not imply fair, or equal, or accurate representation. A military dictatorship may represent the interests of only a very small portion of the state's population; nevertheless, it represents a particular "interest." See Moravcsik, "Taking Preferences Seriously," 518 ("No government rests on universal or unbiased political representation; every government represents some individuals and groups more fully than others").

to their international obligations. The decision whether to achieve a particular policy solution by laws binding on states alone or by laws and institutions aimed directly at individuals and groups would depend on an empirical determination as to which strategy would be most effective in altering either the behavior of individuals and groups as represented by states, or the mode and scope of state representation.

Rationalism versus Constructivism

The families or paradigms of IR theories set forth above define themselves in terms of assumptions about who the principal actors in the international system are and what forces and factors determine the outcomes of interactions between them. Realism and Institutionalism both specify states as the primary actors, but then diverge to focus on the relative impact of state power versus international institutions in determining outcomes. Liberalism focuses on individuals and groups and the way in which their preferences are represented by state actors; it further regards the intensity of those represented preferences as the determinant of international outcomes.

What these paradigms do not specify is how the actors they identify behave, the internal or external mechanisms by which the stipulated factors actually generate or produce the stipulated outcomes. What actually happens? How do state leaders actually reason about and decide on a particular course of action?

To illustrate the point, assume that power is the most important factor determining outcomes in the international system. Do state leaders assess the balance of power, calculate their position relative to other states, and decide to increase military spending to improve their position? Or does a particular balance of power prevailing in either the system as a whole or a particular region create a culture of mistrust within states long used to being dominated, instilling an automatic defensiveness and suspicion in leaders of such states?

Calculation and socialization

Two quite different causal mechanisms are at work in this example. In the case of leaders whom we imagine assessing the prevailing balance of power and determining their defense policies accordingly, the behavioral mechanism at work is calculation. In the case of leaders whom we imagine acting, or rather reacting, reflexively, from an ingrained psychological or cultural impulse, the mechanism is socialization. Further, these two mechanisms are likely to operate through different thought processes, or logics.

Social scientists James March and Herbert Simon distinguish between a "logic of consequences" versus a "logic of appropriateness."[48] The logic of consequences involves instrumental calculation concerning how best to advance a predetermined set of interests. If a particular course of action is selected, how will those interests be affected? Or even more bluntly, "How do I get what I want?"[49] This logic is quickly complicated by the prospect of strategic intervention, in which multiple actors are calculating consequences and attempting to factor in the consequences of each other's calculations.

The logic of appropriateness, by contrast, involves socialization, in the sense that the actor seeks to determine what is "the right thing to do" consistent with that actor's identity or sense of self. The presumed thought process that occurs is to ask: "What kind of a situation is this? And what am I supposed to do now?"[50] Further, "What would other people like me–members of the same social class, the same profession, the same moral community, the same nationality–do?" In this conception, interests can be neither fixed nor predetermined; rather, the perception of interests is likely to flow from a felt identity. Yet neither is identity itself fixed, as it often flows from a felt identity with others, suggesting that it could fluctuate either through different associations or through changing self-perception.[51]

These are differences that make a difference. In thinking about norms, for instance, it is possible to imagine norms operating through both types of mechanisms, but with a different type of impact and for quite different purposes. If actors are calculating how best to advance their interests, they are quite likely to establish norms as a means of reducing informational uncertainty, providing a focal point for coordinated action, and decreasing transaction costs. If actors are asking instead what would be the appropriate course of action, then they might actively seek to identify a pre-existing norm as a behavioral guide. In the calculation scenario,

---

[48] See James G. March and Johan P. Olsen, "The Institutional Dynamics of International Political Orders" in Katzenstein, Keohane and Krasner, *Exploration and Contestation*, pp. 309–12.

[49] Martha Finnemore and Kathryn Sikkink, "International Norm Dynamics and Political Change" (1998) 52 *International Organization* 887, reprinted in Katzenstein, Keohane and Krasner, *Exploration and Contestation*, pp. 274–75.

[50] *Ibid.*   [51] March and Olsen, *Institutional Dynamics*, 312.

interests come first and norms help advance those interests. In the socialization scenario, norms come first and shape both identity and interests.

As discussed at the outset of this essay, Robert Keohane has distilled these differences into two "optics," an "instrumentalist optic" and a "normative optic."[52] He initially advanced this distinction as a way of distinguishing between IR and IL. But again, that division is easy to dissolve. Within IL, consider the debate between positivists and natural lawyers, or functionalists and culturalists. Many international lawyers are entirely comfortable with an image of states as rational calculators, consenting to treaties or engaging in customary practices that they have determined will advance their individual and collective interests. Many others, however, will insist that states are profoundly shaped by the carapace of norms and institutions that they acquire when they gain and exercise their sovereignty.[53]

The debate is, if anything, even more heated and partisan among IR scholars. It is framed in terms of Rationalists versus "Constructivists." Constructivists are so named, or rather so name themselves, because of their emphasis on the way interests and identities are constructed, rather than fixed or given. Constructed identities and interests, in turn, are contingent – on ideas, culture, norms, law – a host of factors that humans, including scholars, activists, leaders, can influence.

The elements of Constructivism

As with the other paradigms set forth above, a number of scholars have sought to define Constructivism.[54] They generally agree that Constructivism, like Rationalism, is an *ontology* rather than a theory, in the sense

---

[52] Robert O. Keohane, "International Relations and International Law: Two Optics" (1997) 38 *Harvard Int'l L. J.* 487.

[53] Abram Chayes and Antonia Handler Chayes, *The New Sovereignty: Compliance with International Regulatory Agreements* (1995), pp. 27–28.

[54] See e.g., Peter J. Katzenstein, Robert O. Keohane and Stephen D. Krasner, "Preface: International Organization at Its Golden Anniversary" in Katzenstein, Keohane and Krasner, *Exploration and Contestation*, pp. 34–36 (describing Constructivism as a sociological orientation that illuminates sources of conflict and cooperation while producing normative consequences); John Gerard Ruggie, "What Makes the World Hang Together? Neo-utilitarianism and the Social Constructivist Challenge" (1998) 52 *International Organization* 185 ("constructivism is about human consciousness and its role in international life ... [N]ot only are identities and interests of actors socially constructed, but ... they must share the stage with a whole host of other ideational factors that emanate from the human capacity and will"); Finnemore and Sikkink, "International Norm Dynamics," 272–73 (arguing that "notions of duty, responsibility, identity, and obligation" are all social constructions that may, just as does self-interest and personal gain, motivate behavior);

that it is a general conception of what exists rather than what causes what. According to Alexander Wendt, one of the pioneers of a constructivist approach to IR, Constructivism is both anti-materialist, in the sense that it focuses on ideas and ideals rather than material interests, and anti-rationalist, in the sense that it rejects the idea of instrumental calculation based on fixed preferences.[55]

Beyond these general claims, Wendt specifies the elements of Constructivism as follows. He begins by accepting all five of the basic Realist assumptions set forth by Mearsheimer: the international system is anarchic; states possess offensive capabilities; they can never be certain of each other's intentions; they wish to ensure their own survival; and they are rational. He underlines two additional assumptions that Mearsheimer would accept: a commitment to states as the basic units of analysis in the international system and a commitment to "systemic theory," meaning theory that focuses on the interaction of states within the structure of the international system.[56]

It is the definition of structure, however, that differentiates Constructivism from Realism, or rather Constructivist Realism from Rationalist Realism. As Wendt explains, Neorealists define the structure of the international system as consisting only of the distribution of material capabilities. For Constructivists, by contrast, that structure is also composed of

---

Alexander Wendt, "Constructing International Politics" (1994–95) 19 *J. Int'l Security* 5 (describing Constructivism as a "concern with how world politics is 'socially constructed,' which involves two basic claims: that the fundamental structures of international politics are social rather than strictly material (a claim that opposes materialism), and that these structures shape actors' identities and interests, rather than just their behavior (a claim that opposes rationalism)"); Alexander Wendt, "Anarchy is What States Make of It" (1992) 46 *International Organization* 391, reprinted in Charles Lipson and Benjamin Cohen (eds.), *Theory and Structure in International Political Economy: An International Organization Reader* (1999), p. 79 (defining Constructivism as an approach which accepts that actors' identities and interests are constructed and transformed under anarchy "by the institution of sovereignty, by an evolution of cooperation, and by intentional efforts to transform egoistic identities into collective identities"); Alexander Wendt, *Social Theory of International Politics* (1999), p. 7 (identifying four "sociologies" involved in the debate over Constructivism, namely Individualism, Holism, Materialism and Idealism); Peter J. Katzenstein (ed.), *The Culture of National Security* (1996), p. 46 (suggesting that for some scholars, foreign policy discourses are a process of production and reproduction of state identities and the primacy of the territorial boundaries in the calculus of the interests of states); Emanuel Adler and Michael Barnett (eds.), *Security Communities* (1998) (applying Constructivism to the study of security communities); Michael N. Barnett, *Dialogues in Arab Politics: Negotiations in Regional Order* (1998) (applying Constructivism to the analysis of the Arab regional system).

[55] Wendt, *Social Theory*, pp. 22, 34–35.
[56] Wendt, "Constructing International Politics," 8.

social relationships. These social relationships, in turn, are composed of "shared knowledge, material resources, and social practices."[57]

To get a more concrete sense of what these differences actually mean, it is helpful to turn to John Ruggie's account of Constructivism. For Ruggie, the distinction between Constructivism and what he calls Neo-utilitarianism, or instrumental calculation, is straightforward. "[C]onstructivism is about human consciousness and its role in international life."[58] The realities of international politics are understood "inter-subjectively," meaning through the collective perception of states or any other actors in the international system. Collective perception, in turn, depends on ideas and principled beliefs as well as material interests, "social facts" as well as physical facts. "Social facts include money, property rights, sovereignty, marriage, football, and Valentine's Day, in contrast to such brute observational facts as rivers, mountains, population size, bombs, bullets, and gravity, which exist whether or not there is agreement that they do."[59] In other words, much of the world is what we make of it.[60]

Ruggie also emphasizes that ideas and principled beliefs have normative as well as instrumental dimensions. They affect behavior through a process of felt obligation as well as instrumental calculation. This felt obligation is itself a part of the socialization mechanism, which can "lead states to redefine their interests or even their sense of self." Learning is a key part of this process, learning that is not simply instrumental, in the sense of problem solving, but transformative, in the sense of changing the definition of what the problem is and what it would mean to solve it. Finally, humans engage in deliberation and persuasion, which requires a concept of actors who are "not only strategically but also discursively competent."[61] Talking matters as much as calculating.

Martha Finnemore and Kathryn Sikkink, on the other hand, reject the dichotomies of materialism versus ideational factors or norms versus rationality.[62] They insist that individuals whom they call "norm entrepreneurs" routinely engage in strategic calculation about how to advance their ends; conversely, calculation on the basis of fixed preferences can include ideas and normative commitments as well as material interests. They present the heart of Constructivism as an account of how norms work: how they emerge, how they influence behavior, and how they are internalized to become part of the social structure that conditions actor

---

[57] Ibid. [58] Ruggie, "What Makes the World," 216.
[59] Ibid. [60] See Wendt, "Anarchy", 79.
[61] Finnemore and Sikkink, "International Norm Dynamics," 274–75. [62] Ibid.

choice.[63] The fights between Constructivists and non-Constructivists, in turn, involve the precise link "between rationality and norm-based behavior, the particular logic that drives action, and the degree to which norms operate by constraining choice or by internalizing a different set of choices."[64] At its most basic, this is the old debate about free will versus determinism dressed in new clothes.

Not surprisingly, many lawyers are drawn to Constructivism. Many lawyers are norm entrepreneurs; virtually all lawyers engage daily in deliberation and persuasion – a world of discourse. Many lawyers are intuitively uncomfortable with purely Rationalist instrumental accounts, believing deeply and verifying empirically through their practice the ways in which the rules that they shape in turn shape the identity and interests of the actors who operate within those rules. For these lawyers, Constructivism provides a deeply satisfying account of how and why what they do matters. For other lawyers, however, legal rules are indeed tools to enable clients – individuals, corporations, NGOs, governments or international organizations – to pursue their interests and values. There is nothing wrong with "rules as tools"; instrumental rationality celebrates the human capacity to escape the constraints of structure and the weight of collective expectations. IR theory can never resolve these debates, any more than can law or philosophy, but lawyers can find Constructivist or Rationalist variants within all three of the major IR paradigms.

Marrying Constructivism with Realism, Institutionalism and Liberalism

The major paradigms of Realism, Institutionalism and Liberalism each encompass more specific theories that rely on Constructivist as well as Rationalist causal mechanisms. However, it remains true that most standard overviews of IR theory privilege the Rationalist versions of each of the paradigms. Constructivist variants are thus most often found in the role of critique.

It often seems particularly difficult to square Realism with Constructivism, given Realism's uncompromising insistence on the role of power in determining state behavior. However, as noted above, Wendt is willing to embrace the principal assumptions of Realism. He would also agree that at least in some parts of the international system, states behave according to Realist precepts. The difference is that Wendt insists that states

[63] Ibid. at 255–66. [64] Ibid. at 271.

pursue power because they have learned, or been taught, to pursue power. The need to amass power to ensure survival does not flow ineluctably from the fact that other states have power, but from the learned perception of that power as a threat. The structure of the international system comprises these perceptions and resulting practices, accreting over decades and centuries to determine behavior. Rationalist Realists accept the enduring fact of some distribution of power across the system and insist that the implications of that distribution are unalterable absent a central coercive authority. Constructivist Realists believe that those implications can be changed as a result of learning to think about them differently.

The debates between Rationalists and Constructivists are most developed within Institutionalism. To take only one example, consider Andrew Hurrell's critique of Rationalist regime theory.[65] Hurrell claims that although the Rationalist account of international institutions develops the idea of self-interest and reciprocal benefits, it "downplays the traditional emphasis on the role of community and a sense of justice."[66] A view of rules primarily as tools for reducing transactions costs, increasing information, and decreasing opportunities for cheating cannot account for a "sense of community" and the emergence of cooperation through the growing perception of common interests.[67] Nor can it address fundamental perceptions of justice and equity in the formation of state preferences. Finally, Rationalist approaches can neither integrate the importance of domestic politics in creating institutions and making them work, nor elaborate the relationship between legal rules and the broader structure of the international system. Constructivist approaches, however, which Hurrell embraces as part of the older tradition of sociological institutionalism, focus on all these factors.[68]

---

[65] Andrew Hurrell, "International Society and the Study of Regimes: A Reflective Approach" in Robert J. Beck, Anthony Clark Arend and Robert D. Vander Lugt (eds.), *International Rules: Approaches from International Law and International Relations* (1999), pp. 206–24.

[66] *Ibid.* at p. 210.   [67] *Ibid.* at pp. 214–15.

[68] For another account of Constructivist Institutionalist theory, see Stephen D. Krasner, *Sovereignty: Organized Hypocrisy* (2000), pp. 56–67. Krasner describes Rational Choice Institutionalism as an approach that conceives of norms and rules as the voluntary choices of calculating actors who perceive resulting institutions as stable equilibria that generate shared expectations and outcomes beneficial over a range of policy options. Similarly, Neoliberal Institutionalism is a rational and contractual response to externalities, collective goods problems and informational imperfections that works to provide information, reduce transaction costs and offer opportunities for issue linkages, thereby promoting more efficient institutional designs. Finally, Sociological Institutionalism functions to socialize relevant actors by embedding them in networks of intersubjectively shared

Finally, Liberalism readily incorporates both Rationalist and Constructivist causal mechanisms. In Moravcsik's account of different types of Liberal theory, he includes "ideational liberalism" as well as commercial and republican Liberalism.[69] Ideational Liberalism "views the configuration of domestic social identities and values as a basic determinant of state preferences, and, therefore, of interstate conflict and cooperation."[70] "Social identity," in turn, refers to the different ways individuals constitute themselves as a nation, as a particular type of political system, or as a particular type of economic order. How and why they constitute themselves this way is left open. "Liberals take no distinctive position on the origins of social identities, which may result from historical accretion or be constructed through conscious collective or state action, nor on the question of whether they ultimately reflect ideational or material factors."[71] In practice, ideational Liberal theories focus on the role of nationalism, ideology and economic libertarianism versus social welfare economics in determining state preferences. Many of these theories are explicitly Constructivist in their explanations of how individuals and states come to identify themselves as part of a particular nation, as adherents of a particular political ideology or as proponents of more-or-less economic regulation.

The road ahead

Looking beyond the specific paradigms to actual work marrying international law with international relations theory, the landscape is becoming increasingly interesting. I advance five basic propositions about the role of law in shaping international politics, the role of politics in shaping international law, the prospects for a new generation of international institutions and the fate of the state. Each of these propositions draws on recent work in both international law and international relations scholarship, and often on work either done by joint teams of lawyers and political scientists or by single scholars with full training in both disciplines. Each is formulated as a definitive proposition of a kind likely to be helpful to

---

cognitive constructs so as to define their interests and capabilities and thereby determine "the patterns of appropriate economic, political, and cultural activity engaged in" by individuals, organizations, interest groups and ultimately states – for some Sociological Institutionalists, actors create the institutions, whereas for others it is the institution that generates the agents.

[69] Moravcsik, "Taking Preferences Seriously," 524–33.
[70] *Ibid.* at 525.   [71] *Ibid.*

practicing lawyers and policy-makers. At the same time, however, each is advanced as a proposition under active debate, a debate that is advanced by the essays in this volume.

International lawyers can profit from an analysis of power

Perhaps unsurprisingly, lest the global order crowd get too carried away, the Realists have raised their heads again to remind the legal and policy-making community of the critical role of power in determining international outcomes. This time, however, with a twist. Whereas the traditional Realist-Legalist debate has been conducted in terms of whether law could play any autonomous role in shaping international outcomes, this round focuses more on the role of power in shaping law. In other words, even if Realists remain uninterested in law as an independent variable, a number are suddenly interested in law as a dependent variable – perhaps from the recognition that, for whatever reasons, the prevailing great powers at this historical moment are keen to use legal rules and institutions to advance their interests and institutionalize their power. Thus, as Richard Steinberg writes, "most realist explanations of international law focus on the distributive consequences of international negotiations – and how powerful states have advanced their interests. Realist predictions center on the kind of international legal developments that may be expected as power disperses or concentrates in particular international organizational or historical contexts, or as the interests of powerful states change."[72]

This approach is represented in this volume by several contributions, most notably the essay by Downs and Jones (Chapter 5). Downs has a well-deserved reputation for forcing international lawyers to think hard about the real sources of cooperation, most notably in his debates with Abram and Antonia Chayes about the relative role of enforcement versus management in ensuring compliance.[73] He and Jones extend this analysis by taking a more nuanced look at the role of reputation in enhancing compliance, noting that many IR and IL scholars believe empirically that states are concerned to protect their reputations for compliance with existing agreements so as to be included in negotiations on new agreements. They argue, by contrast, that states can develop multiple reputations,

---

[72] Richard H. Steinberg (ed.), *The Greening of Trade Law? International Trade Organizations and Environmental Issues* (2000), p. 8.
[73] See Chayes and Chayes, *The New Sovereignty*; George W. Downs, David M. Rocke and Peter N. Barsoom, "Is the Good News About Compliance Good News About Cooperation?" (1996) 50 *International Organization* 379.

"often quite different, in connection with different regimes and even different treaties within the same regime."[74] As a result, developing countries may suffer less from non-compliance in specific issue areas than might be expected. Conversely, however, more powerful developed countries can also defect from relatively less important agreements with little reputational consequence. While Downs and Jones do not track the differences in treaty compliance explicitly in terms of the distribution of economic and military power in the international system, their findings underline differential treatment for powerful and less powerful states. Abbott and Snidal also find that differences in the relative power of the prospective parties to an agreement affect the choice of a particular regime design.

Legalized rules and institutions operate differently from non-legalized rules and institutions

As political scientists discovered and embraced regime theory in the 1980s and 1990s, many international lawyers questioned the value of lumping "rules, norms, principles and decision-making procedures" together, thereby denying any difference between a legal obligation and an informal agreement.[75] Michael Byers, for instance, insists that "international relations scholars need to be told that international law is different from the other factors they study."[76] A growing number of political scientists now accept this proposition (in addition to the many, particularly outside the United States, who never doubted it!). Translated into American political science jargon, the question then becomes how "legalized" regimes differ from "non-legalized regimes" in both their origins and impact on state behavior. Alternatively, how does "law" differ from "norms"? Relatedly, when should policy-makers seek to legalize? And for what purposes?

Note that this debate is not over whether law matters relative to power, interest, geography or a host of other factors in international life. It is conducted among scholars who take as a matter of empirical observation,

---

[74] As elaborated on by George W. Downs and Michael A. Jones in Chapter 5.
[75] See e.g., Tom J. Farer, "An Inquiry into the Legitimacy of Humanitarian Intervention" in Lori Fisler Damrosch and David J. Scheffer (eds.), *Law and Force in the New International Order* 196 (1991). In addition to the various political scientists and international lawyers engaged in the legislation debate, see Anthony Arend, "Do Legal Rules Matter? International Law and International Politics" (1998) 38 *Virginia J. Int'l L.* 107; also Arend, *Legal Rules*.
[76] Michael Byers, "Taking the Law out of International Law: A Critique of the Iterative Perspective" (1997) 38 *Harvard Int'l L. J.* 201, 205.

logic or faith that rules and institutions affect state behavior. The question is a narrower one: How do *legal* rules affect behavior differently from non-legal rules, or, more broadly, norms? On the other hand, the debate in practice is actually broader than most international lawyers would likely assume. "Legalization" refers not only to the obligatory status of a rule as part of the system of international law, but also, in one formulation, to the rule's relative precision and the delegation of its interpretation and application to a third party tribunal.[77] For other political scientists, as well as lawyers, the question involves the "judicialization" of international affairs as much as "legalization."[78] But for present purposes, and in plain English, the issue of interest is the significance and impact of law and courts in the international system, as compared to less formal and binding prescriptions and dispute resolution mechanisms. The answers to these questions, however tentative and incomplete, are of intrinsic interest to any international lawyer and may also prove very important to the larger field of regime design, discussed below.

Several of the contributions to this volume significantly enrich the debate over legalization, particularly regarding the role of international judges. Abbott and Snidal, leading contributors to the original legalization volume, have refined their analysis further in thought-provoking and productive ways. Their analysis of three different pathways to cooperation – framework conventions, plurilateral agreements and soft law – strengthens one of the important conclusions of the original volume: that no necessary teleological progression exists from soft law to hard law.

---

[77] The special issue of *International Organization* devoted to the phenomenon of "legalization" distinguishes "legalized" institutions from non-legalized institutions along three dimensions: "the degree to which rules are obligatory, the precision of those rules, and the delegation of some functions of interpretation, monitoring, and implementation to a third party." Judith Goldstein, Miles Kahler, Robert O. Keohane and Anne-Marie Slaughter, "Introduction: Legalization and World Politics" (2000) 54 *International Organization* 385, 387. Compare Alec Stone Sweet's definition of legal norms as a "subset of social norms," a sub-set "distinguished by their higher degree of clarity, formalization, and binding authority." Alec Stone Sweet, *Governing with Judges: Constitutional Politics in Europe* (2000), p. 11. The *International Organization* volume thus defines the phenomenon of legalization more broadly than simply the increased appearance and influence of legal rules in international affairs.

[78] Alec Stone Sweet is the most prominent scholar studying the "judicialization" of politics, both within specific countries, across countries and in the international realm. See Alec Stone, *The Birth of Judicial Politics in France* (1992); Alec Stone Sweet, "Judicialization and the Construction of Governance" (1999) 32 *Comparative Political Studies* 147; Alec Stone Sweet, *Governing with Judges: Constitutional Politics in Europe* (2000).

In many cases, agreements instantiating cooperation will be more effective if they contain legally binding obligations from the beginning. On the other hand, excessive legalization can backfire, whereas soft law can provide necessary escape valves to help ensure compliance. It is noteworthy in this regard that Edith Brown Weiss does not list the "legal" nature of an agreement in her extensive list of eleven factors that affect compliance.

Eyal Benvenisti takes a different tack, one that is likely to be very welcome to scholars of international relations but that may seem heretical to international lawyers. By training a game theoretic lens on international courts and arbitral tribunals, he finds that international judges contribute directly to creating more "efficient" international legal rules by simply "finding" customary international norms that are in fact unsupported by actual state practice and *opinio juris*, with the happy by-product that these rules are more likely to be complied with. A corollary implication, which he does not emphasize, is that international judges are only empowered to hear cases arising from fully legalized agreements, suggesting that their valuable role in "leap-frogging" existing state practice will be missing in issue areas dominated by soft law.

Soft law is as important as hard law in global governance but plays a different role

An important corollary of the legalization debate is the relationship between soft law and hard law, or, in a parallel conception, low legalization and high legalization. The debate over soft law among international lawyers is extensive and growing, too extensive to chronicle here.[79] However, much if not most of this literature either seeks to respond to

---

[79] See e.g., Dinah Shelton (ed.), *Commitment and Compliance: The Role of Non-Binding Norms in the International Legal System* (2000). Of particular value within this important volume are Naomi Roht-Arriaza, "'Soft Law' in a 'Hybrid' Organization: The International Organization for Standardization" (p. 263); Laurence Boisson de Chazournes, "Policy Guidance and Compliance: The World Bank Operational Standards" (p. 281); Lyuba Zarsky, "Environmental Norms in the Asia-Pacific Economic Cooperation Forum" (p. 303). Other notable examples include Kenneth Abbott and Duncan Snidal, "Hard and Soft Law in International Governance" (2000) 54 *International Organization* 421; P. Dupuy, "Soft Law and the International Law of the Environment" (1991) 12 *Michigan J. Int'l L.* 420; Antonio Cassese and Joseph H.H. Weiler (eds.), *Change and Stability in International Law-Making* (1988); Oscar Schachter, "The Existence of Nonbinding International Agreements" (1977) 71 *Am. J. Int'l L.* 296.

the gauntlet thrown down by Prosper Weil in 1983, arguing that soft law would ultimately destabilize and undermine the entire international legal system,[80] or tries within a doctrinal framework to determine whether soft law is law at all.[81] More recent IR/IL scholarship moves away from this jurisprudential debate and instead explores the relative advantages of soft law and hard law in different situations.[82] It also seeks to establish the conditions under which soft law may ripen into hard law.[83]

In previous work, Abbott and Snidal emphasize that "international actors often deliberately choose softer forms of legalization as superior institutional arrangements."[84] Soft law, in their definition, means "soft legalization," or any legal arrangement "weakened along one or more of the dimensions of obligation, precision, and delegation."[85] Why would states choose such softer arrangements? In a word, "Soft law offers many of the advantages of hard law, avoids some of the costs of hard law, and has certain independent advantages of its own."[86] More specifically, a number of different factors condition states' choice of soft law, including "transactions costs, uncertainty, implications for national sovereignty, divergence of preferences, and power differentials."[87]

In this volume, as noted above, Abbott and Snidal describe a soft law pathway to cooperation in conjunction with two other pathways that begin with hard law agreements but that either deepen or widen over time. They analyze the development of the international human rights regime as an example of how soft law obligations – even if close to the purely hortatory – can gradually become "harder" over decades of political mobilization and pressure. It is not at all clear from their analysis, however, that soft law

---

[80] Prosper Weil, "Towards Relative Normativity in International Law?" (1983) 77 *Am. J. Int'l L.* 413.

[81] See e.g., Dupuy, "Soft Law"; Ved P. Nanda, "Development as an Emerging Human Right under International Law" (1996) 13 *Denver J. Int'l L. and Policy* 161.

[82] Abbott and Snidal, "Hard and Soft Law."

[83] Jutta Brunnee and Stephen Toope, "Environmental Security and Freshwater Resources: A Case for International Ecosystem Law" (1994) 5 *Yearbook of Int'l Environmental Law* 41; Jutta Brunnee and Stephen Toope, "Environmental Security and Freshwater Resources: Ecosystem Regime Building" (1997) 91 *Am. J. of Int'l L.* 6; Stephen Toope and Jutta Brunnee, "Freshwater Regimes: The Mandate of the International Joint Commission" (1998) 15 *Arizona J. Int'l and Comparative L.* 273.

[84] Abbott and Snidal, "Hard and Soft Law." [85] *Ibid.* at 422.

[86] *Ibid.* at 423. As Abbott and Snidal acknowledge, they are building here on the pioneering work of Charles Lipson, "Why Are Some Agreements Informal?" (1991) 45 *International Organization* 495. Lipson's work presaged the current debate by almost a decade.

[87] Abbott and Snidal, "Hard and Soft Law."

strategies are more or less effective than the framework convention or the plurilateral approaches.

Regime design matters

The broad legalization debate and the more focused study of the choice of hard versus soft law can both be understood as sub-sets of, or perhaps precursors to, the growing field of regime design. Much IR/IL scholarship through the 1990s drew on IR theory to help explain the structure and function of existing international institutions. These authors sought to catalogue and explain what particular international legal institutions *do* and why they are structured as they are. Kenneth Abbott pioneered this approach in legal scholarship by examining, through the lens of Rationalist regime theory, the functions performed by international trade law[88] and by the "assurance" and "verification" provisions of major arms control agreements.[89] He also teamed up with political scientist Duncan Snidal to explore the functions performed by formal international organizations.[90]

Although this type of analytical work is important in enhancing a general understanding of why the international institutional landscape looks the way it does, it is more important for most international lawyers and policy-makers to know how specific institutional features can enhance or detract from the performance of the institution's designated function. This type of knowledge can then be directly incorporated into regime design, the architectural blueprints for reforming old institutions and creating new ones in response to the changing needs of the international community. As Ronald Mitchell frames the issue:

> Why do states design regimes the way they do? How should they design them in the future? Why do some regimes appear to rely on tough sanctions, others on financial incentives, and others on what appear to be little more than exhortation? Should states strengthen the nuclear non-proliferation regime

---

[88] See Kenneth W. Abbott, "The Trading Nation's Dilemma: The Functions of the Law of International Trade" (1985) 26 *Harvard Int'l L. J.* 501.
[89] See Kenneth W. Abbott, "'Trust But Verify': The Production of Information in Arms Control Treaties and Other International Agreements" (1993) 26 *Cornell Int'l L. J.* 1, 2.
[90] Kenneth W. Abbott and Duncan Snidal, "Why States Act Through Formal International Organizations" (1998) 42 *J. Conflict Resolution* 3. See Anne-Marie Slaughter, Andrew S. Tulumello and Stepan Wood, "International Law and International Relations Theory: A New Generation of Interdisciplinary Scholarship" (1998) 92 *Am. J. Int'l L.* 376 (1998), for a review of other work in the same vein.

by tightening export controls, offering security guarantees, or developing clear and public bombing plans? Should the Convention on the Rights of the Child threaten countries that violate its terms or engage them in long-term normative dialogue?[91]

Many authors in this volume wrestle with these kinds of questions, with valuable results. Petros Mavroidis, for instance, engages in a sustained analysis about the impact of a commitment to negative integration in the WTO rather than positive integration, on states' abilities simultaneously to fulfill their obligations under international environmental and human rights agreements. Abbott and Snidal explicitly address the basic issue of what general type of regime – a framework convention, a plurilateral agreement or a soft law declaration – may be best tailored to different issue areas. Brown Weiss contributes data on the important role of Secretariats in enhancing compliance with some regimes. Benvenisti's arguments about the role of the International Court of Justice (ICJ) in establishing efficient norms suggests the advantages of including a dispute resolution clause conferring jurisdiction on the ICJ in areas such as global commons issues where it has traditional authority. And Milner, building on John Ruggie's seminal work on embedded Liberalism,[92] demonstrates the crucial value of escape clauses that are explicitly designed with domestic political pressures in mind.

Domestic politics are as important for international lawyers as international politics

International lawyers and international relations scholars alike are paying increasing attention to domestic politics. Even a brief survey of recent work indicates the broad scope of this work and the range of opportunities for further research. To take only one example, in Ronald Mitchell's work on compliance with the international oil pollution regime, he emphasizes that while compliance by private actors varied considerably between the two regimes, state compliance did not. The equipment regime was markedly more *effective* than the discharge regime because it tapped into the power of private actors who had little reason not to follow the Treaty

---

[91] Ronald B. Mitchell, "Situation Structure and Regime Implementation Mechanisms," paper presented at the American Political Science Association Conference, Atlanta, Georgia, September 1999.
[92] See John G. Ruggie, "International Regimes, Transactions, and Change: Embedded Liberalism in the Postwar Economic Order" (1982) 36 *International Organization* 379.

rules but had significant influence over the ultimate targets of the regime: shippers.[93]

Relatedly, the special International Organization issue on legalization spotlights the role of domestic actors and domestic politics more generally both in generating a demand for legalization, as discussed earlier in this chapter, and in determining its consequences. On the demand side, as Abbott and Snidal point out: "In many issue-areas, from trade and investment to human rights and the environment, individuals and private groups are the new actors most responsible for new international agreements – and for resisting new agreements in favor of the status quo."[94] Regarding the consequences of legalization, Miles Kahler summarizes the many ways in which writers on legalization link compliance with legal rules to domestic politics, and particularly to specific configurations of domestic politics.[95] In her study of compliance with IMF regulations, for instance, Beth Simmons finds that "regimes that were based on clear principles of the rule of law were far more likely to comply with their commitments."[96] Yet these results do not flow from some magic incantation of "the rule of law." On the contrary, as Kahler notes, rule of law societies "construct" specific channels of compliance that connect international legal commitments to specific groups of domestic actors, denominated as "compliance constituencies."[97]

This growing literature highlights three cutting edge issues for both international lawyers and political scientists, each of which supports the claim that domestic politics are as important for international lawyers to understand and integrate into their work as international politics:

(1) First, one of the most promising pathways for enhancing the effectiveness of an international legal regime is by bolstering or even triggering domestic political activity.
(2) Second, international law is made by states, but state positions do not spring fully formed from chancelleries or foreign ministries. Different

---

[93] Ronald B. Mitchell, *Intentional Oil Pollution at Sea: Environmental Policy and Treaty Compliance* (1994), pp. 299–300.
[94] Abbott and Snidal, "Hard and Soft Law," 450. See also Miles Kahler's extensive discussion of domestic politics and legalization, discussed above in the section on legalization. Miles Kahler, "Conclusion: The Causes and Consequences of Legalization" (2000) 54 *International Organization* 661, 675–76.
[95] Ibid. at 674–77.
[96] Beth A. Simmons, "The Legalization of International Monetary Affairs" (2000) 54 *International Organization* 573, 599.
[97] Kahler, "Conclusion," 675.

social and governmental actors who actually succeed in being represented at the state policy-making level are the real sources of international law. Thus international law-making is better understood as a "bottom up" than a "top down" process.
(3) Third, the state itself must be reconceptualized as a two-level entity, a set of interaction between actors in domestic and transnational society and a wide array of government institutions.

Milner takes the two-level approach to trade law and policy as their point of departure, identifying the domestic motives that prompt leaders to sign trade agreements in the first place. Further, she notes the ways in which publicizing non-compliance before domestic publics can reinforce compliance. Second, as mentioned above, she focuses on the specific need to accommodate domestic constituencies in regime design. Brown Weiss also points to the differential role of domestic constituencies in strengthening or weakening compliance. And Hirsch argues that the sociological perspective on compliance operates through domestic actors very like Kahler's "compliance constituencies," a mechanism that is strengthened by globalization. Finally, Mavroidis makes clear that the critical variable in improving human rights is domestic actors responding to international pressure; as long as WTO obligations do not actively impede these actors, it is difficult to attribute human rights violations or failure to ameliorate them to the WTO itself.

Conclusion

A decade ago, it was relatively rare for international lawyers and international relations scholars to come together in any format other than a "political science" panel at the annual meeting of the American Society of International Law and an "international law" panel at the annual meeting of the American Political Science Association. That has changed remarkably. Enterprises such as this volume, where political scientists and international lawyers come together to study a common problem, write together, and publish together, have enriched both disciplines. International lawyers, as Eyal Benvenisti makes explicit in his chapter, have learned to deploy political science techniques and draw on empirical data to make positive claims about how law works. At the same time, they are still able, and in my view required, to shift gears to make normative arguments about what the law or a legal institution should be or do, building on their positive claims. Political scientists, on the other hand, such as Downs and

Jones, have learned to listen to international lawyers' insights about how phenomena such as compliance actually work, and to build those insights into their theories and models.

As a scholar, it is relatively easy to survey the literature, the conferences, and the collaborations and to evaluate the academic value of such cross-fertilization. The real test, however, is the world. Both international lawyers and international relations scholars confront pressing global problems, issues of such urgency and import that lives and lands hang in the balance. Compliance with international environmental regimes is not an abstract subject, however much data we collect; however many models we build; however sophisticated the rules we devise. Designing regimes that are effective at actually addressing the problems they purport to regulate and promoting or even enforcing compliance with those regimes are global – indeed planetary – imperatives. If conferences and volumes such as this one improve the ability of individuals in all fields to diagnose problems and develop effective solutions, they will perform the dual function, well known to international lawyers, of advancing knowledge and making a genuine difference in the world.

3

Pathways to international cooperation

KENNETH W. ABBOTT AND DUNCAN SNIDAL

How do states and other international actors move from one level or type of cooperation (which might be the absence of cooperation) to stronger levels or types? While international cooperation sometimes occurs in "big bangs," in which states jump suddenly from low to high levels of cooperation on an issue,[1] cooperation typically advances incrementally through one, or sometimes several, way stations, such as non-binding declarations, vague undertakings and narrowly plurilateral agreements.[2] These incremental processes can be understood in terms of movement along three

---

For valuable comments on an earlier draft of this chapter, we thank participants at the Conference on the Impact of Norms and Institutions on Cooperation in International Environment and Trade at Hebrew University, Jerusalem, as well as seminar participants at the University of Virginia and University of California at Berkeley Law Schools, the University of Wisconsin, and the University of Chicago Program on International Politics, Economics and Security (PIPES).

[1] Two recent, but very different examples of "big bang" cooperation are the following:

(a) TRIPS. Before the Uruguay Round, the GATT trade regime did not address intellectual property at all. When the Round was over, all members of the new World Trade Organization had adopted the Agreement on Trade-Related Aspects of Intellectual Property Rights (TRIPS), which prescribes detailed rules and institutional requirements. This result was achieved through interest-based bargaining and the exercise of political power by Western industry groups and governments.

(b) Land mines. The 1997 Ottawa Convention on the Prohibition of Anti-Personnel Mines, like TRIPS, was created in a relatively short time and largely from whole cloth (although in both cases negotiators could look to models in other agreements). Here, success was achieved largely through the work of norm entrepreneurs like the International Campaign to Ban Landmines and certain Canadian government officials, who utilized moral arguments and mobilized broad public support.

[2] Not infrequently, of course, the process is halted at one of these intermediate points. We argue elsewhere that, at least in the context of soft law, this should not automatically be regarded as a failure; states and other actors may simply prefer softer forms of cooperation (or lower levels of cooperation) as superior solutions to the political problems they face. See Kenneth W. Abbott and Duncan Snidal, "Hard and Soft Law in International Governance" (2000) 54 *International Organization* 421.

important dimensions of cooperation: substantive content, participation and – of special importance for this volume – legalization. In this chapter we identify three alternative routes to cooperation – "pathways" – that correspond to these three dimensions and examine the circumstances under which particular strategies of gradual cooperation will be more effective and are therefore more likely to be chosen as pathways to cooperation.

Our general argument is that states often cannot move directly to a cooperative solution because of informational, bargaining and distribution problems that hamper collective action.[3] We begin with one such problem: the uncertainties that actors commonly face regarding the nature of particular issues, the nature and capabilities of potential cooperators, and political reactions at home and abroad. The three stylized gradual processes we identify here have as their key features that they (i) allow states to limit their commitments at any point in time to the level of cooperation they find appropriate given their uncertainty, and (ii) provide states with opportunities to resolve these uncertainties and undertake greater (joint) cooperative commitments as they are ready to do so. Each pathway offers advantages for dealing with particular types of uncertainty.

Each pathway also has advantages for different actors – not only for states, but also for the domestic agencies, international governmental organizations (IGOs) and non-governmental organizations (NGOs) that are often the key protagonists in campaigns for cooperation. This means that, whatever the issue, different actors will prefer to pursue cooperation along the pathways on which they are most advantaged. However, their ability to do so will be strongly conditioned by the availability of appropriate institutional arrangements. Thus the choice of a pathway in a particular setting depends jointly on the nature of the problem, the actors and the available institutions.

We begin from the observation that an international agreement is only effective when it alters the behavior of participant states in ways that affect outcomes. This requires that (a) the agreement include some substantive content governing the area of behavior that needs to be modified, (b) the agreement includes participation by at least some states whose behavior is consequential for the issue, and (c) the participating states

---

[3] For an elaboration of this argument, see Kenneth W. Abbott and Duncan Snidal, "Filling in the Folk Theorem: The Role of Gradualism and Legalization in International Cooperation," paper presented at the American Political Science Association Annual Meeting, Boston, August 30, 2002.

feel compelled to change some aspect of their behavior because of the agreement. The absence of any of these conditions renders an agreement virtually meaningless. Thus we adopt these three dimensions as key elements of cooperation.[4]

Our first dimension is *substantive content*. As Downs, Rocke and Barsoom have forcefully argued,[5] the existence of an international agreement, even one with which participating states regularly comply, does not necessarily mean that those states have accepted substantively significant commitments. Many treaties manifestly include only shallow content and others require states to do little more than they would have done unilaterally without any agreement. Conversely, the absence of a formal, legally binding agreement does not necessarily imply the absence of substantive content: witness the Universal Declaration of Human Rights, the Rio Declaration on Environment and Development, and the Beijing Declaration on the rights of women.

Our second dimension is *broad participation*. Depending on the nature of the problem, agreements require different levels of participation in order to be effective. In a setting where only bilateral cooperation matters, such as the regulation of the Great Lakes, the element of participation essentially drops out of the analysis – there is either a bilateral agreement or no agreement at all. At the other extreme, agreements on some issues (such as global environmental problems or combating terrorism) depend on nearly universal participation to be effective. Many problems fall between these two poles: while universal participation in an agreement is not necessary, successful cooperation requires that at least a core group of states participate, and cooperation may be further enhanced by additional parties. We use the term "broad participation" in relation to the size of the group, multilateral or plurilateral, that would be optimal for cooperation on an issue.

Our third and most controversial dimension is international *legalization*. It is controversial because, while traditional legal scholars and constructivist political scientists take international law to be binding on its subjects through its own normative force, rational choice legal scholars and political scientists are skeptical that legal rules or agreements

---

[4] As discussed further below, the dimensions of substantive content, participation and obligation or commitment figure prominently in the recent literature on cooperation.
[5] See George Downs, David Rocke and Peter N. Barsoom, "Is the Good News About Compliance Good News About Cooperation?" (1996) 50 *International Organization* 379.

per se have the ability to change behavior.[6] Instead, rationalists argue that legal rules are only effective insofar as the underlying incentives of the actors are properly aligned – making the rules themselves largely epiphenomenal.[7]

Elsewhere we have argued that international legalization is interesting precisely because it combines elements of both the normative and rationalist lines of argument.[8] For present purposes, however, it is sufficient to note that international agreements and undertakings are almost invariably "legalized" to a greater or lesser degree.[9] Indeed, many significant international agreements are quite highly legalized: they take legal form (typically as treaties), are understood to be binding as a matter of international law on states that accept them, and are implemented through legal discourse, procedures and institutions. Moreover, both enthusiasts and skeptics generally agree that states do in fact honor their legal commitments.[10]

---

[6] Examples in the former category include Martha Finnemore and Stephen J. Toope, "Alternatives to 'Legalization': Richer Views of Law and Politics" (2001) 55 *International Organization* 743; Thomas M. Franck, *The Power of Legitimacy Among Nations* (1990); and Harold Koh, "Why Do Nations Obey International Law" (1997) 106 *Yale L.J.* 2599. Examples in the skeptical category include Downs, Rocke and Barsoom, "Good News"; Jack Goldsmith and Eric Posner, "A Theory of Customary International Law" (1999) 66 *U. Chi. L. Rev.* 1113; and "Symposium, Rational Choice and International Law" (2002) 31 *J. Legal Studies* (No. 1, January), Pt. 2.

[7] Sophisticated skeptics, however, accept that international agreements can perform the coordinating functions of "cheap talk" in appropriate circumstances. See Jack L. Goldsmith and Eric Posner, "Moral and Legal Rhetoric in International Relations: A Rational Choice Perspective" (2002) 31 *J. Legal Studies* S115.

[8] Kenneth W. Abbott and Duncan Snidal, "Values and Interests: International Legalization in the Fight Against Corruption" (2002) 31 *J. Legal Studies* S141. Our work is part of a broader intellectual project to better understand the role of law in international relations. Two recent volumes that indicate the range of these efforts include Special Issue, "Legalization and World Politics" (2000) 54 *International Organization* (No. 3) reprinted as Judith L. Goldstein, Miles Kahler, Robert O. Keohane and Anne-Marie Slaughter (eds.), *Legalization and World Politics* (MIT Press, 2001); and "Symposium, Rational Choice."

[9] In the recent volume on *Legalization and World Politics*, our co-authors and we developed a conceptualization of legalization as involving three elements: legal *obligation*, *precision* of commitments and *delegation* of authority to third party institutions (including judicial/quasi-judicial, executive and rule-making institutions). Each of these elements can be independently varied; they can then be combined to create a fine-grained continuum of forms or levels of legalization. See Kenneth W. Abbott, Robert O. Keohane, Andrew Moravcsik, Anne-Marie Slaughter and Duncan Snidal, "The Concept of Legalization" (2000) 54 *International Organization* 401.

[10] See Louis Henkin, *How Nations Behave* (1968); Hans J. Morgenthau, *Politics Among Nations* (1978).

Because states treat international legal commitments as if they were binding, however, they often moderate and modulate their level of commitment by expressing their undertakings as "soft law."[11] States can limit their legal obligation through hortatory language, exceptions, reservations and the like. They can reduce it still further by expressly designating their undertakings as not legally binding,[12] or by adopting them in forums that lack clear law-making power, such as the UN General Assembly. States can reduce the constraining effect of substantive provisions by drafting them in imprecise terms. And they can preserve discretion to interpret and apply their undertakings by limiting the delegation of authority to courts or quasi-judicial institutions, or to any formal institutions at all. Through this striking variety of arrangements, states can achieve fine gradations in the level of their commitments along the dimension of legalization.[13]

We focus on these three elements – substantive content, participation and legalization – as essential elements of effective agreements. In doing so, we deliberately side-step the question of compliance which is so central to international relations and law.[14] Each of our three dimensions provides a means for states to avoid being seriously constrained by an agreement until they are willing to undertake stronger commitments. That is, compliance issues are largely moot if an agreement has little content, or if states are not parties to it, or if it imposes no legal obligations. Our focus, then, is not on whether states comply with agreements, but rather on how they reach agreements where compliance becomes an issue.

Three dynamic pathways

In this section we introduce three pathways along which states and other actors can incrementally strengthen international cooperation over time.

[11] In our conceptualization, "soft law" includes forms of legalization in which one or more of the elements of legal obligation, precision and delegation are weak or non-existent. Elsewhere we have analyzed why states agree on different combinations of these elements to meet their needs in particular settings. See Abbott and Snidal, "Hard and Soft Law."

[12] Significant examples include the Helsinki Final Act and the "Non-Legally Binding Authoritative Statement of Principles" on the sustainable development of forests, adopted at the Rio Conference on the Environment and Development.

[13] In the remainder of this Chapter we treat legalization as a summary dimension, where increases reflect overall movement towards a hard legal arrangement (i.e., an increase in obligation, precision, delegation, or some combination thereof), without differentiating the specific forms of softer legalization.

[14] See e.g., Beth Simmons, "Compliance with International Agreements" (1998) 1 *Ann. Rev. Pol. Sci.* 75.

These pathways are defined in terms of the three major dimensions of successful international cooperation identified above: (i) substantive content, (ii) participation and (iii) legalization.

The three pathways are ideal types constructed to highlight the essential character of different routes to heightened cooperation and to dramatize the contrast among them. Each pathway begins with an initial arrangement in which one of the three elements is weak but the other two are at least moderately strong. This means that, at the starting point of each pathway, states are not significantly constrained by the agreement because a necessary element for cooperation is not yet in place. Analyzing ideal type pathways thus allows us to focus on the political processes involved in incrementally strengthening particular elements. We label the three pathways "Framework Convention," "Plurilateral," and "Soft Law," corresponding, respectively, to the initially weak elements of substantive content, participation and legalization.

In the real world, of course, the three pathways are not mutually exclusive; multiple elements may be initially weak and strengthened together over time. For example, "real" Soft Law processes (which focus on increasing legalization) often incorporate elements of both the Plurilateral (broadening participation) and the Framework Convention (deepening substantive content) approaches. While we have deliberately constructed our ideal types to isolate the distinctive logics underlying the respective pathways, we will return to the possibility of blended approaches later in the chapter.

Deepening substantive content: the Framework Convention (FC) Pathway

A "framework convention" – such as the Framework Convention on Climate Change – is a legally binding agreement that includes a wide range of participants but does not contain significant substantive commitments. Without deep substantive content, framework conventions are unlikely to change behavior significantly in the near term. However, proponents argue that such agreements can initiate powerful dynamic processes based on, among other things, information gathering and exchange, normative dialogue, participation in a normative community and activation of domestic supporters. Over time, participating states may come to new understandings of their own interests and of shared interests; internalize any agreed norms in their domestic law and bureaucracies and in the value systems of individual officials and citizens; and even take on new identities, as, for example, "green," "liberal" or "European." As these processes take hold, states become willing to make greater substantive commitments, which can be added to the framework convention in the form of protocols, amendments and the like.

From this approach we extract the ideal type *Framework Convention Pathway*:

> begin with an agreement that has broad participation and is at least moderately legalized (legally binding) but includes only shallow substantive commitments, and deepen the substantive content over time.

This approach is often associated with constructivist scholars such as Jetta Brunnee and Stephen J. Toope, who specifically urge the use of the Framework Convention (FC) Pathway – in the form of environmental framework conventions – to develop ecosystem-oriented international law in areas such as the protection of freshwater resources.[15] Brunnee and Toope go so far as to argue that it is undesirable to negotiate seemingly strong international environmental treaties without first going through incremental processes like those of the FC Pathway. Unless advocates have first "imagined and nurtured a normative community," they assert, even formal legal commitments are unlikely to be meaningful; states may simply assent with no intention of complying. Rather than obtaining immediate but superficial national commitments through interest-based bargaining – or worse, the exercise of power – the most effective route to international cooperation is the formation of "contextual" regimes within which national interests and identities can gradually converge, through dialogue, persuasion and learning.

For such normative convergence to take place, it is important that regime processes be viewed as legitimate; hence broad participation on a basis of equality (which at the outset tends to limit the adoption of strict behavioral standards) is essential.[16] Once a so-called "contextual" agreement initiates the dynamic subjective processes of the FC Pathway,

---

[15] Jutta Brunnee and Stephen J. Toope, "Environmental Security and Freshwater Resources: Ecosystem Regime Building" (1997) 91 *Am. J. Int'l L.* 26. Although the FC Pathway is associated with constructivism, we argue below that it may also be understood from a more rationalist perspective as a means of reducing uncertainty about the world before proceeding with deeper substantive commitments.

[16] Harold Koh describes a somewhat different "vertical" legal process, also inspired by constructivism, in which international norms are internalized by domestic legal institutions and by individual national officials and citizens. In this process too, dynamic normative processes change calculations of national interests and reconstitute national identities. See Koh, "Why Do Nations."

however, Brunnee and Toope are optimistic that it will evolve in the direction of deeper substantive commitments. As Anne-Marie Slaughter observes, their argument is strongly teleological.[17]

The FC Pathway is utilized most frequently in international environmental agreements. The classic example is the international ozone regime. Here the process began with the multilateral and legally binding, but substantively shallow, Vienna Convention for the Protection of the Ozone Layer. As understanding of the threat posed by ozone depletion grew, both in a normative and in an instrumental sense, the Convention was supplemented by the Montreal Protocol, which set precise, substantively significant limits on emissions of ozone-depleting substances. The Protocol itself has subsequently been strengthened and extended numerous times through amendments, technical annexes and declarations. Proponents of a regime for climate change have attempted to follow the same model with (as the recent American rejection of the Kyoto Protocol attests) somewhat less success.[18]

Expanding membership: the Plurilateral (PL) Pathway

Since many multilateral treaties, including some cited for their high compliance rates, have very shallow substantive content, George Downs and his colleagues have cast doubt on the robustness of the FC Pathway.[19] As an empirical matter, these scholars question the causal role of international framework agreements. In the case of the ozone regime, they argue that scientific discoveries, technological developments and domestic politics, rather than the Vienna Convention, were responsible for the adoption of stronger international rules. In theoretical terms, their analysis is based on

---

[17] Anne-Marie Slaughter, "International Law and International Relations" (2000) 285 *Recueil des Cours* 9 (Hague Academy of International Law). Slaughter contrasts Brunnee and Toope's position with Abbott and Snidal, "Hard and Soft Law," which argues that states and other actors can freeze international cooperation at the level of legalization that best suits their political needs.

[18] Other examples of the FC Pathway include the European Long-Range Transboundary Air Pollution regime (LRTAP), which has been strengthened by protocols setting additional limits on particular pollutants; the Biodiversity Convention, recently supplemented by a protocol on trade in genetically modified organisms; and the Antarctic Treaty, which included significant commitments from the outset in the area of international claims, but over the years has been supplemented by numerous conventions, protocols, recommendations and other actions on environmental protection and other subjects.

[19] See e.g., Downs, Rocke and Barsoom, "Good News"; George W. Downs, Kyle W. Danish and Peter N. Barsoom, "The Transformational Model of International Regime Design: Triumph of Hope or Experience?" (2000) 38 *Colum. J. Transn'l L.* 465.

a rational choice approach, and emphasizes the pursuit of interests rather than norms or values. They argue that significant cooperation among large numbers of participants is extremely difficult to maintain when there are incentives to defect. Because decentralized multilateral cooperation is so fragile, cooperation can only be maintained through stronger monitoring and enforcement procedures. Because *most* states are unwilling to accept such intrusive institutional arrangements, Downs *et al.* reject the argument that substantively shallow cooperation will develop into stronger cooperation over time.[20]

These criticisms suggest an alternative approach. The relatively few states that are committed to substantively deep cooperation on an issue – perhaps because they have been differentially affected by technological or domestic political developments – and are therefore willing to accept the monitoring and enforcement needed to implement deeper cooperation can begin by reaching agreement among themselves. If wider multilateral participation is desirable, they can later seek to bring additional parties into the agreement. Indeed, if the agreement is beneficial to members, its very existence will enhance the incentives for other states to join.

From this we derive the ideal type *Plurilateral Pathway*:

> begin with an agreement that includes deep substantive commitments and is highly legalized, but has limited membership, and expand participation in the agreement over time.

The best example of this approach, and the one most frequently relied upon by scholars, is the formation and enlargement of the European Union (EU).[21] Rationalist proponents of the Plurilateral (PL) Pathway argue that enlargement of the EU was less the result of intersubjective processes like persuasion, normative dialogue, learning and the creation of "European" identities[22] than it was of simple economic and political calculation. Once EU states are seen to receive significant economic

---

[20] One reason for the divergence between the proponents of the FC and PL Pathways is that the two groups of scholars are relying on very different theories of international cooperation. We argue below that both approaches contain relevant insights regarding all three pathways defined here.

[21] Of course, the substantive scope and depth of EU cooperation, and indeed its degree of legalization, have increased over time parallel to the continuing expansion of membership.

[22] Indeed, if Brunnee and Toope's "normative community" approach (text at note 15) turns on the conduct of such processes within a unifying contextual regime, it cannot apply to the case of the EC, since potential new Member States were by definition outside the regime until they joined it.

benefits from membership, then non-members will seek to join the regime.[23] For the same reasons, supporters of the PL Pathway suggest that other regional economic arrangements may be expanded in a similar fashion, as illustrated by the current negotiations to create a Free Trade Area of the Americas to supersede NAFTA, Mercosur and other sub-regional groupings.[24]

Strengthening legalization: the Soft Law Pathway

Numerous international regimes have followed a third pathway based on the gradual strengthening of legalization in broadly inclusive multilateral arrangements that include significant substantive undertakings. For example, in 1985 the Food and Agriculture Organization (FAO) adopted a voluntary Code of Conduct on pesticides, soon revised to call for prior informed consent (PIC) by importing countries for exports of restricted products. In 1987, the United Nations Environment Programme (UNEP) adopted voluntary guidelines for chemicals, emphasizing PIC. The two organizations harmonized their PIC provisions in 1989. After a decade of follow-up and negotiation, these voluntary norms were integrated into a legally binding Convention on PIC for pesticides and chemicals.[25] On a larger scale, the UN human rights regime began with the substantively deep but aspirational Universal Declaration of Human Rights, and only later took the form of more highly legalized treaties, such as the "covenants" on civil-political and economic-social-cultural rights.

We therefore define the ideal type *Soft Law Pathway*:

> begin with an agreement that contains significant substantive commitments and has wide participation, but is not highly legalized, and strengthen legalization over time.

---

[23] See Walter Mattli, *The Logic of Regional Integration: Europe and Beyond* (1999).
[24] Lloyd Gruber, *Ruling the World: Power Politics and the Rise of Supranational Institutions* (2000), puts a less optimistic Rationalist spin on regime expansion: when a small group of states creates an economic integration arrangement, it changes the options for outsiders, often unintentionally. Gruber interprets this as a form of coercion. Thus, for example, when the United States began to negotiate a free trade agreement with Mexico, Canada felt it had no choice but to participate, even though prior to the American move Canada had been strongly opposed to free trade with Mexico.
[25] See Mohamed Ali Mekouar, "Pesticides and Chemicals: The Requirement of Prior Informed Consent" in Dinah Shelton (ed.), *Commitment and Compliance: The Role of Non-Binding Norms in the International Legal System* (Oxford, 2000), pp. 146–63.

Because legalization is itself complex, it can be increased in various ways. Most commonly, as in the examples above, legalization is enhanced by replacing non-legally binding (or only weakly binding) instruments with binding treaties or other agreements. Legalization is sometimes strengthened further by delegating greater authority to legal institutions, as illustrated by creation of the WTO dispute settlement system and the International Criminal Court to implement trade and humanitarian law respectively.

The Soft Law Pathway, like legalization more generally, combines normative and rationalist strategies to enhance cooperation. Advocates of cooperation typically seek to enshrine norms in law because law can operate both through the manipulation of incentives (e.g., through sanctions, issue linkage and reputational concerns) and through normative mechanisms (e.g., legitimacy, persuasion and internalization). Many of these processes can be utilized in soft law arrangements,[26] but highly legalized regimes can partake of even greater legitimacy and impose more potent sanctions. Strong delegation like that found in the WTO is generally limited to hard law regimes. In addition, many treaties require parties to incorporate their obligations into domestic law, allowing normative and incentive techniques to be replicated at the national level. Hence, whether motivated by interests or values, actors will work to strengthen legalization over time, and will deploy both interest-based and normative strategies to do so.

In the same spirit, neither the Framework Convention nor the Plurilateral Pathway is as tightly tied to a particular understanding of the mechanisms of cooperation as the preceding summary suggests. As we argue below, FC processes can proceed by Rationalist mechanisms of learning as well as by processes of normative convergence. And PL expansion can proceed by persuading and "converting" states outside the initial arrangement as well as by demonstrating potential economic gains. Constructivist and Rationalist approaches are not only compatible, but are tightly interwoven across all three pathways.

Table 3.1 summarizes the characteristics of the three ideal type pathways. In each case, two elements of the initial agreement are at least moderately strong while one element (in bold) is weak. As noted above, the pathway is defined in terms of the strengthening of that weak element.

---

[26] An example is the international peer review implementation procedure, such as that administered by the Financial Action Task Force, which draws on all the mechanisms mentioned above.

Table 3.1 *Ideal type pathways to international cooperation*

	Characteristics of initial instrument		
Pathway	Substantive content	Participation	Legalization
Framework Convention	**Shallow**	Broad	Moderate
Plurilateral	Deep	**Limited**	Strong
Soft Law	Deep	Broad	**Weak**

Choosing among pathways

The previous section described three ideal type pathways to international cooperation. These pathways share an assumption that states face some common problem that can be ameliorated or resolved through cooperation. The pathways differ in proposing alternative routes to cooperation, but it would be a mistake to interpret the scholarly debate as meaning that one of the pathways to international cooperation described here is "correct" while the others are not. As their proponents generally recognize,[27] different pathways may be appropriate in different circumstances.[28]

This section investigates the circumstances that lead concerned states and other advocates to select a particular pathway. This is by no means an exhaustive analysis of relevant circumstances, but merely a first step in developing a deeper understanding of the choices advocates make among alternative dynamic strategies of cooperation.

Of course, cooperative processes invariably produce losers along with winners. While we emphasize the perspective of advocates of cooperation, most issues also engage actors who oppose cooperation. Their opposition may be to particular cooperative proposals that do not benefit them as much as alternative cooperative possibilities. Or they may be sufficiently satisfied with the status quo that they will oppose virtually any change – especially given the uncertainties that inevitably arise. For these reasons, opponents will try to block the use of any pathway, force issues into pathways where cooperative efforts can be stalled, and try to delay movement along any pathway.

We present our analysis in positive terms, but it has significant normative implications. First, our analysis should translate directly into lessons

---

[27] See e.g., Downs, Danish and Barsoom, "Transformational Model," 508–9.
[28] Again, in real-world settings it may be necessary or desirable to combine two or more pathways. We consider that possibility below.

for actors choosing a strategy for international cooperation. These lessons are relevant not only to proponents but also to those who would block cooperation. Second, our analysis should also have implications for institutional design: how early-stage arrangements on a particular pathway should be structured to address its special problems.

We focus on three categories of factors that influence the choice among pathways: (a) the nature of the issue; (b) the identity of the actors seeking legalization; and (c) the institutional setting. We assume that actors choose the most effective pathway given their capabilities. Because actors typically cannot achieve their goals immediately, however, an important consideration for them is to select a pathway that both begins a cooperative process and empowers them for continuing action.

Nature of the issue

Uncertainty is a major reason why states find it difficult to create highly legalized arrangements with deep substance and broad participation. They may not understand the problem well, or even be sure that it exists; they may not know what solutions are possible, or what costs and risks potential solutions entail. They may not be sure they will be able to carry out particular commitments – for example, whether they will face serious domestic political opposition – and they may doubt whether other actors will perform on their commitments. In circumstances like these, actors will be reluctant to bind themselves too tightly to particular solutions and will seek greater flexibility while they learn about the issue.[29]

The Framework Convention, Plurilateral and Soft Law Pathways are effective for addressing different types of uncertainty.[30] They encourage

[29] Barbara Koremenos, Charles Lipson and Duncan Snidal, "The Rational Design of International Institutions: Introduction" (2001) 55 *International Organization* 761, discuss how institutions must be designed to address uncertainty and other dimensions of cooperation problems such as distributional and enforcement issues. Their analysis implicitly focuses on the problem of maintaining established cooperative outcomes (e.g., at the endpoints of our pathways), whereas our analysis is about the process of getting to those cooperative outcomes.

[30] Barbara Koremenos, "Loosening the Ties that Bind: A Learning Model of Agreement Flexibility" (2001) 55 *International Organization* 289, discusses how to deal with problems of uncertainty through hard law arrangements that include renegotiation clauses. That is a viable alternative where the uncertainty can be characterized fairly precisely (e.g., as a distribution of possible outcomes) but is less effective when ignorance is more profound, such as doubt as to whether any benefits exist or what the possible outcomes are. Nevertheless, such arrangements as elements of ultimate agreements are natural complements to the pathways discussed below.

different kinds of learning, appropriate to the underlying problems, to help resolve uncertainty over time, and they provide different means of achieving desired flexibility in the interim. Here we distinguish *technical*, *actor* and *political* uncertainty, which are best addressed by the FC, PL and SL Pathways, respectively. In each case, we analyze uncertainty both in rationalist terms, as a question of information, and in normative terms, as a matter of defining appropriate roles, behaviors and identities. Table 3.2 (see p. 71 below) summarizes the relation between the pathways and different types of uncertainty.

Technical uncertainty and the Framework Convention Pathway

Technical uncertainty refers to doubts or partial ignorance as to the existence and nature of a problem, as well as appropriate solutions. Ozone depletion, for example, is now accepted as a significant problem, but a consensus on that point was slow to develop. The situation was similar for climate change until recently: significant disagreement persisted over the seriousness of the problem and over the sorts of actions appropriate against it. This lack of clear understanding impeded the development and implementation of deep substantive commitments, and offered opponents a way to delay a coordinated attack on the problem.

The FC Pathway (beginning with legally binding multilateral agreements but limited substantive content) is a natural response to technical uncertainty. Reluctance to make substantive commitments in an uncertain situation is easy to understand, but why would actors take on binding legal obligations? The reasons are two-fold. First, states and other concerned actors have a mutual interest in learning about the problem (or that there isn't a problem) and therefore in sharing information about the problem and what to do about it. Those who will contribute to the production of such information also have an interest in establishing clear cost-sharing obligations. Second, actors want to assure each other that if the problem turns out to be important, they will cooperate more substantively in the future. A legally binding agreement enhances the credibility of commitments to future cooperative processes in the event they are needed, and facilitates their implementation when they are needed.

However, a framework convention also provides a way for skeptics to resist calls for expansive action by arguing that the problem is not yet clearly understood. With its limited substantive content, there is a possibility that the "assurances" sought from a framework convention can be insincerely given or ignored at relatively low cost. This appears to have happened with the American rejection of the Kyoto Protocol, although even the Bush administration felt compelled to accompany its refusal to participate with a promise to propose alternative ways to implement the Framework Convention on Climate Change. Many other states have ratified the Protocol, however, and the overall FC process has advanced (though obviously not resolved) collective understanding of climate change – and strengthened the reaction against the shift in American policy.

Actual framework conventions devote careful attention to promoting the kinds of technical learning that will reduce uncertainty. Framework conventions usually establish procedures for research by the parties and by institutions associated with the convention, for sharing information among the parties, and for conferences and other meetings at which the parties can consider the information produced. Because of the technical nature of the tasks, "epistemic communities" of scientists and other experts play an important role in producing and analyzing information.[31] These experts come not only from national governments and international organizations but also from the private sector, including NGOs and academic research institutes. The scientific expertise and authority of epistemic communities allow them some independence from the states that empower them. This provides them with some (limited) autonomous capacity to move the issue forward, but it is also a reason why states are hesitant to establish such processes in the first place. Opponents, in particular, do not want to resolve uncertainty where that would strengthen the case for cooperative projects they oppose.

Some framework conventions contain very little substance other than initiating research. Others contain broad principles that the parties agree to apply whenever specific solutions are needed. Some principles may be attuned to the problem at hand (e.g., the precautionary principle in the Climate Change Convention), while others are more general (e.g., considering the special needs and capacities of developing countries). In addition, virtually all framework conventions establish lower cost procedures for taking future substantive action if that is determined to be necessary. These include procedures for adopting protocols, technical annexes and other modes of action that can expand the substantive content of the regime short of a full treaty-negotiation process.

While our analysis of technical uncertainty has thus far been rationalist and interest-based, such uncertainty may also have a more subjective character. With truly novel problems (emerging technology issues like cloning

---

[31] See Peter M. Haas (ed.), "Knowledge, Power and International Policy Coordination" (1992) 46 *International Organization* (No. 1) (Special Issue).

are an example) states may simply have no prior conception of their "interests." In other areas, different ways of thinking about problems – slavery in the nineteenth century, nuclear weapons in the twentieth century, and perhaps genetic modification in the twenty-first century – raise new questions of fundamental "values." New problems may also present trade-offs among values that neither states nor even normative entrepreneurs have ever addressed. In such circumstances, states will be unclear on what role they should play in an issue area, and what standards of behavior they are expected to follow and should expect of others. Deep commitments are clearly premature (and might well be disregarded) in these circumstances, but a legally binding agreement still commits states to cooperate in learning about the problem and provides assurances of future action if that proves desirable.

On an ongoing basis, the structural elements of framework conventions promote the emergence of common interests and norms. Cooperation in information-gathering, information-sharing and consultation regarding appropriate responses can all help develop a sense of common enterprise. Transnational epistemic communities can speed this development and spread the sense of a common project through domestic arenas. Brunnee and Toope note a further advantage of operating under a legal agreement: international law brings to bear norms of participation and fair process that increase the legitimacy of evolving norms.[32] Finally, the process of developing new norms over time can encourage gradual acceptance and internalization that will facilitate compliance as more substantive agreements are reached.

Actor uncertainty and the Plurilateral Pathway

The Plurilateral Pathway (which begins with legalized commitments and deep substance, but limited membership) addresses an important form of *political* uncertainty, distinct from the technical uncertainty of the FC Pathway. States contemplating an international cooperative arrangement must invariably consider the question: which other states can be relied on to participate in the venture? Willingness to accept a substantively meaningful and highly legalized agreement provides a valuable screening device to determine which states are sincere in their commitment to cooperate.

The substantive requirements of the screening agreement (e.g., requiring prospective members of an economic integration arrangement to meet certain economic goals before joining) also provide a check on the

---

[32] See Brunnee and Toope, "Environmental Security."

ability of prospective members to implement the agreement. If the screen is necessary and effective, not all states will be willing and able to sign on. The plurilateral strategy then uses membership criteria as an ongoing screening device that allows states to join the arrangement in the future when they are ready and willing. Important examples include NATO[33] and the European Union,[34] which have expanded over time by admitting new states that met the prevailing membership criteria.[35]

The Plurilateral Pathway begins with a core group of initiators who expect to benefit from cooperation on the problem and are willing to accept the institutional arrangements necessary to assure the success of the group. Typically, this group will be kept relatively small, both to limit participation to truly committed states and especially to facilitate enforcement of the arrangement. The signature examples are international trade agreements such as the EC and NAFTA. Success of trade arrangements among small initial groupings of states has led to a growing consensus on the benefits of economic integration and made additional states eager to join.

Several significant limits to the plurilateral approach follow directly from its necessary conditions. One is that the core group of participants must cover a sufficient portion or scope of the problem to create collective benefits for the group. In trade, as few as two parties can jointly benefit from a bilateral arrangement; in arms control, the core group may have to include all potential military players to be successful. A plurilateral arrangement on ICBMs that did not include Russia would not accomplish much.

Conversely, the core group must be able to exclude non-participants from benefits; otherwise, incentives to free-ride will undermine the arrangement. Again, trade agreements can be fairly (though not completely) effective at excluding non-members. However, a plurilateral agreement on global warming would be undermined if major polluters could enjoy the benefits of others' reductions while not contributing themselves. Such a situation would create incentives for every state to

---

[33] See Andrew Kydd, "Trust Building, Trust Breaking: The Dilemma of NATO Enlargement," (2001) 55 *International organization* (No. 4) 801.
[34] See Downs, Danish and Barsoom, "Transformational Model."
[35] The plurilateral arrangement also responds to the enforcement problem among the members (with or without uncertainty) by reducing the size of the group. Koremenos, Lipson and Snidal, "Rational Design," discuss this under their membership dimension of institutionalization. Interestingly, their empirical summary concludes that the enforcement role of membership appears less important than its informational role.

remain outside the agreement. One remedy, of course, is to construct an agreement under which each actor's participation is contingent upon universal participation. However, that would undercut the very essence of a pure plurilateral approach, which is based on restrictive initial membership as a path to building larger participation. More importantly, this remedy would suffer either from severe instability or from credibility problems: would the community of states really end a beneficial cooperative relationship to punish one deviant state?[36]

While providing benefits to the core group of initiators and restricting benefits to non-participants are the proximate goals, the broader strategy in most cases is to bring a wider set of states under the agreement. The "demonstration effect," whereby outsiders observe the benefits that (only) members reap from the plurilateral arrangement, increases incentives for additional states to join. However, it is also necessary that insiders be willing to accept new members and that the agreement be structured for expansion. New members increase collective benefits, but they may also create new costs and raise domestic political problems. Although both NAFTA and the EU are moving forward with expansion, for example, such obstacles have slowed the pace of progress.

Prospects for expansion depend on the nature of the issue. If there are increasing returns to scale (e.g., when a new member's participation creates public benefits within the group) then existing members have positive incentives to admit new members. But if there are declining benefits from successive members, distributive problems become severe. New members must receive lower benefits than earlier members or existing members have no incentives to admit them.[37] In some cases, this problem can be remedied by organizing parallel plurilateral clubs. The possibility nevertheless remains that distributive issues will impede collective benefits, especially if competition among clubs has other negative externalities, as has been feared with regional trading blocs.

The Plurilateral Pathway has been discussed in the literature largely in rationalist, interest-based terms. From this perspective, as just discussed,

---

[36] Downs, Danish and Barsoom, "Transformational Model," 502, cite the Montreal Protocol and the MARPOL Treaty on ocean pollution from ships as examples where environmental agreements successfully followed a plurilateral route despite the incentives to free-ride. However, they do not explain how the plurilateral process led to this result.

[37] A significant but less severe problem occurs in the increasing returns case if core group members extract the rents from admitting new members. Thus China was asked to make human rights adjustments in order to enter the WTO that were not required of existing WTO members.

it will only succeed for a special class of problems where the issue and its solution are well-understood, an effective core group exists, exclusion is possible, and an expansion path is viable. An approach that combines plurilateralism with softer normative techniques, however, may be more effective. Indeed, many international agreements combine a core group of states committed to a legalized and substantively deep agreement with surrounding soft law arrangements that partially incorporate states less sure of their interest and ability to participate. Exceptions, waivers, special categories of transitional membership and phase-ins are standard techniques to engage other states in the process, while insulating the core plurilateral group.[38]

More generally, the Plurilateral Pathway can be augmented by normative strategies that overcome limitations of a purely interest-based approach. First, the core group often arises in a pre-existing community of states whose shared values and experiences allow them to place the interests of the group ahead of individual incentives that would undermine the effort. Second, the core group – by its existence, rhetoric and activities as a normative community, including relations with those outside – can modify the understandings, interests and identities of outsiders towards acceptance of its norms, leading them to join the agreement. Thus, persuasion becomes an important accompaniment to interest-based demonstration effects.

Plurilateral legal arrangements can create *normative* demonstration effects, based on outsiders' observations that particular standards of behavior are accepted by an influential sub-set of states, and for that group are regarded as helping to define a "good" or "modern" state. In this perspective the legalization of a plurilateral arrangement is valuable not only for enhancing the credibility of commitments among core members, but also for signaling to outsiders that the core group as a whole is committed to this common enterprise. States that aspire to join the core group then also have instrumental reasons to join the effort, even before they share its normative vision.

---

[38] In a similar vein, David G. Victor, Kal Raustiala and Eugene B. Skolnikoff (eds.), *The Implementation and Effectiveness of International Environmental Commitments: Theory and Practice* (1998), notes several cases where states wanted to exclude go-slow states from hard law negotiations but found it too costly to do so for political or symbolic reasons. Because it was less costly to exclude them from a soft law process, the group used the SL Pathway to implement a deeper substantive agreement (albeit one that was not legally binding).

Indeed, plurilateral agreements may have an impact on non-members through normative channels even if they never participate. Although the United States remains outside of the Land Mines Treaty, for example, its behavior on this issue will likely be affected by the creation of a set of standards shared by the broader community. Advocates of a comprehensive ban on land mines and participating governments are clearly aware of this possibility and have structured their operations accordingly. Thus even where the membership of other states is in doubt, the normative channel suggests the desirability of structuring plurilateral agreements to maximize their normative impact, so that outsiders will act in light of them and internalize their fundamental norms even if they cannot formally accede to them at the present.

Political uncertainty and the Soft Law Pathway

In addition to uncertainty as to whether others can be relied on as cooperators, states dealing with an international problem face many other types of domestic *political* uncertainty. They (or at least their experts in the subject area) may agree technically on the existence of a problem and on potential solutions, and they may therefore be able to draft quite detailed substantive provisions. But they may still be uncertain about the political costs and benefits of those solutions (and of inaction), and about their distribution. While costs and benefits are likely to have a material or technical basis (e.g., the impact of reducing carbon emissions by x percent through certain types of regulation), their importance for governments lies in their political consequences: how much opposition (and support) will particular proposals arouse among domestic audiences?

As an immediate consequence, states will be unsure whether they want to undertake or will be able to carry out new obligations, because of domestic political opposition or because of weaknesses in domestic institutions, including reluctance on the part of local officials to carry out required measures. In addition, states will also have doubts as to whether *other* states (and which other states) are sincere in their commitments or will be able to implement them.[39] Governments will be rightly concerned that a legally binding agreement might cost them heavily in domestic politics, and that those costs will be heightened if other states fail to deliver

---

[39] This differs from the Plurilateral Pathway, which is valuable when states know their own situation but not that of other states. The Plurilateral Pathway is not effective for handling political uncertainty, because under that condition members of the core group cannot readily identify themselves, and no membership screening device can be effective *ex ante*.

on their commitments. This assurance problem makes it doubly risky for states to enter international commitments in conditions of political uncertainty. The problem is compounded to the extent that states find it costly to extricate themselves from international legal commitments in the event that (some) others renege.

Soft law provides a means to manage such political uncertainty in the early stages of cooperation.[40] Governments can introduce rules on a tentative basis, test political reactions to them and preserve deniability if the responses are adverse. They can also explore the implementation of the proposed rules while maintaining an ability to drop out or back off if they encounter unpleasant surprises. Soft law provides an opportunity to see whether other states are willing and able to proceed with implementation, and a setting in which to pressure any laggards to do so. Such pressure can include the threat of slowing one's own implementation in response – a threat that may be more credible than under a legally binding commitment. Finally, soft law provides breathing space for supporters and relevant governmental agencies to organize for implementation before an arrangement is adopted on a binding basis. As the uncertainties are resolved, states can move over time to more highly legalized commitments.

Many of the same points apply in a parallel subjective or normative analysis. Soft law creates a setting for normative entrepreneurs to persuade skeptics. It also provides them with standards, approved by the international community, that strengthen efforts to promote new values within domestic bureaucracies and among the public. Whereas an interest-based analysis emphasizes the use of soft law as a "trial balloon" to test (fixed) preferences, a normative analysis conceives of a deeper subjective change based on the introduction of new norms legitimated through broad international approval. In addition, norm entrepreneurs can use soft law standards to assess government behavior and to mobilize political pressure when conduct falls short.

Soft law procedures work by advancing political or normative learning. They focus less on gaining technical understanding than on using soft "managerial" procedures to publicize and promote the agreed rules and to encourage states to try them out and gather feedback about their workability. Moderate delegation to international institutions (e.g., the United Nations Environment Programme) can create forums where experiences can be shared, pressure applied to encourage states to perform,

---

[40] Victor, Raustiala and Skolnikoff, *Implementation and Effectiveness*, p. 686, observes essentially the same phenomenon in its review of international environmental treaties.

Table 3.2 *Pathways and types of uncertainty*

	Technical uncertainty	Actor uncertainty	Political uncertainty
Pathway preference	Framework Convention	Plurilateral	Soft Law

and arrangements modified where they are found too costly. As with other gradual pathways, the drawback to soft law arrangements is that states can agree to them (sincerely or not) and face limited penalties or pressure if they fail to perform, even at a minimal level. As a result, soft law arrangements can also be used to pay lip service to commitments that states are unwilling to undertake in binding form.

Character of the advocates

International cooperation is promoted and contested by a diverse array of actors. These include states or governments viewed as unitary entities, individual government officials or ministries, international Secretariats, technical experts, and issue-oriented NGOs and other civil society groups. As noted above, in a given issue area, some actors are advocates for new or strengthened international rules and institutions, while others resist them, preferring either a different cooperative outcome or the status quo.

Each advocate ideally prefers a hard legal arrangement with broad participation and deep substantive commitments that correspond to its objectives. In practice, of course, even powerful actors can rarely achieve all their goals, and must compromise with others. Gradual pathways like our three ideal types are important forms of compromise: each pathway allows advocates to initiate a process that may lead to desired forms of cooperation over time, while allowing resisters to defer action on at least one important element of cooperative arrangements.

Assuming they act purposively to advance their interests or values, each advocate will press for the selection of a pathway that will maximize both its own continued influence on the process and the likelihood of reaching its preferred outcome. The kind of process actually initiated will depend on the nature of the issue (as discussed above), the institutional setting (as discussed in the next section), the relative power of the actors and many other factors. It is therefore empirically difficult to disentangle actor preferences over pathways from the constraints actors face and the compromises they must make. Still, it is possible to make some general observations regarding the pathways different advocates would prefer, *ceteris paribus*.

States typically prefer Framework Convention and Plurilateral approaches, as both are formal treaty-making processes over which states maintain the greatest control. In particular, both strategies allow states to limit formal participation in the process by NGOs that might disrupt their pursuit of a set of goals. The Plurilateral Pathway further limits the participation of less committed or less capable states that might disrupt or impede cooperation on the issue. Nevertheless, state advocates often agree to follow the Soft Law Pathway as a compromise with others. States may also have independent reasons to prefer this approach. For example, soft law may be a superior way to deal with political uncertainty, as discussed above, while legally binding commitments may entail sovereignty costs states are unwilling to bear. Alternatively, soft law may offer a way to defuse demands for action on an issue in domestic or international politics (e.g., from NGOs or other states) without making binding commitments.

Government ministries and officials with specific substantive agendas, if blocked from moving directly to satisfactory legal obligations, will generally prefer the Soft Law Pathway. This approach allows them to advance their agenda "below the radar" of the national government as a whole, avoiding the elaborate negotiating and approval processes often required for treaty-making. Soft law allows national officials flexibility to build domestic political coalitions with other agencies in their own government, transgovernmental coalitions with their counterparts in other states and informal alliances with business and civil society groups. Officials of international Secretariats often benefit equally from these political advantages. National and international officials with specific substantive agendas sometimes play major roles at international soft law conferences like the 1995 Fourth World Conference on Women in Beijing, where they participate along with civil society groups in framing soft law declarations that governments almost certainly would not approve in a more formal manner.

Technical experts prefer the Framework Convention Pathway because it plays to their comparative advantage of expertise. In addition to framing the problem as one of scientific uncertainty, thus empowering technical experts to play a leading role in the process, the associated institutional arrangements, both national and international, provide important resources to them.

Non-governmental actors gain the greatest benefits from the Soft Law Pathway. First, soft law procedures give NGOs much greater access to the process than do treaty negotiations. NGO participation in UN conferences with a predominantly soft law focus (in addition to the increasingly common parallel NGO conferences) has become particularly visible and influential. Some 1,400 NGOs were accredited to the 1992 Rio Conference on Environment and Development, some 4,000 to the 1995 Beijing Conference on Women. In both cases civil society organizations had significant input into the final declarations. NGOs are also being afforded greater (though still limited) access to the organs of international organizations.[41]

Soft law agreements also include more substantive content than framework conventions. Such international standards, even if not themselves highly legalized, enable a "transnational legal process" through which NGOs use legal strategies to incorporate norms into binding domestic or international law.[42] These strategies include persuading national legislatures to enact international standards into domestic law; persuading domestic courts to adopt international standards (perhaps by treating them as customary international law, as in the well-known *Filartiga* case in the United States) or to use them in interpreting national statutes; or persuading national executive agencies to use international standards for interpreting or issuing national regulations.

Soft law also enables a "transnational political process" that empowers NGOs. Soft law often includes more detailed and ambitious standards than more highly legalized treaties, against which it is easier to expose failures to perform.[43] Transnational advocacy networks use substantive international standards, including those that are legally soft, to hold governments accountable and to mobilize domestic and international reactions to failures of performance.[44] Even groups with purely domestic objectives find it valuable to invoke international standards in domestic politics (the "boomerang effect"). These "shaming" strategies do not require legally binding obligations, since the "enforcement" effect comes

---

[41] See Chadwick Alger, "The Emerging Roles of NGOs in the UN System: From Article 71 to a Millennium People's Assembly" (2002) 8 *Global Governance* 93.
[42] See Koh, "Why Do Nations"; "Bringing International Law Home" (1998) 35 *Houston L. Rev.* 623.
[43] See Victor, Raustiala and Skolnikoff, *Implementation and Effectiveness*.
[44] See Margaret E. Keck and Kathryn Sikkink, *Activists Beyond Borders: Advocacy Networks in International Politics* (1998).

Table 3.3 *Actor preferences across pathways*

Actor type	Unitary states	Government officials/ agencies	Technical experts	NGOs
Pathway preference	Framework Convention, Plurilateral	Soft Law	Framework Convention	Soft Law

through the rhetorical appeal to and mobilization of political pressure from third parties.

Alternative pathways are less amenable to NGO tactics. The central role of states in creating binding plurilateral agreements tends to crowd out NGOs' influence, both as the details of the agreements are worked out and again as they are implemented through state-to-state arrangements. Moreover, because plurilateral agreements are explicitly limited to a few states, it is harder to bring them to bear on non-party governments. Because framework conventions are substantively shallow, they offer few international standards as "hooks" for NGO political action. The FC Pathway also moves the venue of action to channels of expertise where the more political tactics of NGOs are often rendered less effective.

Table 3.3 summarizes the preferences of different types of actors across our three pathways.

Institutional arenas

The institutional setting in which advocates pursue international cooperation strongly influences the selection of a dynamic pathway. When actors are operating in a particular institutional framework,[45] they will enhance their likelihood of success by selecting a pathway for which the institution: (i) permits the initial combination of legalization, substance and participation, (ii) provides a process for strengthening the weak dimension over

---

[45] While advocates can often pursue cooperative arrangements in multiple forums, either simultaneously or *seriatim*, they sometimes limit their activities to a single institution for a variety of reasons: e.g., because that institution is the only body with authority to consider the issue, because it is the only body that can act effectively on the issue, because it is a body to which advocates have special access or because advocates need to concentrate their limited resources.

time, and (iii) offers the organizational support necessary for strengthening cooperation. We discuss each of these considerations below. At the end of this section, we consider the possibility of (iv) forum-shopping, where actors have a choice among institutional venues, and make that choice in part based on the pathways that different institutions can support.

Initial arrangement

Some institutions do not permit the initial combinations of legalization, substantive commitment and participation from which particular pathways originate. For example, in forums like the UN General Assembly and Asia-Pacific Economic Cooperation (APEC) (based respectively on constitutional authority and organizational ethos) it is virtually impossible for advocates to initiate cooperation with a binding legal instrument. As a result, the Framework Convention and Plurilateral Pathways are simply unavailable. Conversely, the WTO regards itself as a "hard law" forum: it is an essential feature of the organization that all agreements are legally binding[46] and subject to the quasi-judicial dispute settlement process and enforcement procedures. This makes it very difficult to initiate a soft law process in the WTO.[47]

A Plurilateral Pathway can only work if the institution's membership incorporates a feasible core group, i.e., it must include all the essential states and a sufficient number of states overall to generate cooperative benefits. Thus, while regional organizations may be well suited to address trade liberalization and localized problems like pollution of watercourses, they rarely encompass a core group capable of addressing broader global problems. The OECD is a valuable plurilateral organization because it includes all the advanced industrial nations, an ideal core group for addressing a wide range of problems.

Conversely, broadly multilateral institutions like the United Nations and the WTO often resist agreements among sub-sets of members, rendering the Plurilateral Pathway infeasible. Although the GATT/WTO regime as a whole has expanded by adding members over time, the WTO was

---

[46] However, the text of some WTO rules, especially those giving special treatment to developing countries, is quite vague, even hortatory.

[47] For example, while the OECD was able to achieve an international Convention on transnational bribery and corruption through a soft law process, the WTO, with its hard law ethos, has still not addressed the problem. See Kenneth W. Abbott and Duncan Snidal, "International Action on Bribery and Corruption: Why the Dog Didn't Bark in the WTO" in Daniel L.M. Kennedy and James D. Southwick (eds.), *The Political Economy of International Trade Law: Essays in Honor of Robert E Hudec* (2002); Kenneth W. Abbott, "Rule-Making in the WTO: Lessons from the Case of Bribery and Corruption" (2001) 4 *J. Int'l Econ. L.* 275.

actually founded on the notion of a "package deal," with all its members adhering to all its agreements. The organization has administered some plurilateral arrangements, notably with respect to liberalizing government procurement, but these are being phased out and new ones are restricted.

Strengthening the weak element

Some institutions do not provide the processes necessary to strengthen the weak elements in particular pathways over time. Here again, in soft law forums like the UN General Assembly and APEC, advocates can initiate cooperation with arrangements that combine deep substance and broad participation with weakly legalized commitments, but they face great difficulty in moving to more highly legalized arrangements – even just legally binding agreements – over time. Organizations of this kind can call separate law-making conferences to negotiate binding treaties, but this adds a costly step to the process.

Plurilateral organizations like the Association of Southeast Asian Nations (ASEAN), the Council of Europe and the OECD can initiate cooperation through a legally binding, substantively deep agreement among the member states, but it is often difficult to expand participation beyond that core group. The organization may be defined by limiting criteria like geography or economic status; it may not be structured to deal with expansion; and the substance of the particular agreement may be tailored to the narrow interests of the core group. For example, the EC anti-bribery treaties addressed corruption that affected "the financial interests of the Community"; as a result, it made little sense for non-member states to adhere.

Administrative support

Each pathway has its own institutional requirements: for reaching the initial agreement, for supporting activities at low levels of cooperation and for moving to higher levels of cooperation over time. Table 3.4 summarizes these requirements. At the same time, each institution has distinct organizational structures, operating procedures, capabilities and ethos, rooted in its constitutional authority and organizational culture. Advocates can enhance the likelihood of success by selecting a pathway whose requirements are aligned with the institutional capacities of the forum.

The Soft Law Pathway usually requires capable institutions to facilitate the initial multilateral agreement, even though this is not legally binding. Whether the agreement is adopted by a formal organization like the World Health Assembly or an ad hoc diplomatic conference, the logistics can be demanding. Still, only supportive administrative services are typically needed.[48] Thereafter, assuring the impact of the soft law norms and making progress to more highly legalized cooperation may require institutions with at least modest authority to promote agreed norms in the ways described above and to facilitate legal development. Many soft law agreements are connected to organizations like the UN Secretariat, Financial Action Task Force and UNEP for just these purposes. In other cases, though, opponents of cooperation deliberately keep the institutional structure weak to prevent further development.

The Framework Convention Pathway also requires supportive institutions to facilitate initial agreement. Since these initial commitments are legally binding (even if not substantively deep), governments are likely to be even more cautious, placing greater demands on the institutions. Further progress along the FC Pathway is highly dependent on a supportive institutional structure, although this need not be elaborate. To the extent that efforts at deepening substantive commitments focus on building a normative consensus, the institutional framework may simply entail ongoing opportunities for interaction, discussion, persuasion and community-building, as well as continuing support for the negotiation of protocols. But insofar as these efforts require the development and dissemination of scientific and other forms of technical knowledge, they may require more substantial institutions designed to promote research, verify data, encourage information-sharing, provide access for epistemic communities and perhaps even monitor certain behavior on a cooperative basis.

Reaching an initial plurilateral agreement may require supportive institutions, as in the other pathways. Since the core group is limited in number and is composed of like-minded members, however, modest support will often suffice. In contrast, both operations among the initial members and subsequent expansion pose strong and quite distinct institutional requirements. Because a plurilateral agreement entails significant substantive commitments that participating states have incentives not to perform, the supporting institution must include informational and reporting capacities that encourage members to comply, and perhaps even some capacity for enforcement of the agreed rules. The institution may

---

[48] For a discussion of the types of services provided by formal organizations, see Kenneth W. Abbott and Duncan Snidal, "Why States Act Through Formal Organization" (1998) 42 *J. Confl. Res.* 3.

Table 3.4 *Institutional requirements of the pathways*

	Framework Convention	Plurilateral	Soft Law
Initial agreement	**Medium** Negotiation support (legal agreement)	**Low** Negotiation support (small core group)	**Low** Negotiation support (non-legal agreement)
Early operation	**Low** Research; information-sharing	**High** Monitoring; implementation; exclusion	**Low** Norm promotion
Strengthening cooperation	**Medium** Information dissemination; verification protocols	**Medium** Persuasion; expansion and transition procedures	**Medium** Norm promotion; legal development

also be required to police exclusion of non-members from the benefits of cooperation. To develop successfully from plurilateral to multilateral, moreover, the institution must include workable criteria and procedures for expansion. It may also be called on to persuade non-members of the benefits of participation, and to administer transitional rules for new and potential members.

A significant issue in the selection of dynamic strategies is that particular pathways demand different levels of institutionalization at different stages in the development of cooperation. Thus a forum that is adequate early on may become less satisfactory in later phases, and vice versa. For example, the Plurilateral Pathway requires only modest institutional support to reach initial agreement because of the limited number of like-minded states involved. However, it is the most institutionally demanding of all the pathways during early operations, and often during the expansion phase as well. In contrast, the Framework Convention Pathway requires significant administrative support to reach an initial multilateral agreement, but it can be less demanding at later stages.

Forum shopping

In many issue areas, advocates – especially powerful advocates, whether states or non-governmental actors – have a choice among institutional arenas. Instead of selecting a pathway based on the character of the institution in which they are operating, this allows advocates to "shop" for an institution in which they can pursue the pathway(s) that are appropriate to the nature of the issue and afford them the greatest influence. When the United States wants to pursue an economic issue, for example, it can frequently decide whether to take it to the WTO, OECD, G-8, Transatlantic Economic Partnership or another organization. Even where the issue definition suggests a "natural" institutional home, actors may choose another body that better serves their purposes. For example, the United States and the EU by-passed WIPO to address intellectual property rights in the WTO because of its dispute settlement mechanism. In addition, advocates can frequently pursue an issue in multiple forums, following a different pathway in each.

Institutions are sometimes pro-active in making themselves effective (and therefore attractive) forums for the pursuit of cooperation along certain pathways. The UN Secretary-General's Office is attempting this with the Global Compact as a way to enlist international business in adhering to a range of labor, environment and human rights standards. In a sense, this opens a Soft Law Pathway for the extension of international norms to private actors. Conversely, institutions may resist efforts by advocates to use them in pursuing pathways they view as inconsistent with their institutional mission and authority. The WTO, for example, has been wary of becoming engaged in environmental and labor issues that might undermine its success on trade issues.

Finally, when no existing institution is appropriate, proponents may seek to create a new one. Advocates for a ban on anti-personnel land mines did this successfully when they abandoned the "natural" home of the issue, the UN disarmament process, to create a new forum; so did supporters of a comprehensive campaign against HIV/AIDS when they caused the issue to be transferred from the WHO to the newly created UNAIDS, a consortium of UN agencies. In both cases, the advantages of an appropriate forum outweighed the difficulties and costs of creating a new institutional arrangement. However, creating institutions is not easy, and opponents will often be successful in blocking the initiation of new arrangements.

Blending and sequencing the pathways

Our three ideal types are constructed to highlight the logic of each pathway and to dramatize distinctions among them. In practice, however, many processes for strengthening international cooperation over time are more complex, drawing on elements of two or more pathways. Pathways can be "blended": combined during a single time period, or "sequenced": pursued *seriatim*, with one process establishing the preconditions that allow a subsequent process to be successful. Distinguishing "blends" from "sequences" can be difficult, and even somewhat arbitrary, however, as processes frequently overlap. Because many combinations of elements are possible, the significance of blends and sequences is best illustrated by example.

Soft Law and Framework Convention

We have elsewhere analyzed the process leading up to the 1997 OECD Anti-Bribery Convention, which combined elements of the Soft Law and Framework Convention Pathways.[49] The initial instrument adopted by the OECD Council, the 1994 Recommendation on Bribery in International Business Transactions, was relatively weak on two of our three characteristics: it was not legally binding or otherwise highly legalized, and it included limited substantive content.[50] OECD governments gradually added content, as in the FC Pathway, through a series of soft law instruments, including additional Recommendations in 1996 and 1997 and the "Agreed Common Elements," a set of recommended principles for national legislation. Once participating states reached agreement on these elements in 1997, they were able to move to a legally binding Convention, as in the SL Pathway. This example also illustrates how gradually deepening substantive content in a Soft Law context may facilitate the negotiation of more highly legalized commitments.

Another common sequence occurs when a series of soft law instruments leads, not to a substantively deep and legally binding agreement like the OECD Anti-Bribery Convention, but to a framework convention under which participating states initiate a further process of rule creation.

---

[49] See Abbott and Snidal, "Values and Interests"; "International Action" ; "Filling in the Folk Theorem."

[50] The OECD process also appears Plurilateral, since only 29 states are members of the organization. Some non-member states did ratify the Convention, and the agreement provides for further expansion, as discussed further below. But the Convention was designed to address the "supply side" of the corruption issue, regulating transnational bribery by firms based in major goods- and capital-exporting states. The OECD includes virtually this entire class of states.

International regulation of tobacco products provides one example. Over several years, the World Health Assembly adopted a series of non-binding resolutions calling on member states to regulate the manufacture, sale, trade and use of tobacco products, on a harmonized basis where possible. The World Health Organization recently began negotiations on a legally binding convention on tobacco control.[51] However, this is intended to be a framework convention,[52] which will contain principles on which consensus can currently be reached and can be supplemented by specific protocols over time.[53]

Framework Convention and Plurilateral

These two pathways are combined when parties to a framework convention deepen its substantive content over time through protocols, amendments and similar mechanisms, and simultaneously take in additional participants. An example is the Council of Europe and its Convention on Human Rights and Fundamental Freedoms, adopted in the early 1950s. The original Convention contained many significant substantive commitments, but participating states added important protocols over the years, notably on institutional matters such as mandatory jurisdiction and private petitions to the European Court of Human Rights. At the same time, many Central and Eastern European states joined the Council and ratified the Convention. The European Union, with several enlargements plus vastly increased substantive undertakings, provides a similar example.

Framework conventions that add substantive content through protocols also incorporate an element of the Plurilateral Pathway by making certain protocols optional. Each optional protocol functions as a plurilateral agreement linked to the underlying convention. The optional character of the protocols increases flexibility for participating states while ensuring that only those states with serious intentions adhere to them;

---

[51] For information on the WHO Tobacco-Free Initiative, see www5.who.int/tobacco/.
[52] See Allyn L. Taylor, "An International Regulatory Strategy for Global Tobacco Control" (1996) 21 *Yale J. Int'l L.* 257 (proposing a SL-FC sequence). Taylor is currently Health Policy Advisor to the Tobacco-Free Initiative, focusing on the Convention.
[53] The current chair's draft text of the Convention, however, contains numerous substantive provisions, more than would be expected in a normal framework convention; the text is also rather vague on the process for adopting protocols. To the extent that later protocols are made optional, the Convention will blend in an element of the Plurilateral Pathway as well.

the connection to the broader treaty framework promotes wider participation over time.

The 1980 Geneva Convention on Conventional Weapons with Excessively Injurious or Indiscriminate Effects illustrates this combination. The original Convention was adopted with several protocols attached; any state adhering to the Convention is required simultaneously to accept at least two of them as the "price of admission," but it can freely choose which ones. By allowing states a choice, the Convention lowers the costs and uncertainty of initial adherence, while engaging states in an ongoing process of cooperation. The Convention also provides for new protocols on additional categories of weapons to be adopted over time; parties are also free to choose whether to accept them.

Plurilateral and Soft Law

Regional organizations and other institutions with limited initial membership often pursue soft law rule-making processes while simultaneously adding new members. For example, Miles Kahler has described how ASEAN, with only five member states at its founding in 1967, proceeded largely through informal diplomatic collaboration for much of its history, then moved to somewhat deeper and more highly legalized cooperation with the formation of the ASEAN Free Trade Area in 1992. Membership in ASEAN has also doubled, mainly during the 1990s. In addition to its own activities, ASEAN played a central role in the 1989 creation of the much larger super-regional organization APEC, although APEC has to date adhered strictly to a Soft Law model, not taking on the legal commitments associated with the Free Trade Area.[54]

Another common sequence occurs when a Soft Law or Framework Convention process (or a blend of those processes) produces a plurilateral agreement that the parties hope to expand by encouraging or allowing other states to join. The OECD process on anti-bribery rules also illustrates this sequence. To some extent, broadening of participation was blended into the process that led to the original Convention: OECD governments allowed five non-member states to join the negotiations and to sign and ratify the Convention along with members. But the Convention

---

[54] See Miles Kahler, "Legalization as Strategy: The Asia-Pacific Case" (2000) 54 *International Organization* 549.

also permits non-member states that meet certain criteria to accede in future years.⁵⁵

These aspects of the OECD process illustrate some of the problems of the Plurilateral Pathway, both on its own and in combination with other processes. The OECD recognized that wider adherence to its anti-bribery rules would be desirable, both for controlling corruption and for competitive reasons. But expansion would also create difficulties. In particular, several potential members (and at least one of the five non-member ratifiers) lacked adequate capacity to frame and implement the required domestic criminal legislation, and would therefore have required special attention and assistance from the OECD. Absorbing one or two such states might be feasible, but adding a larger number would impair the effectiveness of the organization's follow-up process and raise doubts about the implementation of the Convention.

Blends and sequences in complex cooperation

Finally, it is worth noting that the development over long periods of time of elaborate institutional arrangements such as the EU or WTO almost invariably involves complicated blends and sequences. The GATT, for example, was intended as an interim agreement; it imposed weak legal obligations and included almost no institutional capacity. GATT took on greater permanence only because direct movement to a more institutionalized arrangement was not viable. This trade agreement was expanded through a series of rounds that focused on increasing substantive commitments, both by requiring members to further reduce tariffs and other trade barriers and by expanding the range of covered commodities. GATT (and subsequently the WTO) also expanded participation by taking on additional members, sometimes making special allowances for their transition to full participation. Finally, the move from GATT to the WTO represented a substantial increase in the legalization of the regime (as well as further expansion of substantive commitments). The agreement establishing the WTO is a fully binding treaty, and the WTO itself is a true international organization. The Dispute Settlement Mechanism is a

---

⁵⁵ New adherents must accept the other OECD (soft law) instruments dealing with bribery and corruption, must agree to become full participants in the OECD Working Group on Bribery in International Business Transactions, and must satisfy the rules of the organization regarding participation by non-members in its subsidiary bodies.

significant quasi-judicial body, and non-cooperating states can no longer block findings that they are in default under WTO agreements.

The overall GATT/WTO history illustrates the importance of gradual movement towards cooperation when "big bang" cooperation is impossible. Of course, the complicated combination of blends and sequences observed here are a far remove from the simple ideal type pathways we have developed in this chapter to understand smaller issues. However, the logic of breaking cooperation into a series of steps defined in terms of substantive commitments, participation and legalization is the same.

4

Customary international law as a judicial tool for promoting efficiency

EYAL BENVENISTI

Introduction

The 1997 decision of the International Court of Justice (ICJ) in the *Gabcikovo-Nagymaros* case[1] reshaped international law on transboundary resources in the disguise of adhering to customary principles. Aside from praise for the efficient norms it prescribed, the decision raises a fundamental puzzle: from where did the ICJ draw its authority to rewrite international law? Clearly, the ICJ paid no attention to the traditional sources of international law – general and consistent state practice coupled with *opinio juris*, namely the "belief that this practice is rendered obligatory"[2] – to trace the evolution of customary law. Such faithful inspection could not have led the ICJ to the same conclusions. In September 1997, when the *Gabcikovo-Nagymaros* decision was rendered, state practice and *opinio juris* were rather precarious stilts to serve as the foundation of modern transboundary resources law. Instead of compiling, inspecting and analyzing state practice, the ICJ took a short cut by invoking the 1997 Convention on the Law of the Non-Navigational Uses of International Watercourses ("the Watercourses Convention")[3] under the unsupported assertion that

---

[1] *Gabcikovo-Nagymaros Project (Hungary/Slovakia)*, Judgment, [1997] ICJ Reports 7, reprinted at www.icj-cij.org/idocket/ihs/ihsjudgement/ihsjudframe1.htm; (1998) 37 ILM 167.
[2] *North Sea Continental Shelf (FRG v. Denmark/Netherlands)* [1969] ICJ Reports 3, at para. 77. The Permanent Court of International Justice (PCIJ) first enunciated the doctrine of *opinio juris* in the *Lotus* case *(France v. Turkey)*, (1927) PCIJ Reports, Series A, No. 10 at 28: "only if such [practice] were based on their being conscious of having a duty to abstain would it be possible to speak of an international custom." See also *Military and Paramilitary Activities in and Against Nicaragua (Nicaragua v. United States)*, Merits, Judgment, [1986] ICJ Reports 14, at para. 207; *The Paquete Habana*, 175 U.S. 677 (1900).
[3] United Nations Convention on the Law of the Non-Navigational Uses of International Watercourses (adopted on May 21, 1997), reprinted in (1997) 36 ILM 700. See *ibid.* for the details of the votes cast.

the Watercourses Convention reflected contemporary customary law.[4] This was a bold move: the Watercourses Convention had been adopted less than four months earlier, had no signatories at the time, and its entry into force was far off. Even more disturbing, it had numerous opponents, which included key regional players – China and Turkey – as well as pairs of riparians such as Egypt and Ethiopia, France and Spain, India and Pakistan, and other states involved in regional disputes over water, such as Bolivia, Israel and Uzbekistan.[5] The puzzle becomes even more complex when one examines how the ICJ read and applied the Watercourses Convention: the Court distorted the logic of the Convention and treated it as an empty vessel into which it injected its own contradictory vision, pouring "new law in old bottles."[6] In spite of all this, the decision withstood scholarly scrutiny and was received with resounding enthusiasm.[7]

This chapter responds to the puzzle by arguing that in its decision in the *Gabcikovo-Nagymaros* case, despite these unexplained doctrinal irregularities, the ICJ was acting within its general authority under international law. The ICJ activated its unique legislative role in the international system, the role that empowers it to "leapfrog"[8] over international law when seized with questions of management or control of global and transboundary resources. This is the power, under certain conditions, to create new law on the pretext of "finding" the customary international norms. The ICJ has, in fact, the authority to invent the custom. It can fulfill this function when these leaps produce more efficient norms, provided that at the relevant time it is the only institution capable of making the leaps. This residual function becomes relevant when high transaction costs prevent states from negotiating bilateral or multilateral agreements. The

---

[4] *Gabcikovo-Nagymaros* case, note 1, at para. 86.

[5] Obviously, these states abstained from committing to regional cooperation in a general framework convention before entering into direct negotiations over the use of their regional resources. On some of the disputes among these riparians see Eyal Benvenisti, *Sharing Transboundary Resources: International Law and Optimal Resource Use* (Cambridge University Press, 2002).

[6] A.E. Boyle, "*The Gabcikovo-Nagymaros* Case: New Law in Old Bottles," (1998) 8 *Yearbook of International Environmental Law* 13. *See* in general, Benvenisti, *Sharing Transboundary Resources*, ch. 7.

[7] Boyle, "The *Gabcikovo-Nagymaros* Case." See also Charles B. Bourne, "The Case Concerning the Gabcikovo-Nagymaros Project: An Important Milestone in International Water Law" (1997) 8 *Yb. Int'l Envt'l L.* 6, 11; A. Dan Tarlock, "Safeguarding International River Ecosystems in Times of Scarcity" (2000) 3 *U. Denv. Water L. Rev.* 231, 244–47.

[8] David Caron, "The Frog that Wouldn't Leap: The International Law Commission and its Work on International Watercourses" (1992) 3 *Colo. J. Int'l Envt'l L. & Policy* 269.

Watercourses Convention is but one recent example of the predicament in which states taking part in multilateral negotiations over a framework agreement refuse to make concessions or even indicate future readiness to offer concessions, because the situation does not ensure reciprocal concessions. In global processes of this kind, states stick to non-cooperative positions in anticipation of the subsequent negotiations over the more local issue of resources they share with their neighbors. The result (in our first example, the Watercourses Convention) can only be disappointing. In such circumstances, the ICJ is often the sole institution capable of taking the necessary steps towards the development of the law, a sort of trustee acting in the best interests of the states and the global community. States accept this role and welcome such leaps, because they have a general interest in such a residual judicial-legislative function.

This chapter combines a positive analysis and a normative one. In addition to proving that this is what international adjudicators have been doing, I argue that this is exactly what they should do. The chapter proposes that when bilateral or multilateral negotiations fail to reach efficient outcomes or when such negotiations never take place due to conflicting state interests, the international legal system has granted the ICJ the power – and duty – to legislate efficient norms and remedies. Moreover, the use – or, put correctly, the abuse[9] – of customary international law is the main vehicle for executing this function. The chapter explores the link between efficiency and the doctrine of customary international law. Despite recent challenges to its utility and value,[10] this chapter argues that the doctrine plays a crucial role in the international arena. It analyzes why face-value application of the doctrine often fails to yield customary norms, suggests that in such circumstances the ICJ or other tribunals "cheat" by inventing what they refer to as custom, and explains why they are fully authorized and expected to do so. Further, the chapter suggests that when these judges "cheat," they follow the principle of efficiency – but not fairness – as their undeclared guideline. My argument, ultimately, is that this legislative function of international adjudicators is itself grounded in customary international law.

---

[9] One could argue that the doctrine on customary international law is more important for enabling its own abuse than for performing its stated goal of offering customary norms: if general and consistent state practice exists, there is little need for a doctrine that would render that practice obligatory.

[10] Jack L. Goldsmith and Eric A. Posner, "A Theory of Customary International Law" (1999) 66 *U. Chi. L. Rev.* 1113.

Customary international law as a proxy for efficiency

The argument developed in this section is that the doctrine on customary international law is inherently linked to the principle of efficiency. Efficiency justifies the doctrine. Put differently, efficiency is the underlying principle – the *grundnorm* – of customary international law.

An efficient norm in this context is a norm that offers the optimal allocation of the world's resources among states. A legal and political environment consisting of sovereign states is one important constraint imposed on the range of possible optimal outcomes: state sovereignty, as it is understood today, entails the authority of states to use resources under their sole ownership at their discretion, even inefficiently.[11] The second constraint is the lack of global mechanisms for the redistribution of welfare among states. Hence, the efficient outcome is that which allocates resources optimally among states rather than among individuals. It can be expected, but not guaranteed, that this external pull towards optimality will in itself create a pull within states towards optimal allocation among individuals. As I argue below, considerations of fairness in the allocation of resources among states do not play a role in this context, although in recent years human rights considerations (including considerations of human subsistence) do emerge as an important constraint marginally affecting the range of optimal outcomes. The third and final constraint concerns the institutional limitations of the ICJ and other tribunals. Their choice of strategies to develop customary law is influenced by their limited enforcement and managerial powers.

At the foundation of the argument linking custom with efficiency lies the observation that general and consistent state practice – the necessary component for constituting customary international law – will develop if, and only if, such practice is efficient from the perspectives of most of the governments taking part in the process.[12] This observation is consonant with the same observation regarding the evolution of so-called social norms.[13] When general and persistent state practice takes shape, it moulds itself around rules that the strongest and most active governments find

---

[11] Nico Schrijver, *Sovereignty over Natural Resources* (1997).
[12] Goldsmith and Posner's story about customary international law (note 10) begins and ends with this observation. Their story fails to notice the real bite of the doctrine: its potential for serving as an empty vessel for judicial application of efficiency considerations.
[13] Robert D. Cooter, "Decentralized Law for a Complex Economy: The Structural Approach to Adjudicating the New Law Merchant" (1996) 144 *U. Pa. L. Rev.* 1643.

to be efficient.[14] Regarding such rules as legally binding reduces coordination costs, and also imposes costs on inactive or weak actors who did not take part in shaping the rules or on actors who seek to deviate from them. When a certain practice becomes inefficient due to changed circumstances, states begin to exert pressure, or act unilaterally, to modify the custom so that it reflects the efficient practice under the new conditions. The prime and perhaps oldest examples of efficient state practice yielding to clear customary norms are the laws on warfare and on diplomatic immunity.

The norms on diplomatic immunity or on the conduct of hostilities reinforce themselves through reciprocity, without the need to invoke legal arguments or to resort to adjudication. The mistreatment of prisoners of war, for example, or the opening of the diplomatic mail, will trigger similar responses from the adversary. These examples suggest that state practice can often be used as a relatively reliable proxy for efficiency. Indeed, when Hugo Grotius invented in his celebrated treatise *De jure belli ac pacis* (1632)[15] the method of observing state practice as a basis for determining the law,[16] he was in fact using state practice to discover efficient norms. At that time, in a world ruled by papal edicts, state practice as such enjoyed no legitimacy. Grotius referred to state practice in the classic world because he thought it would make sense for states in the emerging Westphalian order to study and emulate general and consistent behavior. The Grotian invention caught on not only because it paved the way to "neutral" – i.e., not religiously based – rules, but also because it made sound economic sense: consistent state practice was a good proxy for efficient behavior.

That the Grotian enterprise was clearly bent on efficiency is made explicit in his first treatise *Mare liberum*, published in 1609,[17] arguing for the norm of freedom of navigation on the high seas. At that time, this issue had crucial economic implications and therefore proved a bone of contention among European powers. Having little state practice to base

---

[14] As Michael Byers observed, "[T]he customary process operates to maximise the interests of most if not all States by creating rules which protect and promote their common interests." Michael Byers, *Custom, Power and the Power of Rules* (1999), p. 19.

[15] Hugonis Grotii, *De ivre belli ac pacis libri tres. In quibus jus naturae et gentium: item juris publici praecipua explicantur* (1632).

[16] David J. Bederman, "Reception of the Classical Tradition in International Law: Grotius' de jure belli ac pacis" (1996) 10 *Emory Int'l L. Rev.* 1.

[17] Hugo Grotius, *The Freedom of the Seas* (Ralph von Deman Magoffin (trans.), James Brown Scott (ed.), Oxford University Press, 1916).

his claim upon, Grotius grounded the principle of freedom of navigation directly on considerations of efficiency, using the following analogy:

> If any person should prevent any other person from taking fire from his fire or light from his torch, I should accuse him of violating the law of human society, because that is the essence of its very nature . . . *why then, when it can be done without any prejudice to his own interests, will not one person share with another things which are useful to the recipient, and no loss to the giver?*[18]

Grotius presented this principle, which he imported from Greek sources, as grounded in "the law of human society," a *grundnorm* of the newly asserted law of nations. At the same time, it was, of course, a definition of efficiency later reformulated by Pareto. Per Grotius, then, international law is based on efficiency and the doctrine on customary law is one of the tools for reflecting efficiency.

But this proxy, as with any proxy, is not always an accurate reflection of efficiency. Market failures often prevent states from adopting a consistent practice or from adapting an existing practice to changed circumstances. In such circumstances, the faithful application of the doctrine on customary international law will produce inefficient norms. I contend that when this happens, and the proxy fails, international adjudicators, especially the ICJ judges, create new norms implicitly. When they identify a market failure that prevents the formation of an efficient practice, these international tribunals step in and try to change the Nash equilibrium[19] of the interstate game or at least try to create conditions that will bring about a change in the equilibrium and thus correct the failure. I further argue that the international community has recognized such a role as lawful.

Note that I do not argue that judicial intervention will *in and of itself* yield a law that is always or even often efficient.[20] Relatively high litigation costs, a lengthy adjudication process and various political costs associated

---

[18] *Ibid.* at p. 38 (emphasis added).

[19] A Nash equilibrium is defined as "a steady state of the play of a strategic game in which each player holds the correct expectation about the other players' behavior and acts rationally." Martin J. Osborne and Ariel Rubinstein, *A Course in Game Theory* (1994), p. 14.

[20] Cf. The continuing debate whether the common law is efficient: Paul H. Rubin, "Why Is the Common Law Efficient?" (1977) 6 *J. Legal Stud.* 51; John C. Goodman, "An Economic Theory of the Evolution of the Common Law" (1978) 7 *J. Legal Stud.* 393; George L. Priest, "The Common Law Process and the Selection of Efficient Rules" (1977) 6 *J. Legal Stud.* 65; Robert Cooter and Lewis Kornhauser, "Can Litigation Improve the Law Without the Help of Judges?", (1980) 9 *J. Legal Stud.* 139; Eric A. Posner, "Law, Economics, and Inefficient Norms" (1996) 144 *U. Pa. L. Rev.* 1697; Cooter, "Decentralized Law."

with such litigation often prevent potential claimants from bringing suit, especially if the gains from judicial intervention are public goods[21] or if one or both litigants are poor. But these costs work in both directions, and in fact, in the international context, these costs deter more the states that subscribe to the old, inefficient norm from bringing a suit against the state whose efficient breach heralds the dawn of the new norm. The valid expectation that international tribunals will approve efficient practices as binding law provides an additional assurance for potential defendant states to act unilaterally and "leapfrog" over the prevailing customs. Thus, potential judicial intervention *indirectly* facilitates the evolution of state practice towards efficiency.

One important caveat to this argument concerns the courts', especially the ICJ's, own institutional limitations. Similar to domestic courts, international tribunals are concerned with their own reputation. They have an acute sense of the limits on their enforcement and managerial powers, and they do not wish to produce judgments that will remain unheeded and ineffective. Therefore they adopt two types of norms. One type promotes litigation, in those contexts where litigation is likely to offer efficient outcomes. For other contexts, where direct or indirect negotiation is likely to yield efficiency more than litigation, the courts will adopt a different set of norms. Thus, for example, the determination of where lies the boundary between two states is rather a simple exercise of judicial authority, which is likely to be respected by the litigants and yield efficient outcomes. On the other hand, courts would be much less successful in establishing, for example, joint management institutions to manage transboundary resources. When judicial intervention is likely to resolve disputes efficiently, as in cases of boundary delimitation, judges will favor clear rules that assign well-defined private property rights to states, such as the rule of *uti possidetis juris* that calls for a simple cartographic exercise. The more vague the norm, the more uncertain will be the outcome of the potential litigation, and therefore the parties to the dispute will prefer to negotiate.[22] Hence, when judicial intervention is less likely to provide efficient outcomes, and direct or indirect negotiations seem to be preferable, tribunals will tend to adopt vague standards, essentially assigning states shares in "club-goods" or "common-pool resources." Thus, for example, because joint management is generally a more efficient modality for using

---

[21] For a similar argument in the domestic context see Cooter, "Decentralized Law," 1694.
[22] See Eyal Benvenisti, "Collective Action in the Utilization of Shared Freshwater: The Challenges of International Water Resources Law" (1996) 90 *Am. J. Int'l L.* 384.

transboundary resources than litigation, the evolving customary law has kept the applicable norms on the vague side, keeping states away from litigation.[23]

Customary international law and market failures

The often-high transaction costs in the global market prevent the development of general and persistent state practice in many areas. In the context of the allocation and management of global or transboundary resources there are two different sources of market failure: international and transnational. The international market failure results from conflicts of interests *among* states, conflicts that preclude states from agreeing on certain practices as legally binding. In a diffuse global environment, international collective action is required for the creation and enforcement of international norms. Such cooperation is costly, and yields public goods that all can share. Therefore, effective international norms depend on the readiness of the few to supply and enforce goods for all to share, and such goods tend to be under-provided. The lack of effective norms results in poorly defined property rights of states in transboundary and global resources.

The second type of market failure, the transnational market failure, is a result of conflict of interest *across* states, as certain domestic interest groups, such as employers and investors, impose externalities on other, usually larger, domestic interest groups, using their stronger influence on the respective national governments.[24] Thus, for example, industries in neighboring countries that have influence on their respective governments are likely to push for a treaty (or state practice) that condones pollution regardless of the environmental damage. Because in most states there are obstacles to giving ample voice to the larger, less enfranchised domestic groups, state practice tends to favor the relatively more effective minorities of the international community. This is particularly true in the sphere of transboundary resource management, where transnational conflicts are abundant.[25]

The first international type of market failure will fail to yield general and persistent practice in the first place, or fail to modify that practice

---

[23] As indeed is the outcome of the *Gabcikovo-Nagymaros* case, note 1.
[24] On this issue, see the discussion in Eyal Benvenisti, "Exit and Voice in the Age of Globalization" (1999) 98 *Mich. L. Rev.* 167.
[25] See Eyal Benvenisti, *Sharing Transboundary Resources: International Law and Optimal Resource Use* (Cambridge University Press, 2002).

to accommodate technological and other changes, because some states will refuse to recognize as legally binding practices that benefit other states. Such disputes will result in conflicting conceptions regarding the binding customary norm. The second transnational type of market failure may yield general and persistent practice only if the groups with similar interests control all governments involved. In such circumstances, state practice can only reflect efficient outcomes for the elite and small domestic interest groups that capture their governments. That practice is not likely to reflect an optimal allocation of resources from a global perspective.

When either type of market failure prevents the formation of general, persistent *and efficient* state practice, efficiency, as the *grundnorm*, calls upon adjudicators, primarily the ICJ, to step in and impose an efficient norm. Their decisions have the capability to alter the equilibrium at which states are situated in the game to a more efficient one. The key to the potential contribution of these adjudicators is their readiness to invent "customary law." Judges respond to this call to create new law, and the international community subsequently endorses their response. A number of decisions illustrate this point.

The first example relates to the issue of freedom of navigation on a river shared by two or more states. One possible equilibrium is reflected in a norm denying the existence of freedom of navigation and prescribing that each state has the sovereign power to prevent any foreign ship from access to the river at its discretion, or to charge access fees. A different equilibrium is reflected in a norm under which ships of all states enjoy freedom of navigation on the river. The second equilibrium, which is similar to the reduction of other trade barriers, is more efficient than the first because it reduces the costs of interstate commerce and hence improves overall welfare. As is often the case, however, states refuse to agree to move from the first inefficient equilibrium to the second, more efficient one. A lower riparian, for example, who controls access to the sea, may demand concessions that not all of the upstream riparians would like to shoulder. It is at this juncture that judicial intervention can be instrumental. The judgment handed down by the Permanent Court of International Justice (PCIJ) in the *Case Relating to the Territorial Jurisdiction of the International Commission of the River Oder*[26] is a case in point. This case involved a dispute concerning the scope of authority assigned in the Versailles Treaty to an international commission established to administer international navigation on "the Oder." Poland, the upstream state, refused to recognize the

---

[26] (1929) PCIJ, Ser. A, No. 23.

commission's jurisdiction over the tributaries of the river situated wholly within its territory. The PCIJ had to interpret the relevant treaty provision with little guidance from the text or from state practice. Moreover, in light of its previous landmark decision in the *Lotus* case,[27] Poland's adversaries were the ones with the burden of proving Poland's obligation to defer to an international regime. Despite these hurdles, the PCIJ opted for the efficient outcome, invoking the desire to allow international access to all navigable parts of the river, explaining that such an outcome was mandated by "the requirements of justice and the considerations of utility."[28] This decision has since been resorted to, without any hesitation, as proof of the existence of a duty to allow free navigation on international watercourses,[29] and even as a basis for the rather radical assertion that international rivers are shared resources.[30]

The *Trail Smelter Arbitration* is yet another example of adjudication that nudges states towards a more efficient equilibrium despite a lack of relevant state practice.[31] In this case, the tribunal found Canada in violation of a duty to prevent activities within its territory from causing injury in or to the territory of another state. Absent clear pronouncements of this principle by other international tribunals, the tribunal followed, "by analogy," in the footsteps of three decisions handed down by the US Supreme Court.[32] Although it did not rely explicitly on the efficiency argument, the tribunal did point to the saliency of this factor as part of its reasoning. It asserted that "great progress in the control of fumes has been made by science in the last few years and this progress should be taken into account."[33] Despite meager evidence of state practice to support the decision, the norm prescribed was never questioned. It has since become a cornerstone of international environmental law.[34]

A third example is the arbitration in the matter of *Lac Lanoux*.[35] Spain argued that its Treaty with France, as interpreted according to general international law, provided it with the right to approve any changes, however slight, France would want to introduce to the flow of a shared river

---

[27] See note 2. [28] See note 26, at 27.
[29] Lucius Caflisch, "Regles Generales du Droit des Cours d'Eau internationaux" (1989-VII) 219 *Recueil des cours* 9, 32–33, 109–10.
[30] *Gabcikovo-Nagymaros* case, note 1.
[31] *Trail Smelter (United States v. Canada)* (1905) 3 UN Reports of Arbitral Awards, reprinted in (1938–40) Annual Digest of Public International Law Cases 315.
[32] *Ibid.* at 318.   [33] *Ibid.*
[34] Phillipe Sands, *Principles of International Environmental Law* (1995), p. 191; Patricia W. Birnie and Allan E. Boyle, *International Law and The Environment* (1992), pp. 89–90.
[35] *Lake Lanoux Arbitration* (1957) 24 ILR 101.

CUSTOMARY IL AS A JUDICIAL TOOL FOR PROMOTING EFFICIENCY 95

before it entered Spanish territory. Spain hoped its refusal would lead France to offer her a larger share of the revenues from its planned hydro-electrical project. The tribunal viewed this as an inefficient claim, one that if accepted would have reduced the upper riparian's incentive to use transboundary resources more efficiently. The tribunal rejected Spain's claim. In doing so, the tribunal did refer to "international practice" and to customary international law,[36] yet it did not provide any example of such practice to support its findings. Instead, it emphasized the inefficiency of Spain's assertion of what the tribunal regarded as "a 'right of veto,' which at the discretion of one State paralyses the exercise of territorial jurisdiction of another."[37] Despite its weak doctrinal foundations, the *Lac Lanoux* decision is hailed as an important milestone in the development of international freshwater law.[38]

The final example explores a slightly different context in which international adjudicators are given the opportunity to intervene in a situation of market failure and set a new, more efficient norm. This is the case of a challenge to the validity of an established customary norm in light of new technology, new scientific findings or a change in natural conditions that render past practices inefficient and require the adoption of new, more efficient rules. Such developments create a time lag between what is established as customary law and the more efficient behavior dictated by the new reality. At such junctures, a wedge is created between efficiency and custom, as well as corresponding pressure to amend the law. Absent market failures, such pressure ultimately leads to efficient outcomes. But when market failures prevent such legal modifications, judges are given the opportunity to intervene. Such an opportunity seemed to present itself to the ICJ judges who presided over the *Fisheries Jurisdiction* case in 1974.[39]

Reacting to over-fishing by British and German fishing fleets in the North Sea, Iceland, in 1972, extended its Exclusive Fisheries Zone from a twelve- to fifty-mile limit. This move was in clear violation of the old customary norm of freedom on the high seas. But it was in line with the demands of efficiency and sustainability: it was aimed at preventing a tragedy of the commons due to over-fishing. Iceland had been preoccupied with this possible tragedy since 1948, when the Althing passed

---

[36] See e.g., Birnie and Boyle, *International Law*, p. 130.   [37] *Ibid.* at p. 128.
[38] Sands, *Principles*, pp. 348–49; Birnie and Boyle, *International Law*, pp. 102–3.
[39] *Fisheries Jurisdiction (United Kingdom v. Iceland)* [1974] ICJ Reports 2. See also the parallel and almost identical *Fisheries Jurisdiction (Federal Republic of Germany v. Iceland)* [1974] ICJ Reports 175.

the Law concerning the Scientific Conservation of the Continental Shelf Fisheries.[40] Furthermore, the Althing's resolution in 1972 provided, inter alia, that "effective supervision of the fish stocks in the Iceland area be continued in consultation with marine biologists and that the necessary measures be taken for the protection of the fish stocks and specific areas in order to prevent over-fishing."[41] The extension of the zone of unilateral appropriation resulted in about 90 percent of the fisheries in the North Sea becoming the private property of Iceland, the coastal state. Commanding sole authority over the exclusive zone, Iceland could now manage alone the harvests and thereby prevent depletion and ensure sustainable yields. This outcome was also in the long-term interests of states with large fishing fleets who had already started to compete among themselves and over-fish. Approval of Iceland's unilateral measure was mandated on efficiency grounds. But it was contrary to prevalent state practice at the time. The ICJ, however, refused to leapfrog the law and side with efficiency and sustainability. Instead, it resorted to the traditional search for past practice accepted as law. Coming as no surprise, in examining past practice, the Court could detect no customary norm that allowed coastal states to extend their exclusive spheres of economic interest beyond the twelve-mile territorial sea zone. Iceland, and the efficiency principle, lost. At that very stage, however, the law was transforming rapidly, as the ICJ itself indicated in subsequent judgments. Between 1976 and 1979, about two-thirds of the exclusive economic zones and exclusive fishery zones of up to two hundred miles had been unilaterally created,[42] with the relevant states choosing not to wait for the results of the ongoing negotiations of the UN Convention on the Law of the Sea. This practice enabled the ICJ, a decade after its *Fisheries Jurisdiction* decision, to rule that a custom had emerged in support of the legality of an exclusive economic zone of two hundred miles.[43]

The reason for the decision in the *Fisheries Jurisdiction* case was not the ICJ's disregard for the principle of efficiency. Rather, the judges chose to defer to the governments that were negotiating the Third Conference on the Law of the Sea. They explicitly acknowledged that their legislative role is residual and becomes relevant only after states have failed to come to an agreement:

---

[40] *Ibid.* at para. 19.   [41] *Ibid.* at para. 29.
[42] R.R. Churchill and A.V. Lowe, *The Law of the Sea* 144–46 (1988), pp. 144–46.
[43] *Continental Shelf (Libyan Arab Jamahiriya/Malta)*, Judgment, [1985] ICJ Reports 13, para. 34.

The very fact of convening the third conference on the Law of the Sea evidences a manifest desire on the part of all States to proceed to the codification of that law on a universal basis, including the question of fisheries . . . Such a general desire is understandable since the rules of international maritime law have been the product of mutual accommodation, reasonableness and co-operation. In the circumstances, the Court, as a court of law, cannot render judgment *sub specie legis ferendae*, or anticipate the law before the legislator has laid it down.[44]

Iceland's extension of its exclusive fisheries zone did, indeed, deviate from the prevailing practice at the time; but I submit, this measure was not unlawful. It was the quintessential first step towards the establishment of a new, more efficient norm through new state practice, the first challenge to the old law heralding the birth of the new law. Iceland's unilateral act, like the previous Truman Proclamation of 1945, which had stated the United States' unilateral extension of its jurisdiction to its continental shelves,[45] was an exemplary case of how science and technology postulate the need to change international law.[46] It was, therefore, commensurate with the abstract, basic norm of efficiency. Nevertheless, in view of the fact that multilateral negotiations on a new law were under way, there was no immediate need for judicial intervention. As it turned out, this specific international market in fact proved efficient, and no judicial intervention was ultimately required.

These examples, like the previously mentioned 1997 *Gabcikovo-Nagymaros* decision,[47] provide ample evidence for the argument that international courts and tribunals often decide to take the leap and declare new law. They take this responsibility in light of the adverse environmental and health consequences of the continuation of the prevailing practice of states, provided no contemporaneous negotiations render their intervention unnecessary.

These international adjudicators also have to pretend that they are not doing what they actually are doing. They conceal the new law in "old

---

[44] *Fisheries Jurisdiction* case, note 39, at para. 53.   [45] Whiteman, (1946) 4 *Dig. Int'l L.* 752.
[46] H. Scott Gordon, "The Economic Theory of a Common-Property Resource: The Fishery" (1954) 62 *J. Pol. Econ.* 124; Colin W. Clark, "Restricted Access to Common-Property Fishery Resources: A Game-Theoretic Analysis" in Pan-Tai Liv (ed.), *Dynamic Optimization and Mathematical Economics* (1980), p. 117. See also Yoram Barzel's analysis of the conversion of the North Sea into owned property, Yoram Barzel, *Economic Analysis of Property Rights* (2nd ed., 1997), pp. 101–2.
[47] See note 1.

bottles."[48] They play down their legislative role in a wise effort to escape controversy and questions about their personal accountability. After all, the legal system within which they operate does not explicitly recognize their legislative role. By stressing their conformity with the duty to apply "international custom, as evidence of a general practice accepted as law,"[49] these judges invoke their unique expertise – as the oracles of the mystic "custom" – that few can challenge. Although at first their norms are novel, these leaps that are consistent with efficiency are likely to be accepted as reflecting the law and to produce consistent *future* practice. The aftermath of these decisions and the fact that the decisions are subsequently widely and undisputedly accepted as valid pronouncements of international law despite their weak doctrinal basis suggest that states accept the role of tribunals as legislators of efficient norms. Put differently, this positive reaction to the judicial leaps suggest the existence of a custom that tribunals are authorized to prescribe efficient norms when market failures preclude states from reaching such norms independently.

To conclude, when states or any other players interact, they rationally find themselves in Nash equilibria that may be inefficient. A judicial declaration of one equilibrium as the one that is binding as custom is likely to lead all players to modify their activities to conform to the judicially sanctioned equilibrium. This equilibrium will thus become the new practice, the new custom. This suggests that one state's deviation from prior practice in favor of a more efficient one need not be regarded as a breach if the deviation conforms to the underlying norm of efficiency. Rather, such a deviation has a very good chance of becoming, sooner rather than later, and certainly with the help of an intervening court, the new practice, the new norm.

But my argument is not only descriptive, but also prescriptive. In the following section, I argue that in prescribing new norms concerning the allocation of transboundary and global resources, international adjudicators exercise a legitimate function under customary international law. International adjudicators, at the ICJ or elsewhere, are fully authorized to divert from current practices and "detect" a new custom when their prescription creates a new equilibrium that allocates resources more optimally. The justification for their authority lies in the efficiency of their norm and in the fact that the norm would soon be reflected in state practice.

---

[48] Boyle, "The Gabcikovo-Nagymaros Case."
[49] Article 38(1)(b) of the Statute of the International Court of Justice.

Judicial findings on efficiency

There are two major questions regarding the legitimacy of judicial prescription of efficient norms: How can adjudicators assess that the proxy, customary international law, no longer reflects efficiency, and adopt an efficient alternative despite the fact that persistent and general practice is yet to be formed? Why should we expect these adjudicators to seek these goals and trust their judgment?

To answer the first question, I argue that adjudicators can and do resort directly to scientific evidence. An assessment of the relevant data and its scientific evaluation raises evidentiary issues, but such issues are not foreign to the adjudication process, which often involves expert evidence. The litigants or the tribunals themselves can appoint expert witnesses and even assistants to the tribunal. In the *Trail Smelter Arbitration*, for example, the two sides appointed scientists, one from each side, to assist the tribunal.[50] When undisputed scientific findings show that a new norm can promise more efficient outcomes, outcomes states cannot reach due to market failures, it is up to the judges to base their decisions on the best available scientific evidence as providing the neutral and efficient norm. This scientific evidence can then be seen as offering direct guidelines to efficient norms. The study of economics and game theory, sociology and psychology, replaces the study of historical facts in the intellectual quest to establish a neutral foundation for international law.

Thus, for example, this science-based theory on the sources of international law suggests that if economic efficiency postulates effective joint management of shared ecosystems, international law should endorse it and fashion norms that will reduce the transaction costs involved in negotiating and establishing such cooperative regimes. Because states balk at conceding to this postulate without eliciting concessions from their neighbors, state practice will often prove to be inefficient. The equilibrium is reluctance to cooperate. Judges and other third parties can overcome this impasse. This observation explains the shortcomings of the 1997 Watercourses Convention and, in contrast, the landmark decision in *Gabcikovo-Nagymaros*.

In fact, the ICJ seems to have hinted that it has done exactly this. The link between science, sustainable development and the law is captured best in the following passage:

---

[50] See note 31, at 318.

> Owing to new scientific insights and to a growing awareness of the risks for mankind – for present and future generations – of pursuit of such interventions at an unconsidered and unabated pace, new norms and standards have been developed, set forth in a great number of instruments during the last two decades. Such new norms have to be taken into consideration, and such new standards given proper weight ... not only when States contemplate new activities but also when continuing with activities begun in the past. This need to reconcile economic development with protection of the environment is aptly expressed in the concept of sustainable development.[51]

In the same vein, the ICJ should use the same science-based approach to shape and mold other legal issues. One example, related to transboundary resources, involves transboundary gas and oil deposits straddling land or maritime boundaries. It is beyond dispute that so-called "unitization" – namely, the formation of a single authority to exploit such deposits – is a prerequisite for efficient utilization of oil and gas deposits.[52] Such a single authority will be able to exploit the underground pressures to propel captured deposits to the surface to benefit all riparians. When such deposits straddle international boundaries, unless a joint development agreement is reached among the coowner states, only a fraction of the deposit can be exploited. Does this suggest that states sharing such resources have a duty under international law to form such joint regimes? If one follows the doctrine on customary law, the answer will be negative. Indeed, a recent examination of state practice typically concluded with the following observation:

> [The] survey of bilateral state practice indicates, as a preliminary conclusion, that a rule of customary international law requiring cooperation specifically with a view toward joint development or transboundary unitization of a common hydrocarbon deposit has not yet crystallized.[53]

Although such a conclusion may be a fair description of an existing situation, judges or arbitrators who have the power and duty to modify the law in the face of market failures cannot share it. They cannot let pass the opportunity to transform the existing equilibrium of the interstate game into a new and self-enforcing equilibrium of cooperation. A hint in that direction was recently given in the second phase of the arbitral

---

[51] See note 1, at para. 140.
[52] Gary D. Libecap, *Contracting for Property Rights* (1989); Rainer Lagoni, "Oil and Gas Deposits Across National Frontiers" (1979) 73 *Am. J. Int'l L.* 215, 224.
[53] David M. Ong, "Joint Development of Common Offshore Oil and Gas Deposits: 'Mere' State Practice or Customary International Law?" (1999) 93 *Am. J. Int'l L.* 771, 792.

award in the *Eritrea-Yemen Arbitration*.⁵⁴ In the process of delimiting the maritime boundary between the two states, the tribunal considered the possibility that petroleum deposits would be found to straddle the boundary. Although it admitted that so far no general customary law has been developed to require unitization, the tribunal carefully tailored a specific norm pertaining only to the two litigants. It found that the parties are bound to inform one another and to consult one another on any oil and gas and other mineral resources that may be discovered that straddle the single maritime boundary between them or that lie in their immediate vicinity. Moreover, the historical connections between the peoples concerned, and the friendly relations of the parties that had been restored since the Tribunal's rendering of its award on sovereignty, together with the body of state practice in the exploitation of resources that straddle maritime boundaries, imported that Eritrea and Yemen should give every consideration to the shared or joint or unitized exploitation of any such resources.⁵⁵

Recourse to science, of course, is not a panacea. The available scientific evidence may eventually be proven wrong. Experts may, for example, agree at a certain point in time that based on state-of-the-art scientific knowledge, joint management is the most efficient way to resolve conflicts concerning international common pool resources, be it fisheries, forest, freshwater or oil. Such an opinion may, in principle, eventually be proven wrong. At that stage, a new theory will suggest a more efficient norm that will then become the new norm. Another complication factor is risk and its assessment. The recourse to science does not eliminate all uncertainties concerning the potential risks of a new use or a new technology. Thus, science does not relieve decision-makers of their duty to make policy choices regarding the potential nature of the risks and their allocation. International adjudicators are less capable of making such choices for the litigants and thus tend to let the states negotiate these choices directly.

Why do judges in the ICJ, in other judicial institutions, or ad hoc arbitrators subscribe to the goal of efficiency? Why should we trust their judgment? Here I can only hint at possible responses. I would suggest that judges in international institutions, and particularly in the ICJ, are relatively immune to inducements that would lead them to favor partiality (aside from ad hoc judges that are expected to give a voice to their state's

---

⁵⁴ *Eritrea-Yemen Arbitration* (Award Phase II: Maritime Delimitation), December 17, 1999, available at www.pca-cpa.org/ERYE2.
⁵⁵ *Ibid.* at para. 86.

concerns). Reaching the height of their professional career, ICJ judges act behind an almost perfect Rawlsian veil of ignorance. As lawyers whose reputation is global, arbitrators too have no strong incentive to promote partial and inefficient norms. Be the reason as it may, ultimately they adopt the goal of efficiency.

Efficiency and the contemporary crisis of customary international law

The emphasis on efficiency, as lying at the heart of customary international law, can salvage the doctrine from grave doubts about its authority and utility. As all international lawyers know, the doctrine on customary international law does not provide clear answers as to what constitutes custom. The doctrine is malleable, open to conflicting policy considerations, to wishful thinking, to abuse.

On the most immediate level, viewing customary law as a proxy for efficiency resolves the inherent paradox concerning the evolution of custom:[56] if custom evolves and is modified through unilateral action, how does the doctrine explain the first deviation from the previous custom? Is it an illegal defection? Does subsequent practice absolve the deviating state from responsibility? Must a tribunal, faced with a complaint against the deviating state, find against the harbinger of the new law and, thereby, arrest the development of the law? Grounding the doctrine of customary international law on efficiency offers a solution to the seeming paradox: if the deviating state asserts a new norm that is more efficient than the old one, the deviation should not be considered a violation. Thus, in the example of the *Fisheries Jurisdiction* cases,[57] the ICJ was in a position to accept Iceland's unilateral move as legal, prior practice notwithstanding. As I argued, the ICJ should have done so, and its refusal to do so can only be justified in light of the simultaneous efforts to negotiate this matter multilaterally.

The emphasis on efficiency also responds to the growing criticisms of the utility of the doctrine: Robert Jennings warned of the inconsistency between doctrine and reality, suggesting that "Perhaps it is time to face squarely the fact that the orthodox tests of custom – practice and *opinio juris* – are often not only inadequate but even irrelevant for the

---

[56] On this paradox, see Byers, *Custom, Power*, pp. 130–33. [57] See note 39.

identification of much new law today;"[58] W. Michael Reisman warned against resorting to custom as a tool for clarifying and implementing policies in an advanced and complicated civilization.[59] The particular discrepancy between state practice and appropriate norms in the sphere of the environment has been noted by Oscar Schachter, who wrote, "[t]o say that a state has no right to injure the environment of another seems quixotic in the face of the great variety of transborder environmental harms that occur every day."[60] Other commentators have conceded that the list of customary norms concerning the environment is rather short[61] and that the actual identified norms lack precision: "their legal status, their meaning, and the consequences of their application to the facts of a particular case or activity remain open."[62]

The doctrine on customary law does, indeed, fail if its role is to provide positive norms based on general and persistent state practice simply because on many important questions there is no such practice. This shortcoming tempts scholars to employ a less rigid scrutiny of state behavior, peppered with value judgments. This practice is as ancient as its inventor, Grotius.[63] But breaking loose from the doctrinal examination of state practice exposes the judge to the opposite danger: the danger of subjectivity and, hence, loss of legitimacy.[64] Attempts to reconcile inconsistent practice by invoking normative arguments deliver a blow to the

---

[58] Robert Y. Jennings, "The Identification of International Law" in Bin Cheng (ed.), *International Law: Teaching and Practice* (Stevens, London, 1982), pp. 3, 5.
[59] See W. Michael Reisman, "The Cult of Custom in the Late 20th Century" (1987) 17 *Cal. W. Int'l L.J.* 133, 134.
[60] Oscar Schachter, "The Emergence of International Environmental Law" (1991) 44 *J. Int'l Aff.* 457, 462–63.
[61] Sands, *Principles*, p. 184, lists the following norms as customary: the responsibility of states not to cause environmental damage and the principle of good neighborliness and international cooperation. These are the only principles sufficiently established to give rise to customary obligation. Birnie and Boyle, *International Law*, pp. 92–94, suggest that the customary duty of states is to take adequate steps (due diligence) to control and regulate sources of serious global environmental pollution or transboundary harm within their territories or subject to their jurisdictions.
[62] Sands, *Principles*, p. 236.
[63] Bederman, "Reception of the Classical Tradition," 37–39: "Grotius assigned varying significance to natural law dictates and to customary international law evidences in his consideration of different international law doctrines ... He purported to scientifically approach the historical record of State practice, although he was prepared to modify (and even distort) that evidence in order to fashion rules of enduring significance to modern nations. Grotius thus embodied the contemporary ambivalence of legal scholarship."
[64] Jonathan I. Charney, "Universal International Law" (1993) 87 *Am. J. Int'l L.* 529, 545–46.

effort to establish a value-neutral basis of international law, digestible by all states. In a divided globe, this is a source of crisis for the doctrine. The search for prevalent state practice necessitates a choice between past-looking and inefficient neutrality on the one hand, and teleological forward-looking subjectivity on the other.

Basing the doctrine of customary international law squarely on efficiency redeems it from a third and final flaw. Presented as a neutral doctrine, the only normative basis the doctrine on customary international law can have is state consent: custom reflects the express or implied consent of states to be bound by it. But clearly, state consent can no longer provide the normative basis, the *grundnorm*, for international obligations. State consent is no more a satisfying normative basis than the idea of positivism in domestic law. A global system redefined as subject to basic principles of human rights cannot be described as preserving the unfettered discretion of states to accept or decline the evolution of the law in conformity with the basic norms. If we regard sovereignty as having no inherent value, but instead having only an instrumental value, as a useful concept for allocating powers among peoples in a global system, then also state consent, in itself, cannot have any normative value.[65] In other words, the seemingly positive, neutral basis of the doctrine not only yields indeterminate outcomes, but also is not satisfactory from a normative perspective. Basing the doctrine on efficiency relieves the need to reconcile custom with consent. It provides an alternative, neutral ground for determining "custom."

Efficiency, equity and fairness: contradiction or affinity?

Thus far I have argued that efficiency is the underlying principle of customary international law. This argument serves as the basis for the claim that the process of defining and redefining customary international law could be based on a study, informed by scientific assessments, of the efficient rules. But can we argue that efficiency is the only principle that nurtures the evolution of customary law? What about equity considerations – should judges who leapfrog international law factor in equity considerations? At first blush the response should be positive, given the fact that the doctrine on equity in international law is well developed and quite often used. The prevalence of equity in different legal contexts

---

[65] See Martti Koskenniemi's critique of the principle of state consent in Martti Koskenniemi, *From Apology to Utopia* (1989), pp. 270–73.

of international law may suggest that an underlying policy of equity – equity-as-fairness – permeates quite a number of international norms, constituting "an important, redeeming aspect of the international legal system"[66] that may clash with and even take precedence over efficiency. Where a trade-off between efficiency and fairness is possible, emphasis on fairness may lead to the adoption of policies that are less efficient, but distribute more equitably the benefits and risks across the relevant groups. The interplay between equity-as-fairness and efficiency also raises the question as to whether in addition to moving international law to the "Pareto frontier," namely, to the zone of the most efficient outcomes, tribunals can also choose among the efficient outcomes the outcome that distributes the gains most equitably. These questions call for an inquiry into the relationship between the two principles: equity-as-fairness and efficiency.

These two questions are more acute in the international context than in the national one. In national systems, governments pursue efficiency not because they eschew fairness, but because they design legal or market-based mechanisms to redistribute risks and benefits among citizens. Thus, they achieve fair results without sacrificing efficiency. But in the international system, such a solution is problematic because there are no readily available institutions for making and implementing decisions on distributing or redistributing among states the added benefits from the more efficient allocation of global resources. In addition, international tribunals may be less informed than national courts or legislatures to be able to make responsible choices on the Pareto frontier. In the international context, therefore, we often face a tough choice between efficiency and fairness.

My observation is that international law, due to its institutional limitations in assessing fairness, favors efficiency over it, and recognizes not a doctrine of fairness (or equity-as-fairness), but a doctrine of *equity-as-efficiency* which is far removed from fairness considerations. The international legal doctrine on equity does not require the subjecting of efficiency to fairness arguments. Rather, equity in international law is a doctrine used to achieve efficiency. Hence, I argue, there is a convergence, rather than a clash, between the two concepts. A careful analysis of the use of the concept of equity in international law supports and complements my previously outlined observation that efficiency considerations stand at the basis of customary international law.

---

[66] Thomas M. Franck, *Fairness in International Law and Institutions* (1995), p. 79.

The gist of my argument is that the concept of equity in international law does not serve distributive functions. Instead, equity in the application of the law (as distinct from equity *ex aequo et bono*, namely, equity rendered outside the law)[67] serves two functions, both of which are mandated by efficiency. First, equity grants discretion to decision-makers, primarily judges and arbitrators, where existing norms are too crude to be applied to specific matters, such as in cases dealing with the delimitation of maritime boundaries. Second, equity creates incentives for users of global or transboundary resources to act efficiently by cooperating with their neighbors.

Equity as discretion

Just as the doctrine of administrative discretion provides authority to administrative agencies to implement statutory policies in specific instances, so the doctrine of equity allows negotiating states to seek ways to resolve their differences within the confines of international norms that provide only rough principles. Similar to administrative discretion, this delegation of authority minimizes the costs of legislation. The doctrine of equity authorizes judges or arbitrators to balance all the considerations which international law prescribes as relevant to the intricacies of the particular case.[68] "Equité peut être définie comme la solution qui convient le mieux á chaque cas qui se presente. Elle est donc autre chose que l' 'Equity' du Droit anglo-saxon."[69] In other words, equity provides decision-makers with the discretion to implement general policies on an ad hoc basis. The use of equity does not guarantee outcomes that are "fair," if by "fair" we mean that at least some attention is paid to distributive effects. It guarantees an economy of law prescription and enforcement.

This function of equity-as-discretion is evident in the areas of territorial and maritime boundary delimitation. In the delimitation of territorial boundaries in the decolonized world, equity considerations have played

---

[67] On the different contexts of equity, see Ruth Lapidoth, "Equity in International Law" (1987) 22 *Isr. L. Rev.* 161.

[68] *Continental Shelf (Tunisia/Libyan Arab Jamahiriya)*, Judgment, [1982] ICJ Reports 18, at para. 24 (Jimenez de Arechaga, J., sep. op.). See also Masahiro Miyoshi, *Considerations of Equity in the Settlement of Territorial and Boundary Disputes* (1993), p.173.

[69] A. Alvarez, "Preliminary Communication" (1937) 40 *Annuaire de l'Institut de Droit International* 151.

only a marginal role. The reigning principle is *uti possidetis juris*, namely, the supremacy of pre-independence boundaries.[70] This principle promotes stability and certainty and, hence, is efficient. It eschews fairness considerations, even if a most precious resource is kept only on one side of the border. Equity considerations become relevant only when the *uti possidetis* rule fails to provide a clear answer.[71] And even then, equity allows decision-makers the discretion to weigh a host of *natural* factors, none having to do with distributive concerns.[72]

The doctrine on equity is also effective in settling questions of maritime delimitation of continental shelves or exclusive economic zones between two or more neighboring states with opposite or adjacent coasts. Here, again, equity grants discretion to judges and authorizes them to balance all the relevant conflicting factors and interests.[73] The judges do not necessarily use their discretion to achieve fair outcomes. An examination of the many decisions rendered by the ICJ, its Chambers and other tribunals reveals that the major consideration has been the geography of the particular area, again in an effort to offer clarity. In one such decision, the ICJ explicitly rejected as irrelevant the consideration of the relative wealth of the two neighboring states. It ruled out the possibility that the relative economic wealth of the two litigants would influence its decision "in such a way that the area of continental shelf regarded as appertaining to the less rich of the two States would be somewhat increased in order to compensate for its inferiority in economic resources," explaining that:

---

[70] Miyoshi, *Considerations of Equity*, pp. 153–54.
[71] *Frontier Dispute (Burkina Fasu/Mali)*, Judgment, [1986] ICJ Reports 536, para. 149 ("to resort to the concept of equity in order to modify an established frontier would be quite unjustified").
[72] *Land, Island and Maritime Frontier Dispute (El Salvador/Honduras: Nicaragua intervening)* [1992] ICJ Reports 351, para. 58 ("economic considerations of this kind could not be taken into account for the delimitation of continental shelf areas . . . still less can they be relevant for the determination of a land frontier").
[73] See e.g., *North Sea Continental Shelf* case, note 2, at 3, para. 93; *Continental Shelf (Tunisia/Libyan Arab Jamahiriya)*, note 68, para. 107; *Application for Revision and Interpretation of the Judgment of 24 February 1982 in the Case Concerning the Continental Shelf (Tunisia v. Libyan Arab Jamahiriya)*, Judgment, [1985] I.C.J. Reports 192, at para. 35. On the role of equity in balancing different factors in the context of maritime delimitation, see generally Francisko Orrego Vicuna, *The Exclusive Economic Zone* (1989), pp. 211–22; Prosper Weil, *Perspectives du droit de la Delimitation Maritime* (Paris, 1988), pp. 282–85; Malcolm D. Evans, *Relevant Circumstances and Maritime Delimitation* (Oxford, 1989), pp. 90–94; Miyoshi, *supra* note 68.

[s]uch considerations are totally unrelated to the underlying intention of the applicable rules of international law. It is clear that neither the rules determining the validity of legal entitlement to the continental shelf, nor those concerning delimitation between neighbouring countries, leave room for any considerations of economic development of the States in question.[74]

Geographic considerations prevailed because the continental shelf and the exclusive maritime economic zones in question were viewed as the natural prolongation of the land-mass. Sovereignty over the land-mass is the starting point for judicial discretion. The ICJ developed a notion of a conceptual nexus between the land – sovereignty over land being the basis for the claim – and the shelf or the exclusive economic zone to be delimited.[75] As the ICJ stated:

> Since the land is the legal source of power which a State may exercise over territorial extensions to seaward, it must first be clearly established what features do in fact constitute such extensions.[76]

Judicial disregard of the relative economic conditions in the relevant countries has been most clearly manifested in the case concerning the delimitation of the continental shelf between Libya and Malta.[77] The ICJ emphasized that equity entails:

> the principle that there is to be no question of refashioning geography, or compensating for the inequalities of nature; . . . the principle that . . . [equity does not] seek to make equal what nature has made unequal; and the principle that there can be no question of distributive justice.[78]

---

[74] *Tunisia* v. *Libyan Arab Jamahiriya*, note 73, at para. 50. See also *Tunisia* v. *Libyan Arab Jamahiriya*, note 68, at para. 107; Louis F. E. Goldie, "Reconciling Values of Distributive Equity and Management Efficiency in the International Commons" in Rene-Jean Dupuy (ed.), *The Settlement of Disputes on the New Natural Resources* (1983), pp. 335, 338–39; L.D.M. Nelson, "The Roles of Equity in the Delimitation of Maritime Boundaries" (1990) 84 *Am. J. Int'l L.* 837; Derek W. Bowett, "The Economic Factor in Maritime Delimitation Cases" in 2 *International Law at the Time of its Codification: Essays in Honour of Roberto Ago* (1987), pp. 45, 61–62.

[75] *North Sea Continental Shelf* case, note 2, at paras. 19, 96. See also *Aegean Sea Continental Shelf* (*Greece* v. *Turkey*), [1978] ICJ Reports 3, at para. 86; Research Centre for International Law, University of Cambridge, *International Boundary Cases: The Continental Shelf*, vol. 1 (1992), p. 12; Elihu Lauterpacht, *Aspects of the Administration of International Justice* (1991), pp. 124–30; Weil, *Perspectives du Droit*, pp. 56–61; Evans, *Relevant Circumstances*, pp. 99–103. Sovereignty over the land as the source of title over the territorial waters was confirmed by the ICJ in *Anglo-Norwegian Fisheries* (*United Kingdom* v. *Norway*) [1951] ICJ Reports 116, at 133.

[76] *North Sea Continental Shelf* case, note 2, at para. 96.

[77] See note 43.   [78] *Ibid.* at para. 46.

Thus, the considerable difference in the economic strength of Libya and Malta was regarded as an irrelevant consideration.[79] A Chamber of the ICJ did consider the economic interests of communities residing within the disputed area (i.e., the local population that relies on the fisheries for subsistence), but made it clear that these interests would not be assigned great significance and would influence the decision only marginally:

> What the Chamber would regard as a legitimate scruple lies rather in concern lest the overall result ... should unexpectedly be revealed as radically inequitable, that is to say, as likely to entail catastrophic repercussions for the livelihood and economic well-being of the population of the countries concerned.[80]

Theoretically, the concept of equity-as-fairness could have been invoked in the sphere of delimitation of contiguous river boundaries. Equal access to navigable watercourses could have constituted quite a cogent principle. It is, therefore, rather telling that the *Beagle Channel Arbitration* mentions it as the *last* consideration guiding its decision, giving precedence to geographic considerations. According to the Tribunal, it was guided "in particular by mixed factors of appurtenance, coastal configuration, equidistance, and also of convenience, navigability, and the desirability of enabling each Party so far as possible to navigate in its own water."[81]

Equity as an efficient incentive

The second function of equity is demonstrated in the sphere of allocation of transboundary resources such as freshwater. In this context, the claim for equity-as-fairness seems to be most evident, as in the call in the Watercourses Convention for "equitable and reasonable utilization"[82] of shared watercourses. But also here I argue that equity serves the goal of efficiency.

---

[79] Ibid. at para. 50. See also Evans, *Relevant Circumstances*, p. 186, and the decision of the ICJ in *Maritime Delimitation in the Area between Greenland and Jan Mayen (Denmark v. Norway)* [1993] ICJ Reports 38, at paras. 79–80.

[80] *Delimitation of the Maritime Boundary in the Gulf of Maine Area (Canada v. United States)* [1984] ICJ Reports 246, at para. 237; Evans, *Relevant Circumstances*, pp. 189, 200; Weil, *perspectives du droit*, pp. 274–80.

[81] *Beagle Channel Arbitration (Argentine v. Chile)* (1977) 52 ILR 93, para. 110. See also the *Case Relating to the Territorial Jurisdiction of the International Commission of the River Oder*, note 26, at 27–28; Elihu Lauterpacht, "River Boundaries: Legal Aspects of the Shatt-Al-Arab Frontier" (1960) 9 *I.C.L.Q.* 216–22.

[82] Watercourses Convention, Article 5, heading.

The Watercourses Convention sets forth as its objective "attaining optimal and sustainable utilization [of international watercourses] and benefits therefrom."[83] This reflects a long-standing conception, in the words of the Institut de droit international, "that the maximum utilization of available natural resources is a matter of common interest," as well as the aspiration to "assur[e] the greatest advantage to all concerned."[84] Equity is a convenient notion in the quest for achieving "maximum benefit to each basin State from the uses of the waters with the minimum detriment to each,"[85] while being sensitive to the divergent economic conditions among riparians. Thus, the International Law Association (ILA), in its 1966 Helsinki Rules, emphasize that states are bound by "a duty of efficiency which is commensurate with their financial resources."[86] This is further explained by the ILA as follows:

> State A, an economically advanced and prosperous State which utilizes the inundation method of irrigation, might be required to develop a more efficient and less wasteful system forthwith, while State B, an underdeveloped State using the same method might be permitted additional time to obtain the means to make the required improvements.[87]

Furthermore, the report of the International Law Commission explicitly emphasizes that,

> Attaining optimal utilization and benefits does not mean achieving the "maximum" use, the most technologically efficient use, or the most monetary valuable use ... Nor does it imply that the State capable of making the most efficient use ... should have a superior claim to the use thereof. Rather, it implies attaining maximum possible benefits for all watercourse States and achieving the greatest possible satisfaction of all their needs, while minimizing the detriment to, or unmet needs of, each.[88]

---

[83] Watercourses Convention, Article 5(1).

[84] See the Institute of International Law's Resolution on the Utilization of Non-Maritime International Waters (Except for Navigation) adopted at its session at Salzburg, September 3–12, 1961, (1961) 49 (II) *Annuaire de l'Institut de Droit International* 370 (translated in (1962) 56 *Am. J. Int'l L.* 737), Preamble and Article 6.

[85] *Ibid.* at 486.

[86] "Commentary on the Helsinki Rules, ILA *Report of the Fifty-Second Conference* (1967), pp. 484, 487.

[87] *Ibid.* at 487.

[88] ILC Report on the Law of the Non-Navigational Uses of International Watercourses, [1994] II *Yearbook of the International Law* Commission, Pt 2, 85, 97. See also Commentary on the Helsinki Rules, note 86, at 487: "A 'beneficial use' need not be the most productive use to which the water may be put, nor need it utilize the most efficient methods known in order to avoid waste and insure maximum utilisation."

This concern with "equity of needs" is reflected in the list of factors mentioned as relevant in the process of determining what constitutes "reasonable and equitable" allocation. Included among these factors are "the social and economic needs of the watercourse States concerned"[89] and of "the population dependent on the watercourse in each watercourse State."[90] Although these factors are preceded by "geographic, hydrographic, hydrological, climatic, ecological and other factors of a natural character,"[91] such natural factors play a minor role. It is generally accepted that the natural factors provide only the factual basis for the analysis of the respective needs,[92] a telling contrast to the equity analysis in the sphere of maritime boundary delimitation.[93]

Equity as "equity of needs" is well entrenched in the practice related to federal or international freshwater.[94] In fact, there exists no evidence to support the contrary proposition, namely, that waters should be allocated, for example, according to the contribution of each state to the basin's waters or according to the length of the river in each state's territory.[95] "Equity of needs" is efficient because it creates the proper incentives for

---

[89] Watercourses Convention, Article 6(1)(b). A similar consideration appears in Article V(2)(e) of the 1966 Helsinki Rules, note 86.

[90] Watercourses Convention, Article 6(1)(c). A similar consideration appears in Article V(2)(f) of the 1966 Helsinki Rules, note 86.

[91] Watercourses Convention, Article 6(2)(a). The Helsinki Rules specify these natural factors as the first three on the list: Article V(2)(a)–(c).

[92] See Bonaya A. Godana, *Africa's Shared Water Resources* (1985), p. 58: "Factors (a) to (c) mentioned in Article V of the Helsinki Rules merely re-emphasise the need for an accurate assessment of the nature and extent of the interdependence between utilisation in the different basin states."

[93] On maritime boundary delimitation see text to notes 73–81.

[94] See e.g., Gerhard Hafner, "The Optimum Utilization Principle and the *Non-Navigational Uses of Drainage Basins*" (1993) 45 *Aust. J. Publ. Int'l L.* 113, 124–26; Patricia Buirette, "Genese d'un Droit Fluvial International General" (1991) 95 *R.G.D.I.P.* 5, 38; Gunther Handl, "The Principle of 'Equitable Use' as applied to Internationally Shared Natural Resources: Its Role in Resolving Potential International Disputes Over Transfrontier Pollution" (1978) 14 *Rev. Belge de Droit International* 40, 46, 52–54; Jerome Lipper "Equitable Utilization" in A. Garretson, R. Haydon and C. Olmstead (eds.), *The Law of International Drainage Basins* (1967), pp. 16, 41, 45; Charles Bourne, "The Right to Utilize the Waters of International Rivers" (1965) 3 *Can. Yb Int'l L.* 187, 199; William Griffin, "The Use of Waters of International Drainage Basins Under Customary International Law" (1959) 53 *Am. J. Int'l L.* 50, 78–79 1959.

[95] Lipper, "Equitable Utilization," 44: "Factors unrelated to the availability and use of waters are irrelevant and should not be considered. For example, the size of a particular state in relation to a co-riparian or the fact that the river flows for a greater distance through one state than another is not in itself a factor to be considered in determining what is an equitable utilization (although it may prove relevant on the issue of 'need')."

users to invest in efficient uses of a shared watercourse: efficient (or "beneficial") existing uses enjoy qualified supremacy in the balancing of the riparians' equitable shares. As Article 8(1) of the ILA Helsinki Rules states:

> [a]n existing reasonable use may continue in operation unless the factors justifying its continuance are outweighed by other factors leading to the conclusion that it be modified or terminated so as to accommodate a competing incompatible use.[96]

As explained in the commentary to the Helsinki Rules:

> failure to give any weight to existing uses can only serve to inhibit river development. A State is unlikely to invest large sums of money in the construction of a dam if it has no assurances of being afforded some legal protection for the use over an extended period of time.[97]

But only efficient projects deserve protection. The principle of optimal utilization – that protects only "beneficial uses"[98] – implies that existing uses that are wasteful do not merit continued respect.[99] Thus, existing uses enjoy priority:[100]

> [b]ut a contemplated use will nevertheless prevail over an existing use if the former offers benefits of such magnitude as is sufficient to outweigh the injury to the existing use.[101]

"Equity of needs" is also efficient for the creation of the "constructive ambiguity" of the legal norm that is so important for creating the proper incentives for states to commence negotiations. As noted earlier,[102] the vague standard "equity of needs" increases the uncertainty of litigation, and therefore draws riparians to negotiate and thereby – hopefully – begin a process that may lead to long-term cooperation in the management of the shared resource. Such a vague standard that instructs states to provide

---

[96] The 1966 Helsinki Rules, note 86, Article 8(1). In the same vein, see the Institute of Internaltional Law's Salzburg Resolution, note 84, Articles 3, 4.
[97] Commentary to the Helsinki Rules, note 86, at 493.
[98] As Lipper defines this term, "a use, to be entitled to protection, must afford sufficient economic and social benefit to the user so that it is reasonable, under all the circumstances, that its continuation be considered." "Equitable Utilization," 63.
[99] *Colorado v. New Mexico*, 459 U.S. 176, 103 S.Ct. 539, 74 L.Ed.2d. 348 (1982) (a more efficient future use may outweigh an existing wasteful one); Lipper, "Equitable Utilization," 46 (a more efficient use by another state is not dispositive, but it is a relevant consideration).
[100] *Ibid.* at 58. See also Caflisch, "Regles Generales," 158–60.
[101] Lipper, "Equitable Utilization," 58.   [102] Text to notes 22–23.

information not only on the natural characteristics of the shared transboundary resource but also on their existing and potential needs, prompts an informed discussion over existing and potential needs, which sensitizes negotiators to the constraints of their partners and the limitations on their room for political maneuvering and enables them to explore ways to accommodate the interests of all parties. Therefore the vague standard offered by the "equity of needs" doctrine increases the potential for initiating efficient bilateral or regional cooperation.

Finally, "equity of needs" raises the potential of domestic support for negotiated or judicial allocation of entitlements. Domestic users, especially the strong agricultural interest groups, will simply resist new allocations that severely curtail their existing uses. Moreover, it would be much more difficult to implement reallocation plans. The conditional priority assigned to existing uses assists in reducing domestic opposition to the ratification and implementation of agreements.

For these reasons, the use of the "equity of needs" principle in the transboundary resources sphere facilitates efficiency. It creates efficient incentives for users of the resource to act collectively, and increases the likelihood that the negotiated settlement will be domestically ratified and obeyed. In other words, invocation of "equity of needs" was not – or not only – motivated by fairness considerations but rather was designed to achieve efficient allocation of transboundary resources.

Efficiency and human rights

A question of trade-off seems to exist when the goal of efficiency clashes with human rights considerations. The human rights perspective generates a host of principles concerning, for example, the management of transboundary resources affecting individual and group rights. This perspective informs us about the obligation to ensure the bare necessities on a per capita basis to all individuals who depend on specific transboundary resources. In particular, it mandates a sufficient supply of clean air and water for personal consumption for all individuals, regardless of nationality, financial resources or other distinguishing factors. It requires minimum and equally distributed exposure to risks. It entails the protection of minority groups, their property and culture, against government-sponsored development projects that disregard them.[103] At these junctures, efficiency may seem to be subordinated to basic human

[103] See Benvenisti, *Sharing Transboundary Resources*, ch. 7.

rights considerations. There can be no trade-off, for example, between water for basic domestic needs and water for irrigated cash crops. In the same vein, the unequal distribution of risks of pollutants among different regions or groups of people infringes on the principle of equal treatment of individuals. Damming rivers or diverting flows from one basin to another may increase the availability of water for some people, but, at the same time, create adverse environmental and social effects for others. In such cases, equality requires a careful balancing between the interests of the different communities and fair representation of the affected groups in the various stages of the decision-making process. Granting voice in the decision-making process and paying respect to individual and communal interests enhance the quality of the decisions that take due account of their concerns, increase the legitimacy of such agreements, and, thus, strengthen the durability and success of collective action. This is why, ultimately, human rights considerations uphold the principle of efficient allocation of resources. Under conditions of growing scarcity, recurring crises and natural disasters, the law of human rights postulates sustainability as a goal of international law. In the context of transboundary resource management, states are required to pursue policies that provide efficient and sustainable uses.

The doctrine in national courts: serving a different function

One important caveat to the thesis presented here involves the use of customary law by national courts. National courts use the fuzziness of international custom not as a tool for achieving efficiency in the use of transboundary and global resources, but as a means to forward national goals. As I demonstrated previously, based on a comparative analysis of national courts' jurisprudence in this regard, customary international law is one of the principal "avoidance doctrines" these courts use in order to defer to their executive branch.[104] Thus, the method of inquiry used by a national court in examining the existence of a custom is likely to reflect its national affiliation. Even when the national courts use similar approaches to identifying custom, they reach different conclusions, and in any event, the outcome is likely to conform with national interests. It is especially rare for a national court to invoke customary law against its own executive. Moreover, even cases in which enforcement of international customary

---

[104] Eyal Benvenisti, "Judicial Misgivings Regarding the Application of International Norms: An Analysis of Attitudes of National Courts" (1993) 4 *Eur. J. Int'l L.* 159.

law was sought against a foreign government or foreign officials, courts hesitated, and acquiesced only where encouraged to do so by the executive.

This parochial attitude towards customary international law is one component of a general hands-off judicial policy. Judicial interference with the executive's performance in the international realm is deemed an illegitimate intervention in international affairs, regardless of the domestic implications. The basic attitude has been that in international affairs, "[o]ur State cannot speak with two voices on such a matter, the judiciary saying one thing, the executive another,"[105] and the executive's voice is preferred because of an inherent "advantage of the diplomatic approach to the resolution of difficulties between two sovereign nations, as opposed to the unilateral action by the courts of one nation."[106]

International adjudicators understand intuitively the institutional constraints within which national courts operate, and hesitate to invoke them as evidence of the emergence of customs despite the fact that such judicial decisions are officially recognized "as subsidiary means for the determination of rules of [international] law."[107] They do refer to national courts' decisions when these are decisions of federal courts seized with disputes over allocation of resources among states or provinces.[108] In such litigation, federal courts are institution-wise in a situation that is similar to international tribunals.

Concluding observations

Efficiency, in the sense of efficient allocation of resources among states, has been all along the driving force behind the development of international law in general, and customary international law in particular. State practice has often proven a reliable proxy for determining what constitutes efficient behavior for all states to follow. This proxy enabled international tribunals and other actors to impose sanctions on free-riders or others seeking to deviate from the efficient norm. But this proxy fails when global or regional conditions lead states to pursue inefficient behavior. In

---

[105] *The Arantzazu Mendi* [1939] App. Cas. 256, 264 (HL) (granting immunity to the nationalist government of Spain by the British House of Lords following recognition by the Foreign Office as a de facto government).
[106] *United States* v. *Alvarez-Machain*, 504 U.S. 655, 669 n.16 (1992). On this see Eyal Benvenisti, "Exit and Voice in the Age of Globalization" (1999) 98 *Mich. L. Rev.* 167.
[107] Statute of the International Court of Justice, Article 38(1)(d).
[108] See e.g., *Trail Smelter* case, note 31 (relying on the US Supreme Court's cases dealing with interstate pollution).

such situations, tribunals and other third parties can make a difference by pushing states towards new, more efficient Nash equilibria. The argument developed in this chapter is that the judicial authority to nudge states towards efficient equilibria exists in international law. This authority is derived from the principle of efficiency that nurtures much of international law and particularly its customary law. Where state practice fails to follow the efficient mode of behavior, international adjudicators are authorized to inform themselves directly on the best available scientific research. Judges in international tribunals, especially at the ICJ, therefore have a unique role in the advancement of international law. They have the genuine opportunity of translating science into law, an opportunity the states themselves often fail to seize. In a sense, tribunals have the opportunity to declare as law what states would have agreed upon had they decided behind a Rawlsian veil of ignorance under the assurance of reciprocity. This explains why judicial solutions may offer far greater promise than internationally negotiated framework conventions. The history of the evolution of international freshwater law culminating in the ICJ decision in the *Gabcikovo-Nagymaros* case[109] demonstrates this point.

This analysis also explains why states pay so much attention to the decisions of the ICJ, despite the fact that ICJ decisions are technically not binding on states that have not taken part in the specific litigation and also the fact that the ICJ is not bound by its own prior decisions.

This analysis further demonstrates the need to redirect the focus in the study of customary international law. The analysis of customary law cannot remain confined to the study of past precedents. In order to remain true to the underlying goals of international law, it must encompass the scientific insights in the fields related to the subject matter under scrutiny, in the quest of refining knowledge about the efficiency or inefficiency of prevailing practices.

[109] See note 1.

5

Reputation, compliance and development

GEORGE W. DOWNS AND MICHAEL A. JONES

Introduction

Many international relations and international legal theorists believe that the concern a state has for its reputation as a reliable treaty partner provides the key to understanding the evolution of multilateral cooperation in the international system. Even in situations with considerable incentives to defect and unavailable reciprocal and institutional sanctions, the prospect of exclusion from future agreements and/or having participation in current agreements discounted suffices to insure compliance.

These theorists tend to find the process by which reputation operates to promote compliance normatively attractive as well. It is considered less coercive than either reciprocal or institutional sanctions, and requires far lower transaction costs than more institutionalized alternatives, such as a multilateral organization's dispute resolution process. Perhaps most importantly, reputational recalibration promises to operate more democratically than other enforcement mechanisms. While large developed states may be politically insulated from institutional sanctions by the multilateral organizations that they dominate and may be invulnerable economically to reciprocal sanctions from weaker developing states, they cannot so easily escape the consequences of their own reputations. Yet despite these attractive features, reputation is more often viewed as an enemy than as a friend of developing states. In general, developing states have poorer compliance records than developed states – records that may well worsen before they improve, as multilateral agreements promise to proliferate more quickly than developing state economies improve. According to the traditional view of the character and power of reputation, these records will eventually lead to their exclusion from the benefits of future multilateral agreements. If traditional theory is correct, reputation is more an enemy than a friend of these states.

This chapter presents a political economy argument for believing that the situation is less bleak for developing states than the traditional view of reputation suggests. States, it argues, have reason to revise their estimate of a state's reputation following a defection or pattern of defections, but they tend to do so only in connection with agreements that they believe (1) are affected by the same or similar sources of fluctuating compliance costs and (2) are valued the same or less by the defecting state. Consequently, the reputational implications of any given incident of non-compliance are more restricted than the literature suggests and, with time, states develop several, often quite different, reputations, in connection with different regimes and even different treaties within the same regime.

The existence of multiple reputations protects developing states from many of the reputational costs that traditional theory predicts they will have to pay because of their frequent non-compliance. Developing states will still tend to have poorer compliance records than developed states and thus suffer more reputational damage; however, a poor record of compliance with several environmental treaties will not necessarily impact a state's attractiveness as a prospective member of a multilateral trade agreement.

Unfortunately, the same process that insulates developing states from a generalized deterioration in their reputation also insulates developed states, so that reputation will be less able to insure the compliance of powerful states than traditional theory suggests. In addition, since the reputational repercussions of defecting from an important relationship are greater than those of defecting from a less important relationship, reputation perversely protects developed states more than developing states.

Development and compliance

Considerable direct and indirect evidence shows that a state's level of development is related to its record of compliance with multilateral agreements. For example, Weiss and Jacobson examine the compliance record of nine states in connection with five prominent multilateral agreements and find a disproportionate amount of developmental non-compliance.[1] Although "weak compliance" – the lowest of three categories – is the

---

[1] Edith Brown Weiss, and Harold Jacobson (eds.), *Engaging Countries: Strengthening Compliance with International Environmental Accords* (MIT Press, Cambridge, MA, 1998). Meaningful comparisons of the compliance rates of developed and developing states are sometimes difficult to conduct. One reason for this is that the responsibilities of developing and developed states are often different. The Montreal Protocol, for example, required virtually

exception rather than the rule for all the agreements, the only states assigned to this category are developing states, several of which are persistent non-compliers. Cameroon, for example, was found to be only in weak compliance with the World Heritage Agreement, CITES and the Tropical Timber Agreement. Brazil and China were in weak compliance with both CITES and the Tropical Timber Agreement. In contrast, the three most developed states, Japan, the EU and the United States, were each found to be in substantial or moderate compliance with five agreements.[2]

Other studies of multilateral environmental regulation tend to reinforce these findings. Although the International Tropical Timber Agreement created in 1983 employs a conservationist rhetoric in emphasizing the sustainable utilization and conservation of tropical timber forests, producer states – all developing countries – have paid little more than lip service to the Agreement's sustainability aims and have consistently blocked developed-country efforts at enforcement. Eight years after the Agreement's entry into force, only 1 percent of all tropical timber was harvested sustainably.[3]

This pattern is much the same in the area of human rights. A glance at the Human Rights Watch website or at an inventory of US State Department country reports clarifies that even with a correction for their greater numbers, the vast majority of human rights problems in recent years have arisen in developing states, particularly those in the throes of ethnic civil war or interstate conflict. Of the thirty-one reports that Human Rights Watch generated in the last six months of 1999, twenty-five or about 80 percent deal with problems in developing states. The list of problems is long: lack of freedom of the press and assembly in Croatia, forced emigration from East Timor, high rates of domestic violence and the routine torture of children in Pakistani detention facilities, political repression in Uganda, attacks on Christians in India, ethnic cleansing in Yugoslavia, the displacement of 10 percent of the population in Angola due to the breakdown of the Lusaka peace process, and widespread murder, mutilation and rape due to civil war in Sierra Leone.

nothing of developing states for the first ten years. In other cases, international institutions do not collect reliable compliance information from the poorest states.

[2] This is not to imply that the records of some developing states are not better than those of some developed states. Brazil, for example, has a higher compliance rate with both the London Convention and Montreal Protocol than does Russia, and India has a better compliance record with CITES and the Tropical Timber Agreement than does Japan (Brown Weiss and Jacobson, *Engaging Countries*, p. 519).

[3] Marcus Colchester, "The International Tropical Timber Organizations: Kill or Cure for the Rainforests?" (1991) 43 *Transnational Organizations* 4.

The literature that seeks to understand why states fall into noncompliance also corroborates this picture, albeit more indirectly. Consider: the Chayeses, creators of the managerial approach to solving compliance problems, argue that the majority of treaty violations are not the product of any calculated exploitation but rather are caused by three factors: (1) the ambiguity and indeterminacy of treaty language, (2) limitations on the capacity of the parties to implement their commitments, and (3) social, economic and political departures from the expectation embodied in regulatory treaties.[4] If the Chayeses' explanation of noncompliance is basically correct – and no one has yet taken issue with their argument on the substantial role of such factors – one can clearly anticipate that developing states will experience far more compliance problems than developed states. Almost invariably, developing countries have less administrative and financial resources with which to implement and then enforce an agreement, and their generally higher levels of economic and political instability make it almost inevitable that they will experience greater and more frequent departures from their expectations upon entering a given agreement. Developing states are also more likely to interpret incorrectly the provisions of an agreement, because they are rarely involved to any significant extent in its initial design. Even when an agreement's requirements are completely transparent, developing states are more likely to err in estimating the cost of achieving different levels of compliance with a complicated agreement like CITES or WTO.

The compliance of developing states is also affected by external shocks and unexpected events that the Chayeses do not discuss but are consistent with their basic argument. Violent conflict, which disproportionately affects developing states, is one source of these shocks. Interstate wars and civil wars divert the administrative and financial resources required for regulation costs and overseeing compliance. The longer the wars, the more pronounced this effect. Severe and/or prolonged conflicts virtually cripple a state's capacity to comply with many multilateral commitments, and increase the incentive of desperate parties to engage in opportunistic violations of human rights and arms agreements.

The gradual evolution of agreements toward more cooperation further compounds these problems for developing states. As economies improve and the middle class expands and grows wealthier, developing states often become more positively disposed to cooperation in areas

---

[4] Abram and Antonia H. Chayes, *The New Sovereignty: Compliance with International Regulatory Agreements* (Harvard University Press, Cambridge, MA, 1995), p. 10.

such as the environment and willingly join more developed states in more ambitious regulatory standards. Unfortunately, due to their more volatile economies and the less developed administrative capacity of their governmental apparatus, developing states remain more vulnerable than developed states to any number of "shocks," such as recessions and political unrest, that can lead to non-compliance. As a result, the reputation of developing states may deteriorate even as their overall level of contribution to the effectiveness of an agreement increases.

The reputational consequences of non-compliance: the traditional view

While positions vary in the literature about the role of reputation in promoting compliance, the dominant view is that reputational concerns are very important.[5] The logic underlying this belief is that actors possess a general reputation for cooperativeness that determines their attractiveness as a treaty partner both now and in the future. Knowing that a defection in connection with any agreement will impose reputation costs that affect all current and future agreements, states are motivated to comply with their commitments even in circumstances in which they would otherwise defect.

Thus, the literature is rife with references to the price a state pays for losing its reputation of reliably maintaining commitments and being considered "law abiding." Reflecting on the exemplary record of compliance associated with most agreements, Barrett states that, "A damaged reputation resulting from noncompliance can make it difficult for a deviant to enter into future agreements. Even a single deviation carries the risk of precipitating general erosion in law abidance, to the detriment of all states."[6] In discussing the implications of India's failing to adhere to the CTB after its prominent multidecade campaign for the agreement's passage, Williamson speaks of the "severe costs to the nation's reputation and perception as a trustworthy member of the international community."[7]

---

[5] Authors often oscillate in their characterization of reputational effects between the "traditional" view that states possess a single reputation and a more regime-specific perspective in which states have a different reputation in connection with different regimes. Therefore, our association of a given author with a given perspective should be taken only as indicating our interpretation of a specific text.

[6] Scott Barrett, "International Cooperation and the International Commons" (1999) 10 *Duke Int'l L. and Policy Forum* 139.

[7] Richard L. Williamson, Jr., "Law and the H-Bomb: Strengthening the Nonproliferation Regime to Impede Advanced Proliferation" (1995) 28 *Cornell Int'l L. J.* 71.

Hurrell and Kingsbury argue that, "states generally comply with international obligations . . . because of their broader concern with their reputation as reliable partners and their interest in a rule governed . . . international system."[8] Parker speculates that states complied with the IATTC Tuna-Dolphin Program, even after suspending their formal participation, in order to "preserve their reputation as reliable negotiating partners."[9]

The Chayeses also believe that the power of reputational concerns to promote compliance is considerable and rivals the deterrent effect of expectations about reciprocal defection: "But in international organizations, as in other political settings, specific reciprocity is not the only or even the most important form of exchange. When a member of an organization goes back on a commitment, it compromises in some degree its reputation as a reliable partner and jeopardizes its ability to continue to reap organizational benefits."[10] Elsewhere they observe: "More subtle and perhaps more menacing, in an increasingly interdependent world where not many states can achieve many of their objectives by their own exertions, are various kinds of reputation effects."[11]

This expansive vision of the power of reputation is understandably exciting for international legal theorists because it helps allay persistent doubts about the enforceability of international law while reducing the need to rely on compliance-enhancing strategies, such as the integration of international law into domestic legal systems. However, the implications for developing states are more frightening than reassuring. It leads us to expect that developing states, which experience far more compliance problems than developed states experience, will quickly acquire a reputation of overall unreliability as treaty partners which will reduce the likelihood of their being invited to participate in future agreements in areas ranging from military alliances to membership in trade organizations such as NAFTA and the EU. In addition, it suggests that developed states will quickly learn to discount developing state participation in existing agreements which will, in turn, reduce the developed states' incentive to meet their own commitments to developing states.

Fortunately for developing states, there is reason to doubt that this is really how reputation operates. If the cost of a general reputation for

---

[8] Andrew Hurrell and Benedict Kingsbury, *The International Politics of the Environment* (Oxford University Press, New York, 1992), p. 24.

[9] Richard W. Parker, "The Use and Abuse of Trade Leverage to Protect the Global Commons: What We Can Learn from the Tuna-Dolphin Conflict" (1999) 12 *Georgetown Int'l Envtl L. Rev.* 2.

[10] Chayes and Chayes, *The New Sovereignty*, p. 273.   [11] *Ibid.* at p. 152.

non-compliance were as high as the general theory suggests, one would expect developing states to avoid joining any multilateral agreement that they were not confident that they could comply with so as to avoid the substantial reputational penalty. Yet there is no evidence that developing states are reducing the rate at which they join new agreements or that developed states have begun to bar them systematically from membership in new multilateral agreements or reduce their own level of cooperation in existing agreements because of developing state non-compliance.[12] How might we account for this?

The case for multiple reputations

One way to account for the muted reputational response to development state non-compliance is to argue, as some have, that there really is no such thing as state reputation, and that it is largely the figment of the imaginations of a handful of theorists. This seems increasingly unlikely, however. A growing number of empirical studies, including Milgrom, North and Weingast,[13] on the reputation-setting role of merchant guilds in managing trade cooperation, English[14] on the role that reputational expectations played in leading American states to repay their foreign debts during the 1840s, and Kyle and Sachs[15] on the decision of sovereign states to reschedule rather than default completely on foreign debts, suggest that reputational concerns are quite real.

An alternative approach acknowledges the reality of reputation but tries to formulate a theory of reputation that is more consistent with the facts. One possibility is that having noticed that the compliance of virtually every state varies considerably across agreements, states assign each other different reputations in different areas. As a result, they do not automatically

---

[12] Some might argue that developing states avoid the expected reputational penalties by convincing other members of the multilateral agreement that their non-compliance was due to factors "beyond their control." However, reputational penalties in the international system are not as easily cancelled out by a legitimate excuse as a reciprocal or institutional penalty might be. Whether a state's frequent violations of a trade agreement are intentional or not, other states still have reason to reduce the expected value of that state as a partner in future trade agreements.

[13] Paul R. Milgrom, Douglas C. North and Barry R. Weingast, "The Role of Institutions in the Revival of Trade: The Medieval Law Merchant, Private Judges, and Champagne Fairs" (1990) 2 *Economics and Politics* 1.

[14] William B. English, "Understanding the Costs of Sovereign Default: American State Debts in the 1840s" (1996) 86(1) *Am. Economic Rev.* 259.

[15] Steven Kyle and Jeffrey D. Sachs, "Developing Country Debt and the Market Value of Large Commercial Banks" (1984), NBER Discussion Paper 1470.

expect that a state that has recently failed to comply with a provision of the CITES agreement is likely to renege on its WTO commitments as well. States are free, of course, to act "as if" they thought otherwise and lower the offending state's reputation in connection with every agreement, as traditional theory suggests, but know that doing so would be inefficient in that it would require them to sacrifice some cooperative gains that they could obtain by acting differently.

To understand why this might be appropriate, one need only consider the Chayeses' explanation of why states violate treaties. A common characteristic of their three external factors is that their relevance varies greatly across the universe of agreements. Treaty ambiguity and contract ambiguity are obviously contract specific in the sense that each agreement has its own associated level of ambiguity, which can vary enormously depending on such factors as the agreement's complexity. Capacity limitations are similarly agreement specific. Some, like CITES, for example, are extremely costly to implement for states with large borders and high levels of border traffic like Brazil or the United States. Others, such as the agreement prohibiting nuclear weapons in space, are essentially cost-free for every state to implement. Volatile economic and social consequences also have a diverse effect. A severe recession, for example, might affect a state's willingness to abide by its trade and environmental commitments without affecting its willingness to stand by security commitments.

Just as states may have different levels of reliability in connection with treaties in different areas, they may also have a different record for reliability with different treaties in the same regulatory area if they contain different amounts of ambiguity, require widely differing levels of resources from states in order to implement, or are subject to different political and economic shocks. Unless one is willing to say that reputation is based on something different than compliance reliability, states, for all practical purposes, will often have different reputations with different agreements. We can, of course, simply ignore this fact and proceed to evaluate every prospective agreement using a single reputation, but this would be wildly inefficient. Information about which agreements were in treaty areas with higher and lower than average reliabilities would be lost and the overall value of future portfolios of agreements would be less than it might have been as a result.

A second characteristic of the Chayeses' three factors is that their impact varies over time, even in connection with a particular agreement. Social, economic and political departures from the expectations embodied in a given treaty are by their very nature stochastic shocks. The ambiguity and indeterminacy of a treaty also varies over time, at least in the sense that different administrations encounter different problems of interpretation and resolve them in different ways. Finally, capacity limitations vary depending on the economy, the weight of expenditure demands in other major categories of expenditures, such as defense and education, and the impact of major administrative reforms that occur periodically in many countries.

In theory, designers can cope with the potential effect of these transient shocks by setting such a high penalty for non-compliance that a state experiencing a shock would prefer to comply despite the added hardship involved in doing so. However, if such shocks are prevalent enough and are suffered by the majority of states, the total benefits of a system's high penalties are often less than one that permits intermittent non-compliance at modest cost. That is, states are better off establishing a penalty that is high enough to prevent opportunistic non-compliance but low enough for states to still defect when necessary. The duration or severity of the penalty optimizes the expectation over time of the fluctuations of the cost and/or benefit structure. As a result, there is a system of treaties in which states exhibit high, but not perfect, levels of reliability.[16]

Thus, it has been argued that the weak enforcement norm of GATT was designed to deal with the existence of just the kind of political and economic shocks described above. Many (if not most) states did not want aggressive enforcement of GATT because they knew that there would be times when they would find it advantageous to depart temporarily from a free trade standard. The political, if not the economic, benefit of free trade varies with changes in the state of the economy, particularly changes in unemployment in sectors that are import competitive. When unemployment is high, the domestic pressures to apply tariffs become strong and politicians find that they are often better off – at least until the economy recovers – responding to those demands with temporary protectionist policies.[17]

The transient and differential impact of the transient shocks caused by the operation of the Chayeses' three factors is not the only thing that operates to create multiple reputations and limit the power of reputation. The fact that agreements are heterogeneous with respect to the value

---

[16] George W. Downs and Michael A. Jones, "Reputation, Compliance, and International Law" (2002) 31 *J. Legal Studies* (No.1, Pt 2) S95.

[17] George W. Downs and David M. Rocke, *Optimal Imperfection? Domestic Uncertainty and Institutions in International Relations* (Princeton University Press, Princeton, NJ, 1995), pp. 88–89.

that they represent to states plays a similar role. That states do, in fact, attach different values to different agreements is obvious enough, but formal models of reputation rarely focus on this because it complicates the mathematics considerably and often distracts the reader from the point being made. Still, in order to understand reputation, it is worth considering the implications of the fact that such variation is the rule rather than the exception. The United States does not value NATO the same as it does SEATO; nor does it value the WTO the same as a bilateral fishing treaty with a small country.

When there is no stochastic benefit or cost component, ignoring this heterogeneity makes little difference but when there is a stochastic benefit or cost component, it can make quite a difference. The benefits attached to a given agreement operate to offset the stochastic costs of compliance that are tied to the Chayeses' sources of non-compliance.[18] If the surplus is large enough to offset the shock, cooperation will continue uninterrupted. A given cost increase that is not offset by the surplus of cooperative benefits that a state receives from cooperation will lead to defection.

It follows that an exogenous shock that slightly raises compliance costs will precipitate defection from an agreement that produces a low level of benefits, but will have no effect on an agreement that produces a much higher level of benefits. This means that when benefit heterogeneity exists among agreements in an environment where stochastic shocks exist, states will (1) defect from low benefit relationships more frequently than they will from high benefit relationships and (2) defect from low benefit relationships whenever they defect from high benefit relationships but not vice versa.

If the above characterization of how reputation operates in connection with cooperation is roughly correct, its power to ensure that states comply with their international agreements is smaller and considerably more variable than many commentators suggest. The fact that reliability is an endogenous strategy that emerges from a specific context means that any simple characterization of a state's reputation for overall cooperation will either not be very general or, if it pretends to be, not very accurate. The well-known fact that the reliability of any particular state can vary substantially across different treaties should have made this obvious (as well as suggesting that the magnitude of reputational punishments was usually small). This does not deny that it can be a useful rhetorical convenience

---

[18] Adjusting the distribution of the costs can also absorb the stochastic nature of any beneficial payoffs.

or an effective political strategy to speak of a state as if it had a single reputation – especially when the context is understood as, for example, during a discussion of human rights – but it will be descriptively misleading if taken too seriously.

Under most circumstances, the reputational consequences of a given state's non-compliance in connection with a given agreement are bounded. Other states will revise their estimates of the state's reliability but only in connection with agreements that they believe (1) are affected by the same or similar sources of fluctuating costs and (2) are valued the same or less by the defecting state. The first tends to limit the reputational consequences of even sharp decreases in compliance with a given treaty to other treaties in the same area. This prediction is in keeping with the already existing tendency of a substantial minority of scholars to confine their discussion of reputational consequences to their impact on a specific regime.[19] It helps explain why, despite the prevalence of the unitary reputation assumption, examples of a state's defection from an agreement in one area (e.g., environment), jeopardizing its reputation in every other area (e.g., trade and security), are virtually non-existent in the literature. More importantly, it helps account for why states often have widely divergent reputations in different areas. Thus, the United States has one simple reputation for making good on its financial commitments with workers in the UN Secretary-General's office and another quite different simple reputation with officials of European states in connection with its financial commitments to NATO. Neither group is much concerned with characterizing the reliability of the United States in meeting its financial commitments in general. Those inside the Secretary-General's office are probably aware that the United States has paid its NATO bills and NATO workers know that the United States is behind on its UN dues, but both groups mostly comment on the United States' reputation in the sub-set of contexts important to them.

Our claim that reputational inferences are segmented helps explain why members of the North Atlantic community could show solidarity over Milosevic's Yugoslavia while they were squabbling over tariffs on the sale of bananas. While there was no shortage of dispositional-like statements about EU "protectionism" and "lack of commitment to multilateralism"

---

[19] Whether the underlying logic of these authors who implicitly treat reputational implications as being confined to a specific regime is the same as that described here is unclear since they rarely give the reasons for their position. It is possible that some of them actually embrace the unitary perspective and only appear to believe in regime specific reputations in the context of a given article whose focus is a specific regime area.

in the Congressional Record and elsewhere, such judgments had few consequences for the allies' ability to conduct the war. In this case, both the utility and stochastic elements of the trade and security treaties were not sufficiently related for reputational consequences of one treaty to affect the other treaty.

One might object to this picture of multiple, relatively independent, reputations by pointing to situations where states have responded to non-compliance in one area by retaliating in another (e.g., sanctions against Iraq for violating the weapons inspection provisions of its agreement with the United Nations). However, we would argue that these represent linkage penalties rather than a reputational penalty. A linkage penalty might seem equivalent to a reputational punishment because it occurs as a consequence of a pattern of non-compliance, but it is actually different. The states punishing the guilty state are *not* doing so based on anticipation that the state that violated the human rights agreement will be unreliable in the trade treaty or fail to repay its loans. Rather, states are simply trying to coerce the guilty state into changing its behavior in the same way that they might try to coerce a state into altering behavior in an area with *no* treaty (e.g., sanctions against South Africa during the waning years of Apartheid).

Another perspective is to consider that if the states inflicting the linkage penalty were worried about the defecting state's reliability, they would *defensively* reduce their level of cooperation in the area where the violator's defection would cost them the most domestically. Instead, when a linkage penalty is involved, the states *offensively* reduce their level of cooperation in the area where it will inflict the most damage on the violating state. The rarity and selective nature of these linkages are testimony to their strategic nature. Even when the United States periodically threatened to oppose China's entry into the WTO because of its human rights record, it did not simultaneously threaten to oppose China's participation in environmental or arms agreements; the vast majority of states did not threaten to do anything at any time.

Reputation, multilateralism and development

If reputation operates in the way we suggest, it helps allay some of the concerns raised by the traditional theory of reputation about the future of multilateralism as a movement and the role of developing states. With respect to multilateralism, states have learned that multilateral agreements are only loosely coupled with each other and that a treaty partner's non-compliance with one treaty is not expected to reduce the likelihood that it will comply with another treaty, unless the agreements are in the same area and valued the same or less by the defecting state. The rule holds except for exceptional circumstances – an unusually great shock, such as a major war or worldwide depression or conditions that support the use of an extra-reputational linkage strategy. Multiple reputations may not have the power to support as much cooperation as supporters of the traditional theory believe, but they help guarantee that multilateral cooperation is not a brittle house of cards that is likely to be shattered by the same forces that sustain it.

The scattered evidence we have corroborates this picture. Retaliatory or reputational penalties do not commonly spread from one multilateral agreement to another across regimes and the rate at which multilateral organizations are being created continues to be high despite notable non-compliance in areas such as the environment and human rights. There is not even evidence that policy-makers – as opposed to academics – are inclined to think of multilateral cooperation as an undifferentiated category. If anything, the contrary is true: policy-makers' beliefs about the health of multilateralism and compliance exhibit every sign of being compartmentalized in a regulatory area. Compliance problems in one area only spill over into other areas of cooperation in those few cases where some enforcement agent strategically links the two issues.

If non-compliance is not generally a threat to the reputation of multilateralism, is it nonetheless a threat to multilateralism and multilateral progress within some areas of cooperation? Some evidence supports our theory's prediction that compliance problems in connection with a major agreement in a particular regulatory area can have major implications for cooperation in that area. For example, prior to the creation of the WTO, any number of commentators on trade cooperation – the area in which cooperation has evolved the furthest – expressed fear that the trade system that was painstakingly established since World War II was beginning to unravel, partially due to increasing non-compliance. Today, there are those who fear that if a serious recession strikes Europe, the ability of states to meet the performance standards embodied in the EMU will decline and European integration, and regional integration generally, could suffer a serious, long-term setback. Yet even in the human rights area, which has the most violations and the weakest cooperation, there is little sign that non-compliance is about to destroy the entire regime.

On the whole, the existence of segmented or multiple reputations is good news for developing states because it mitigates the reputational costs that traditional theory predicts they will have to pay because of their greater vulnerability to the factors that make compliance more difficult. A state's poor environmental record may have reputational consequences for the value that other states assign to its willingness to sign a new environmental treaty, but it will not affect how states evaluate it in connection with a pending trade or security treaty. More comforting still, because states have learned to pay attention to the importance as well as the nature of the underlying stochastic shocks that caused the non-compliance, developing states can suffer a severe reputational loss in connection with a particular regional trade or security treaty and still preserve a good reputation in connection with others that they value more.[20] This reputational insulation all but eliminates the possibility that non-compliance caused by economic, political or social shocks will plunge a developing state into a reputational purgatory from which it would never be given a chance to escape.

Unfortunately, not all of the implications of the multiple reputation model are quite so beneficial for developing states, especially as compared to developed states. The first negative implication follows immediately from the previous discussion. The same limitations on reputational reliability that protect developing states from being ostracized from the environmental community for a poor compliance record with a particular treaty or type of treaty also limit the liability of developed states. In their case, however, limited liability from reputational consequences does not so much free developed states from the specter of cooperative isolation – their compliance record is unlikely to deteriorate to such an extent that this will be a problem – as limit the size of the reputational penalty that they will have to pay for defecting from any given agreement. As a result, developing states cannot rely on the increasingly dense network of multilateral agreements and global interdependence to function as a counterweight to offset the greater economic power of developed states. Reputation can still operate to constrain developed states as well as developing states, but it will not level the playing field as much as many hope.

A second negative implication is that developing states have to pay much closer attention than do developed states to any non-compliance by

---

[20] The tendency of the magnitude of the reputational implications of a defection to be directly proportionate to the perceived opportunity costs of defection also means that the contribution that reputation makes to sustain international law cooperation is greatest in agreements that states think are the most beneficial and has the least effect in agreements that produce the smallest amount of benefits.

their developing state partners in connection with third parties because they are always more likely to be the next victim. The only time that developed states have to worry is when the "victim state" represents the same value to the defecting state as they do. In all likelihood, this will only happen when the victim is another developed state or a very large developing state.

Reputational repercussions of defecting from an important relationship are greater than those of defecting from a less important relationship, which means that reputation, and to some extent international law, tend to protect developed states more than developing states. This is really not so surprising. From the standpoint of predicting future behavior, it does not seem unreasonable that the reputational implications of a person reneging on an agreement with a close friend would be greater than they would be if the person were a casual acquaintance. Nonetheless, from a normative perspective, the fact that reputation offers the most protection to those who need it least is still disconcerting.[21]

The objection might be raised that associating development with importance does not necessarily hold. One can argue that what determines the importance of a relationship is the gains to trade that the parties derive, and quite possibly, for any number of reasons, a developing state might derive more such gains from a given relationship with another developing state than from a similar treaty with a developed state. Shouldn't this make the state more protective of its reputation with the developing state? While this argument is correct as far as it goes, the reputational argument hinges on more than the value of any particular treaty relationship. Rather, it involves the benefits of a cooperative relationship in its totality, including all current treaty relationships and expectations for further cooperation. The fact that states tend to have *more* transactions with developed states that can potentially be disrupted by a reputational recalibration than with developing states operates to make developed states more valuable.

The above discussion is primarily applicable to multilateral agreements that regulate essentially private goods with few externalities, such as trade agreements and alliances.[22] It is in connection with this type of agreement

---

[21] Not only does a defection against developing states tend to have the fewest reputational consequences for the violator, but the reputational penalties that developing states pay for their defections will tend to be quite large, because other states will soon learn that they are vulnerable to a high percentage of compliance cost shocks.

[22] Alliances are not, of course, pure private goods since conflict in one state can potentially spread to another state. Alliances do, however, tend to contain a larger private goods component than the average environmental treaty.

that reputation will operate to protect large and powerful states the most – assuming that these relationships are most likely to be highly valued by their treaty partner – and small states the least.

In multilateral agreements that regulate public goods, defection from a given agreement affects every treaty partner the same, so small states are somewhat less disadvantaged, at least in that there is no reputational penalty protecting developed states more than developing states. However, developing states will still suffer more *frequent* reputational penalties than developed states because they are likely to violate public goods agreements more frequently for the same reason that they violated private goods agreements more frequently. That is, they are subject to more frequent economic, political and social shocks than are developed states. A second reason why developing states will violate public goods agreements more often is more unique to public goods. On average, the demand for environmental goods is less in developing states than in developed states because demand tends to be positively related to income. Since developing states assign a lower value to environmental treaties, a smaller shock will cause them to defect.

Conclusion

The international relations and international law communities place great stock in the power of reputation to enforce compliance, even in the absence of adequate institutional mechanisms or reciprocal punishment. No state, they reason, can afford to ignore the reality that failure to keep a particular commitment will affect other states' estimates of its reliability (and value) as a partner in all other current and future agreements. This view of reputation promises an increasingly bright future for international cooperation as the number of multilateral agreements continues to proliferate. However, the largely unnoticed implications for developing states are anything but bright. It suggests that the characteristically higher rates of compliance failures that take place in the most economically and politically unstable developing states will increasingly isolate them from the benefits of cooperation that an increasingly integrated community of nation states will generate.

This chapter has argued that reputation will do less to insure compliance than traditionalist theory suggests but that the implications for developing states are correspondingly less bleak. Rather than updating a single estimate of a state's expected reliability when a state defects from an agreement, other states only revise its reputation vis-à-vis agreements that they believe to be "similar," where similarity is a function of the source of non-compliance and the value of the agreement for the defecting state. Consequently, states possess multiple reputations rather than one reputation. This dilutes the reputational consequences of any given defection and hence the power of reputation to promote compliance, but it also creates firewalls that prevent a developing state's poor reputation in one area from lowering its reliability rating in every other area. Thus, despite very poor compliance records in connection with a sub-set of the agreement to which they are a party, developing states are not regularly excluded from new agreements.

Of course, the limited reach of reputational implications is not an unalloyed benefit for developing states. While limiting their liability, it also limits the protection that reputation could provide from the opportunistic defection of developed states. Not only will a developed state that defects from a trade agreement with a developing state escape reputational punishment in areas other than trade, but since reputational consequences only extend to agreements and/or partners that the defecting state is believed to value the same or less, the defecting developed state will only suffer a reputational loss among other developing states. Since this may be a very small penalty indeed, the hope that reputational concerns will level the playing field between rich and poor states is unlikely to be realized.

6

Rethinking compliance with international law

EDITH BROWN WEISS

Approximately 40,000 bilateral and multilateral agreements are registered with the United Nations.[1] The widespread assumption, at least among international legal scholars, is that states substantially comply with these obligations.[2] But the evidence suggests that the picture is far more mixed, and that sometimes there is minimal compliance at best. Many human rights treaties are in effect, but gross violations of human rights continue, as witnessed by the torture and death of hundreds of thousands of people from El Salvador to Bosnia, Rwanda to East Timor. A consular convention protects citizens of other countries domestically, but local authorities widely ignore its obligations.[3] A treaty bans international

---

The author thanks Nathalie Bernasconi, Daniel Michalchuk and Lisa Eisen for research assistance. I am especially grateful to the late Harold K. Jacobson, my collaborator for the research on national compliance with international environmental accords, on which this chapter builds.

[1] According to the Treaty Section of the United Nations Office of Legal Affairs, personal contact, August 2, 2002.

[2] See Louis Henkin, *How Nations Behave* (Council on Foreign Relations, 1979). Henkin asserts: "It is probably the case that almost all nations observe almost all principles of international law and almost all of their obligations almost all of the time." *Ibid.* at 47. For a reaffirmation of substantial compliance see Abram Chayes and Antonia H. Chayes, *The New Sovereignty: Compliance with Treaties in International Regulatory Regimes* (Harvard University Press, 1995).

[3] Vienna Convention on Consular Relations, Vienna, April 24, 1963, 596 UNTS 261. The United States, for example, has been brought before the International Court of Justice (ICJ) on three occasions for alleged violation of the Convention. In the first case, authorities in the State of Virginia arrested Angel Francisco Breard, a Paraguayan national, on charges of homicide without informing Breard of his rights under Article 36 (1)(b) of the Consular Convention, which include the right to inform one's consulate upon arrest. Breard was tried in Virginia State Court and sentenced to death. Paraguay lodged a claim against the United States before the ICJ. As a provisional measure, the ICJ ordered the United States to take all measures at its disposal to ensure that Breard was not executed, pending a final decision by the ICJ. The US Supreme Court, however, refused to block the execution, which took place as scheduled on April 14, 1998. Prior to the issuance of a final decision by the ICJ, Paraguay

trade in endangered species of fauna and flora, but the trade in some species continues to flourish, especially with a handful of importing countries.[4] Countries join the World Trade Organization and subscribe to GATT 1994,[5] but without necessarily having the capacity to comply.[6] WTO disputes, over matters such as the sale and distribution of bananas,[7]

---

and the United States came to an agreement on the matter and the case was removed from the ICJ docket. *Case Concerning the Vienna Convention on Consular Relations (Paraguay v. United States)*, Order of April 9, 1998, Request for the Indication of Provisional Measures [1998], ICJ Reports 266, reprinted in (1998) 37 ILM 810, available at ICJ website www.icj-cij.org; *Paraguay v. United States*, Order November 10, 1998, Discontinuance, available at www.icj-cij.org. See also *Breard v. Green*, 523 U.S. 371 (1998) (refusing to block Virginia's execution of Breard).

In the second case, two brothers, Karl and Walter LaGrand, German nationals and permanent residents of the United States, were arrested on homicide charges. Again, local authorities in Arizona did not fully comply with the provisions of the Vienna Convention. Both brothers were convicted and sentenced to death in Arizona State Court. One was executed, but before the other one was executed, the ICJ ordered the United States to take measures to prevent the execution pending a final decision by the ICJ. Nevertheless, the execution went forward. The ICJ found that the United States breached its obligations to Germany and to the brothers under the Convention. Moreover, for the first time, the Court specified that orders indicating provisional measures are legally binding. *LaGrand (Germany v. United States)*, June 27, 2001, available at ICJ website, www.icj-cij.org; *La Grand*, Order of March 3, 1999, Request for the Indication of Provisional Measures, reprinted in (1999) 38 ILM 308, available at www.icj-cij.org. The ICJ also found a breach of the Consular Convention in the third case, *Case Concerning Avena and Other Mexican Nationals (Mexico v. United States)*, March 31, 2004, available at www.icj-cij.org.

Violations of the Consular Convention also occur in many other countries. See Detlev F. Vagts, *The United States and its Treaties: Observance and Breach* (2001) 95 A.J.I.L. 313 (arguing that the number of American breaches of treaty commitments is not large in relation to the number of obligations and that the death penalty cases are "rather exceptional").

[4] Convention on International Trade in Endangered Species of Wild Fauna and Flora (CITES), Washington, DC, March 3, 1973, 993 U.N.T.S. 243, reprinted in (1973) 12 ILM 1088. See Edith Brown Weiss and Harold K. Jacobson (eds.), *Engaging Countries: Strengthening Compliance with International Environmental Accords* (MIT Press, 1998) (detailing compliance with CITES).

[5] As of April 23, 2004, 147 nations were members of the WTO. *Understanding the WTO: The Organization Members and Observers*, available at WTO website, www.wto.org/english/thewto_e/whatis_e/tif_e/org6_e.htm (last visited January 14, 2004). GATT, which existed from 1947 through January 1, 1995 when it was replaced by the WTO, had 128 signatories. *GATT Members* (August 1, 2002), available at www.wto.org/english/thewto_e/gattmem_e.htm (last visited January 14, 2004).

[6] See discussion below. See also Edith Brown Weiss, "Strengthening National Compliance with Trade Law: Insights from Environment" in Marco Bronckers and Reinhard Quick (eds.), *New Directions in International Economic Law* 463–7 (Kluwer Law International, 2000), pp. 463–67.

[7] *European Communities: Regime for the Importation, Sale and Distribution of Bananas*, WTO Appellate Body Report WT/DS27/AB/R (adopted September 27, 1997), reprinted in (1998) 37 ILM 243, available at WTO website http://docsonline.wto.org/gen_search.asp (last visited January 14, 2004).

the use of beef hormones by North American cattle producers,[8] and the prohibition of certain shrimp imports in order to protect endangered sea turtle populations,[9] lead to results that the losing party is either loath to comply with or finds difficult for domestic reasons. We need to understand why countries comply or don't comply with international law in order to determine what strategies may be effective in strengthening compliance with international law. While the analysis will focus mostly on compliance with environmental agreements and to a lesser extent with trade agreements, the framework for assessing compliance strategies applies across all fields of international law. The latter part of this chapter presents data on the evolution of various compliance strategies in international agreements across environment, trade, human rights and arms control. This chapter is based in substantial part on the research undertaken by the author with the late Harold K. Jacobson and scholars from eleven countries on compliance with international environmental agreements.[10]

The international system

The international system is changing. This changing structure affects the role of international law and the preferred strategies for seeking compliance. Three paradigms, which serve as starting points for analysis, may be distinguished: the classical, the non-hierarchic network and, arguably, the individualist. Each will be considered briefly.

---

[8] *EC Measures Concerning Meat and Meat Products (Hormones)*, WTO Appellate Body Reports WT/DS26/AB/R, WT/DS48/AB/R (adopted January 16, 1998), available at WTO website http://docsonline.wto.org/gen_search.asp (last visited January 14, 2004). See also Edith Brown Weiss and John H. Jackson (eds.), *Reconciling Environment and Trade* (Transnational Publishers, 2001).

[9] *United States: Import Prohibition of Certain Shrimps and Shrimp Products*, WTO Appellate Body Report WR/DS58/AB/R (adopted October 12, 1998), available at WTO website http://docsonline.wto.org/gen_search.asp (last visited January 14, 2004).

[10] Brown Weiss and Jacobson, *Engaging Countries*. There is also a growing body of scholarship on compliance with international agreements. See also Ronald B. Mitchell, *Intentional Oil Pollution at Sea: Environmental Policy and Treaty Compliance* (MIT Press, 1994); Thomas Franck, *Equity in International Law* (Kluwer International, 1995), pp. 3–25 (noting the importance of equity to compliance); Chayes and Chayes, *The New Sovereignty*; James Cameron (ed.), *Improving Compliance with International Environmental Law* (Earthscan, 1996); Rudiger Wolfrum (ed.), *Enforcing Environmental Standards: Economic Mechanisms as Viable Means?* (Springer, 1996); Harold H. Koh, "Why Do Nations Obey International Law?" (1997) 106 *Yale L.J.* 2599; David G. Victor, Kal Raustiala and Eugene B. Skolnikoff, *The Implementation and Effectiveness of International Environmental Commitments: Theory and Practice* (MIT Press, 1998); Eleonore Kokotsis, *Keeping International Commitments: Compliance, Credibility and the G7, 1988–1995* (Garland, 1999) (analyzing compliance with selected G7 Summit commitments).

The classical paradigm

The classical paradigm of international law is dualist: there is an international sphere and a domestic sphere. The international system consists of sovereign, independent states, which are in theory equal in their relations with each other. International law rests on the consent of states, as an expression of sovereign will.[11] The classical paradigm assumes that countries join international agreements only when their governments regard them as in their interest. It follows from this that countries generally comply with their obligations under the treaties; if they do not, sanctions are the preferred strategy. Sanctions are used to punish offenders and deter future violations.

The reality differs from these assumptions. Classical theory does not adequately reflect the many other reasons why countries find compliance to be in their self-interest. These reasons affect their willingness to comply. Countries may join a treaty because others are doing so, contributing to a "bandwagon" effect. Other governments may use leverage to pressure countries into compliance. Domestic interests may force the issue. In some cases, countries may join with no intention of immediately changing their behavior to conform to international obligations. Frequently, countries simply lack the capacity to comply.

The traditional view of compliance is hierarchic. States negotiate international agreements, which are made effective through implementing legislation or regulations. States ensure that the actors comply with these regulations. The traditional view is also static. A snapshot at a given point in time accurately captures a country's record of compliance. This view of compliance is outmoded across all areas of international law, as empirical research on international environmental agreements indicates.

The network paradigm[12]

An alternative paradigm is one in which power is organized non-hierarchically in the form of networks. More than fifteen years ago, the political scientist Harold Jacobson noted that "effective power is

---

[11] See *S.S. Lotus (France v. Turkey)* (1927) PCIJ (Series A, No. 10) 18 (September 7). See also James L. Brierly, *Law of Nations* 7–16 (6th ed., Oxford, 1963), pp. 7–16.

[12] This analysis draws upon Edith Brown Weiss, "The Changing Structure of International Law," paper presented at Georgetown University Law Center, May 23, 1996 (elaborating non-hierarchic networks); and Edith Brown Weiss, "The Rise or the Fall of International Law" (2000) 69 *Fordham L. Rev.* 345.

increasingly being organized in a non-hierarchical manner."[13] In this paradigm, there are many important participants in addition to states, and they perform increasingly complex tasks.[14] All of the actors – states, international organizations, non-governmental organizations, industry associations, ad hoc associations and even individuals – are linked together in transnational networks that flow across national borders. At the same time, the international system is also increasingly fragmented, which elevates the importance of local communities, ethnic groups and other associations in securing compliance with international agreements.

International law, not surprisingly, then flows both from the consent of sovereign states and increasingly from the consent of transnational non-state actors and individuals. It encompasses both public and private international law, and so-called "soft law," in addition to binding agreements and customary rules.

In this paradigm, compliance is a dynamic process in which states and their sub-units, intergovernmental institutions, non-governmental organizations, businesses, other associations and individuals interact in complex ways. Patterns vary among agreements and among and within countries. The degree of compliance for any country changes over time.[15] Moreover, the agreements themselves evolve over time, so that the obligations with which states must comply also change.

The individualist paradigm

A third paradigm is emerging for discussion: namely, the individual as the key participant and sovereign unit in the international system. Individuals give consent to governments, and even to international bodies. Democracy is the political vehicle. International law is focused on the individual and the rights of individuals.[16] According to this view, international law

---

[13] Harold K. Jacobson, *Networks of Interdependence: International Organizations and the Global Political System* (2nd ed., Knopf, 1984). See also Anne-Marie Slaughter, "The Real New World Order" (1997) 76 *Foreign Affairs* 183 (stressing the importance of domestic actions and transnational linkages); Robert Keohane and Joseph Nye (eds.), *Governance in a Globalizing World* (Brookings Institution Press, 2000).

[14] See generally James N. Rosenau and Ernst Otto Czempiel (eds.), *Governance Without Government: Change and Order in World Politics* (Cambridge University Press, 1992), pp. 160–94.

[15] Brown Weiss and Jacobson, *Engaging Countries* (concluding as a major finding of the research that national compliance changes over time).

[16] For development of this paradigm, see Paul W. Kahn, "Speaking Law to Power: Popular Sovereignty, Human Rights and the New International Order" (2000) 1 *U. Chi. Int'l*

draws upon international human rights law. It follows then that we are witnessing the demise of the sovereignty of states and the rise of the sovereignty of individuals and the protection of their rights.

If we were to accept such an individualist paradigm, compliance would then focus primarily on educating and mobilizing civil society to pressure governments, international organizations and other relevant actors to comply with their international obligations. Compliance strategies that focus on transparency and capacity-building help empower individuals, non-governmental organizations and other non-state actors to comply.[17] Non-state actors can use information technology to organize collectively and raise global awareness. It is not clear what role traditional sanctions play, because the state, to whom sanctions are addressed, has a less central role.

Understanding compliance with international environmental agreements

Understanding national compliance with international agreements requires empirical research. Hypotheses need to be devised and tested. In a recent international, multidisciplinary, collaborative study, forty scholars from eleven countries sought to understand the factors affecting national compliance with international environmental agreements.[18] The research focused on compliance with five agreements by eight countries and the European Union. The focal countries included those that have contributed most to the anthropogenic effects that induce global environmental change (Japan, the Russian Federation, the United States and the states in the European Union) and those that have the most potential to do so (Brazil, China and India). Two of the countries studied, Cameroon and Hungary, represented the small industrializing countries, which comprise the largest number of states in the international system. Together, the five agreements covered both pollution control and natural resource conservation. Each had been in effect long enough to gather empirical data on national compliance, and each contained both procedural obligations,

---

L. Rev. 1. See also Christopher W. Morris, "The Very Idea of Sovereignty: 'We the People' Reconsidered" (2000) 17 Soc. Phil. & Pol. 1. For related theory as it pertains to the legal system in the United States, see Mark Tushnet, *Taking the Constitution Away from the Courts* (Princeton University Press, 1999).

[17] Of course, individuals or organizations that do not want to comply can also use transparency to work against compliance.

[18] Brown Weiss and Jacobson, *Engaging Countries*. This section is based especially on ch. 15.

such as reporting, and substantive obligations. The substantive obligations varied from precise targets and timetables for controlling pollutants to general obligations concerning the conservation of resources. Each of the agreements had many parties to it. Moreover, most of the states studied were parties to all of the agreements. The five agreements were the London Convention of 1972 (which controls ocean dumping), the World Heritage Convention (which protects internationally designated natural and cultural sites), the Convention on International Trade in Endangered Species (CITES) (which controls trade across national borders in endangered species of fauna and flora), the International Tropical Timber Agreement (ITTA) (primarily a commodity agreement with provision for sustainable forestry), and the Montreal Protocol on Substances that Deplete the Ozone Layer (which regulates chemicals that deplete the high-level ozone layer).[19] The findings from this study are relevant to all areas of international law, as will be detailed later.

The first step in analyzing compliance is to distinguish between implementation, compliance and effectiveness. Implementation refers to the measures states take to give effect to the agreement in domestic law. Compliance goes beyond implementation. It refers to whether states in fact adhere to the agreement's obligations and to domestic implementing measures. Some obligations are procedural (such as national reporting); others are substantive (such as phasing out ozone-depleting substances or controlling the dumping of pollutants in the ocean). Even if there is technical compliance with the obligations, there may be a question of compliance with the spirit of the agreement. Countries may technically comply, as the former Soviet Union did with the provisions of the London Convention on marine dumping, but the dumping by the Russian military of radioactive wastes in the Arctic did not comply with the spirit of the agreement.[20]

---

[19] Convention for the Protection of the World Cultural and Natural Heritage, Paris, November 16, 1972, 1037 UNTS 152, reprinted in (1972) 11 ILM 1358, available at http://whc.unesco.org/world_he.htm (last visited January 14, 2004); Convention on International Trade in Endangered Species of Wild Fauna and Flora (CITES), Washington, DC, March 3, 1973, 993 UNTS 243, reprinted in (1973) 12 ILM 1088; International Tropical Timber Agreement, Geneva, November 18, 1983, 1393 UNTS 67; Convention on the Prevention of Marine Pollution by Dumping of Wastes and Other Matter (London Convention 1972), London, December 29, 1972, 1046 UNTS 138, reprinted in (1972) 11 ILM 1294; and Montreal Protocol on Substances that Deplete the Ozone Layer, Montreal, September 6, 1987, 1522 UNTS 3, reprinted in (1987) 26 ILM 1516.

[20] William Zimmerman, Elena Nikitina and James Clem, "The Soviet Union and the Russian Federation: A Natural Experiment in Environmental Compliance" in Brown Weiss and Jacobson, *Engaging Countries*, pp. 291–325.

On the other hand, countries can use compliance with the spirit of the agreement to try to escape accountability with the precise obligations in the agreement, as with regulations implementing CITES. Effectiveness is related to compliance but differs. States may comply with an agreement, which may nonetheless be ineffective in achieving the objectives. For example, if states complied with the export and import requirements for trade in endangered species, CITES would still not necessarily protect endangered species. The species could be consumed domestically without violating the agreement. For example, an endangered species of monkey could be eaten within the country and become extinct without violating CITES. Even if all countries complied with an agreement controlling trade in certain endangered species, it would not necessarily protect biological diversity, which is the stated purpose of CITES.

The empirical study of the five agreements revealed that over time states devoted greater attention to implementing and complying with the agreements' obligations. Generally this meant fuller compliance. However, this was not always true for all countries at all times. Compliance declined in certain countries during particular times for specific agreements. Factors such as economic chaos, political instability and sudden decentralization caused compliance to decrease, particularly with agreements for which there was no strongly vested interest in securing compliance.

Factors that affect compliance

Many factors affect national compliance. They can be grouped into four categories: the characteristics of the problem (a few large producers of ozone-depleting chemicals or thousands of traders in endangered species); the characteristics of the agreement (hard or soft obligations, reporting requirements, funding arrangements); the international environment (concern with compliance); and national factors (political, economic, administrative, etc.). The dynamic and complex interactions of these factors can be captured in Figure 6.1, which is excerpted from the book, *Engaging Countries*.

The research on the five agreements confirmed the following propositions.

(1) The smaller the number of countries or firms involved, the easier it is to monitor and regulate the activity concerned. Activities conducted by large transnational corporations are easier to control than those conducted by small private entrepreneurs.

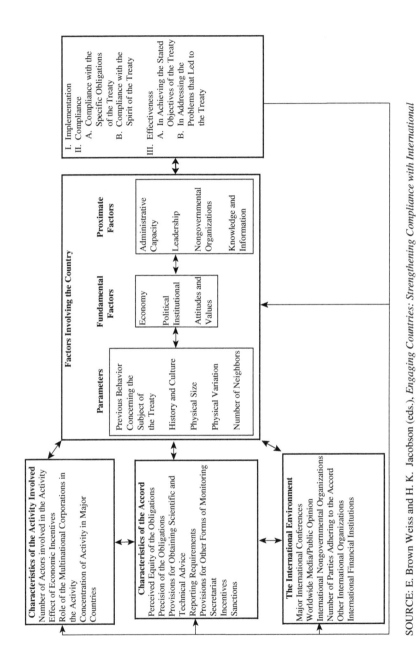

SOURCE: E. Brown Weiss and H. K. Jacobson (eds.), *Engaging Countries: Strengthening Compliance with International Environmental Accords* (MIT Press, Cambridge, MA, 1998), p. 536

Figure 6.1 A comprehensive model of factors that affect implementation, compliance and effectiveness

(2) What a country has traditionally done about the issue significantly affects its capacity to comply when it joins the agreement.

(3) A country's administrative capacity, namely, whether it has an educated and trained bureaucracy with financial resources, is important for effective compliance. Thus, relatively wealthy countries are more likely to be in compliance than those that are less economically well-off.

(4) Economic chaos or collapse greatly impedes compliance, although changes in GNP or rate of growth appear to have few immediate consequences.

(5) Markets are important to compliance, but their effect is complicated. Market demand can harm compliance, as with the demand for endangered species under CITES, but market demand for environmentally acceptable products can also help compliance, as with the substitutes for the chlorofluorocarbons that are required to be phased out under the Montreal Protocol.

(6) A country's size and political system affects compliance. Large countries have a more complex task in complying than smaller ones. Central governments have difficulty controlling areas at the periphery. There is a great need to coordinate widely dispersed activities and several levels of political authority within countries. Decentralization does not necessarily enhance compliance, at least in the short term, because local authorities may have other priorities and be subject to other pressures. Over the long term, decentralization can lead to greater and more efficient compliance.

(7) Non-governmental organizations are important, although not all NGOs necessarily boost compliance. Because NGOs dedicated to environmental protection and an informed and engaged citizenry are conducive to compliance, democratic countries are more likely to be in substantial compliance than those that are not democratic. But democracy does not necessarily lead to better compliance, since those opposed to the agreement may also be empowered in fighting compliance. Individuals also make an important difference, whatever the political system.

(8) The international environment affects compliance. When more countries participate actively in an agreement, it encourages other countries to join and to comply. International conferences, such as the 1972 United Nations Conference on the Human Environment (Stockholm Conference) and the 1992 United Nations Conference on Environment and Development (Rio Conference) raise public consciousness and help compliance.

(9) International Secretariats to the agreements play important roles in promoting compliance. While formally they are responsible to states

party to the agreement and act at their request, they are certainly not puppets on strings pulled by governments. Secretariat officials are often the most knowledgeable sources about who is doing what and where under the agreement. Increasingly, they investigate complaints, jawbone various actors into compliance and advise both public and private actors on how to comply. Secretariats serve as focal points for interactions among governments, non-governmental organizations or corporations and others. In recent years, Secretariats have spent more time on monitoring, training, assistance and compliance-related activities.

(10) If there are large countries that contribute the most to the problem, it is especially important that they join the agreement and comply with it.

(11) Finally, "leader" countries, especially among the large countries, may be essential to negotiating an effective agreement and then to promoting implementation and compliance with it. They are, of course, not sufficient.

Differentiating among countries party to international agreements

In applying these findings to the problem of strengthening countries' compliance with international obligations, we need to differentiate among countries. In so doing, we can more effectively design international instruments that encourage compliance. Two dimensions are particularly important: intention to comply and capacity to comply. Countries are in quite different positions when they join an agreement, and these positions change during the life of the agreement. Some countries clearly intend to comply with their obligations. These countries have considered issues of compliance and they either believe themselves already to be in substantial compliance or they have a clear idea about steps needed to bring their practices into compliance. Other countries accept obligations without having thought through how to bring their practices into compliance. Still others may be more cynical, in that they sign agreements knowing they will not comply. Sometimes a government may be divided: the foreign ministry intends to comply while other branches have no intention of abandoning practices that contravene the accord.

Capacity to comply is essential. Some countries have the resources, while others do not. Many assets are important for effective compliance, such as an effective and honest bureaucracy, economic resources and

	Capacity	
	Strong	**Weak**
Strong	Sunshine (Sanctions)	Incentives (Sunshine)
Weak	Sanctions / Sunshine (Incentives)	Incentives / Sanctions / Sunshine

(Row label: **Intention**)

SOURCE: E. Brown Weiss and H. K. Jacobson (eds.), *Engaging Countries: Strengthening Compliance with International Environmental Accords* (MIT Press, Cambridge, MA, 1998), p.550

Figure 6.2 Strategies to strengthen compliance, taking account of intention and capacity to comply

public support. Countries have different amounts of these resources when they join an agreement, and these amounts change over time. Bureaucracies that are effective and honest can become ineffective and corrupt. Surpluses in government budgets may disappear and be replaced by deficits. Public support for leadership or particular policies may increase or diminish. Sometimes the foreign ministry may intend to comply while the ministry that actually implements the agreement does not, or vice versa. Or the federal government may want to comply, but the state or provincial government does not, or does not have the resources to comply. At other times, it is a matter of priority. The country might want to comply, but compliance with the agreement is simply low priority compared to more pressing problems such as safe drinking water, adequate sewerage, etc.

We can use a matrix to analyze countries according to intent and capacity: see Figure 6.2.

In the first quadrant are countries with both a strong intent and strong capacity to comply. Other countries may have a strong intent but little capacity. They are in the second quadrant. Some countries may not intend to comply or their intention may be weak but they have the capacity to comply – the third quadrant. Others lack both intent and capacity to comply – the fourth quadrant. In each of these categories there will be variations in the strength of the intent and of the capacity to comply. The object is to incorporate into agreements those strategies that encourage all countries to have both strong intent and strong capacity to comply.

Compliance strategies

Three strategies encourage countries to take actions to comply with international environmental agreements: transparency or sunshine methods, positive incentives and coercive measures. Different strategies are appropriate for different levels of intent and capacity. The strategies appear in all fields of international law, although different ones are emphasized in each. Moreover, as will be detailed later, there has been a general increase across all fields of international law in the use of both sunshine methods and positive incentives to encourage compliance.

Transparency or sunshine methods, which are associated with democratic systems, are intended to bring the behavior of states and other targeted actors into the open for appropriate scrutiny. The so-called "sunshine" strategy relies on the "reputation" factor to induce states to comply. Sunshine measures include:

- national reporting on substantive and procedural obligations;
- scrutiny of national reports by parties, Secretariats and/or non-governmental organizations;
- on-site monitoring by parties, Secretariats and/or non-governmental organizations;
- publication of violations (as with CITES), which also serves as informal coercion through "shame;"
- regional workshops and monitoring networks;
- corporate and private sector monitoring;
- on-site consultants responsible to the parties;
- public access to information about the agreement and compliance efforts;
- media and electronic coverage to provide public awareness and to educate civil society about the agreement's obligations and national implementing measures; and
- informal persuasion by member states and by Secretariats for the agreements.

Sunshine methods work through non-governmental organizations, expert communities, corporate actors and individuals, as well as states, to promote compliance with international obligations.

Monitoring is essential to the sunshine strategy. It may take many forms: national reports, on-site monitoring, corporate monitoring to ensure level-playing fields in business, or off-site monitoring through advanced technologies that track scientific baselines or other criteria. In international environmental law, national reporting has served as the primary means for monitoring compliance with international agreements. Reporting, however, has limitations. Countries may not want to report problems of non-compliance, or they may lack the capacity to deliver comprehensive and accurate reports. Moreover, too much time may be spent on preparing reports to fulfill the requirements of international agreements rather than on addressing the problems targeted by the agreement. On the other hand, reporting requirements ensure that officials in the bureaucracy become engaged in implementing the agreement. Preparing the report can also educate officials about the agreement.

Increasingly, international agreements include positive incentives to encourage countries to join and to comply with the obligations. The incentive strategy assumes that many compliance problems exist because states do not have the capacity to comply. Incentives build capacity. They may also be effective in favorably shaping a country's intention to comply and in making the obligations seem equitable, and hence acceptable.

Incentives take many forms: special funds for financial or technical assistance; training programs and materials; access to technology; and bilateral or multilateral assistance outside the framework of the agreement, whether from other states party to the agreement, multilateral development banks or the private sector. Many international agreements such as the Montreal Protocol on Substances that Deplete the Ozone Layer,[21] the World Heritage Convention,[22] or the International Tropical

---

[21] Montreal Protocol on Substances that Deplete the Ozone Layer, note 19; Adjustments and Amendments to the Montreal Protocol on Substances that Deplete the Ozone Layer, London, June 29, 1990, reprinted in (1991) 30 ILM 537, available at www.unep.org/ozone/Montreal-Protocol/Montreal-Protocol2000.shtml (last visited January 14, 2004).

[22] Convention for the Protection of the World Cultural and Natural Heritage, note 19. See Edith Brown Weiss, "The Five International Treaties: A Living History" in Brown Weiss and Jacobson, *Engaging Countries*, pp. 89–172.

Timber Agreement 1994[23] provide special funds to assist states in complying. Others, such as the Framework Convention on Climate Change[24] or the Convention on Biological Diversity,[25] rely on the multilateral Global Environmental Facility (GEF) for special funding.[26] Most, but not all, agreements have programs that provide limited training and materials to relevant national and local officials to comply with the agreements.

Traditionally, states have relied or threatened to rely on coercive measures to obtain compliance with international obligations. Coercive measures include sanctions, penalties and measures such as the withdrawal of membership privileges. They may also include publication of violations and other measures that induce "shame;" to this extent, some of the sunshine methods serve also as coercive measures. Sanctions are available to enforce two of the international environmental agreements studied: CITES and the Montreal Protocol. In addition, under the World Heritage Convention, the guidelines provide that parties can remove a site from the World Heritage List if the home country is not conserving the site. Although this is not referred to as a sanction and has never been used, it offers an informal means of coercion to conserve the site. This, however, assumes that the state still wishes its site to be listed on the World Heritage List. Otherwise sanctions would serve to relieve the state of responsibility under the Convention. Notably, sanctions are rarely used in international environmental law agreements. Some writers have suggested that sanctions are largely irrelevant to compliance with international agreements, including international environmental agreements.[27] But sanctions may

---

[23] International Tropical Timber Agreement, Geneva, January 26, 1994, UN Doc TD/TIMBER.2/L.9, reprinted in (1994) 33 ILM 1014. The Agreement establishes the Bali Partnership Fund. It replaces the 1984 agreement.

[24] Framework Convention on Climate Change, New York, May 9, 1992, 1771 UNTS 107, reprinted in (1992) 31 ILM 849.

[25] Convention on Biological Diversity, Rio de Janeiro, June 5, 1992, 1760 UNTS 79, reprinted in (1992) 31 ILM 818. Although Article 21, Financial Mechanism, does not explicitly refer to the Global Environmental Facility (GEF), the GEF has subsequently been designated as the mechanism.

[26] The GEF provides funding to cover the costs of agreed measures in four focal areas: biological diversity, climate change, international waters and ozone layer depletion. In addition, the GEF's mandate includes land degradation issues as they relate to the four focal areas. See Global Environment Facility, 1996, *Operational Strategy for the Global Environment Facility*, available at www.gefweb.org/Operational_Policies/Operational_Strategy/operational_strategy.html (last visited January 14, 2004).

[27] Chayes and Chayes, *The New Sovereignty*, pp. 32–33. Chayes and Chayes conclude that "[i]n sum, sanctioning authority is rarely granted by treaty, rarely used when granted, and likely to be ineffective when used." *Ibid.*

have value as a "weapon of last resort" and as a latent threat to make other methods of achieving compliance more effective.[28] In the environmental field, the parties to CITES have used the threat of suspending trade in species to try to spur a country's compliance.[29] The threat of sanctions is also relevant in environmental agreements where non-parties could substantially benefit from free-riding and/or where free-riding could hamper the effectiveness of the treaty. In these cases, treaty provisions that penalize parties for trading with non-parties serve effectively as a sanction on parties engaging in such trade.[30]

In addition to the above strategies, international environmental agreements have introduced significant institutional innovations for strengthening compliance. These include such institutional structures as a body to consider national problems in discharging the obligations of the agreement, procedures for addressing non-compliance, fora in which parties can consider violations and develop appropriate ways to handle them, and the use of non-governmental organizations to monitor compliance.

The Montreal Protocol on Substances that Deplete the Ozone Layer is a path-breaking agreement, in part because it provides for institutional means to address issues of implementation and of non-compliance by states party to the agreement. Under the Protocol, parties have established an Implementation Committee of ten states, which meets biannually, and agrees upon procedures to address cases of non-compliance (known as Non-Compliance Procedures).[31] The procedures can be activated by one state against another, by the Secretariat, or by a state with respect to itself. The Implementation Committee reviews the annual reports submitted by parties on consumption and production of controlled chemicals and

---

[28] See George Downs et al., "Is the Good News About Compliance Good News About Cooperation?" (1996) 50 *International Oraganization* 379. See also George Downs, "Enforcement and the Evolution of Cooperation" (1998) 19 *Mich. J. Int'l L.* 319.

[29] See Christine Crawford, Note, "Conflicts Between Species and the GATT in Light of Actions to Halt the Rhinoceros and Tiger Trade" (1995) 7 *Geo. Int'l Envtl L. Rev.* 555. See also Brown Weiss and Jacobson, *Engaging Countries*, ch. 5.

[30] See e.g., CITES, note 19; Montreal Protocol on Substances that Deplete the Ozone Layer, note 19; Basel Convention on the Control of Transboundary Movements of Hazardous Wastes and their Disposal, Basel, March 22, 1989, 1673 UNTS 57, reprinted in (1989) 28 ILM 649.

[31] Decision Concerning the Non-Compliance Procedure for the Montreal Protocol on Substances that Deplete the Ozone Layer, adopted at Copenhagen, November 25, 1992, UNEP/OzL.Pro.4/15, Annex IX, available at www.unep.org/ozone/mop/mop-reports.shtml (last visited January 14, 2004). See Edith Brown Weiss, "The Five International Treaties: A Living History" in Brown Weiss and Jacobson, *Engaging Countries*, pp. 125–37.

considers alleged violations of these procedural obligations or of the substantive targets and timetables for reducing or phasing out the chemicals. Members can make on-site visits to countries believed to be in non-compliance. In response to violations of either procedural or substantive obligations, the Committee can use a variety of measures ranging from incentives such as technical assistance to coercive measures such as warnings or suspension of rights and privileges under the Protocol. Some of these institutional innovations are reflected in subsequent environmental agreements, such as the Framework Convention on Climate Change and the 1996 London Protocol to the 1972 London Convention on marine dumping.[32]

Research in international environmental law suggests that compliance strategies must be targeted at insuring that all states party to an agreement have both strong intent and strong capacity to comply. Different strategies need to be emphasized for different countries in the context of different agreements. The mix of appropriate strategies to be included in an agreement depends on the profile of potential parties to the agreement with respect to intent and capacity to comply. A variety of strategies should always be available, particularly because countries' positions with respect to intent and capacity may change over time.

If states have both the intent and the capacity to comply, sunshine methods are particularly effective and appropriate. These measures are useful in monitoring behavior and in building public support for compliance. However, care is needed to ensure that they do not lead to large administrative burdens or assist those who oppose compliance by circumventing the agreement.

Even if countries have the intent and capacity to comply, sanctions may be needed to prevent countries from regressing. The threat of sanctions arguably makes sunshine methods effective. Publicizing violations serves as an indirect sanction in this context.

If countries intend to comply but lack the capacity, incentives are especially important. Many low-income countries are in this category. Incentives build capacity and may encourage countries to give higher priority to compliance. Sunshine methods may also be important in mobilizing actors other than states to press for compliance and in enabling governments, non-state actors (including industry) and individuals to monitor progress toward building the capacity to comply.

---

[32] London Protocol to the International Maritime Organization Convention on the Prevention of Marine Pollution by Dumping of Wastes and Other Matter, London, November 7, 1996, IMO LC/SM1/6, reprinted in (1997) 36 ILM 1.

If countries intend not to comply or to comply only weakly, but have the capacity to comply, targeted coercive measures may be useful. Sunshine methods may help build pressures to comply. In some cases, positive incentives may help change a country's views about compliance or its priorities, or strengthen its resolve to comply.

For countries weak both in intent and capacity, a group that includes many low-income countries, all of the compliance strategies are relevant. Positive incentives build compliance. Sunshine measures foster a culture of compliance and discourage regression. The threat of sanctions may empower those within the government to take actions to comply. The strategies may also be used to combat corruption in various forms that hinder compliance.

Over time, the attention to compliance and the mix of compliance strategies that are included in international environmental agreements has changed. For comparison purposes, it is useful to use 1988 as a benchmark. This is the year when the Cold War began to end, the Bruntland Commission had recently released its report on environment and development,[33] and the preparations for the United Nations Conference on Environment and Development were in the nascent stage. A review of fifty-nine multilateral environmental treaties drafted before 1988 and of more than thirty-two agreements concluded after 1988 indicates a stronger focus on compliance since 1988: see Figure 6.3.

The attention to sunshine methods and to incentives has increased dramatically, such that in the post-1988 period, all of the agreements include one or more sunshine methods, while provision for technical assistance is included in more than 60 percent of the agreements and for education and training in more than 40 percent. Sanctions have never played an important role in the agreements, although since 1988 a slightly greater percentage of agreements include provisions for membership sanctions.[34]

Applying compliance strategies to the WTO[35]

In contrast to environment, states party to the GATT and, since the end of 1994, the WTO, have relied on the threat (or occasional use) of sanctions to enforce obligations. Increasingly they are expanding the positive incentives for compliance, such as training and technical assistance. With

---

[33] Bruntland Commission, *Our Common Future* (Oxford University Press, 1987).
[34] Edith Brown Weiss, unpublished study (2001), data available from author.
[35] This section is adapted from Edith Brown Weiss, "Strengthening National Compliance with Trade Law: Insights from Environment" in Bronckers and Quick, *New Directions*, pp. 463–67.

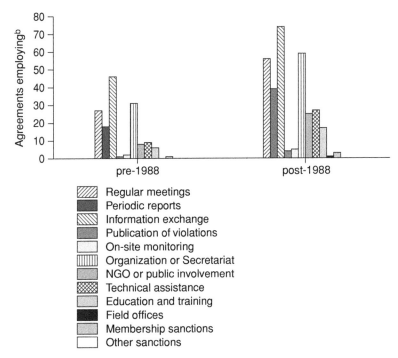

bOut of 59 treaties drafted before 1988 and out of 91 treaties drafted before and after 1988.

Figure 6.3 Compliance measures in multilateral environmental agreements pre-1988 v. post-1988 (as of July 2002)[a]
[a]Compliance measures:
  Sunshine methods: includes periodic reports, publication of violations, existence of organization or Secretariat, involvement of NGOs or the public, regular conferences between states parties, exchange of information between parties.
  Positive incentives: includes technical assistance, education or training programs, and field offices or presence to assist with compliance.
  Sanctions: includes revocation of membership status or other sanctions.
Sources: Edith Brown Weiss et al., *International Environmental Law, Basic Instruments and References* (Transnational Publishers, 1992); Edith Brown Weiss et al., *International Environmental Law, Basic Instruments and References, 1992–1999* (Transnational Publishers, 1999); United Nations Environment Program: www.unep.org

more developing countries and countries in transition becoming parties to the WTO, member states have recognized the need to build the capacity of both groups of countries to comply. However, the WTO relies less on the sunshine methods associated with environmental, human rights and other international agreements. Like environmental agreements, though, the WTO agreements provide in some cases for special and differential treatment for the least developed countries, such as longer transition periods and less far-reaching commitments, although many developing countries are dissatisfied with these provisions.

Figure 6.4 shows the compliance measures employed by the GATT prior to 1988, and those employed by the GATT after 1988 and by the WTO post-1994. As Figure 6.4 indicates, there has been much more emphasis in the WTO than in the GATT on incentives for compliance, such as technical assistance, education and capacity-building. Sunshine methods have generally not been an important component of inducing compliance.

The threat of sanctions has always lurked as the primary means of inducing states to comply with their obligations under GATT and the WTO. Prior to the WTO, the dispute settlement procedures were such that parties had to adopt a panel report by consensus for it to be binding. Building consensus was difficult. Nonetheless, even in the absence of a formal decision, the threat of coercive measures against the losing party pushed parties toward compliance with panel reports.

Some states use coercive or retaliatory measures unilaterally against foreign practices that might threaten the development or maintenance of a level playing field. The United States Trade Act of 1974, as amended in subsequent years, provides for a "Section 301 Procedure" that authorizes the US Trade Representative to investigate barriers to American trade. Section 301 also authorizes the US Trade Representative to take retaliatory action.[36] The Omnibus Trade and Competitiveness Act of 1984 created a "Super 301," which requires identification of "priority practices," the elimination of which has the greatest potential to increase American exports, and of "priority foreign countries" for targeting investigations into their trade practice.[37] In 1984, the European Council adopted a measure similar to Section 301, which is aimed at protecting against "illicit commercial practices."[38]

Since the WTO's adoption of the Dispute Settlement Understanding (DSU), it is increasingly likely that sanctions will be employed in response

---

[36] United States Trade Act of 1974, Public Law 930618, Approved January 3, 1975, 19 U.S.C. §§ 2101–2487, 88 Stat. 1978.

[37] United States Omnibus Trade and Competitiveness Act of 1988, Public Law 100–418, Approved August 23, 1988, 102 Stat. 1107.

[38] Council Regulation 2641/84/EEC on the Strengthening of the Common Commercial Policy with Regard in Particular to Protection Against Illicit Commercial Practices, [1984]. OJL252/1 (September 20, 1984).

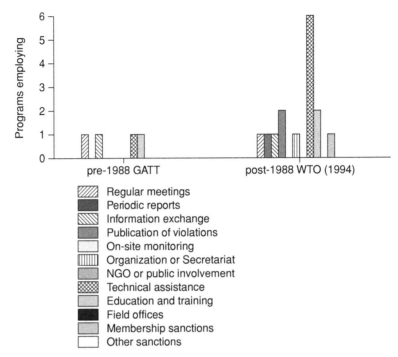

Figure 6.4 Compliance measures in trade programs pre-1988 GATT v. post-1988 GATT and WTO (1994) (as of July 2002)[a]

[a]Compliance measures:

  Sunshine methods: includes periodic reports, publication of violations, existence of organization or Secretariat, involvement of NGOs or the public, regular conferences between states parties, exchange of information between parties.

  Positive incentives: includes technical assistance, education or training programs, and field offices or presence to assist with compliance.

  Sanctions: includes revocation of membership status or other sanctions.

Sources: WTO website: www.wto.org; WTO, *Manual on Technical Cooperation* (1998); *Annual Report on the International Trade Centre* (1988); World Bank website: www.worldbank.org

to a country's refusal to adapt its behavior to a binding decision under the DSU. In part this is because the new procedure provides for an appellate body to review a panel decision and for the appellate body's report to become binding unless there is a consensus among the WTO parties to the contrary. Thus it is reasonable to expect that nearly all decisions will be binding. If a state does not comply with the decision, it is also reasonable to expect coercive measures to be taken by the state(s) bringing the complaint. Coercive measures are appropriate because the goal is to shape the intent of the country to comply with the decision, rather than to build capacity to comply.

The WTO has also increasingly turned to compliance strategies that utilize incentives to build the capacity of states and enterprises within states to comply with the WTO obligations. While several of the programs were started under the GATT, at least four significant programs have been initiated since the WTO was formed. The programs of technical assistance and other incentives generally have grown over time.

The three pre-WTO programs include the following: trade policy courses given for officials from developing countries to foster understanding of the trading system and the legal requirements; technical assistance to countries under the Trade Policy Review Mechanism; and supporting activities of the WTO/UNCTAD International Trade Centre (ITC), which focus on enterprise-related measures, such as market development and support services. The trade policy courses have been offered in Geneva since 1955. As of the beginning of the year 2000, the programs had trained more than 1,700 officials.[39] In the period before the WTO, the courses were given on average twice each year; since 1995, three courses have been held each year, and additional "special" courses have been held for transitional countries. In fall 2002, two courses were held in parallel for the first time.[40]

The Trade Policy Review Mechanism (TPRM) was established in December 1988. The Marrakesh Agreement provides that the four member states of the WTO with the largest share of world trade are to be reviewed every two years, the next sixteen countries every four years, and other countries every six years. While TPRMs serve primarily to monitor national trade policies, they also provide implementation incentives in the form of information, insights and technical assistance. The TPRM process may also exert informal coercion on some countries. While there has been a general increase in the number of TPRM reviews since 1991, the rise is neither even nor dramatic. This slow growth is likely due, at least in part, to resource constraints.

---

[39] *WTO Trade Policy Courses*, available at WTO website www.wto.org/english/tratop_e/devel_e/train_e/tradepolicycource_e.htm (last visited January 14, 2004) (last date for which composite figures were available).
[40] *Ibid.*

Since 1995, the WTO has created four new capacity-building programs for member countries. In June 2001, it created the WTO Training Institute, which significantly expands upon the capacity-building programs already in existence, particularly the Trade Policy Courses.[41] Under the Institute's auspices, the WTO is initiating a training-of-trainers program designed to build local capacity to educate officials to WTO requirements and a pilot program in distance-learning services.[42] In addition, the WTO Secretariat offers, upon request, technical assistance to developing countries to strengthen their understanding and implementation of international trade rules. In 1998, most of these activities (more than 80 percent) were financed by dedicated trust funds established by WTO members. The other two new WTO programs involve links with other international organizations. The Integrated Framework for Trade-Related Technical Assistance to Less-Developed Countries receives requests for trade assistance from developing countries and coordinates the programs among six organizations: WHO, UNCTAD, ITC, IMF, World Bank and UNDP. Many of the activities are similar to those performed by the WTO. The WTO also joined with the World Bank in two new initiatives to assist developing countries in complying with their WTO commitments: the Trade and Development Centre, which is designed to assist developing countries in participating more effectively in the WTO; and the WTO 2000 capacity-building project, launched in January 1999, to help developing countries participate more effectively in the next round of WTO negotiations. Taken together, these programs suggest a growing emphasis on building national capacity to comply with WTO agreements. As noted before, if countries lack the capacity to comply, it is essential to adopt compliance strategies that address this problem. Moreover, if countries develop the capacity to comply, it may also strengthen their intention to comply.

There has been little reliance in trade agreements on the transparency approach to ensure compliance. The Trade Policy Review Mechanism is an important exception in that the WTO subjects a country's trade policies to WTO monitoring and review. The reviews are public and can be purchased by anyone. Most country trade officials and WTO officials are not accustomed, however, to providing complete information about the operation of trade agreements to the public or to having non-governmental

---

[41] See *WTO Training Institute*, available at WTO website www.wto.org/english/tratop_e/devel_e/train_e/train_e.htm (last visited January 14, 2004).
[42] *Ibid.*

organizations participate in monitoring of adherence to commitments or implementation of the agreement.

There is still little transparency in the dispute settlement process. The country submissions are rarely made public, although confidentiality rules do not preclude WTO members from disclosing their positions to the public. Under Article 18 of the DSU, a member state may request that a party to a dispute provide a non-confidential summary of information contained in its written submissions that could be disclosed to the public. Nationally, the United States, for example, is obligated under domestic law to require such a non-confidential summary in any WTO dispute if a party has not already made its submission public. Moreover, most submissions are essentially transcribed in the panel reports. Timely access to the reports, if not the submissions, and perhaps access to the proceedings by non-state actors and the press would increase transparency and could make dispute settlement findings more acceptable to the public. This in turn should encourage national implementation of and compliance with the decision.[43] The recent decision by the Appellate Body on asbestos moved in the direction of increased public participation by permitting non-governmental organizations to submit *amicus curiae* briefs.[44] The Appellate Body report is controversial among many governments.

The WTO agreements obligate countries to provide notice to the Secretariat of certain actions.[45] The notifications may be ad hoc, one-time only, or regular and periodic. The notification requirements are procedural obligations. But notification may also be viewed as a form of reporting and as such serves as an example of a "sunshine" compliance strategy. For example, pursuant to the Technical Barriers to Trade Agreement (TBT),[46]

---

[43] See Thomas Cottier, "The WTO Dispute Settlement System: New Horizons" (1998) 92 *Am. Soc'y Int'l Proc.* 86. Similarly, see Robert E. Hudec, "The New Dispute Settlement: An Overview of the First Three Years" (1999) 8 *Minn. J. Global Trade* 1.

[44] *European Communities: Measures Affecting Asbestos and Asbestos-Containing Products*, WTO Appellate Body Report WT/DS135/AB/R (March 12, 2001), available at WTO website http://docsonline.wto.org/gen_search.asp (last visited January 14, 2004).

[45] In June 1995, the WTO Secretariat prepared a list of all notifications required under Agreements in Annex 1A of the WTO Agreement (G/NOP/W/Rev.1). Included are specific Agreements on Agriculture; the Application of Sanitary and Phytosanitary Measures; Textiles and Clothing; Technical Barriers to Trade; Trade-related Investment Measures; Implementation of Article VI of the GATT 1994; Implementation of Article VII of the GATT 1994; Pre-shipment Inspection; Rules of Origin; Import Licensing Procedures; Subsidies and Countervailing Measures; and Safeguards.

[46] Agreement on Technical Barriers to Trade, available at WTO website www.wto.org/english/docs_e/legal_e/final_e.htm (last visited January 14, 2004) ("TBT Agreement").

countries must notify the WTO Secretariat when they adopt binding technical regulations that are not based on existing international standards. The notice must be provided sufficiently in advance of the adoption of the regulation to give interested exporting countries an opportunity to comment on the draft. Likewise, under the Agreement on the Application of Sanitary and Phytosanitary Measures (SPS),[47] member countries must provide interested exporting countries with an opportunity to comment on draft standards.

Compliance with the notification requirements varies greatly. However, it appears to be improving, at least for some agreements. As of March 1999, member countries were progressively and more comprehensively meeting their notification requirements under the SPS agreement.[48] The Committee meetings for both the TBT and SPS help to secure compliance, because they provide the opportunity for officials to get to know each other, point out potential compliance problems with the procedural obligations, informally discuss problems on a continuing basis and generate feelings of responsibility to comply. In international environmental agreements, meetings of the parties and of sub-committees have been effective means for enhancing compliance. Such compliance methods also may be increasingly useful in the context of trade agreements as a means of influencing a country's intent to comply and in complementing capacity-building measures.

Considering compliance strategies in other international agreements

In both international environmental and international trade law, states show growing interest in strengthening national compliance with international obligations. This trend also appears in other areas of international law, such as human rights, labor and arms control.

Human rights and labor

As is the case with international environmental agreements, the agreements concerned with human rights and with labor have long been

---

[47] Agreement on the Application of Sanitary and Phytosanitary Measures, available at WTO website www.wto.org/english/docs_e/legal_e/final_e.htm (last visited January 14, 2004) ("SPS Agreement").

[48] Committee on Sanitary and Phytosanitary Measures, Review of the Operation and Implementation of the Agreement on the Application of Sanitary and Phytosanitary Measures, *Report of the Committee* (March 11, 1999).

associated with compliance strategies that focus on transparency or sunshine methods. Most agreements contain one or more sunshine measures including provisions for investigation, reporting and the publication of violations. A review of agreements before and after 1988 indicates increased attention to incentive measures, such as technical assistance, education and training, and the establishment of field offices: see Figure 6.5. Human rights agreements have not explicitly provided for sanctions.[49]

Most international and regional human rights agreements offer technical assistance as a means to encourage compliance with obligations. For the most part, this assistance is used by new member states, or by those who lack the capacity to implement treaty requirements. Only a few human rights instruments explicitly invite requests for technical assistance. In practice, however, many other treaty regimes accept and even encourage requests for assistance from state parties. These regimes offer several types of technical assistance. States may receive assistance in reforming national legislation with the aim of establishing a national legal framework consistent with international standards. Assistance is also available for states having difficulty complying with the periodic reporting requirements – the sunshine measures required by many human rights agreements. Similarly, the International Labor Organization (ILO) assists countries in their efforts to bring labor standards in line with ILO guidelines. The ILO also responds to requests for assistance with reporting requirements.

Many international human rights regimes as well as the ILO offer a variety of educational and training programs to assist compliance. For example, the United Nations High Commissioner for Human Rights, through the Center for Human Rights, offers human rights training for police officers, military personnel and national legislatures. Regional human rights regimes sponsor similar educational programs. The ILO also provides training and educational opportunities at the ILO International Training Center in Turin, Italy. The center offers training on a range of ILO issues, including international labor standards and human rights, the periodic reporting and supervisory system of the ILO, and specific labor topics such as women's and children's rights. In addition, the ILO maintains Regional Labor Administration Centers, which offer similar training programs.

---

[49] Edith Brown Weiss, unpublished study (2001), data available from author. See also Katarina Tomasevski, *Responding to Human Rights Violations: 1946–1999* (Kluwer, 2000) (detailing use of multilateral and unilateral sanctions to enforce human rights).

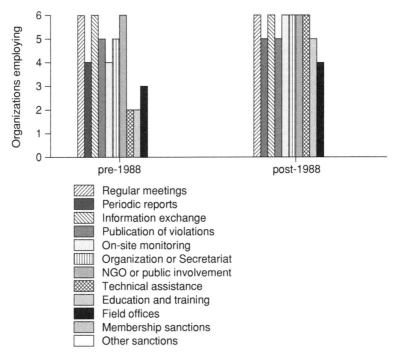

Figure 6.5 Compliance measures in human rights and labor organizations pre-1988 v. post-1988 (as of July 2002)[a]

[a]Compliance measures:

Sunshine methods: includes periodic reports, publication of violations, existence of organization or Secretariat, involvement of NGOs or the public, regular conferences between states parties, exchange of information between parties.

Positive incentives: includes technical assistance, education or training programs, and field offices or presence to assist with compliance.

Sanctions: includes revocation of membership status or other sanctions.

Sources: United Nations: www.unhchr.ch; International Labor Organization: www.ilo.org; Organization for Security and Cooperation in Europe: www.osce.org; Organization of American States: www.oas.org; Organization of African Unity: www.oau-uao.org; Council of Europe: www.coe.fr

The Council of Europe's Program of Assistance with the Development and Consolidation of Democratic Stability (ADACS) for Central and Eastern European states and states of the former Soviet Union developed unusual, multidisciplinary incentive programs with the potential to build robust capacity for complying with international agreements. ADACS programs, pursued in cooperation with the Commission of the

European Communities, focus on six central themes: (1) human rights protection, with a view to the harmonization of national legislation with the European Convention and the case law of the European Court of Human Rights; (2) legal cooperation to develop institutions and practices based on the rule of law, legislative reform and reform of the judiciary; (3) protection of independence and pluralism of the media; (4) protection of civil society; (5) development of efficient grassroots democracy; and (6) educational programs on human rights.[50] Since 1993, ADACS programs have been developed in two regionwide initiatives and in several individual member states: Albania (since 1993); Estonia, Latvia and Lithuania (since 1994); the Russian Federation (since 1996); and the Ukraine (since 1995).[51]

Arms control agreements

As is the case with human rights and labor agreements, arms control agreements have consistently utilized sunshine methods. A review of multilateral arms control agreements indicates that 80 percent of those treaties drafted before 1988 and all of the treaties drafted after 1988 utilize one or more sunshine method: see Figure 6.6. Along with reporting requirements, many arms control agreements set forth monitoring procedures and systems by which one party may verify compliance by another party.

Incentive measures are also increasingly common in arms control agreements. Several treaties that came into force in the late 1990s rely on incentives to increase the capacity of states party to the agreement. For example, the 1997 Convention on the Prohibition of the Use, Stockpiling, Production and Transfer of Anti-Personnel Mines and on their Destruction (Land Mines Convention) provides that each state party may seek assistance from other parties and from the United Nations in obtaining equipment, material and scientific methods to clear mines; in clearing and destroying mines; in caring for and rehabilitating mine victims; and in running national mine awareness programs.[52] Under the Convention,

---

[50] See Council of Europe in Central and Eastern Europe, Programmes of Assistance with the Development and Consolidation of Democratic Stability, available at the Council of Europe website www.coe.int/DefaultEN.asp (last visited January 14, 2004).
[51] See Joint Programmes between the Council of Europe and the Commission of the European Communities, available at the Council of Europe website, note 50.
[52] Convention on the Prohibition of the Use, Stockpiling, Production and Transfer of Anti-Personnel Mines and on their Destruction, Oslo, September 18, 1997, Article 6, 2056 UNTS 211, 244, reprinted in (1997) 36 ILM 1507, 1511 ("Landmines Convention").

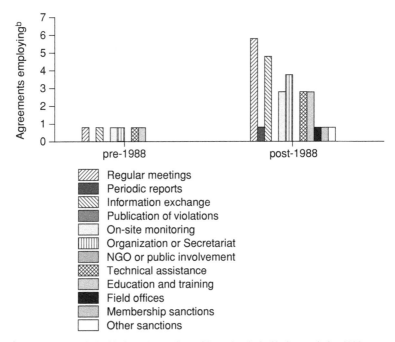

bOut of 2 treaties drafted before 1988 and out of 8 treaties drafted before and after 1988.

Figure 6.6 Compliance measures in arms control agreements pre-1988 v. post-1988 (as of July 2002)[a]

[a]Compliance measures:

Sunshine methods: includes periodic reports, publication of violations, existence of organization or Secretariat, involvement of NGOs or the public, regular conferences between states parties, exchange of information between parties.

Positive incentives: includes technical assistance, education or training programs, and field offices or presence to assist with compliance.

Sanctions: includes revocation of membership status or other sanctions.

Sources: Treaty on the Non-Proliferation of Nuclear Weapons 1970, 729 UNTS 169; Strategic Arms Reduction Treaty 1982 www.state.gov; Treaty on the Conventional Armed Forces in Europe 1992 www.state.gov; Convention on the Prohibition of the Development, Production, Stockpiling and Use of Chemical Weapons and on their Destruction 1993, 1974 UNTS 45; Wassenaar Arrangement on Export Controls for Conventional Arms and Dual-Use Goods and Technologies 1996 www.wassenaar.org; Comprehensive Test Ban Treaty 1996 (not presently in force) www.state.gov; Convention on the Prohibition on the Use, Stockpiling, Production and Transfer of Anti-Personnel Mines and on their Destruction 1997, 2056 UNTS 211; Inter-American Convention Against the Illicit Manufacturing of and Trafficking in Firearms, Ammunition, Explosives and other related Materials 1997 www.state.gov

the United Nations can also provide guidance and clarification regarding countries' obligations under the Convention.[53] The 1993 Convention on the Prohibition of the Development, Production, Stockpiling and Use of Chemical Weapons and on their Destruction (CWC)[54] utilizes both positive incentives and sunshine measures. The CWC provides for an internship program to educate scientists from developing and transitional countries; supports laboratories with equipment, training and consultants; sponsors seminars and symposia; and runs a course program for personnel from national authorities responsible for implementing the Convention.[55]

Political incentives also appear in earlier treaties. For example, nuclear powers party to the Nuclear Non-Proliferation Treaty (NPT)[56] pledge to provide security assistance to non-nuclear parties, so that they do not have to develop nuclear weapons. This is an incentive in the classical sense. Overall, more than 60 percent of all modern arms control treaties provide for some form of incentive to comply. Some of the agreements use sanctions as well. Sanctions are included in 25 percent of arms control agreements negotiated after 1988.[57]

Arms control treaties also show a trend toward the use of multiple compliance strategies. For example, major Cold War era arms control agreements, such as the Treaty on the Limitation of Anti-Ballistic Missile Systems, the NPT and the Treaty on Conventional Forces in Europe, use mostly sunshine provisions in the form of verification measures, provision of information, a special commission attached to the agreement or meetings of the parties to help facilitate compliance. By contrast, the Landmines Convention and the Comprehensive Test Ban Treaty, which were completed after 1996, provide for a variety of measures to strengthen compliance, which focus especially on sunshine and positive incentives. Many of these new agreements have also created separate international bodies to help facilitate compliance.

---

[53] *Ibid*. Article 8, 2056 UNTS at 246, reprinted in (1997) 36 ILM 1513.
[54] Convention on the Prohibition of the Development, Production, Stockpiling and Use of Chemical Weapons and on their Destruction, Geneva, January 13, 1993, 1974 UNTS 45, reprinted in (1993) 31 ILM 800.
[55] See *International Cooperation and Assistance*, available at OPCW website www.opcw.org/html/db/icprot_frameset.html (last visited January 14, 2004).
[56] Treaty on the Non-Proliferation of Nuclear Weapons, Washington, DC, London and Moscow, July 1, 1968, 729 UNTS 161, reprinted in (1968) 7 ILM 509.
[57] Edith Brown Weiss, unpublished study (2001), data available from author.

Explaining the trends in compliance

Overall, as evidenced by agreements in the areas of environment, trade, human rights, labor and arms control, states are increasingly focusing on measures to enhance compliance in the negotiation, design, and implementation of international agreements. States' use of all of the compliance strategies described previously is increasing. In particular, there is an accelerating emphasis on measures that make a country's compliance with its international obligations transparent and on programs that build the capacity of countries to comply. How do we explain the growing focus on compliance with treaty obligations? Why are countries increasingly turning to sunshine methods and to incentives to strengthen compliance?

While many factors contribute to these trends, two may be critical. First, there were 191 member states of the United Nations as of April 23, 2004, as compared to 51 when the United Nations was formed.[58] This means that many more states must develop the capacity to comply with international agreements. Many of these newer states are developing countries that often lack the capacity to comply with the agreements they join. In some cases, they also have other priorities. Incentives, such as technical assistance and education, build national and local capacity to comply. Special funds may also help to shift a country's priorities so that compliance with particular international obligations is given greater importance.

Secondly, as the non-hierarchical network paradigm for the international system revealed, civil society is seen as increasingly important in securing compliance with international agreements (or conversely in undercutting compliance). Sunshine or transparency methods can be targeted to enhance civil society's role in securing compliance. Such measures are also likely to strengthen the capacity of civil society to abide by implementing legislation and regulations. In many cases, these measures will facilitate compliance by the relevant sectors of civil society.

The analysis of national compliance with international environmental agreements suggests that states should consider compliance issues throughout the life of an international agreement: from the negotiations, to the design of the agreement, to the strategies for encouraging or strengthening compliance by member states at the national and local levels. Sunshine measures, incentives and sanctions should be considered,

---

[58] United Nations, *Growth in United Nations Membership 1945–2000*, available at www.un.org/Overview/growth.htm (last visited April 23, 2004). For a list of the 191 current members, see www.un.org/overview/unmember.html (last visited April 23, 2004).

so that the mix of measures can be tailored to a state's intent and capacity to comply at any given time.

States are moving in this direction. In February 2002, the UNEP Governing Council adopted Guidelines on Compliance with and Enforcement of Multilateral Environmental Agreements.[59] The Guidelines, prepared by UNEP and finalized by the Intergovernmental Working Group of Experts, are comprehensive and cover all stages in an international agreement: from preparatory work for negotiations through the drafting of the agreement to national implementation after the agreement is concluded.[60] They draw upon the three compliance strategies of sunshine measures, incentives and sanctions, although the focus is on the first two. The guidelines offer a wide range of options for countries to consider, and in this sense are relevant to agreements in areas other than the environment.

The World Summit on Sustainable Development in Johannesburg, South Africa, held from August 26 to September 4, 2002, considered measures for strengthening national implementation of international environmental agreements. These focused particularly on public-private partnerships. Research on compliance affirms the importance of involving civil society as well as governments in this daunting task and suggests that international agreements need to provide a range of options for promoting national compliance with all international obligations.

---

[59] See United Nations Environment Programme, Report of the Governing Council on the Work of its Seventh Special Session/Global Ministerial Environment Forum, February 13–15, 2002, UNEP/GCSS.VII/6 (March 5, 2002), available at www.unep.org/governingbodies/gc/specialsessions/gcss_vii/Documents/K0260448.doc (last visited January 14, 2004) (adopting the guidelines and authorizing the Executive Director to seek funds for the implementation of the guidelines); Draft Guidelines on Compliance with and Enforcement of Multilateral Environmental Agreements, UNEP/GCSS.VII/4/Add.2 (November 23, 2001), available at www.unep. org/governingbodies/gc/specialsessions/gcss_vii/Documents /K0100451.e.doc (last visited January 14, 2004).

[60] Draft Guidelines, note 59, at §§ D.1 (Preparatory Work for Negotiations), D.4 (Compliance Considerations in Multilateral Environmental Agreements) and E.1 (National Measures).

7

Compliance with international norms in the age of globalization: two theoretical perspectives

MOSHE HIRSCH

Introduction

The subject of compliance with international norms has recently attracted significant attention of scholars from both the international law and international relations disciplines. The former, rather skeptical attitude of many scholars regarding the compliance of states with international law has largely shifted to a more favorable appraisal. The widespread view in the current literature[1] embraces the famous statement of Louis Henkin that "almost all nations observe almost all principles of international law and almost all of their obligations almost all of the time."[2] Less preoccupied with the question of how much compliance, scholars now pose the more intriguing question of why compliance is prevalent in the international community. This question challenges scholars of international law and international relations to identify the major factors that motivate states to observe or violate their international obligations.

The process of globalization raises numerous questions for social scientists regarding the ramifications of this phenomenon in a variety of spheres, including international law and international relations. The principal aim of this chapter is to analyze the likely repercussions of the process of globalization upon compliance with international norms. More precisely, the central question here is whether globalization is expected to

---

[1] See e.g., George W. Downs, D. M. Rocke and P. N. Barsoom, "Is the Good News About Compliance Good News About Cooperation?" (1996) 50 *International Organization* 379; Beth A. Simmons, "Compliance with International Agreements" (1998) 1 *Annual Rev. Political Science* 75, 76–77, 79; H. Morgenthau, *Politics Among Nations* (5th ed., 1973), pp. 290–91.

[2] Louis Henkin, *How Nations Behave* (2nd ed., Columbia University Press, NY, 1979), p. 47.

enhance or lessen compliance with international norms (assuming that the process of globalization proceeds).[3]

The answer to this important question is dependent to a significant measure upon the answer provided to the above question regarding the factors that affect compliance with international norms. This subject is disputed among eminent scholars of international relations and international law. Thus, before analyzing the effects of globalization on the observance of international norms, we will consider the two principal paradigms that explain state behavior in the international arena. After a review of the fundamental tenets of the rational choice model and the sociological perspective in social sciences, we shall briefly discuss the international relations theoretical streams that draw upon these two paradigms. We shall then examine the uniqueness of each of these approaches to the question of compliance with international norms. Finally, equipped with the relevant knowledge regarding the principal features of globalization, as well as with the main factors that affect compliance in accordance with each of these theories, we shall analyze the likely effects of globalization upon the prospects of compliance with international norms.

Globalization: processes and characteristics

The phenomenon of globalization is extensively discussed in numerous books and articles published in the last decade. Therefore we shall only trace the broad contours of this process and identify the core characteristics particularly important to the subject of compliance. There is some controversy among scholars regarding the extent and the impact of the changes generated by globalization. The two extreme camps are the "hyperglobalizers" and the "skeptics." These titles well reflect the general position of the proponents of each approach towards globalization.[4]

As opposed to these two camps, this study will generally adopt a middle version of globalization, which is closer in many respects to the third

---

[3] On the continuing process of globalization following the attacks on September 11, 2001, see "Measuring Globalization: Who's Up, Who's Down?" (2003) *Foreign Policy* 60, 62–64 (January/February); "Measuring Globalization: Economic Reversals, Forward Momentum" (2004) *Foreign Policy* 54 (March/April).

[4] See on this controversy, David Held, Anthony Mcgrew, David Goldblatt and Jonathan Perraton, *Global Transformations: Politics, Economics and Culture* (Polity Press, Cambridge, 1999), pp. 6–9; Stephen Castles, "Studying Social Transformation" (2001) 22 *Int'l Political Science Rev.* 13, 20–22.

stream in this field, the "transformationalist" approach. This stream perceives the phenomenon of globalization as a process (or set of processes) that constitutes the central driving force behind the social, political and economic changes that gradually reshape modern societies and world order. This phenomenon, it should be noted, does not necessarily reflect linear-development logic.[5] Accordingly, we shall attempt to delineate the major trends encompassed by the process of globalization, without attempting to provide far-reaching predictions regarding "the end of state," "the end of history," etc.

Globalization is a multifaceted concept that encompasses technological, political, economic and social trends. The term principally refers to a process of "widening, deepening and speeding up of worldwide interconnectedness in all aspects of contemporary social life."[6] This process has accelerated in the last four decades. The rapid changes in technology, economic activity and governance significantly increased the speed (and decreased the costs) of international communication and transportation. Consequently, cross-border flows (of trade, investment, migrants, cultural artifacts, environmental factors, etc.) have reached unprecedented levels. International trade and investment has dramatically expanded during recent decades and trade grew much faster than global output. The operation of increasingly transboundary labor markets and the rapid changes in transportation have also led to a significant increase in international immigration.[7]

The extensive changes in the above spheres are naturally accompanied by increased interpersonal contacts across national boundaries and enhanced interconnectedness among societies.[8] The result is that, nowadays, people in different states are more significantly affected by activities that take place in other states, and often, in other parts of the globe. In

---

[5] Held *et al.*, *Global Transformations*, pp. 7–10; Castles, "Studying Social Transformation."

[6] Held *et al.*, *Global Transformations*, p. 2.

[7] See on these changes, Castles, "Studying Social Transformation", 21; Jan Art Scholte, "The Globalization of World Politics" in John Baylis and Steve Smith (eds.), *The Globalization of World Politics* (2nd ed., Oxford University Press, 2001), pp. 13, 14–15; Peter Willets, "Transnational Actors and International Organizations in Global Politics" in Baylis and Smith, *Globalization of World Politics*, pp. 356, 373; Thomas D. Lairson and David Skidmore, *International Political Economy* (2nd ed., Hardcourt Brace College Publishers, Fort Worth, 1997), pp. 109–10; Jonathan D. Aronson, "The Communications and Internet Revolution" in Baylis and Smith, *Globalization of World Politics*, pp. 541, 544–46; *WTO Annual Report 1998* (WTO, Geneva, 2000), pp. 33–35; *WTO Annual Report 2003* (WTO, Geneva, 2003), pp. 12–14; *Human Development Report 2000* (United Nations Development Program, NY, 2000), pp. 32–33; Held *et al.*, *Global Transformations*, pp. 283–326.

[8] Held *et al.*, *Global Transformations*, p. 5.

this sense, the world is perceived to be "shrinking."⁹ Consequently, one of the most striking developments noted by scholars studying the phenomenon of globalization is the decreasing importance of distance and of international borders. As stated by Scholte:

> [G]lobalization refers to processes whereby many social relations become relatively delinked from territorial geography, so that human lives are increasingly played out in the world as a single place.¹⁰

States are not the only major actors in the process of globalization. Other transnational actors, like multinational corporations, non-governmental organizations (NGOs), and transnational social movements have increased their strength and influence upon international events. Thus, for instance, major multinational corporations dominate global production and markets, and NGOs play a major role in the sphere of international environment, as well as in human rights protection.¹¹ The increasing influence of non-state actors, as well as the above-mentioned unprecedented flows of factors across boundaries (e.g., communication, environmental factors) decrease the power of sovereign states to control activities within their territories.¹² In the sphere of international economics, for instance, the expansion of international trade and investment has increasingly constrained the policy choices available to national decision-makers regarding social schemes.¹³

Finally, it is important to emphasize that not all states participate equally in the process of globalization. This process is clearly uneven and unbalanced. Generally, globalization is more profoundly felt in industrialized states (North America, Europe and the Pacific Rim) than in Africa and regions in Asia.¹⁴ This gap is particularly prominent in the

---

⁹ Steve Smith and John Baylis, "Introduction" in Baylis and Smith, *Globalization of World Politics*, pp. 1, 7.
¹⁰ Scholte, "The Globalization of World Politics," 14–15; see also, with regard to global economic developments, David N. Balaan and Michael Veseth, *Introduction to Political Economy* (Upper Saddle River, New Jersey, 2001), p. 21.
¹¹ Held *et al.*, *Global Transformations*, p. 9; Lairson and Skidmore, *International Political Economy*, pp. 109–10; Willets, "Transnational Actors," 369–80.
¹² See e.g., Scholte, "The Globalization of World Politics," 21–22; Willets, "Transnational Actors," 363–64; Held *et al.*, *Global Transformations*, pp. 8–9; Moises Naim, "Five Wars of Globalization" (2003) *Foreign Policy* 38 (January/February).
¹³ See e.g., Helen V. Milner, "The Political Economy of International Trade" (1999) 2 *Annual Rev. Political Sciences* 91, 109; Dani Rodrik, *Has Globalization Gone Too Far?* (Institute for International Economics, Washington DC, 1997), pp. 5–6.
¹⁴ Scholte, "The Globalization of World Politics," 17; Held *et al.*, *Global Transformations*, pp. 7–8.

field of information technology, where the vast activities related to information and communication technologies that are concentrated in the developed states have created the "digital divide."[15] Furthermore, while, generally, the world is more prosperous (the average per capita income having more than tripled in the past fifty years), and the share of the world's people living in extreme poverty is slowly declining, the gap between poorest and richest people and countries, in terms of income equality, has continued to widen.[16] The latter fact, however, should not necessarily mean that there is a causal connection between globalization and income equality. The effects of globalization on inequality among states are complicated[17] and various empirical studies show that the evidence is still inconclusive.[18] Notwithstanding the uncertain causal link between globalization and inequality, the increasing gap between developing and developed states should be taken into account by any researcher who seeks to analyze expected trends in the international system.[19]

[15] "Measuring Globalization," (2001) *Foreign Policy* 56, 60–62 (January–February); "Measuring Globalization: Who's Up, Who's Down," 68: 70 percent of Internet users live in high-income OECD countries, with 14 percent of the world's population; *United Nations Development Report 2002* (United Nations Development Program, NY, 2002), p. 10.

[16] *UNDP Report 2000*, pp. 25–26, 36; *UNDP Report 2002*, p. 13; "Measuring Globalization," 63–64.

[17] See e.g., Robert O. Keohane, "Governance in a Partially Globalized World" (2001) 95 *Am. Political Science Rev.* 1, 3; Dani Rodrik, "Symposium on Globalization in Perspective" (1998) 12 *J. Economic Perspectives* 3, 5–7; Ngaire Woods, "Order, Globalization, and Inequality in World Politics" in Andrew Hurrell and Ngaire Woods (eds.), *Inequality, Globalization, and World Politics* (Oxford University Press, Oxford, 1999), pp. 20–25; Frances Seward and Albert Berry, "Globalization, Liberalization, and Inequality: Expectations and Experience" in Hurrell and Woods, *Inequality, Globalization, and World Politics*, pp. 150–86; Thomas J. Biersteker, "Globalization as a Mode of Thinking in Major Institutional Actors" in Ngaire Woods (ed.), *The Political Economy of Globalization* (Macmillan Press, 2000), pp. 147, 159–61.

[18] For a comprehensive statistical analysis of the impact of the processes of globalization on both within-country income distribution and between-country inequality, see Kevin H. O'Rourke, "Globalization and Inequality: Historical Trends," NBER Working Paper 8339 (2001). See also on this subject, Gregory Clark and Robert C. Feenstra, "Technology in the Great Divergence," NBER Working Paper W8596 (2001); Glen Firebaugh, "Empirics of World Income Inequality" (1999) 104 *Am. J. Sociology*, 1597.

[19] On the impacts of globalization on within-country inequality, see Robert C. Feenstra and Gordon H. Hanson, "Global Production Sharing and Rising Inequality: A Survey of Trade and Wages," NBER Working Paper 8372 (2001); Samuel Bowles, "Globalization and Redistribution: Feasible Egalitarianism in a Competitive World," PERI Working Paper 34 (SSRN Paper Collection, 2002).

Explaining compliance: the inter-paradigms debate

An analysis of the impact of globalization on the prospects of compliance[20] with international norms[21] requires us to examine in advance which factors motivate or hinder compliance with these norms. Here lies the fundamental question: Why do states obey or violate international norms? Two distinct social sciences paradigms provide two different answers to this important question. The rational choice model and the sociological perspective posit different assumptions regarding the motivation for social behavior in general, and regarding the central factors that affect decision-making processes. Each of these paradigms generated theoretical strands in the various disciplines of the social sciences, including in law and international relations.[22]

---

[20] Following the definition suggested by Edith Brown Weiss and Harold Jacobson, the term "compliance" refers in this chapter to whether countries in fact adhere to the provisions of international agreements and to the implementation measures that they have instituted: Harold Jacobson and Edith Brown Weiss, "A Framework for Analysis" in Edith Brown Weiss and Harold Jacobson (eds.), *Engaging Countries: Strengthening Compliance with International Environmental Accords* (MIT Press, Cambridge, MA, 1998), pp. 1, 4. On the definitions of "implementation" and "effectiveness," see pp. 4–5. On the relationship between compliance and effectiveness, see Kal Raustiala, "Compliance and Effectiveness in International Regulatory Cooperation" (2000) 32 *Case Western Reserve J. Int'l L.* 387, 411–21. On the definition of "compliance" see also Oran Young, *Compliance and Public Authority* (Johns Hopkins University Press, Baltimore, 1979), pp. 4–5; Benedict Kingsbury, "The Concept of Compliance as a Function of Competing Conceptions of International Law" (1998) 19 *Michigan J. Int'l L.* 345, 346–49.

[21] The term "norm" is broader than a binding legal rule and it includes "soft law" rules. On compliance with soft law, see Edith Brown Weiss, "Understanding Compliance with Soft Law" in Dinah Shelton (ed.), *Commitment and Compliance: The Role of Non-Binding Norms in the International Legal System* (Oxford University Press, 2000), p. 535.

The term "norm" refers in the sociological literature to rules and expectations by which a society guides the behavior of its members. Some norms are proscriptive (i.e., prescribing what we should not do) and some norms are prescriptive (i.e., prescribing what we should do): John J. Macionis, *Sociology* (6th ed., International ed., Prentice-Hall International, Inc., New Jersey, 1997), p. 74. See also Friedrich V. Kratochwil, *Rules, Norms, and Decisions* (Cambridge University Press, Cambridge, 1989), pp. 181–211; Martha Finnemore and Kathryn Sikkink, "International Norm Dynamics and Political Change" (1998) 52 *International Organization* 887, 891.

[22] Even within the discipline of sociology, there are proponents of the rational choice approach; see e.g., Peter Abel, "Sociological Theory and Rational Choice" in Bryan S. Turner (ed.), *Social Theory* (Blackwell, Massachusetts, 1996), p. 252; James S. Coleman, "Human Action as Rational Choice" in Richard Munch (ed.), *Sociological Theory: Developments Since the 1960s* (Nelson-Hall Publishers, Chicago, 1990), p. 37. For a criticism of the rational choice approach in sociology, see Josh Whitford, "Pragmatism and the Untenable Dualism of Means and Ends: Why Rational Choice Theory does not Deserve Paradigmatic Privilege" (2002) 31 *Theory and Society*, 324.

Hence, the answer to the question of compliance is dependent to a large extent upon the paradigm employed. This section will briefly discuss the core assumptions of the rational choice model and the sociological perspective. The discussion will be followed by a review of the treatment of these approaches concerning the subject of compliance with international norms, and more particularly, upon the question of what factors are likely to increase or decrease compliance in accordance with each of these theories.

The rational choice model and compliance with international norms

The rational choice doctrine views a person as an instrumentally rational and calculating seeker of preference satisfaction. The standard rational choice model assumes that decision-makers are utility maximizers: they have certain goals ("preferences") that they strive to attain through their actions. They have consistent preferences ordering over the goals and they know the outcomes ("utilities") of their alternative actions. Rational decision-makers select the course of action ("strategy") that maximizes their utility, as determined by their goals and the alternative options available to them. The rational choice model takes individual preferences as predetermined goals. The model does not seek to explain which factors motivate a person to adopt a certain aim and how preferences are modified over time. The process of the emergence and change of preferences is exogenous to rational choice theory.[23] Rational choice theory is widely applied in various social science disciplines, most commonly in economics, but also in sociology, psychology, political science, international relations and international law.[24]

---

[23] Shaun Hargreaves Heap *et al.*, *The Theory of Choice: A Critical Guide* (Blackwell, Oxford, 1992), pp. 4–5, 62–63; Martin Hollis, *The Philosophy of Social Science* (Cambridge University Press, Cambridge, 1994), pp. 116–18.

[24] See e.g., Moshe Hirsch, "The Evolution of Environmental Cooperation Between Former Belligerents in the Middle East and Europe: A Rational Choice Approach" (2001) *Netherlands Int'l L. Rev.* 115; Jeffrey L. Dunhoff and Joel P. Trachtman, "The Law of Economics of Humanitarian Law Violations in Internal Conflict" (1999) 93 *Am. J. Int'l L.* 394; Michael Nicholson, *Formal Theories of International Relations* (Cambridge University Press, Cambridge, 1989), pp. 1–10; James D. Morrow, "A Rational Choice Approach to International Conflict" in Nehemia Geva and Alex Mintz (eds.), *Decision-making on War and Peace: The Cognitive-Rational Debate* (Lynne Rienner Publishers, 1997), pp. 1, 11–17; James S. Coleman, "Human Action as Rational Choice" in Richard Munch (ed.), *Sociological Theory: Developments Since the 1960s* (Nelson-Hall Publishers, Chicago, 1990), p. 37.

Game theory[25] is a formalized strand of rational choice theory that has been frequently applied by social scientists to analyze various phenomena, including international settings.[26] Unlike rational choice theory in general, game theory models only apply to *interactive* ("strategical") situations, i.e. situations in which the outcome depends not only on the decision-maker's behavior or nature, but also upon the moves of other players. Game theory enables social scientists to formalize social structures and determine the implications of the structure on individual decisions.[27]

Each of the major approaches in international relations literature—Realism, Liberalism and Institutionalism—includes specific theories that draw upon the rational choice model.[28] Some leading scholars of international relations emphasize the common rational elements of the Neorealist and Neoliberal Institutionalist approaches, and argue that they have "moved in ever-closer proximity to one another."[29]

---

[25] For a general introduction to game theory, see Robert Gibbon, *Game Theory for Applied Economists* (Princeton University Press, Princeton, 1992); James D. Morrow, *Game Theory for Political Scientists* (Princeton University Press, Princeton, 1994); Shaun P. Hargreaves Heap and Yanis Varoufakis, *Game Theory: A Critical Introduction* (Routledge, London, 1995); R. Duncan Luce and Howard Raiffa, *Games and Decisions: Introduction and Critical Survey* (1957).

[26] See e.g., Pierre Allan and Christian Schmidt (eds.), *Game Theory and International Relations* (Edward Elgar Publishing Company, Vermont, 1994), p. 1; Steven J. Brams, *Game Theory and Politics* (The Free Press, New York, 1975), pp. 13–16. On the prospects and pitfalls of employing game theory to analyze international settings, see Stephan Haggards and Beth A. Simmons, "Theories of International Regimes" (1987) 40 *International Organization* 491, 493–94; James E. Dougherty and Robert L. Pfaltzgraff, *Contending Theories of International Relations: A Comprehensive Survey* (5th ed., Longman, New York, 2001), pp. 568–71. For a game theoretical analysis of the Middle Eastern environmental system, see Moshe Hirsch, "Game Theory, International Law, and Future Environmental Cooperation in the Middle East" (1999) 27 *Denver J. Int'l L. and Policy* 75.

[27] Oscar Morgenstern, "Game Theory: Theoretical Aspects" in David L. Sills (ed.), *International Encyclopedia of the Social Sciences*, Vol. 6 (1968), p. 62; Robert J. Auman, "Game Theory," in John Eatwell, Murray Milgate and Peter Newman (eds.), *The New Palgrave: Game Theory* (Macmillan Press, 1987), p. 1.

[28] As elaborated in Anne-Marie Slaughter's contribution (see Chapter 2 at pp. 37–38), each of these theoretical approaches also include specific theories that rely on the Constructivist paradigm. On the rational variant of the Institutionalist approach, see Robert O. Keohane, "International Institutions: Two Approaches" (1988) 32 *Int'l Studies Q.* 379. On the latter subject, see also, Robert Axelrod and Robert O. Keohane, "Achieving Cooperation Under Anarchy: Strategies and Institutions" (1985) 38 *World Politics* 226; Barbara Koremenos, Charles Lipson and Duncan Snidal, "The Rational Design of International Institutions" (2001) 55 *International Organization* 761.

[29] John Gerard Ruggie, *Constructing the World Polity* (Routledge, London, 1998), pp. 9–11.

In accordance with the rational choice model, compliance with or violation of international norms is dependent upon a comparison of the expected outcomes resulting from these alternative courses of action. In each case, individual policy-makers examine the existing incentives (both positive and negative) for a particular course of action and the period in which they are expected to materialize. Thus, national decision-makers are assumed to calculate the positive and negative effects of compliance with or breach of a particular norm and, consequently, adopt the strategy that best serves the interests of their respective states. The perception of international rules as an instrument to solve shared problems, as well as the rational view of compliance, led scholars to treat such cases of common need as "collective action"[30] problems. Consequently, theoretical tools developed in game theory are increasingly employed by scholars of international relations and international law to analyze the prospects of cooperation in particular international settings.[31]

Models and concepts of game theory are valuable tools that would enable us to analyze systematically the impact of the process of globalization on the prospects of compliance with international norms. The widely used term "cooperation" in game theoretical analysis of collective action problems may also refer to compliance with agreed rules that are expected to further the interests of the involved parties.

There are numerous models of collective action, each presenting a different payoff structure. The models that are considered to reflect the most prevalent patterns of state behavior in the international system are the Prisoner's Dilemma (PD), the Assurance Game, the Coordination Game and the Game of Chicken. This section does not aim to present a detailed analysis of these models but rather to present the predominant characteristics of each model and to highlight the factors that affect compliance in each setting.

---

[30] Collective action occurs when the efforts of two or more individuals are needed to achieve a certain outcome, typically, furthering the interests or well-being of the group. Todd Sandler, *Collective Action: Theory and Applications* (University of Michigan Press, Ann Harbor, 1992), p. 1. See also John Elster, "Rationality, Morality and Collective Action" (1985) 96 *Ethics* 136, 139; John Elster, *The Cement of Society* (Cambridge University Press, 1989), p. 17 *et seq.*

[31] See e.g., Eyal Benvenisti, "Collective Action in the Utilization of Shared Freshwater: The Challenges of International Water Resource Law" (1996) 90 *Am. J. Int'l L.* 384; Hirsch, "Game Theory, International Law, and Future Environmental Cooperation."

The Prisoner's Dilemma[32]

This is certainly the most famous model in the social sciences. The model attracted considerable attention from both game theorists and scientists in various disciplines because its implications apply to a wide range of social phenomena (including the Tragedy of the Commons).[33] The Prisoner's Dilemma (PD) well represents situations characterized by externalities, i.e., settings in which the parties are able to externalize a significant part of the negative impact of their behavior to other parties.[34] An analysis of the PD reveals that international settings that present strong features of this model are susceptible to collective action failure, i.e., violation of agreed rules that generates undesirable consequences for all parties (*Pareto-inferior equilibrium*).

Several factors are likely to enhance the prospects of compliance in settings characterized by features of the PD model. The most prominent are iteration of the interaction among the involved parties ("repeated game")[35] and the capacity of the parties to operate retaliatory measures.[36] Effective countermeasures frequently presuppose reliable information indicating that the other party violated a particular norm. In addition, inducing compliance by threats of retaliation necessitates that the parties will not significantly under-estimate future losses or gains. The variable that represents the current value of future gains

---

[32] On the story that illustrates the Prisoner's Dilemma, see Anatol Rapoport and Albert M. Chammab, *Prisoner's Dilemma: A Study in Conflict and Cooperation* (University of Michigan Press, Ann Arbor, 1965), pp. 24–25; Anatol Rapoport, "Prisoner's Dilemma" in Eatwell, Milgate and Newman, *The New Palgrave* p. 198; Luce and Raiffa, *Games and Decisions*, pp. 94–95.

[33] Garret Hardin, "The Tragedy of the Commons" (1968) 162 *Science* 1243. On the Tragedy of the Commons as a PD, see Thomas C. Schelling, *Micromotives and Macrobehavior* (Norton, New York, 1978), pp. 110–15; Duncan Snidal, "Coordination Versus Prisoner's Dilemma: Implications for International Cooperation and Regimes" (1985) 79 *Am. Political Science Rev.* 923, 929.

[34] Consequently, it is not surprising that the model was applied to environmental collective action problems. See e.g., Benvenisti, "Collective Action in the Utilization of Shared Freshwater"; Hirsch, "Game Theory, International Law, and Future Environmental Cooperation."

[35] Mutual cooperative behavior is expected in infinite iterated games or in finite games in which the players are not certain when the last play will occur.

[36] See e.g., Robert Axelrod, *The Evolution of Cooperation* (Basic Books, New York, 1984), pp. 27–54; Robert Axelrod, "The Emergence of Cooperation Among Egoists" (1981) 75 *Am. Political Science Rev.* 306; Rapoport, "Prisoner's Dilemma," 200–2.

and losses is the "discount factor."[37] Generally, the likelihood of compliance in PD settings is increased together with the increase of the discount rate.

The Assurance Game[38]

The Assurance game represents less conflictual situations than in the PD and, generally, the prospects of compliance in such settings are better than in PD situations. Still, compliance is certainly not assured in Assurance situations. Attainment of the optimal outcomes in the Assurance game requires all parties to comply with the agreed rule. Parties in such settings will comply if assured that the other parties will also follow the particular norm. A party is not expected to conform to the particular rule if it is not certain whether the other parties will comply or not, and particularly if it is determined to avoid the worst outcomes (arising when it complies while the other breaches the norm).[39]

The characteristics of the Assurance Game lead to the conclusion that gaining information regarding the other parties' planned course of action is crucial to compliance in such settings.[40] Parties to Assurance situations attempt to gather information regarding the expected behavior of the other parties. In iterated situations, a party may learn about the other parties' intentions from their past record in the same or similar settings. Contingent strategies are also likely to enhance the prospects of compliance in Assurance situations.[41]

---

[37] The *discount factor* represents the current value of a dollar to be generated at some later stage. The discount factor (usually written as 'δ') falls between 0 and 1 and its relation to the interest rate (r) is $\delta = 1/(1 + r)$. Gibbons, *Game Theory for Applied Economists*, pp. 68, 88; Morrow, *Game Theory for Political Scientists*, p. 38.

[38] On the story that illustrates the Assurance Game, see Drew Fudenberg and Jean Tirole, *Game Theory* (MIT Press, Massachusetts, 1991), p. 3; Russell Hardin, *Collective Action* (Johns Hopkins University Press, Baltimore, 1982), pp. 167–68.

[39] Fudenberge and Tirole, *Game Theory*, p. 20.

[40] Some scholars have therefore argued that the Assurance Game does not constitute a genuine collective action problem and presents only an "information problem": Elster, "Rationality, Morality and Collective Action," 140. See also Michael Taylor, *The Possibility of Cooperation* (Cambridge University Press, Cambridge, 1987), pp. 19, 39; Arthur A. Stein, *Why Nations Cooperate: Circumstances and Choice in International Relations* (Cornell University Press, Ithaca, 1990), p. 30.

[41] See e.g., Sandler, *Collective Action*, p. 83; Hugh Ward, "Testing the Waters: Taking Risks to Gain Reassurance in Public Goods Games" (1988), 33 *J. Conflict Resolution* 274.

The Coordination Game[42]

As in the Assurance and PD Games, all parties in the Coordination Game have to comply with a common rule in order to attain the optimal outcome. The central difference between these game models is that while the Assurance and the PD Games present only one optimal equilibrium position, the Coordination Game presents multiple Pareto equilibria over which the players have divergent preferences. The parties in Coordination settings are interested in "meeting" each other in some agreed rule but have conflicting preferences over the particular agreed rule. This is the case, for instance, in setting common standards for international communication, agreeing on emergency procedures for civil aviation or formulating an international system for the classification of goods for customs purposes.[43]

Such settings represent a clear distributional problem[44] that impedes the process of shaping agreed rules. Furthermore, in contrast to the PD and Assurance Games, the iteration of the same interaction increases the magnitude of the distributional problem, and thus, makes it harder to attain agreement on the desirable rule. But once the parties arrive at an agreement on a particular rule, there are no significant incentives to deviate from the coordinated rule, and the norm is considered to be "self-enforcing."[45]

The Game of Chicken

The unique feature of the Game of Chicken[46] (or hawk-dove) is that the optimal collective outcome is not necessarily attained by mutual cooperative action; the best result may be generated by either unilateral or mutual

---

[42] On the story that illustrates the Coordination Game, see Fudenberg and Tirole, *Game Theory*, p. 18; Luce and Raiffa, *Games and Decisions*, p. 91.

[43] For more situations presenting the features of the Coordination Game, see James D. Morrow, "Modeling the Forms of International Cooperation: Distribution versus Information" (1994) 48 *International Organization* 387, 390–93, 409–13; Snidal, "Coordination Versus Prisoner's Dilemma," 932; Stein, *Why Nations Cooperate*, pp. 42–43; Kenneth W. Abbott, "Modern International Relations Theory: A Prospectus for International Lawyers" (1989) 14 *Yale J. Int'l L.* 335.

[44] Snidal, "Coordination Versus Prisoner's Dilemma," 931–32; Morrow, "Modeling the Forms of International Cooperation," 387, 388.

[45] Snidal, "Coordination Versus Prisoner's Dilemma," 932; Stein, *Why Nations Cooperate*, p. 42. On bargaining problems that arise from distributive difficulties, see James D. Fearon, "Bargaining, Enforcement, and International Cooperation" (1998) 52 *International Organization* 269.

[46] On the story that accompanies the Game of Chicken, see Brams, *Game Theory and Politics*, pp. 39–40; Morrow, *Game Theory for Political Scientists*, p. 93.

cooperative behavior. The competitive character of this game is exacerbated by the fact that, as in the PD, an individual player prefers to defect while the other cooperates. Non-cooperative behavior may, however, be avoided because mutual defection yields the worst payoffs for both players. The parties may be interested in avoiding the worst result by mutual compliance, but this strategy is unstable: when a player anticipates that the other is going to cooperate, he/she has an incentive to defect and gain the best outcome for himself/herself.[47] On the other hand, when a player expects the other to defect, he/she has an incentive to cooperate and avoid the worst result.

A party in infinite iterated games may make credible threats by employing contingent strategies, and compel the other players to cooperate. The effectiveness of such threats is dependent upon the parties' discount factor.[48] Thus, the capacity to operate retaliatory measures and sufficiently high discount factors are likely to promote the prospects of compliance in Chicken situations.

Summary of the factors affecting compliance

The above analysis of collective action models allows us to summarize the impact of the following factors on the prospects of compliance in a wide range of international situations:

(1) Iteration of the interactions among the involved parties increases the prospects of compliance (see the PD, Assurance Game, as well as the Chicken Game).
(2) The capacity to operate retaliatory measures increases the prospects of compliance (see the PD, Assurance Game, and the Chicken Game).
(3) Information regarding the behavior of other parties is crucial for increasing the prospect of compliance. The operation of effective retaliatory measures is dependent upon reliable information. In addition, information may well lead the parties to comply with agreed rules (even without the threat of sanctions) in Assurance situations.
(4) Retaliatory measures, which are crucial to compliance in numerous situations (see above) are also dependent upon the parties' "discount factor" regarding future gains or losses. The likelihood of compliance in such situations grows with the increase of the discount rate.

---

[47] Taylor, *The Possibility of Cooperation*, p. 354; Barton L. Lipman, "Cooperation Among Egoists in Prisoners' Dilemma and Chicken Games" (1986) 51 *Public Choice* 315, 316; Brams, *Game Theory and Politics*, p. 40.
[48] Lipman, "Cooperation among Egoists," 323; Taylor, *The Possibility of Cooperation*, p. 367.

The sociological perspective and compliance with international norms

The second paradigm we shall employ to analyze compliance is distinctly different from the rational choice model. The sociological perspective is generally a structure-oriented approach and considers social structures as irreducibly causal factors that strongly affect personal behavior. Thus, basic units are collective entities rather than individuals. As stated by Emile Durkheim, society is more than the individuals who compose it; society has a life of its own that stretches beyond our personal experience.[49] The central assumption of the classic sociological approach is that individual choices are largely shaped by social factors. Accordingly, individual preferences are of lesser importance in understanding human behavior in society.[50]

Social inquiry emphasizes that norms and roles constrain human behavior. A role is defined as a typified response to a typified expectation, and roles are constituted by the expectations of the members of a society that other persons will behave in a certain manner in a given situation. Under this conception, "roles encode norms, and conformity to norms becomes a motive of behavior."[51] The readiness to abide by norms is dependent to a large measure upon a process of internalization of the relevant social norm, and not upon a calculation whether such behavior is profitable or not.[52] Exploring the social process from a more personal view, well-known experiments in social psychology revealed that people are inclined to conform in order to avoid rejection and gain acceptance. Such experiments also show that people often pay an emotional price for deviation from social norms.[53]

---

[49] Emile Durkheim, *Sociology and Psychology* (Free Press, Glencoe, IL, 1953), p. 55.
[50] Martin Hollis, *The Philosophy of Social Science* (Cambridge University Press, Cambridge, 1994), pp. 112–13; Heap et al., *The Theory of Choice*, pp. 63–64; Macionis, *Sociology*, pp. 4, 25, 115. The importance of the social structure is emphasized by the "structural functional" approach in sociology literature (e.g. Talcott Parsons, see Derek Layder, *Understanding Social Theory* (Sage Publication, London, 1994), pp. 15–33). Individual interpretations are emphasized by the "symbolic interactionist" stream in sociological literature, see pp. 57–74 and Ken Plummer, "Symbolic Interactionism in the Twentieth Century" in Layder, *Understanding Social Theory*, pp. 223–251. See in general on the underlying relationships between individual and society (or "agency and structure") in sociological literature, Layder, *Understanding Social Theory*, pp. 1–7.
[51] Heap et al., *Theory of Choice*, p. 63. See on "norms" in Talcott Parsons writings, Layder, *Understanding Social Theory*, pp. 14–15.
[52] Heap et al., *Theory of Choice*, p. 68.
[53] David G. Myers, *Social Psychology* (6th ed., McGraw-Hill College, Boston, 1999), p. 237.

Social Constructivism, a relatively new stream in international relations theory, developed out of the critique of the rational choice strand in international politics.[54] The Constructivist approach is largely consistent with the sociological perspective. Unlike the rational choice paradigm, social Constructivism does not take interests, preferences and strategies of the parties as given. Rather, these important motivations to behavior are constructed in a social interactive process.[55]

The social Constructivist theory emphasizes the dynamic aspect of social concepts (including interests and preferences). As Adler explains, acceptable social behavior and values may be changed in a cognitive evolutionary process. Cognitive evolution includes three dimensions: innovation, selection and diffusion.[56] Ideas, beliefs and behavior are studied from other people and the source of social learning lies in the ability of groups to transmit to each other the products of their respective cognitive experience.[57]

As to compliance, under the Constructivist approach, decision-makers are motivated by impersonal social factors such as values, norms and cultural practices, rather than a calculation of material interests.[58] Legal

[54] On the origins of Costructivism in international relations theory, see Stefano Guzzini, "A Reconstruction of Constructivism in International Relations" (2000) 6 *European J. Int'l Relations* 147, 150–55; Ruggie, *Constructing the World Polity*, pp. 11–14.

[55] Alexander Wendt, *Social Theory of International Politics* (Cambridge University Press, 1999), pp. 309, 135–139; Emanuel Adler, "Cognitive Evolution: A Dynamic Approach for the Study of International Relations and their Progress" in Emanuel Adler and Beverly Crawford (eds.), *Progress in Postwar International Relations* (Columbia University Press, New York, 1991), p. 43. Martha Finnemore, "Construction of Norms of Humanitarian Intervention" in Peter J. Katzenstein (ed.), *The Culture of National Security: Norms and Identity in World Politics* (Columbia University Press, New York, 1996), pp. 153, 154–61; Steve Smith, "Reflectivist and Constructivist Approaches to International Theory" (2000) 54 *International Organization* 242. See also Harold Hongju Koh, "Why Do Nations Obey International Law?" (1997) 106 *Yale L. J.* 2599, 2633–34. See also chapter 2 at pp. 34–37; Ruggie, *Constructing the World Polity*, pp. 13–25.

[56] "Innovation" refers to the creation of new expectations and values that become collective and accepted by the group. "Selection" refers to a political process that determines the extent to which values and expectations are effectively adopted by the group. "Diffusion" refers to the spread of expectations and values to other states. Adler, "Cognitive Evolutions," pp. 55–56; Emanuel Adler and Peter M. Haas, "Epistemic Communities, World Order, and the Creation of a Reflective Research Program" (1992) 46 *International Organization* 367, 375–85; Dougherty and Pfaltzgraff, *Contending Theories of International Relations*, p. 163.

[57] Adler, "Cognitive Evolution," 50–54; Dougherty and Pfaltzgraff, *Contending Theories*, pp. 167–68. On international socialization, see also Guzzini, "A Reconstruction of Constructivism"; Jeffrey T. Checkel, "Why Comply? Social Learning and European Identity Change" (2001) 55 *International Organization* 553, 560–64.

[58] Robert O. Keohane, "International Institutions: Two Approaches" (1988) 32 *Int'l Studies Q.* 379, 381; Adler, "Cognitive Evolution," 49–51; Vaughn P. Shannon, "Norms are What States Make Them: The Political Psychology of Norms Violation" 44 *Int'l Studies Q.*

obligations are perceived in this context as social standards of appropriate behavior that operate in an intersubjective framework. Thus, state behavior is subjectively interpreted by other states, and a judgment whether a particular state's conduct constitutes a violation or compliance is not only an objective judgment but also an intersubjective appraisal.[59] Furthermore, the essential components of the rational game, i.e., state interests and the range of legitimate strategies available to the parties, are themselves largely shaped by the norms prevailing in a particular society.[60]

States' decision-makers, as part of their relevant identity group, learn the prevailing norms in their group and the expectations of appropriate behavior through the process of "socialization."[61] International socialization refers to the process that is directed toward a state's internalization of the constitutive beliefs, norms and practices institutionalized in its international environment.[62] International socialization is accomplished through state emulation of other successful states, which are praised for conforming to prevailing norms, or condemned for deviating from them. Occasionally, the "peer group" exerts its influence by diplomatic measures, economic pressure or even by social isolation.[63]

In line with the social psychological and sociological perspectives, the proponents of the Constructivist approach argue that decision-makers

---

293, 297–98; Adler, "Cognitive Evolution," 48–52; Finnemore, "Construction of Norms of Humanitarian Intervention," 157–58; Martha Finnemore, *National Interests in International Society* (Cornell University Press, Ithaca, 1996), pp. 1–13; Simmons, "Compliance with International Agreements," 88. On the Constructivist conceptions of international law in general, see Jutta Brunee and Stephen Toope, "International Law and Constructivism" (2000) 39 *Columbia J. Transnational L.* 19, 38–42.

[59] Simmons, "Compliance with International Agreements," 86–88.

[60] Finnemore, "Construction of Norms of Humanitarian Intervention," 154–61; Shannon, "Norms are What States Make Them," 8–9. On some common features shared by the Rational and the Constructivist approaches, see Checkel, "Why Comply?," pp. 558–59; Kingsbury, "The Concept of Compliance," 358–64.

[61] Adler, "Cognitive Evolution," 58–60; Shannon, "Norms are What States Make Them," 9; Finnemore, "National Interests," 128–29. The term "socialization" refers in sociological literature to the process by which the society transmits norms and values to new members of a group of individuals; see Macionis, *Sociology*, p. 144.

[62] Frank Schimmelfenning, "International Socialization in the New Europe: Rational Action in an Institutional Environment" (2000) 6 *European J. Int'l Relations* 109. See also Martha Finnemore and Kathryn Sikkink, "International Norm Dynamics and Political Change" (1998) 52 *International Organization* 887, 902.

[63] Finnemore and Sikkink, "International Norm Dynamics," 902–4; Shannon, "Norms are What States Make Them," 10–11. On the important role of group influence in compliance with *domestic* norms, see Tom R. Tyler, *Why People Obey the Law* (Yale University Press, New Haven, 1990), pp. 22–27. For a Constructivist analysis of state compliance with the Council of Europe's rules regarding dual citizenship, see Sheckel, "Why Comply?" 567–78.

are routinely inclined to obey international norms, and norm conformity is the default option in the international system. Hence, "compliance is the normal organizational assumption."[64] Koh explains the impact of habitual compliance upon the process of shaping states' interests:

> Nations thus obey international rules not just because of sophisticated calculations about how compliance or noncompliance will affect their interests, but because a repeated habit of obedience remakes their interests so that they come to value rule compliance.[65]

The Constructivist approach so well explains compliance as the normal course of events that it may appear hard to understand any breach of norms. Still, such cases do exist in the reality of the international system. Certain social factors may explain why states violate international norms in some cases. These factors include vague norms, conflict of norms, social detachment and inadequate socialization processes.

Occasionally, non-compliance may derive from vague norms as where the social message encoded in a particular norm is subject to different interpretations.[66] Violations of international norms may also arise from the fact that national decision-makers are members of two (or more) social groups. National policy-makers play a role in both their respective national social systems as well as in the international system.[67] The occurrence of "role strain"[68] is not rare and national decision-makers occasionally face a conflict between the norms prevailing in the two groups. Such a conflict may lead national decision-makers to conform to the national norm and breach the international one.[69]

Decision-makers may also violate international norms when they feel socially alienated from the source of these norms. Sociologists explain that social attachment or detachment is important for compliance. Strong

---

[64] Abram Chayes and Antonia Handler Chayes, "On Compliance," (1993) 47 *International Organization* 175, 179; James G. March and Johan P. Olsen, *Rediscovering Institutions* (Free Press, New York, 1989), p. 21.
[65] Koh, "Why Do Nations Obey International Law?," 2634.
[66] Shannon, "Norms are What States Make Them," 12.
[67] For a rational choice analysis of the parallel phenomenon in the context of conclusion of international agreements, see Robert D. Putnam, "Diplomacy and Domestic Politics: The Logic of Two-Level Games" (1988) 42 *International Organization* 427.
[68] In sociological literature, the term "role strain" refers to incompatibility among roles corresponding to a single status: Macionis, *Sociology*, p. 153.
[69] See also Shannon, "Norms are What States Make Them," 299–300; Andrew P. Cortell and James W. Davis, "When International and Domestic Norms Collide: Japan and the GATT/WTO," paper submitted to the Annual Meeting of the International Studies Association, Chicago, February 21–24, 2001, pp. 8–10.

attachments with the group encourage conformity, while weak relationships leave people freer to deviate.[70] Thus, when a group of states is detached and placed in the periphery of the international community, or worse, when such a group perceives itself as an "outgroup," its members are likely to feel aversion towards norms shaped by the "ingroup" states.[71] Parallel literature in international law and international relations underscores the importance of legitimacy as a factor that intensifies or weakens the sense of obligation towards international norms.[72] Naturally, social detachment of a state is likely to diminish significantly the legitimacy of international norms.

Non-compliance may also arise from an insufficient or inadequate socialization process. Thus, for instance, inexperienced decision-makers who have not fully socialized into the international community are less likely to internalize the prevailing norms of the international system. The prior social environment of a decision-maker, particularly in the formative period, may also affect the prospects of compliance. Sociological studies show that any person's tendency towards conformity or deviance also depends upon the relative frequency of association with others who encourage conventional behavior or norm violation.[73] Thus, for instance, policy-makers who were involved in persistent international violence during the course of their political socialization processes are less likely to rapidly internalize the international norm prohibiting the use of force.

The impact of globalization processes on the prospects of compliance

Equipped with the knowledge of the principal features of globalization, and of the main factors that affect compliance in accordance with the rational choice and the sociological perspectives, we can approach the task of analyzing the likely effects of globalization upon the prospects of compliance. The following analysis presupposes that the process of

---

[70] Macionis, *Sociology*, p. 213. See also Shannon, "Norms are What States Make Them," 17.
[71] "Outgroup" is defined in sociological literature as a social group toward which one feels competition or opposition. The term "ingroup" refers to a social group commanding a member's esteem and loyalty. Macionis, *Sociology*, p. 181. See also Henry Taigfel, "Social Psychology of Intergroup Relations" (1982) 33 *Annual Rev. Psychology* 1, 1–2.
[72] See Thomas M. Franck, *The Power of Legitimacy Among Nations* (Oxford University Press, Oxford, 1999), p. 3; Simmons, "Compliance with International Agreements," 87–89.
[73] See on "Southerlands differential association theory" in Macionis, *Sociology*, pp. 212–13.

globalization will proceed, though the pace of this process should certainly not be assumed. In order to address the question of compliance in the process of globalization, we shall first employ the theoretical tools of the rational choice model and analyze its consequences. We will examine the same question using the concepts of the sociological approach.

Rational choice analysis

Iteration

One of the hallmarks of globalization is the widening and deepening of interactions among states and peoples worldwide.[74] The intensification of interactions clearly increases the ratio of "iterated" settings in the international system. As analyzed above, iteration enhances the prospects of compliance with international norms.

Retaliation

An additional prominent feature of globalization is the increasing levels of interdependence among states in a variety of spheres (economy, health, environment, etc.).[75] Generally, the rapid increase of interdependence in numerous domains expands the possibility for states to employ retaliatory measures against states that breach their obligations. In some cases, however, the growing interdependence may also constrain the choice of some states in implementing some countermeasures.[76] The notable increase of interdependence not only increases the possibilities of retaliation within numerous spheres but also expands the capacity to form *linkages* between different domains, thus enabling cross-sector retaliations. Where retaliation is not possible or desirable in a particular domain, the formation of a linkage between different spheres widens the space available for contingent strategies. This is the case, for instance, with the establishment of a linkage between environmental protection and international trade,[77] or with the linkage between human rights protection and international trade.

---

[74] See p. 00.   [75] See e.g., "Measuring Globalization," 57–58.
[76] As analyzed in detail below, as interdependence intensifies, part of the negative effects generated by retaliatory measures may also affect the retaliating state itself. In such cases, the threats of retaliation may be considered as less credible.
[77] See e.g., Article 4 of the Montreal Protocol on Substances that Deplete the Ozone Layer (1987) 26 *ILM* 1550.

As discussed above,[78] widening the possibilities of retaliation in a given area, or cross-sector retaliation in several areas, enhances the prospects of compliance with international norms.

Information

Rapid technological progress, particularly in the spheres of communication and information technology, increases the amount of information available to decision-makers regarding the conduct of other states. New, sophisticated instruments (e.g., remote sensing satellites) make it much harder to conceal violations of international rules.[79] Significantly greater (and more reliable) information regarding the behavior of other parties[80] enables states and international organizations to operate more effective retaliatory measures against states that breach international norms.

The improved mechanisms for gathering and disseminating information are of even greater importance to compliance in situations where retaliatory measures are not indispensable for compliance. As discussed above, the flow of reliable information regarding the other parties' behavior is crucial to compliance in Assurance settings (even without a threat of countermeasures).[81]

Rebounded externalities and structural change

The above analysis of the impact of globalization on compliance is largely based on current structures of prevalent collective action settings. Deeper analysis, however, reveals that changes engendered by the process of globalization are also likely to generate significant *structural change* of current international settings. The following analysis indicates a gradual trend of increasing the ratio of international settings that present features of the

---

[78] See p. 178.
[79] See e.g., on the American satellite data that revealed the cause for the destruction of Sibirian Airlines aircraft in October 2001, Sabrina Tavernise and Michael Wines, "Accident Suspected in Black Sea Crash," *New York Times*, October 6, 2001; Sabrina Tavernise, "Ukrainian Shift Stance on the Cause of Air Crash," *New York Times*, October 7, 2001.
[80] On the impact of transparency methods that reveal information regarding states' behavior on compliance with international environmental agreements, see the contribution of Edith Brown Weiss (chapter 6) at pp. 146–47.
[81] In addition, it should be noted that iteration itself generates more information regarding the past behavior of the parties in similar situations. As discussed above, the amount of iterated interactions is increased in the process of globalization. Thus, in Assurance situations, states in the age of globalization are more likely to have indications regarding the expected behavior of other parties in the international system.

Assurance Game. This change implies important ramifications for the prospects of compliance with international norms.

First, let us very briefly highlight the unique properties of the PD and Assurance Games regarding the parties' capacity to externalize or internalize the effects of their conduct. Both models involve some externalities for other players and the difference in this regard depends upon *the extent to which the acting party is affected by its own behavior*. While in the PD Game the acting party externalizes a considerable part of the effects of its conduct to other parties, the acting party in the Assurance Game does experience the effects that flow from its own behavior.

This difference may be illustrated by two common types of settings in the sphere of international environment. In both cases, the parties share natural resources. A party in the setting that presents strong features of the PD Game is able to externalize to the other party a significant part of the pollution resulting from its industrial activities. This is the case, for instance, where two states share several common natural resources (rivers, seas, etc.), but in each shared resource, one state is the "upstream party" and the other is the "downstream party."[82] The second setting presents strong features of the Assurance Game. Here the parties are not able to externalize a significant part of the pollution. Thus, most of the pollutants emanating from each state *generate negative results for both parties*. This is the case, for instance, where two states share a small lake of freshwater or narrow closed sea,[83] and every significant pollution event generates harm for both states.

The process of globalization intensifies worldwide interconnectedness, and states are increasingly affected by the activities of other states; thus the world seems to be "shrinking."[84] This process certainly increases the number of international settings that generate externalities, and the domain of "internal affairs" is gradually curtailed. As states draw closer, and interconnectedness deepens, an increasingly larger part of externalities rebounds and is felt within the acting states themselves. In a shrinking world, the acting state finds that its externalities are more likely to rebound in a variety of ways that generate effects within its own territory. Thus, while the amount of international externalities grows in the process of globalization, an increasing part of the externalities are expected to be reflected and affect the interests of the acting states.

---

[82] As discussed at p. 178, the capacity of the parties to operate retaliatory measures is of major importance for compliance in such settings.

[83] See e.g., the positions of Israel and Jordan regarding the Gulf of Aqaba; Hirsch, "Game Theory, International Law, and Future Environmental Cooperation," 94–100.

[84] See p. 169.

This trend of rebounded externalities is illustrated in various spheres of the modern international system. Thus, erecting trade barriers by a state is often designed to inhibit import from other states. Such actions generate externalities and harm the economies of other exporting states. Still, with the dramatic expansion of international investment, such a policy is also likely to negatively affect investors of the protectionist states that purchased factories within the exporting states.[85] In the sphere of labor rights, externalization of the process of manufacturing of numerous products from developed states to low labor cost states also generates a process of lowering labor standards within the developed states themselves.[86] The process of rebounded externalities is more likely to take place where the level of mutual interdependence is intensified, particularly where the interdependence relationship involves more than one domain (e.g., both in the spheres of economics and environment).

Hence, the process of globalization generates a growing amount of international externalities, but an increasingly larger part of the resulting externalities rebound and are felt within the acting states. The increasing trend of reflected externalities implies a structural change that is likely to change the apportionment of the prevalent international settings between the PD and Assurance models. Bearing in mind that the PD model represents significant externalization rates, and that the Assurance Game presents significant internalization rates, the above trend of rebounded externalities indicates a structural change from PD situations to Assurance settings.[87] Thus, if the process of globalization proceeds, the ratio of settings belonging to the Assurance type is likely to

---

[85] See on this trend (and similar processes), Helen V. Milner, *Resisting Protectionism* (Princeton University Press, 1988), pp. 18–24.

[86] See e.g., Rodrik, *Has Globalization Gone Too Far?*, p. 13.

[87] An additional possibility to be taken into account is that the process of rebounded externalities will change PD situations to settings in which the parties' dominant strategy is to refrain from actions that generate externalities (whether the other party externalizes or not). This strategy of mutual refraining from action will be materialized where alternative strategies of mutual cooperation are expected to generate inferior outcomes. Mutual cooperative strategies, however, may often offer superior outcomes to both parties. Mutual cooperative strategies frequently allow the parties to undertake their beneficial activities while complying with agreed precautions that significantly diminish (or eliminate) externalized damages. The various processes of globalization, particularly the increasing interaction among states as well as rapid technological innovations, are expected to produce additional mutual cooperative equilibria, thus increasing the amount of Coordination and Assurance settings (rather than Deadlock situations). It should be noted that Assurance Games involve some coordination features since each party to the Assurance Game prefers a cooperative strategy only as long as the other party is expected to do the same.

I am grateful to Duncan Snidal who brought this issue to my attention, provided some explanations, and discussed them with me.

increase at the expense of settings characterized by features of the PD model.

The ramifications of this structural change for the prospects of compliance with international norms are significant. First, as discussed above, the prospects for compliance in Assurance settings are better (than in PD) and compliance by all parties is the optimal alternative for all parties in such situations.[88] Second, information has a crucial role in Assurance settings, and the prospects of compliance are dependent to a significant measure upon the information available to the parties regarding the other parties' behavior. As discussed above, the process of globalization generates more reliable information regarding activities undertaken in other states.

To sum up this section, the combined effect of the structural change towards increasing the compliance rate in Assurance settings in the international system and the increase of information regarding states' behavior, indicates that the prospects of compliance are likely to be enhanced through the process of globalization.

Sociological analysis

Social factors may affect compliance in a variety of ways but we focus here on only two principal social processes that are likely to have a significant impact upon compliance in the course of globalization: conflict between domestic and international norms and socio-economic stratification.

Conflict between domestic and international norms

One of the important motivations to violate international norms stems from a conflict of national and international norms. National decision-makers are members of both their own domestic group as well as of the international society. Naturally, such a dual membership may expose decision-makers to a "role strain" that finds its expression, inter alia, in divergent norms that prevail in the two different communities.[89] Such conflicts occasionally lead national decision-makers to violate international norms.[90]

---

[88] It should be noted that even in cases where the process of rebounded externalities leads both parties to refrain from the externalizing activity (see note 87), such a strategy does not necessarily increase violations of international rules.
[89] On "role strain" and its impact on compliance, see p. 182.
[90] See e.g., Davis, "When International and Domestic Norms Collide."

Norms reflect to a significant degree the societies from which they arise, and the difference between international and national norms reflect, inter alia, the different social and cultural features prevailing in the respective systems. Consequently, we can generally posit that the greater the social and cultural diversity between domestic and international systems, the greater the prospects for non-compliance with international norms. Or, vice versa, the greater the similarity between domestic and international socio-cultural systems, the better the prospects for compliance with international norms.

Sociologists have expressed the opinion that globalization processes, and particularly the increasing interconnectedness between societies, lessen the cultural diversity of the contemporary world.[91] The unprecedented technological capacity to disseminate information leads to a situation in which the level of cultural diffusion has never been greater than it is today.[92] This trend should certainly not lead to a conclusion that the world is approaching a state of a single "global culture" or "cultural homogeneity."

Sociological investigations also reveal that the process of globalization exerts pressure toward both unity and fragmentation of different communities. The term "community" has several meanings[93] but two are paramount in this context: community as a territorial concept and community as a relational concept. The first sense of community refers to *territorial communities* that are located in a specific geographic location with borders, etc. Community in the *relational sense* refers to people who are tied together by webs of communication, friendship, association or mutual support. Relational communities may be geographically scattered and they include, for instance, the gay community, the Jewish community, the academic community, etc. In the past, there was a considerable overlap between these two sorts of communities since people lived, worked, traded and interacted in other ways with other people from the same village or town. This considerable rate of overlapping between the two types of communities is fundamentally changed in the process

---

[91] See e.g., Macionis, *Sociology*, p. 66. See also Andrew Mason, *Community, Solidarity and Belonging: Levels of Community and their Normative Significance* (Cambridge University Press, Cambridge, 2000), p. 178. On Emile Durkheim's view that interdependence enhances solidarity, see Macionis, *Sociology*, pp. 116–17; Roger Cotterrel, *The Sociology of Law* (2nd ed., Butterworths, London, 1992), p. 98.
[92] Macionis, *Sociology*, p. 82. See also Malcolm Waters, *Globalization* (Routledge, London, 1995), pp. 148–50.
[93] See e.g., Mason, *Community, Solidarity and Belonging*, pp. 17–41.

of globalization. The increasingly globalized and mobile society presents less identity between relational and territorial communities.[94]

Sociological analysis reveals that the process of globalization generates increased penetration of external cultural features into the *territorial communities*.[95] This process also supports the establishment and sustaining of *relational communities*. The revolution in communication and transportation enables actors to reach geographically dispersed audiences and allows more individuals to establish "cultural enclaves," and confine most of their interactions to those who belong to these communities.[96]

The processes of unity and fragmentation in territorial and relational communities are of paramount importance for the future development of international law (substantial and procedural norms alike). In terms of the issue of compliance, it is important to mention that the predominant subjects of international law, at present, are states, i.e., territorial communities. Most analysts of globalization agree that states are likely to continue to play a central role in the international system. Here we also have to bear in mind the above process of lessening socio-cultural diversity among states in the course of globalization.

A combination of the above analyses leads to the conclusion that the likelihood of conflict between national and international norms is expected to decrease in the process of globalization. Bearing in mind that the extent of socio-cultural difference affects the prospects of conflict of norms, it is clear that the trend of lessening socio-cultural diversity among states indicates that the likelihood of a conflict between national and international norms is expected to decline. Consequently, the analysis of the factor of conflict of norms indicates that the above two social processes are expected to enhance the prospects of compliance with international norms.

Socio-economic stratification

The pace of globalization is considerably uneven in various regions of the world, and the benefits of this process are largely felt in the industrialized states.[97] Despite tremendous economic progress in the last decades, the

---

[94] Wendy Griswold, *Cultures and Societies in a Changing World* (Pine Forge Press, Thousand Oaks, CA, 1994), pp. 138–39.
[95] As stated by Griswold, "If communities are bound by cultures, and if national cultures are increasingly penetrated from outside, then 'global culture' displaces 'national culture' to an ever greater extent." Griswold, *Cultures and Societies*, p. 147.
[96] Griswold, *Cultures and Societies*, pp. 147–48.
[97] See p. 169.

world today faces huge backlogs of inequality and poverty. The gap between poorest and richest states continues to grow[98] and an estimated 2.8 billion people still live on less than US$2 a day.[99] Although social stratification and economic gaps are common features of every domestic society,[100] it is clear that these gaps are even more pronounced in the international system. Poverty is more extensive and severe in poor countries than in rich nations.[101] Sociologists and international relations specialists are divided regarding the causes of global inequality but it is clear that the current, considerable socio-economic gaps constitute a destabilizing factor in the international system.[102]

The increasing inequality is expected to exacerbate social divisions in the international community. Developing states may further develop social detachment and even hostile feelings toward the system that does not rectify their inferior position. Norms that emerge from the international system in such a context are likely to be perceived as less legitimate by decision-makers in developing states. Bearing in mind the relationship between social attachment to the community and compliance,[103] the growing detachment of developing states from the international community implies increasing polarization and a decline of the prospects of compliance with international norms.[104]

Similar conclusions are drawn from an analysis of the impact of socio-economic gaps upon individuals' decisions whether to comply or breach

---

[98] As discussed at p. 170, this widening economic gap should not necessarily mean that there is a causal connection between globalization and income equality.

[99] *UNDP Report 2002*, p. 28.

[100] See e.g., Andre Beteille, "Inequality and Equality" in Tim Ingold (ed.), *Companion Encyclopedia of Anthropology: Humanity, Culture and Social Life* (Routledge, London, 1994), p. 1100; Macionis, *Sociology*, pp. 292–93.

[101] See e.g., the data cited in *UNDP Report 2000*, p. 13 *et seq.*; Macionis, *Sociology*, p. 296.

[102] Generally, those with fewer resources are more likely to seek change: Macionis, *Sociology*, pp. 237, 313.

[103] See pp. 182–83.

[104] On the current lower level of compliance with international environmental agreements by poor states, see Harold Jacobson and Edith Brown Weiss, "Assessing the Record and Designing Strategies to Engage Countries" in Brown Weiss and Jacobson, *Engaging Countries*, pp. 530–31; Marc A. Levy, "European Acid Rain: The Power of Tote-Board Diplomacy" in Peter M. Haas, Robert O. Keohane and Marc A. Levy (eds.), *Institutions for the Earth* (MIT Press, Cambridge, 1993), pp. 75, 119, 126; Elinor Ostrom, *Governing the Commons* (Cambridge University Press, Cambridge, 1990), p. 35; Hector Rogelio Torres, *Overview of Developing Country Interests in Trade and Environment*, OECD Workshop on Methodologies for Environmental Assessment of Trade Liberalization Agreements, Paris, October 26–27, 1999, p. 6, www1.oecd.org/ech/26-27 oct/docs/torres/pdf

societal norms. Robert Merton, the well-known sociologist who specialized in social deviance, emphasized that some social arrangements are more likely to generate non-compliance. In accordance with Merton's Strain Theory, the scope and character of deviance depend on how well a society makes cultural goals (such as financial success) accessible by providing institutionalized means to achieve them. Conformity is achieved by pursuing conventional goals by approved means. But people who grow up in places in which they see little hope of attaining the society's goals if they "play by the rules," may attempt to attain these aims by illegal activities. The result is a "strain" between the current culture's emphasis on wealth and the limited opportunity to attain this aim, particularly among poor people.[105]

Drawing upon Merton's Strain Theory, it is apparent that national decision-makers in developing states who internalize the importance of a high standard of living (as in the Western states) may find that the likelihood of providing such a standard of living to their people by lawful means (in a reasonable period) is slim. Such "strained" settings are more likely to lead decision-makers to violate international norms.[106] Bearing in mind that socio-economic gaps between developed and developing states are widening, the above analysis indicates that the prospects of compliance with international norms by developing states are likely to decline.

Concluding remarks

The preceding sections explore the impact of globalization upon the prospects of compliance with international norms. The analysis of this challenging subject required us to employ the two major paradigms in social inquiry, the rational choice model and the sociological perspective. Each of these over-arching paradigms generates different sets of variables for analyzing breach and compliance with international norms.

The analyses in this study, undertaken along these theoretical lines, do not lead to a single conclusion. Assuming that the current trends of globalization will proceed, the results regarding the prospects of compliance in the course of globalization are rather mixed. The rational choice

---

[105] Robert K. Merton, *Social Theory and Social Structure* (Free Press, New York, 1968), pp. 188–89; Macionis, *Sociology*, pp. 207–8; Layder, *Understanding Social Theory*, p. 24.
[106] See e.g., data regarding infringements of intellectual property rights by developing states; *Sixth Annual Survey on Global Software Piracy* (2001), www.bsa.org/usa/press/newsreleases/2001-05-21.566.phtml.

analysis reveals that the trends of growing iteration, expanding capacity of retaliation, increasing amounts of reliable information and the process of growing rebounded externalities indicate that the prospect of compliance is likely to be enhanced. The sociological analysis pursued in this chapter shows that the trend of increasing interconnectedness among societies lessens the social and cultural diversities among states and, consequently, reduces the likelihood of conflict between national and international norms. Analysis of the growing socio-economic inequality among states and its impact upon the social attachment of poorer states to the international society, however, implies that this process is likely to decrease compliance with international norms.

Taking all these trends into account, the above analyses suggest that the general level of compliance with international norms among developed states is likely to rise in the course of globalization. This statement applies, though to a significantly lesser extent, to developing states. The resulting "compliance gap" is undesirable and even dangerous to the relations between developing and developed states, as well as to the international community at large. The result of this analysis constitutes an additional justification for the urgent need for redoubled efforts to narrow the socio-economic gap between developing and developed states.

8

Compliance and non-compliance with international norms in territorial disputes: the Latin American record of arbitrations

ARIE M. KACOWICZ

Introduction

Why do states comply with international norms related to territorial disputes, such as *pacta sunt servanda* and the peaceful settlement of international disputes? Why and when do states reject adverse arbitration awards and not comply with their previous international commitments (to abide by the ruling)? This chapter attempts to answer these two questions by examining the strange reality of Latin American (especially the South American) international society, and its unique record of recourse to international arbitration to settle international disputes over territory.

Since independence, the Latin American countries have gradually built a sophisticated and highly developed system of regional international law and institutions, including regional norms that have regulated their international and domestic behavior. Among these regional norms are principles of sovereignty and non-intervention, the recognition of former colonial borders, peaceful settlement of international disputes and commitment to political legalism, democracy and human rights. More than any other regional grouping, the Latin American countries have turned to international arbitration to settle their territorial disputes (about twenty-two times in the last part of the nineteenth and throughout the twentieth centuries), and have complied on almost half of the occasions (ten or eleven out of twenty-two). This is a remarkable record in relative (comparative) terms.

The working assumption of any functional international society with "normal" international relations is that of compliance. Thus, international lawyers assume that "almost all nations observe almost all principles of international law and almost all of their obligations almost all of the time."[1] In other words, in an increasingly complex and interdependent world, negotiations and implementation of international agreements are a major component of the foreign policy activity of every state.[2] Conversely, political scientists tend to be a bit more skeptical on the probabilities, or inherent importance and relevance of compliance with international norms.[3] Whether compliance with international norms is viable or not should be assessed in the context of "hard cases," such as compliance with the award of international arbitration regarding the fate of disputed territories in international conflicts.

In the following pages, I examine, in both theoretical and empirical terms, the issue of compliance and non-compliance in the context of international arbitration, with particular reference to territorial disputes in Latin America. First, I assess alternative explanations to understand, in general, why and when countries comply and do not comply with their international obligations. Second, I review the peculiar Latin American record of arbitration in territorial disputes. Particularly, I review two cases of non-compliance with arbitration awards that were eventually resolved by subsequent mediation efforts and direct negotiations between the parties: (1) the *Oriente/Marañón* question, involving the Ecuadorian rejection of the Protocol of Rio (1942) and the subsequent arbitration award of 1945, followed by armed conflict, negotiations and mediation, up to the conclusion of the Peace Treaty of 1998 between Ecuador and Peru; and (2) the *Beagle Channel* question, as related to the Argentine rejection of the British arbitration award in favor of Chile in 1977, followed by a military crisis, mediation and negotiations, up to the signature of the Peace Treaty of 1984 between Argentina and Chile.

Compliance with international norms: when and why?

Pacta sunt servanda *and compliance in territorial disputes*

As stated above, the fundamental international legal principle and norm of *pacta sunt servanda* means that the rules and commitments specified in legalized international agreements are considered as binding and

---

[1] Louis Henkin, *How Nations Behave* (2nd edn., Columbia University Press, NY, 1979), p. 47.
[2] Abram Chayes and Antonia Handler Chayes, "On Compliance" (1993) 47 *International Organization* 175.
[3] George W. Downs, David M. Rocke and Peter N. Barsoom, "Is the Good News About Compliance Good News About Cooperation?" (1996) 50 *International Organization* 379; John J. Mearsheimer, "The False Promise of International Institutions" (1994–95) 19 *International Security* 5.

obligatory, even if the preferences and interests of the parties change over time.[4] The resilience of this fundamental norm might help explain patterns of compliance with international obligations in most cases, as well as the expansion of legalized forms into new issue areas.[5]

In paradigmatic terms, the question of whether states (and other actors) adopt the norm of *pacta sunt servanda*, so that they comply with their international commitments, has stood at the root of major disagreements between Realist and Neoliberal institutionalist theorists in international relations.[6] From a Realist standpoint, the basic argument is that states might comply (as they do) only when they can ignore relative gains considerations and focus instead on absolute gains, and/or when compliance serves their national interests.[7] Moreover, the high level of compliance and the marginality of enforcement in international relations result from the fact that most treaties require states to make only modest departures (if at all) from what they would have chosen to do in the first place, even in the absence of any written agreement.[8] Thus, the issue of compliance is at best superfluous, if not completely irrelevant. Conversely, Neoliberal institutionalists suggest that when states can jointly benefit from cooperation, we should expect governments to construct international institutions (including international organizations, international regimes and principles and practices of international law such as *pacta sunt servanda*). Such institutions can provide information, reduce transaction costs, make commitments more credible, establish focal points for coordination and in general facilitate reciprocity.[9] For Neoliberals, the issue of compliance is thus directly related to the enhancing of cooperation, even under conditions of international anarchy.

In more practical terms, the question of compliance can and should be assessed across different issue areas of international relations, such as environment, monetary affairs, human rights and territorial disputes.

---

[4] Kenneth W. Abbott, Robert O. Keohane, Andrew Moravcsik, Anne-Marie Slaughter and Duncan Snidal, "The Concept of Legalization" (2000) 54 *International Organization* 401, 409.
[5] Judith Goldstein, Miles Kahler, Robert Keohane and Anne-Marie Slaughter, "Introduction: Legalization and World Politics" (2000) 54 *International Organization* 385, 397, 399.
[6] Beth A. Simmons, "International Law and State Behavior: Commitment and Compliance in International Monetary Affairs" (2000) 94 *Am. Political Science Rev.* 819.
[7] Mearsheimer, "False Promise," 21–22.
[8] Downs et al., "Good News About Compliance," 380.
[9] Robert O. Keohane and Lisa L. Martin, "The Promise of Institutionalist Theory" (1995) 20 *International Security* 39, 42.

Territory is often described as perhaps the most salient of all possible issues. It is often valued for both its tangible contents (geopolitics, economic resources) and intangible values (national identity, history and religion).[10]

If and when states are ready to submit their territorial disputes to international arbitration, they work on the premises of legalization, to the extent that they assume as a working hypothesis that they would comply with any possible subsequent outcome. Thus, any agreement that gives rise to a process of arbitration generally specifies that the subsequent decision (ruling award) should respect the rule of international law, making the arbitral award a legal rather than an explicitly political decision. Moreover, as mentioned above, the decisions that result from arbitration are legally binding, though the previous decision to submit the territorial dispute to legal (judicial) processes is a voluntary political act. Hence, an agreement to submit a dispute to arbitration raises the stakes for each state, in terms of reputation, by publicly committing it *a priori* to the settlement of the dispute by legal means – regardless of the decision.[11] Since territory is considered a paramount issue for many states, their voluntary agreement to comply afterwards brings us back to the initial question of why and when to comply with international commitments.

Why and when do states comply with international commitments in territorial disputes?

The general assumption of compliance is directly related to the possibility (and capability) of states to make a credible commitment over the short and long term. As stated above, compliance is considered the normal organizational presumption in international relations.[12] The alternative explanations for the "normal" tendency of states (like individuals) to comply with their (international) commitments include (1) reciprocity, self-interest and reputation; (2) the impact of the normative framework; (3) the impact of the structure of the international system; (4) the incorporation of international law into domestic law; and (5) the type of political regime (preferably, a democratic/liberal regime).

---

[10] Paul R. Hensel, "Contentious Issues and World Politics: The Management of Territorial Claims in the Americas, 1816–1992" (2001) 45 *Int'l Studies Q.* 81, 85.
[11] Beth A. Simmons, "Territorial Disputes and their Resolution: The Case of Ecuador and Peru" (1999) 27 *Peaceworks* 6 (April).
[12] Chayes and Chayes, "On Compliance," 179.

Why and when do states not comply with international agreements?

Even though non-compliance can be considered a deviant rather than an expected normal behavior, it does occur, both within the realm of interpersonal relations and in international relations as well. According to Chayes and Chayes, the usual causes of non-compliance are to be found in: (1) the ambiguity and indeterminacy in the language and content of treaties; (2) limitations on the capacity of the parties to carry out their obligation; and (3) uncontrollable social or economic changes.[13]

In turn, those causes can be further explained by turning to the Rationalist or psychological approaches. From a Rationalist point of view, the usual (and under-specified) argument is that states violate norms whenever those norms clash with the "national interests" of states – whatever that means for them.[14] Conversely, from a psychological perspective, states might not comply with their international obligations when they can claim an exemption from the norm by invocation of apologies, denials, excuses and justifications.[15] In this sense, the more ambiguous the situation and the norm(s), the easier to detract from compliance by interpreting the norm to justify its possible violation. It should be pointed out, furthermore, that the Rationalist and the psychological approaches complement each other.

The Latin American record of arbitration

After succinctly presenting the theoretical arguments for compliance and non-compliance, we should now examine the Latin American record of international arbitration of territorial disputes. First, I briefly examine the peculiarities of Latin America as an international society. Second, I describe the general Latin American record of arbitration in a comparative perspective. Third, I review two cases of temporary non-compliance with arbitration awards, Ecuador (1941–1998) and Argentina (1977–1984).

The peculiarities of Latin American international society

The reality of a regional international society is puzzling in the Latin American context by evident contrasts between the rhetorical and

---

[13] Ibid. at 188.
[14] Vaughn P. Shannon, "Norms are What States Make of Them: The Political Psychology of Norm Violation" (2000) 44 *Int'l Studies Q.* 293.
[15] Shannon, "Norms are What States Make of Them," 304.

practical levels, and between the international and domestic arenas. No other region of the world has as many bilateral and multilateral documents, treaties and charters imposing obligations for the peaceful settlement of international disputes. Conversely, in practical terms, Latin American nations have been more inclined to adopt prejurisdictional or political forms of settlement, usually through diplomatic negotiations and ad hoc procedures, rather than legal and quasi-legal processes, such as adjudication and arbitration.[16] Still, in comparative terms, Latin America sustains a world record of adjudication and arbitration, in which the disputing countries request a neutral third party to make an authoritative ruling to resolve international conflicts involving territorial questions.

Latin America has long exhibited a strong support for international law, in part to prevent war and to oppose the potential intervention by stronger extra-regional powers, first and foremost the United States. In this regard, Latin Americans have contributed important principles to the (more general) American international law, including (a) non-transfer of territories; (b) *uti possidetis* (recognition of the colonial borders at the time of independence); (c) non-intervention; (d) non-recognition of territorial conquests; (e) use of morality in international relations; (f) solidarity; and (g) equality of states and respect for their sovereignty.

In Latin America, and especially in the South American sub-region, the majority of border disputes throughout the nineteenth and twentieth centuries have been resolved peacefully, leading to some cession or exchange of territories. The basis for a peaceful settlement of these disputes was established through the principle of *uti possidetis, ita possideatis* ("as you possess, you may possess"). According to Cukwurah, "The new states of Latin America, for convenience and expediency, adopted as the basis for their boundaries the administrative divisions of the mother country which existed at the date when the movement for independence broke out. That 'critical date' in the case of South America was generally taken to be 1810."[17] The principle of *uti possidetis* did not preclude the emergence of boundary disputes among the Latin American states. However, by recognizing the same norm of international law, the parties in many cases managed to resolve their border disputes peacefully.

---

[16] Juan Carlos Puig, "Controlling Latin American Conflicts: Current Juridical Trends and Perspectives for the Future" in Michael A. Morris and Victor Millan (eds.), *Controlling Latin American Conflicts: Ten Approaches* (Westview Press, Boulder, 1983), pp. 11–39.
[17] A. O. Cukwurah, *The Settlement of Boundary Disputes in International Law* (Manchester University Press, Manchester, 1967), pp. 112–13.

The norms of peaceful settlement of international disputes, *convivencia* and *concertación* encompass a pattern of regional cooperation that has resulted in mediation, arbitration and diplomatic solutions rather than war. Sometimes peaceful settlement was arranged through international congresses and multilateral diplomacy; more frequently, it took place through bilateral solutions with non-compulsory, ad hoc resources for the management and resolution of international conflicts.

The domain of the Latin American regional society overlaps with a greater vision of the Americas, including the entire Western Hemisphere. This great design of a New World as a continent culturally and politically distinct from Europe has permeated the diplomatic rhetoric, if not the actual foreign policy, of many Latin American states. There have always been discussions about a special "American international law," as distinct from the general international law binding upon the international community.

Latin American (especially South American) countries have managed to establish a unique Latin "diplomatic culture" through a gradual learning process that has helped their governments resolve international conflicts in the region short of war. There is a long tradition in the region of gaining honor by complying with legal obligations, not divorced from considerations of national interest such as prestige and reputation.[18] Latin American nations have thus developed a theory and practice of exceptionalism regarding their recourse to instruments of international law – arbitration of disputes, mediation, bilateral negotiations and other techniques for the peaceful settlement of international disputes – rather than using force in their international relations. Based upon a common historical and cultural framework, Latin American nations have built a strong normative consensus that has been institutionalized in legal instruments since the beginning of the nineteenth century.[19] It should be pointed out, however, that this normative and legal reluctance to engage in war against fellow Latin American nations never implied a lack of serious interstate disputes through the entire region.

In sum, the Latin American countries have reached a high degree of civility in their international relations, juxtaposed with uncivilized (if not brutal) political relations within their own borders until the late 1970s and

---

[18] Kalevi J. Holsti, "Armed Conflict in the Third World: Assessing Analytical Approaches and Anomalies," paper presented at the Annual Meeting of the International Studies Association, Acapulco, Mexico, March 1993, p. 19.

[19] See Arie M. Kacowicz, "Latin America as an International Society" (2000) 37 *International Politics* 143.

the 1980s. Thus, an international society could coexist for many decades with the lack of basic societal relationships between authoritarian regimes and their societies. This paradox stems from the common values and political culture of the region.

In contrast to other regions of the Third World, the basic social, political and economic values of Latin America directly derive from its European tradition; its values are part of the Western Christian culture (or "civilization"). In this regard, the political system of Latin America has developed a culture of legalism. Among the most important factors that have conditioned this legal culture are idealism, paternalism, legalism, formalism and lack of penetration into their own societies. The Hispanic tradition of political monism, organicism, legal idealism and patrimonialism has forged the dominant political value system of Latin America, discouraging the development of pluralistic tendencies in favor of a difficult, if not impossible, collective harmony at the domestic level.[20]

The Latin American record of arbitration in comparative perspective

Latin America in general, and South America in particular, have experienced, in the last part of the nineteenth and throughout the twentieth centuries, exceptionally high rates of peaceful conflict resolution, and/or toleration of conflicts that remain unresolved but are not likely to be settled by recourse to war. Latin American countries mutually agreed to numerous treaties for peaceful settlement of disputes, especially arbitration, above all during the late part of the nineteenth century and the beginning of the twentieth century, though those treaties were not hermetical.[21] Up to the 1930s, there have been approximately 250 treaties for arbitration and for the advancement of peace involving American (i.e., Latin and North American) states, including treaties of a general character and those dealing with particular disputes.[22] More than any other area of the world, border disputes in the region have been subject to formal legal and quasi-legal processes, such as adjudication and arbitration,

---

[20] See Kenneth L. Karst and Keith S. Rosenn, *Law and Development in Latin America: A Case Book* (University of California Press, Berkeley, CA, 1975), pp. 58–65; Roland H. Ebel and Raymond Taras, "Cultural Style and International Policy-Making: The Latin American Tradition," in Jangsuk Chay (ed.), *Culture and International Relations* (Praeger, New York, 1990), pp. 195–200.
[21] See Puig, "Controlling Latin American Conflicts," 15.
[22] See Charles Evan Hughes, *Pan-American Peace Plans* (Yale University Press, New Haven, CT, 1929), pp. 17–19.

in which the disputing states request a neutral third party to make an authoritative ruling resolving their territorial questions.[23] For instance, arbitration procedures have been used at extraordinary high rates compared to other regions of the world. From the 1820s until the 1970s, eight states – Argentina, Bolivia, Brazil, Colombia, Chile, Ecuador, Peru and Venezuela – used arbitration procedures 151 times in a myriad of issue areas.[24] Many of the bilateral border disputes involving Latin American states have been submitted to arbitration (about twenty-two), in itself a puzzling phenomenon given the political sensitivity of territorial issues and their centrality to notions of states' sovereignty and national identity.[25] This is a large number of cases, as compared to one in Europe, two in Africa, two in the Middle East, and three in Asia, the Far East and the Pacific. Of these twenty-two cases, there were ten (or even eleven) in which the parties complied completely with the ruling and twelve (or eleven) in which at least one of the parties partially or utterly rejected the ruling (see Table 8.1).

How can one explain this popular tendency among Latin American countries of recourse to arbitration? First, as mentioned above, a relatively strong tradition in the region exists of using formal legal procedures to resolve territorial disputes. Second, states that have been more symmetrical in their military capabilities have been more likely to submit a territorial dispute to arbitration than highly asymmetric dyads (as in the cases of Argentina and Chile in the late part of the nineteenth century, Costa Rica and Nicaragua, and Costa Rica and Panama). Third, countries with a history of difficulty getting territorial agreements ratified by their national congresses prefer a recourse to arbitration, as a way to by-pass continued domestic obstruction to resolving border disputes. Fourth, prior experience with quasi-legal procedures tends to repeat itself over time (Argentina and Chile turned to arbitration five times, Argentina has been involved in seven of the twenty-two cases).[26] Fifth, in general, Latin American countries have preferred the recourse to arbitration as a peculiar legal instrument to cope with the threats of intervention by the United States and the European powers.

In addition, the Latin American case fits the more general explanations for compliance to explain the relatively successful record of acceptance of

---

[23] Beth A. Simmons, "Territorial Disputes and Their Resolution: The Case of Ecuador and Peru" (1999) 27 *Peaceworks* v (April).
[24] See Puig, "Controlling Latin American Conflicts."
[25] Simmons, "Territorial Disputes and Their Resolution," 6.   [26] Ibid. at 6–7.

Table 8.1 *Cases involving authoritative third party rulings*

Parties	Dates of dispute	Ruling date	By	"Loser"/ Rejecter	Comments
(a) In which the parties complied with the rulings					
1. Argentina/ Brazil	1858–1898	1895	US	Argentina	
2. Argentina/ Chile	1872–1903	1899	US	not clear	Los Andes
3. Argentina/ Chile	1847–1966	1966	UK	Chile	Palena sector
4. Argentina/ Chile	1847–1994	1994	Regional	Chile	Laguna del Desierto
5. Argentina/ Paraguay	1840–1939	1878	US	Argentina	
6. Colombia/ Venezuela	1838–1932	1891	Spain	Venezuela	Compliance delayed
7. El Salvador/ Honduras	1861–1992	1992	ICJ	El Salvador	80% to Honduras
8. Guatemala/ Honduras	1842–1933	1933	Costa Rica/US	not clear	
9. Guyana (UK)/ Venezuela	1880–1899	1899	US	Venezuela	34,000 sq. miles to UK; 8,000 sq. miles to Venezuela
10. Honduras/ Nicaragua	1858–1960	1960	ICJ	Nicaragua	
(b) In which the parties did not comply with the ruling					
1. Argentina/ Chile	1847–1984	1977	UK	Argentina	Beagle Channel
2. Argentina/ Chile	1847–1994	1902	UK	Chile	Partially rejected
3. Bolivia/Peru	1825–1911	1909	Argentina	Bolivia	
4. Chile/Peru	1881–1929	1924	US	Peru	Tacna and Arica
5. Costa Rica/ Nicaragua	1842–1900s	1888	US	Nicaragua	
6. Costa Rica/ Nicaragua	1842–1900s	1916	CACJ	Nicaragua	

Table 8.1 *(cont.)*

Parties	Dates of dispute	Ruling date	By By	"Loser"/ Rejecter	Comments
7. Costa Rica/ Panama	1903–1944	1900	France	Costa Rica	
8. Costa Rica/ Panama	1903–1944	1914	US	Panama	
9. Ecuador/Peru	1842–1998	1910	Spain	Ecuador	Non-compliance threat deters ruling
10. Ecuador/Peru	1842–1998	1945	Brazil	Ecuador	Rejects in 1960
11. Guyana/ Venezuela	1951- present	1899	US	Venezuela	
12. Honduras/ Nicaragua	1858–1960	1906	Spain	Nicaragua	

Source: Beth A. Simmons, "Territorial Disputes and their Resolution: The Case of Ecuador and Peru" (1999) 27 *Peaceworks* 5 (April)

arbitration awards. In the first place, the acceptance of awards enhances the *reputation*, and thus, the *self-interests* of the parties involved, assuming the principle of *reciprocity*. In other words, strengthening legal institutions and mechanisms has generally served the interests of the countries in the region (which submitted their disputes to arbitration on their own volition). Second, there is a strong *normative framework* that socializes and induces states to comply with arbitration awards. Argentina, with the notorious exception of its 1978 rejection of the 1977 award, is a case in point. Traditionally, it has accepted the principles of peaceful settlement of international disputes and pacifism, as well as recourse to international law and moralism.[27] This normative framework is directly related to the "legalist culture" that characterizes the Latin American region. Third, the

---

[27] Norberto Piñero, *La Política Internacional Argentina* (J. Menendez, Buenos Aires, 1924), p. 129; Isidoro Ruiz Moreno, *Historia de las Relaciones Exteriores Argentinas 1810–1955* (Perrot, Buenos Aires, 1961), p. 19; José Paradiso, "El Poder de la Norma y la Política del Poder 1880–1916" in Silvia Ruth Jalabe (ed.), *La Política Exterior Argentina y sus Protagonistas 1880–1995* (GEL, Buenos Aires, 1996), pp. 13, 15.

structure of the international system, characterized by the subordinated position of the Latin American states vis-à-vis Europe and the United States, has also enhanced their disposition to accept the arbitral ruling of the more powerful (United States, United Kingdom) or former colonial powers (Spain). Fourth, the *type of political regime* seems to be indeterminate in the Latin American case, since there has been quite a rule of (international) law and respect for arbitration awards among non-democratic states, well before their transition to democracy in the late part of the twentieth century. Yet, democratization seems to have some positive effect on the tendency to settle disputes peacefully (i.e., Argentina in 1984; Ecuador in 1998) but that remains inconclusive.

At the same time, it should be emphasized that the recourse to arbitration in Latin America, though still useful in a few cases such as Argentina and Chile in the 1990s, has declined in the late part of the twentieth century. As an alternative, states nowadays favor political, ad hoc arrangements that have led to a peaceful resolution of international disputes through mediation and direct negotiations.

Two cases of non-compliance: Ecuador from 1960 to 1995; Argentina from 1977 to 1984

The fact that arbitration has been a popular recourse for the peaceful settlement of international disputes does not guarantee automatic compliance, or a final and peaceful resolution of the territorial conflict. On the one hand, there is an inherent difficulty in turning a political conflict (a territorial dispute) into a legal contention, since many arbitral procedures might result in zero-sum or win-lose outcomes rather than compromises that can be articulated through political negotiations. On the other hand, the recourse to arbitration assumes a strong presumption against turning to violence, or rejecting the award. There seems to be a real cost in terms of prestige and "honor" in refusing peaceful conflict resolution procedures when the other party has accepted them.[28] Yet, as Table 8.1 indicates, there have been many cases of non-compliance with the arbitration award. In the following section, I briefly review two cases of non-compliance following international arbitration in territorial disputes, which were eventually resolved by mediation and bilateral negotiations.

[28] Holsti, "Armed Conflict in the Third World," 170.

The Ecuadorian rejection of the Rio Protocol (1941) and of the Brazilian Arbitration of 1945, from 1960 to 1995

Peru and Ecuador have had an old territorial dispute since their independence in the early nineteenth century, claiming an area of about 80,000 square miles lying to the north of the Marañón River, not far from the Amazon River. Their boundary conflict over the "Oriente" resulted from the ambiguous border definition of the former colonial units and the emergence of wild rubber as a potential resource in the area. Despite occasional efforts at mediation (such as in 1936–1938), no solution was found and border skirmishes became frequent. They escalated in July 1941 into a short but intensive undeclared war, culminating with a Peruvian blitzkrieg into Ecuadorian territory.

On January 29, 1942, Ecuador was compelled to accept the Protocol of Rio de Janeiro, negotiated between the parties through the mediation of the United States, Argentina, Brazil and Chile as "guarantor powers." Its terms were stern. Ecuador recognized Peruvian sovereignty over most of the disputed territory and surrendered another 5,000 square miles. The new boundary line not only caused Ecuador to lose two-thirds of the "Oriente Province," which it considered its own, but also deprived it of an outlet to the Amazon River. In implementing the Rio Protocol, more than 95 percent of the border was demarcated, except for a small section of 78 kilometers along the Cordillera del Cóndor. This area was the subject of an arbitral award authorized by the Rio Protocol and rendered by a Brazilian naval officer, Captain Braz Dias de Aguiar, in July 1945. The two countries initially accepted the award unconditionally, and began to demarcate their common border.[29]

Yet, Ecuador asserted that new geographical information came to light as a result of aerial photography in 1946 regarding the location of a new watershed (the *divortium aquarium*) between the Zamora and Santiago rivers, the Cenepa River, which invalidated the location of the border in the Cordillera del Cóndor area. As a result, Ecuador became increasingly revisionist, formally declaring the Protocol (and the subsequent arbitration of 1945) null and void in August 1960. At that time, Ecuadorian President José María Velasco Ibarra initiated a critical and destructive campaign for re-election, in which he asserted that the Rio Protocol could not be executed, due to its geographical flaws and inherent unfairness. In his view, the Protocol was an unjust settlement forcibly imposed by Peruvian arms

---

[29] Simmons, "Territorial Disputes and Their Resolution," 10–11.

in defiance of international law. Moreover, Ecuador sustained a valid and just claim to territorial rights to the headwaters of the Amazon River. Peru, on its part, regarded the border problem as being definitively resolved by the Rio Protocol. The four "guarantor states" also upheld the validity of the 1942 Treaty and urged the two parties to finish charting the area in question. Thus, Ecuador was in a disadvantaged position, since it demanded revisions of a settlement already recognized by the inter-American and Latin American communities.[30]

The major arguments presented by Ibarra for non-compliance with the Protocol and the subsequent arbitration included legal and equity claims, as follows:

- "Ecuador cannot be far away, maintained apart from the Amazons."[31]
- "Can Ecuador, which discovered and colonized the Amazon basin, be confined to the sea and mountain ranges in the East? Is that justice? Is that Americanism? Is that an expression of Sudamerican cooperation?"[32]
- "Can a treaty be signed when a[n Ecuadorian] province is being invaded? Is it possible to formulate a contract when a pistol is pointed at one of the parties? [Hence,] The Treaty of Rio is a null treaty."[33]
- "In the so-called Declaration of Costa Rica, it is stated that the controversies among the American nations should be resolved by peaceful and juridical means ... Hence, we have the right to say that, according to the inter-American norms, the treaties imposed by force are null and void."[34]
- "The Protocol of Rio de Janeiro is null because it was imposed by force, when the country was invaded and its cities put on fire. Thus, from a legal point of view, it is null and void. This position is entirely legal."[35]
- "The 1942 Protocol contradicts the substance of American [international] law, according to which one cannot earn advantages from military conquests, as was proclaimed in all the Panamerican

[30] Ronald Bruce St. John, "The Boundary between Ecuador and Peru" (1994) 1 *Boundary and Territory Briefs* 1; Gabriel Marcella and Richard Downes, "Introduction" in G. Marcella and R. Downes (eds.), *Security Cooperation in the Western Hemisphere: Resolving the Ecuador–Peru Conflict* (North–South Center Press, Miami, 1999), pp. 1, 7. See also Diego Delgado Jara, *Problema Territorial: Oligarquía y Pueblo* (Universidad de Cuenca, Cuenca, 1985), pp. 17–23.
[31] José María Velasco Ibarra, *Democracia Jurídica Interamericana* (Unión Interamericana de Periodistas para la XI Conferencia de Quito, Quito, 1961), p. 16 (author's translation).
[32] Ibarra, *Democracia Jurídica Interamericana*, p. 17 (author's translation).
[33] Ibid. at p. 17 (author's translation).   [34] Ibid. at p. 23 (author's translation.).
[35] Ibid. at p. 26 (author's translation).

Conferences from 1890 up to the consultation among American Foreign Ministers in 1940."[36]

In sum, Ecuador dismissed the Rio Protocol as legally null because (a) it was imposed by force; (b) it could not be executed on the watershed between the Zamora and Santiago rivers; (c) it was not signed by competent and legitimate representatives; (d) it opposed positive norms of international law in Latin America, regarding the nullity of territorial cessions if effected under pressure or by force; and (e) it opposed legal and historical facts, essentially the principle of *uti possidetis* and the Guayaquil Treaty of September 22, 1829.[37]

Thus, for about thirty years, Ecuadorian foreign policy actively pursued in numerous international fora the nullification of the entire Rio Protocol and the rejection of the 1945 arbitration. The territorial conflict persisted, and further escalated into armed confrontations in 1981 and most recently in January 1995. Only after the brief war of 1995, did Ecuador surprisingly change its revisionist attitude, accepting the Rio Protocol as valid but with "shortcomings."[38] This opened the way to negotiations and mediation, and to the active participation, good offices, and even arbitration of the "guarantor powers," leading to the ultimate resolution of the conflict in the Peace Treaty of October 1998.

With the conclusion of the Rio Protocol of 1942, the Ecuadorian case was closed from a legal standpoint. Hence, its subsequent rejection of the Protocol between 1960 and 1995 could be considered a subversive challenge of the accepted rules of international law, in the name of justice and morality. Unfortunately for Ecuador, it has been the weaker side, both in terms of its legal arguments and in terms of its power relation vis-à-vis Peru, though the results of the war of 1995 slightly changed the power equation between the two countries. The change was more psychological than real and opened the way for some form of political compromise between the two parties. Yet, the final agreement of October 1998 remained within the pre-established legal and territorial parameters of the Rio Protocol of 1942.

Only in the last few years, following the 1995 war, did the parties change their nationalistic rhetoric, agreeing that trade and development were more important than nationalist symbols. Alongside their conflict, a series of common interests and institutions involving the two countries pushed

---

[36] Ibid. at p. 46 (author's translation). [37] Jara, *Problema Territorial*, pp. 16–23.
[38] Marcella and Downes, "Introduction," 7.

them in the direction of resolving their enduring dispute. Both shared a common stance on the Latin American thesis of the 200 miles in the debates on the Law of the Sea; both were partners in the Andean Group and the Amazon Treaty.[39] Moreover, both governments faced a poor economy and few resources to devote to another military round. Ecuador's stronger performance in the 1995 war meant that any concessions it made in the near future would not be interpreted as an act of coercion. As economic and trade integration in the Andean Community proceeded, Ecuador and Peru became increasingly aware of the cost that their dispute exacted by denying them the advantages of normal economic and political relations.[40] Finally, from a normative and legal standpoint, with great help and assistance from the guarantor powers, Peru and Ecuador eventually returned to the original formula already established in the 1942 Protocol: Ecuador would give up its quixotic claims to the disputed land. In return, it would have permanent access, though not sovereignty, to the Amazon River.

The Argentine rejection of the Arbitral Award of 1977 on the Beagle Channel Islands, 1977–1984

The definition of the boundary between Argentina and Chile has historically been a source of conflict between the two states. Longstanding, intractable territorial disputes marked the relations between Chile and Argentina since their early post-colonial days. Throughout the twentieth century, the territorial conflict has centered on three areas in particular. One is the precise location of the Beagle Channel, a strait separating Argentina's part of Tierra del Fuego from Chile's Navarino Island. The dispute involved the possession of a group of three islands in the Channel (Picton, Nueva and Lennox), and the maritime rights regarding their surrounding sea. A second is the Palena area, involving a twenty-four-mile stretch of sparsely inhabited territory along the Andes frontier, eventually resolved in 1966 by an arbitration award that granted Argentina 70 percent of the disputed territory. The Laguna del Desierto region was a third area of conflict, also located on the Andean frontier to the south. It was also resolved in 1994 by a regional arbitration award in favor of Argentina. The most intractable among these three disputes has

---

[39] Félix Denegri Luna, *Peru y Ecuador: Apuntes para la Historia de Una Frontera* (Bolsa de Valores, Instituto Riva-Agüero, Universidad Pontificia Católica del Perú, Lima, 1996), pp. 322–23.
[40] Simmons, "Territorial Disputes and Their Resolution," 21.

been the Beagle Channel, ranging from 1847 through the Peace Treaty of 1984.[41]

Despite the partial settlement of border disputes by the arbitration of 1902, Argentina and Chile continued to dispute possession of the Beagle Channel and its islands, Antarctica and maritime limits until 1984. The dispute erupted again in the late 1960s. In July 1971, the two countries agreed to submit the Beagle Channel dispute to the arbitration of the United Kingdom. Under the terms of the accord (*compromis*), the British government was restricted to accepting or rejecting whatever award was given by an international court of five jurists of the ICJ. The major task of the court was to find the correct interpretation of Article III of the Treaty of 1881 between Argentina and Chile, which specifically referred to the location of the Beagle Channel. The award was to be legally binding on both parties unless based on factual error.

In May 1977, Argentina and Chile received the Arbitration Award, which awarded the disputed islands and territory in dispute to Chile (which was already in possession of them). This seriously damaged Argentina's vital geopolitical concerns in the South Atlantic, directly related to its Antarctic claims and the Falklands/Malvinas conflict with the United Kingdom. On January 25, 1978, Argentina officially rejected the arbitration award, precipitating a serious military and political crisis between the two countries. As Chile became Argentina's major security concern – replacing Brazil and the United Kingdom – the two countries prepared for war, including the massing of troops and equipment in their southern border and the general mobilization of their armed forces. A series of bilateral negotiations in 1978 failed, so war became imminent in December of 1978, when a last-minute mediation by the Pope helped to defuse the crisis. The Montevideo Act of January 8, 1979 paved the way for a peaceful resolution of the dispute. Negotiations were conducted for almost six years with the mediation of the Pope, ultimately leading to the conclusion of the Treaty of Peace and Friendship on November 29, 1984.[42] In the Treaty, Chile's sovereignty over the Beagle Channel Islands was recognized, though there was an explicit limitation about projecting

---

[41] See Robert L. Butterworth, *Managing Interstate Conflict 1945–1974: Data with Synopses* (University Center for International Studies, University of Pittsburgh, Pittsburgh, 1976), p. 235.

[42] See Victor Millán and Michael A. Morris, "Conflicts in Latin America: Democratic Alternatives in the 1990s" (1990) 230 *Conflict Studies* 1, 9–10; James L. Garrett, "The Beagle Channel Dispute: Confrontation and Negotiation in the Southern Cone" (1985) 27 *J. Interamerican Studies and World Affairs* 81; Carlos Washington Pastor, "Chile: La Guerra o la Paz, 1978–1981" in Silvia Ruth Jalabe (ed.), *La Política Exterior Argentina y sus Protagonistas, 1880–1995* (GEL, Buenos Aires, 1996), pp. 259–308.

its sovereignty beyond a surrounding three-mile wide zone. The 1984 Treaty of Peace and Friendship represented a watershed in the relations of Chile and Argentina, who at least three times in their long history had been on the brink of war, although they had never fought against each other.

The Beagle Channel conflict, like the Falklands/Malvinas dispute, was considered in both Chile and Argentina in terms of obligations arising from nineteenth century treaties and standard legal practices in locating sea and other territorial boundaries, including the interpretation of the principle of *uti possidetis*.[43] The unfortunate legal and political conflict between Argentina and Chile shows very clearly that an arbitral award delivered following a pre-established hermetical procedure is neither a guarantee of a final agreement nor an obstacle to further crisis and escalation.[44] Puzzling questions remain: why such an inadequate procedure took place at all, and why statesmen and diplomats in both countries did not realize that "formal" (legal) solutions do not always help resolve a dispute. On the contrary, the unilateral Argentinian rejection of the arbitral award in January 1978 led the two countries to the brink of war.

By unilaterally rejecting the arbitral award of 1977, Argentina violated the principle of *pacta sunt servanda*. It became the renegade party in terms of international law, like Ecuador after 1960. Its normative justification for the unilateral rejection included the following points:

- With publication of the award, Argentina acknowledged that, while it had traditionally upheld international agreements and had a long tradition of peaceful settlement of disputes, it had no obligation to comply with any decision that damaged its vital national interests.[45]
- The award was null and void, and "dictated in violation of international norms." The arguments were based on (1) excess of power, including opinions to questions not submitted to the court, such as the eastern mouth of the Magellan Strait; (2) defects of argumentation; (3) mistakes related to the application of international law ("defective"); (4) the court's reasoning being deemed "contradictory"; and (5) distortion of Argentine arguments.[46]

---

[43] See Holsti, "Armed Conflict in the Third World," 170.
[44] Puig, "Controlling Latin American Conflicts," 302.
[45] Quoted in Garrett, "The Beagle Channel Dispute," 93.
[46] See declaration of Oscar Antonio Montes, quoted in Miguel A. Scenna, *Argentina-Chile: Una Frontera Calient* (Editorial Belgrano, Buenos Aires, 1981), p. 263; Juan Archibaldo Lanús, *De Chapultepec al Beagle: Política Exterior Argentina, 1945–1980* (EMECE, Buenos Aires, 1984), p. 520.

- There were "geographical and historical errors" in the award. Moreover, the court exhibited a clear "imbalance in the evaluation of the respective arguments and evidence submitted by the two parties."[47]

The arguments presented by Argentina in its Declaration of Nullity attempted to justify non-compliance with the execution of an arbitral award, which was remanded to the honor of the parties to accept. Officially, Argentina claimed that its rejection stood "according to the *jus cogens* and a series of international precedents, regarding the rejection of an award if it violates in content and procedures basic rules of international law."[48] In practice, many of these assertions were far more subjective than the Argentine Declaration of Nullity suggests. Argentina was quite aware that its rejection contradicted its longstanding tradition of accepting and executing arbitration awards in the past, even when they ruled against its territorial interests.

From a legal and juridical point of view, the Argentine rights over the Beagle Channel Islands could not be sustained. The legal controversy reached (literally) a dead-end. As Argentine President General Jorge Videla argued, "for Argentina, the arbitral award does not exist any more, the juridical road is finished."[49] At this point, Argentina preferred a political solution that could be reached by peaceful settlement if possible, but by military means if necessary. Paradoxically, the rejection of the award in 1977 and the escalation towards a serious military crisis, as orchestrated by the Argentine military dictatorship, created the conditions for the Papal mediation and the negotiations that led to the political compromise of 1984. The political agreement somehow improved Argentina's position in relation to what was stipulated by the arbitration of 1977. At the same time, the Peace Treaty of 1984 encompassed the basics of the arbitration award by recognizing Chilean sovereignty over the disputed islands.

The Beagle Channel dispute was argued in legal and juridical terms, although it was eventually resolved as a political compromise. In juxtaposition to their legal arguments and claims, the two countries sustained serious geopolitical and economic interests in the disputed area. The award of 1977 changed the geopolitical situation in the region, opening the door for

---

[47] Quoted in Albert S. Golbert and Yenny Nun, *Latin American Laws and Institutions* (Praeger, New York, 1982), pp. 201–2.
[48] Argentina in Hernando Holguín Pelaez, *El Caso del Canal Beagle: Proceso Histórico-Jurídico* (Bloque Editorial Andino Ltda, Bogotá, 1980), p. 178 (author's translation).
[49] Videla in German Carrasco, *Argentina y el Laudo Arbitral del Canal Beagle* (Editorial Jurídica de Chile, Santiago, 1978), pp. 338–39 (author's translation).

Chile to get into the Atlantic Ocean. As Malcolm Shaw has rightly pointed out with respect to the Beagle Channel conflict, the Argentine rejection of the 1977 award was a "reflection of the vital interests it sees at stake here, placing the Argentine naval base of Ushuaia in Chilean-controlled waters and affecting Argentine claims to Antarctica and the oil and fish resources of the 200-mile zone south, toward Antarctica."[50]

From the Argentine standpoint, a stark contradiction existed between its geopolitical interests and compliance with the norms of international law. Coping with the award of 1977, Argentina confronted a particularly difficult dilemma: should it reject the award, and thus violate its honor, reputation, and good name in the Latin American international society? Or should it accept the award, and thus violate what it considered to be legitimate national interests? By choosing to reject the award in January 1978, Argentina, like Ecuador before, emphasized the political dimension of the conflict, although the Declaration of Nullity (like the Ecuadorian arguments) was formulated in legal (or even legalistic) terms.[51]

Summary and conclusions

We can now try to extrapolate from these two cases of Latin American rejection of international treaties and arbitration by applying the more general explanations why and when states do not comply with international agreements. First, the renegade states present the rejected treaties or awards as a "violation of international norms," in contradiction to the very principles they are supposed to uphold. Second, they point to the ambiguity, contradictions and indeterminacy in the language and content of treaties and awards. Third, upon recognizing that it has violated the principle of *pacta sunt servanda*, the rejecting party justifies this in terms of justice and morality, as opposed to law and order. For instance, Argentina in *Beagle Channel*, and Ecuador in *Oriente* introduced arguments of "fairness" and "justice" to justify their defiance of international law. Moreover, they also argued for a "change in conditions" (*rebus sic stantibus*) to justify their violation of the principle of *pacta sunt servanda*. Fourth, the rejecting parties argue that they prefer considerations of geopolitics and national interest to those of compliance with international

---

[50] Shaw, quoted in Puig, "Controlling Latin American Conflicts," 302–3 (author's translation).
[51] See María Teresa Infante Caffi, "Argentina y Chile: Percepciones del Conflicto de la Zona del Beagle" (1984) 17(67) *Estudios Internacionales* 337, 334; Ricardo Alberto Paz y Figueroa, *El Conflicto Pendiente* (EUDEBA, Buenos Aires, 1980), p. xiii.

norms. Fifth, non-compliance might be related to a particular type of political regime (authoritarian, nationalistic, militaristic) that misperceives the surrounding normative milieu, so it is "out of sync" with the current norms of international society, such as Argentina in 1976–1983 and Iraq until 2003.

This chapter has examined the questions of why and when states do or do not comply with their international obligations by reviewing the Latin American record of international arbitration in territorial disputes. In general, the explanations for compliance and non-compliance with international norms can be successfully implemented in the case of the Latin American region. This is quite remarkable, considering that most of the Latin American political regimes have usually not been democratic (at least until the late 1970s and 1980s, with the exceptions of Chile, Uruguay and Costa Rica).

Thus, the Latin American region has proven that non-democratic states can share some, if not all, of the normative perspectives and institutional restraints that seem to characterize democracies. Thus, the Latin American international (regional) society has been a most successful Grotian laboratory to test the presence, effect, impact and resilience of international norms associated with peace and compliance (*pacta sunt servanda*).

Why do states in general, and Latin American countries in particular, comply with international obligations, including the acceptance of arbitral awards? The common explanations include: (1) reciprocity, self-interest and reputation; (2) the regional normative framework; (3) the structure of the international system; (4) the incorporation of international law into domestic law; and (5) the type of political regime. For Latin Americans, there has been a long tradition of gaining (and keeping) honor, prestige and reputation by complying with legal obligations, not divorced from considerations of national interest.

At the same time, states do not always comply with their international obligations, as Argentina and Ecuador showed in their unilateral rejections of arbitral awards and international treaties. The arguments presented for non-compliance are elaborated as legal, normative and rational justifications. National interests and geopolitical considerations are stressed over compliance with international norms. Moreover, the treaties and awards are themselves presented as distortions of the "true" principles of international law, morality and justice – which demand a "just" rejection of an "unjust" award. Interestingly, the stalemate reached by non-compliance with an arbitration award initially leads to further escalation and militarized crises, like Argentina and Chile in December of

1978, and even to war, as in the Peruvian-Ecuadorian "rounds" of 1981 and 1995. Yet, the closing of a legal solution might eventually be followed by an opening (or return) to political (rather than legal) avenues of mediation, good offices and direct negotiations, as in the case of Argentina and Chile between 1979 and 1984 and Peru and Ecuador between 1995 and 1998. Thus, ultimately peace can be achieved, not by semi-legal or juridical means, but by political mechanisms.

9

International trade and domestic politics: the domestic sources of international trade agreements and institutions

HELEN V. MILNER,
B. PETER ROSENDORFF AND
EDWARD D. MANSFIELD

Introduction

Over the past fifty years, barriers to international trade have decreased substantially. While the decline in protectionism since World War II has stemmed partly from unilateral changes in trade policy by countries, it also has been a result of agreements among countries to liberalize their trade policies. International trade agreements and especially the GATT (now the WTO) have played an important role in this liberalization process. This chapter analyzes the conditions under which states have concluded such agreements to lower their trade barriers and joined such international institutions. More generally, it explores the domestic factors affecting international economic cooperation.

We make two central arguments, both relating international trade to domestic politics. The first is that domestic political reasons can provide an important motive for leaders to sign trade agreements and abide by international trade rules. The second is that the internal design of international trade agreements may depend in part on domestic politics. Again, domestic political reasons can be an important motive for leaders in choosing a specific structure for international trade agreements. In particular, we show that the inclusion of escape clause mechanisms in trade agreements can result from domestic incentives. Indeed, most strongly put, without such escape clauses in international agreements, political leaders could not afford to sign trade agreements because of domestic pressures. Hence their inclusion and character are important for such agreements and depend upon the nature of domestic politics in the countries.

We thus join the debate over the causes of economic cooperation. Many studies attribute variations in cooperation to international factors, especially the global distribution of capabilities and international institutions.[1] Some effort also has been made to link these variations to domestic institutional differences among democracies.[2] Others have related international cooperation to domestic politics by showing how such cooperation changes the domestic game that states play.[3] Fewer studies have examined the domestic sources of international cooperation.[4] We seek to fill this important gap in the literature by examining how domestic politics promotes the establishment of trade agreements and shapes their very nature.

International trade agreements often stem from the economic gains that leaders expect to derive from cooperation. Equally important but far more poorly understood, however, are the domestic political gains that also motivate leaders to cooperate in trade. The argument developed here focuses on leaders' domestic political incentives for international cooperation. It follows the "commitment approach to trade agreements," rather than the "traditional economic approach" which focuses on the terms of trade Prisoner's Dilemma faced by states.[5]

---

[1] See Robert Axelrod, *The Evolution of Cooperation* (Basic Books, New York, 1984); Robert Keohane, *After Hegemony: Cooperation and Discord in the World Political Economy* (Princeton University Press, Princeton, NJ, 1984); Stephen D. Krasner, "State Power and the Structure of Foreign Trade" (1976) 28 *World Politics* 317; Helen V. Milner, "International Theories of Cooperation: Strengths and Weaknesses" (1992) 44 *World Politics* 466.

[2] See Helen V. Milner, *Interests, Institutions, and Information: Domestic Politics and International Relations* (Princeton University Press, Princeton, NJ, 1997); Eric Reinhardt, "Posturing Parliaments: Ratification, Uncertainty, and International Bargaining," Ph.D. Dissertation (Columbia University, 1996).

[3] See Lisa Martin and Beth Simmons, "Theories and Empirical Studies of International Institutions" (1998) 52(4) *International Organization* 729 (Autumn); Andrew Cortell and James Davis, "How Do International Institutions Matter?" (1996) 40(4) *Int'l Studies Q.* 454.

[4] See Edward D. Mansfield, Helen V. Milner and B. Peter Rosendorff, "Free to Trade: Democracies, Autocracies, and International Trade" (2000) 94 *Am. Political Science Rev.* 305; Edward D. Mansfield, Helen V. Milner and B. Peter Rosendorff, "Why Democracies Cooperate More: Electoral Control and International Trade Agreements" (2002) 56(3) *International Organization* 477 (Summer); Fiona McGillivray and Alastair Smith, "Trust and Cooperation through Agent-Specific Punishments" (2000) 54 *International Organization* 809 Karen Remmer, "Does Democracy Promote Interstate Cooperation?" (1998) 42 *Int'l Studies Q.* 25; Daniel Verdier, "Democratic Convergence and Free Trade?" (1998) 42 *Int'l Studies Q.* 1; Brett Ashley Leeds, "Domestic Political Institutions, Credible Commitments and International Cooperation" (1999) 43 *Am. J. Political Science* 979.

[5] Kyle Bagwell and Robert Staiger, "GATT-Think," NBER Working Paper (NBER, Cambridge, MA, 2000), pp. 2–3.

First, we explore the domestic sources of trade agreements. Political leaders face two sets of domestic pressures in the trade realm. Special interest groups often want protection, and leaders may feel great pressure to provide protection. Political leaders, especially if motivated by rent-seeking, may therefore impose a variety of trade barriers. Furthermore, even elections may not reduce the responsiveness of leaders to special interests; instead, competitive elections may generate strong pressures for rents in the form of campaign contributions. On the other hand, political leaders desire above all to remain in power, and this depends in part on the reactions of their publics. If members of the public gear their approval of leaders to their economic situation, then leaders may be caught between the pressures of public approval and those of special interest groups. Too much protection may negatively affect the economy, and lead the public to seek new leaders. Hence leaders may be in a sub-optimal position where they have to give more protection to domestic interests than is optimal.

Leaders desire to provide only as much protection to special interests as they can without hurting their prospects of remaining in office. In any political regime, then, leaders may have to balance the policies that would enhance their electoral prospects and those that would meet the demands of special interest groups.[6] But when they have complete discretion over trade policy, leaders may be unable to resist the pressures of special interest groups in the short run, even though they would like to for political survival reasons.

Our claim is that signing an international trade agreement may help leaders overcome this dilemma. This outcome arises because of the way that trade agreements can enhance the utility of both leaders and the public. Trade agreements convey information to citizens about the activities of leaders; such information helps leaders retain office. The public knows that their leaders may be pressured to give more protection than is beneficial for society in general. But social actors face an informational problem; they cannot distinguish perfectly between adverse economic shocks and the extractive policies of leaders. The public may, as a result of this informational problem, remove a leader from office during economic downturns, even if that leader has not been engaged in excessive rent-seeking.

Leaders therefore would like to find a way to indicate that poor economic performance is not the result of their extractive policies. One way

---

[6] Gene M. Grossman and Elhanan Helpman, "Protection for Sale" (1994) *Am. Economic Rev.* 833 (September).

to do so is by entering into a trade agreement with another country. An agreement both commits leaders to less protectionist policies and conveys credibly to the public that a less protectionist policy has been adopted. International cooperation can thus help leaders increase their chances of staying in power, thereby providing a strong reason for them to pursue such agreements.[7]

Our second claim is that the internal design of international trade agreements may also depend much on domestic politics. Domestic influences on the institutional design of international trade agreements may be quite powerful. Almost all international trade agreements include some form of "safeguard" clause, which allows countries to escape the obligations agreed to in the negotiations. Such escape clauses erode both the credibility and the trade-liberalizing effect of international trade agreements, but they also increase the flexibility of the agreement by adding some discretion for national policy-makers.[8] Such increased flexibility may be ideal for leaders because of domestic politics.

An escape clause is any provision of an international agreement that allows a country to suspend the previously negotiated concessions without violating or abrogating the terms of the agreement. They are a prominent feature of many international agreements and are included in virtually all trade agreements. But the nature of the escape clauses often differs across agreements and is usually a subject of vigorous contestation in the negotiations. Since its inception in the 1940s, the GATT (and the subsequent WTO) has slowly built an arsenal of safeguard mechanisms to protect states from import pressures in the wake of extensive trade liberalizing agreements, including an escape clause, countervailing duty (CVD) penalties, anti-dumping (AD) statutes and a national security exception. They are thus means for industries to limit import competition by temporarily abrogating some portion of their treaty obligations under the GATT/WTO. These, and other measures such as the infant industry exemption and the balance of payments exemption in the GATT, are all designed by governments to reduce domestic pressures to withdraw from the entire agreement when protectionist pressures grow at home.

---

[7] See Mansfield, Milner and Rosendorff, "Why Democracies Cooperate More," for a model that shows why democracies in particular are most affected by this dynamic.

[8] For a formal model along these lines, see B. Peter Rosendorff and Helen V. Milner, "The Optimal Design of International Institutions: Why Escape Clauses are Essential" (2001) 55(4) *International Organization* 829 (Summer).

Escape clauses are an essential element of trade agreements when domestic uncertainty is high.[9] When political leaders cannot foresee the extent of future domestic demands for more protection at home, such clauses provide the flexibility that allows them to accept an international agreement liberalizing trade. The use of an escape clause, a flexibility-enhancing device, in institutional design also increases institutional effectiveness whenever there is domestic political uncertainty. Flexibility in this context refers to the ability to adapt and respond to unanticipated events within the context of a well-designed institutional system. The system itself is not subject to renewed bargaining. Alternative flexibility-enhancing devices are, of course, available: sunset provisions or anticipated renegotiations are often used. But these mechanisms are even more costly and hence less used than escape clauses. Indeed, the greater the uncertainty that political leaders have about their ability to comply with international agreements in the future, the more likely agreements are to contain escape clauses.

For escape clauses to be useful they must impose some kind of cost on their use; that is, countries that invoke escape clauses must pay some cost for doing so or else they will invoke them all the time, thus vitiating the agreement. Paying this cost signals their intention to comply in the future. But the different costs of alternative escape clause measures will affect the frequency of their use. Less costly measures will be used more often. If governments understand this, then they should prefer escape clauses that best match the extent of protectionist pressure they expect to experience from domestic interests. The costliness of the escape clause is crucial to the effectiveness of the escape clause regime, and the preferences of the domestic players in the negotiating countries will affect the optimal choice of this cost. Variation in the nature of the escape clause mechanism – i.e., primarily its cost – is an important feature of different agreements. Domestic preferences and institutions thus matter in the design of international institutions. Our argument is similar to the notion of efficient breach in legal theory.

Including escape clauses may also make initial agreements easier to reach. Their flexibility allows states to be reassured about the division of the long-term gains from the agreement. Indeed, without escape clauses of some sort, many trade agreements would never be politically viable

---

[9] See George W. Downs and David M. Rocke, *Optimal Imperfection? Domestic Uncertainty and Institutions in International Relations* (Princeton University Press, Princeton, NJ, 1995).

for countries. Increased flexibility (necessary for dealing with uncertainty about the future) lessens the distributional problems of bargaining that may plague an initial agreement.[10]

In the following two sections, we discuss these two important, yet distinct ways in which international trade agreements are shaped by domestic political considerations.

Domestic incentives for leaders to sign trade agreements

Why do political leaders make international trade agreements? International trade agreements arise in part because of the economic gains that leaders expect to derive from them; there are important terms of trade benefits that come from multilateral agreements.[11] In addition to economic conditions, international factors may motivate leaders to sign trade agreements. Relations between countries are likely to affect whether they cooperate economically. Many observers, for example, argue that the amount of economic exchange between states influences whether they enter a trade agreement. Such functionalist arguments have been common since Haas' early work on the European Community.[12] Political–military relations may also provide incentives for states to form trade agreements. Studies show that countries may be more likely to enter trade agreements with their allies than with other states.[13] Trade liberalization yields efficiency gains that enhance the political–military capacity of participants and alliances help to internalize these security externalities.[14] Since trade agreements liberalize commerce among members, alliance politics may influence the likelihood that states will establish such an agreement. Military disputes are also important since they tend to discourage participants from forming a commercial agreement. All of these factors are important for understanding the motivations of states to cooperate in trade relations. But these economic and international factors are not the focus of our argument.

---

[10] James D. Fearon, "Bargaining, Enforcement and International Cooperation" (1998) 52(2) *International Organization* 269.

[11] See Kyle Bagwell, and Robert Staiger, "An Economic Theory of GATT" (1999) 89 *Am. Economic Rev.* 215; Giovanni Maggi, "The Role of Multilateral Institutions in International Trade Cooperation" (1999) 89(1) *Am. Economic Rev.* 190 (March).

[12] Ernest, Haas, *The Uniting of Europe* (Stanford University Press, Stanford, 1958).

[13] See Edward D. Mansfield, and Rachel Bronson, "Alliances, Preferential Trading Arrangements, and International Trade" (1997) 91(1) *Am. Political Science Rev.* 94.

[14] Joanne, Gowa, *Allies, Adversaries, and International Trade* (Princeton University Press, Princeton, NJ, 1994).

Equally important but far more poorly understood, however, are the domestic *political* gains that also motivate leaders to cooperate in trade. What kinds of domestic conditions create incentives for leaders to sign trade agreements?

International agreements may serve a domestic purpose by constraining leaders. They allow political leaders to commit themselves credibly to actions that the public would otherwise find incredible. Others have argued that international institutions promote cooperation by providing information,[15] but they have been less specific about how this mechanism actually induces leaders to choose cooperation. Here, we identify one mechanism by which such cooperative agreements can convey information to the public about the behavior of their leaders, thus allowing them to better judge their leaders. Other mechanisms might serve this purpose too, but trade agreements do so especially well. The information provided by trade agreements benefits everyone: the public as well as the government. International cooperation can thus generate domestic political benefits for leaders, making them more likely to seek such cooperative agreements in the first place.

The goals of political leaders are to implement that policy which they most prefer and also to remain in power. The leader, whether democratic or autocratic, is interested in both the rents she derives from special interest groups and larger social welfare concerns. Trade policy provides her with one way of getting such rents. She can extract rents from interest groups in exchange for trade barriers that shield these groups from foreign economic competition.

If the leader did not have to worry about staying in office, then she could provide all groups who desired it with protection (even though this would reduce the benefits of protection for any one group). With political survival concerns, however, the leader does not desire to give all groups protection. Indeed, the more protection she gives, the worse the economy may perform and the more endangered her position may become. When she has complete discretion over policy, she may, however, be forced into giving more protection that she would otherwise desire. She thus lacks some credible commitment strategy for limiting the trade barriers that she implements.

Because of survival concerns, leaders have to worry about the public, and the public tends to care mostly about their economic situation. Social groups are likely to have different preferences for trade policy, if they have

---

[15] Keohane, *After Hegemony*.

any preferences in this area at all. Some, say those working in import-competing industries (in the United States, think of those in the apparel industry where about 75 percent of goods are imported or even the auto industry where over 25 percent of cars are imported), are likely to favor protection. Others, working in exporting industries such as electronics, computers and aircraft, are more likely to support trade liberalization. Most of the public is likely to support some level of trade barriers, but as barriers rise it is probable that their support for the leader falls. Protection is well known to impose large costs on the economy overall; the cost to any member of society is small but the cost to the economy as a whole may be large.[16] Choosing too high a level of trade barriers is likely to hurt the economy and thus reduce a leader's support among social groups.

When they have discretion over policy, political leaders are likely to be pushed to adopt too high a level of trade barriers. If the executive chooses a level of trade barriers different from that preferred by most of the public, this has two effects. It reduces her chances of staying in office since it lowers the public's welfare, but it also increases the rents that the leader may derive. Groups that the leader's policy helps are likely to give a portion of the rents they derive to her as either campaign contributions, lobbying expenditures or outright bribes. For these reasons, the executive may deviate from the policy preferred by most of society. But she knows that after setting commercial policy, elements of the public will decide whether or not to keep her in office at some time in the future, so she may want to commit herself to a lower level of protection. How to do this credibly is her problem.

The public faces a principal-agent problem. They help bring leaders to power and then leaders get to choose policies for them. The public has heterogeneous preferences about trade policy; given their factor endowments, some prefer very high levels of protection and some prefer freer trade. Most prefer a positive level of trade barriers but not too much protection. The public, however, cannot directly control trade policy; only their leaders can. The public is unlikely to know the exact level of trade barriers, but they do know the domestic price of the goods they produce and consume. This seems to accord with reality, since it is not obvious that

---

[16] See Gary Hufbauer and Kimberley Anne Elliott, *Measuring the Costs of Protection in the US* (Institute for International Economics, Washington, DC, 1994). For instance, trade barriers against sugar imports in the United States cost the American consumer over US$2 billion per year in higher prices, and despite some consumer groups' protests against them, sugar producers want political leaders to increase their protection. David Barboza, "Sugar Rules Defy Free Trade Logic," *New York Times*, May 6, 2001, A-1, A-4.

most individuals know the exact policy choices of their representatives. For example, American voters are much more likely to know the domestic price of sugar than the level of the quota imposed on imported sugar by the government. The public generally is unlikely to know what trade policies their representatives have enacted, giving the leaders an opportunity to extract more rents from special interest groups. The public has to be concerned, then, with their agent's behavior. When their overall economic welfare is good and rising, members of society may not be too worried about their leaders' behavior. But when economic conditions turn down, they may suspect that their leaders are providing too much protection for special interests and thus weighing down the economy. Economic downturns may thus signal them to vote against or reduce support for their incumbent leaders.

In such an environment, the public faces a problem: they do not know whether the reduction in their economic welfare was caused by an exogenous shock to the economy or by excessive protectionism on the part of the executive. They can only base their decision to support or oppose incumbents on the available information. This implies that they may throw out of office incumbent leaders for events beyond the leaders' control. Executives may pick the optimal policies from the public's point of view, but the economy may experience an adverse shock, thereby degrading their welfare and prompting them to reject the executive. The executive thus faces some prospect of being ousted from office every period, no matter what trade policy she chooses. And the more democratic the country, the more powerful this pressure will be.

In addition to setting their own policies, executives have the capability of negotiating trade agreements with other countries. But an executive will only do this if the gains from an agreement are at least as great as those from setting policy unilaterally. When can a leader gain from a trade agreement? An agreement usually involves a set of mutually acceptable trade policies for the countries involved and an institution that can send signals about the countries' behavior. (It is also possible that signals about compliance can be sent by the foreign countries involved). That is, it comprises a level of trade barriers lower than the executive's optimal unilateral policy. It also includes a mechanism for the foreign country or the international institution to signal to others that the home executive has cheated and raised trade barriers above the agreement level. Trade agreements bind leaders in the sense that they make information about the leaders' behavior more readily available. They need not actually punish leaders for their violations of the agreement; they just make such violations much more public so that they can be dealt with in other domestic fora, as suggested by Benvenisti.[17]

The agreement includes a level of trade barriers below what the leader would otherwise choose and an alarm mechanism that other governments or the trade institution, such as the GATT or WTO, can use whenever the actual trade policy of a country that is party to the agreement exceeds the agreed-upon level. A commercial agreement is public and therefore provides information that at least some social actors can use to monitor the executive more closely.

In particular, monitors of the trade agreement such as an independent agency like the WTO, or even the participating governments themselves, can announce whether the leader in each country is in compliance with the agreement. The WTO does indeed issue such reports on all member countries periodically. Its publicly issued Trade Policy Reviews of member countries are an important aspect of monitoring. The EU also provides such periodic reports on compliance with its policies by member governments. The international institution and its member countries have an incentive to divulge this information and make sure that domestic publics in other countries pay attention to it since this can in turn help to discipline the foreign government. Moreover, the public has some incentive to pay attention to it, since the signal can improve their welfare. These dynamics are increasingly important as countries become more democratic and leaders face growing electoral competition. So an international trade agreement moves countries away from their unilateral policy choices and has important informational features.

The public (at least some of them) now have more information than before. They may adjust their strategies accordingly. Instead of just looking at their overall welfare, they may also listen for the alarm sent by the international institution. If they hear the alarm, then they have more reason to reject the incumbent leader and she is more likely to lose power.

There is some evidence that leaders do worry about the domestic effects of cheating on international agreements. It would be ideal to have data on how such cheating affects public support for incumbents. But in its absence, there is certainly evidence that leaders, when knowing they are going to violate international agreements, try to mitigate the potential impact by invoking imperatives of national security or explaining away such infractions legalistically. (The Bush Administration's handling of

---

[17] Eyal, Benvenisti, "Exit and Voice in the Age of Globalization" (1999) 98(1) *Michigan L. Rev.* 167, 206.

the ABM treaty is a case in point.) If leaders were not worried about the domestic impact of such cheating, they would not expend the effort to rationalize their actions.

The executive faces a new situation relative to her trade policy decision under a trade agreement. By making an agreement, the executive trades some of her policy-setting discretion for the greater certainty that she will not be rejected (unfairly) from office. Interestingly, the leader (who is the potential violator) may benefit from the alarm too because it reduces the prospects of being punished by the public when no rules were broken. When the public's welfare declines but there is no cheating alarm sounded by the international institution, they will be less likely to blame their incumbent leader and more likely to keep her in office.

Complying with the agreement, however, reduces the rents that leaders can collect domestically. The leader now earns some lower value of the rents she gains from this level of trade barriers. With pure discretion, the executive can earn a higher level of rents from setting policy unilaterally and providing more protection for special interests. The value of cooperation over non-cooperation for the executive thus is the difference between the gains from cooperation minus the gains from unilateral policy-making. The executive trades off a greater degree of certainty of remaining in office when she cooperates, for a lower level of rents since she employs a lower level of trade barriers. When the gains from cooperation relative to unilateral policy-making are positive, the leader should choose to make an agreement. When leaders value office highly and fear losing it, international trade agreements may be beneficial to them. They will lower the levels of protection leaders are forced to provide and thereby increase their chances of staying in power.

Even if the government gains, we need to show that the majority of the public gains as well from an international agreement. If the leader always chooses too much protectionism when unconstrained, then any reduction in this level through a trade agreement will be beneficial to most members of society. In addition, the public has a new source of information about their leaders' behavior that allows for better monitoring and acting more informatively. Thus the public should also gain from a trade agreement.

In a world where the public cannot perfectly distinguish between a reduction in their welfare stemming from an adverse economic shock, on the one hand, and excessive government rent-seeking, on the other, leaders and the public will both gain from international trade agreements that provide information about the executive's behavior. There may be other mechanisms that countries could design to provide such information to the public, but it is hard to think of ones that are as credible. Political oppositions in the country itself cannot be counted on since they are unlikely to tell the truth about the incumbent's behavior. Social actors are likely to know this and thus to discount any information domestic oppositions provide. Other domestic institutions, such as courts or the media, may also be seen as less credible since they too may have strategic reasons for providing such information.

International agreements can thus serve a domestic purpose. They allow executives to commit themselves credibly to actions that their publics would otherwise find incredible. They allow leaders to choose a lower level of trade barriers than they could unilaterally. They also convey information to the public about the behavior of their leaders, thus allowing them to better judge their leaders. The information provided by trade agreements benefits all groups: home and foreign publics, as well as leaders in both countries. This is an aspect that few, if any, scholars have discussed concerning the role of international institutions. These mechanisms are more potent in democracies than in autocracies. International cooperation and the institutions created to monitor it can thus generate domestic benefits for leaders, making them more likely to seek such cooperative agreements in the first place.

Domestic influences on the design of international trade agreements

While there has been much debate over the role of international institutions, less has been written about the internal design of such institutions. We know that international institutions differ greatly in their forms; the number of states included, the decision-making mechanisms, the range of issues covered, the degree of centralized control, and the extent of flexibility within them all vary substantially from one institution to the next. What accounts for such variation? We claim that such variation can be accounted for in part as the response of leaders faced with particular domestic problems.

Almost all international trade agreements include some form of "safeguard" clause, which allows countries to escape the obligations agreed to in the negotiations.[18] On the one hand, such escape clauses are likely to erode both the credibility and the trade-liberalizing effect of international

---

[18] Bernard Hoekman and Michel Kostecki, *The Political Economy of the World Trading System* (Oxford University Press, New York, 1995), p. 161.

trade agreements. On the other hand, they increase the flexibility of the agreement by adding some discretion for national policy-makers. When is such increased flexibility optimal for leaders making international trade agreements?

An escape clause is any provision of an international agreement that allows a country to suspend the concessions it previously negotiated without violating or abrogating the terms of the agreement. They are a prominent feature of many international agreements and are included in virtually all trade agreements. However, it is interesting to note that not all international agreements have such clauses; for instance, some international arms control agreements, such as the SALT agreements, do not contain such escape mechanisms. Most trade agreements do contain them, but the nature of the escape clauses often differs across agreements and is usually a subject of vigorous contestation in the negotiations. For example, in both the NAFTA and GATT Uruguay Round negotiations, antidumping and countervailing duty laws were critical issues that impeded agreement among the countries.

Since its inception in the 1940s, the GATT (and the subsequent WTO) has slowly built an arsenal of safeguard mechanisms to protect states from import pressures in the wake of extensive trade liberalizing agreements. These include an escape clause, countervailing duty (CVD) penalties, antidumping (AD) statutes, and a national security exception. For each of these, the GATT (now WTO) specifies the conditions under which a government can grant relief to an industry from import competition, and industries then have the option of choosing under which mechanism to file their complaints. In each of the GATT negotiating rounds, the inclusion and/or modification of these different laws have been the subject of intense debate among the signatories.

Many have noted that these different clauses can be substitutes for one another. Hoekman and Leidy[19] and Hansen and Prusa[20] suggest that CVD and AD laws are really "a poor man's" escape clause. AD and CVD complaints allege that exporting countries are playing unfairly and thus the harmed country avoids the payment of compensation that the GATT requires on use of the escape clause. They are thus means for industries to limit import competition on the cheap: they mean that a country can

---

[19] Bernard M. Hoekman and Michael P. Leidy, "Dumping, Antidumping and Emergency Protection" (1989) 23(5) *J. World Trade L.* 27 (October).

[20] Wendy Hansen and Thomas Prusa, "The Road Most Taken: The Rise of Title VII Protection" (1995) *The World Economy* 295.

abrogate some portion of its treaty obligations under the GATT and pay a lower penalty than if they were to use the escape clause. These, and other measures such as the infant industry exemption and the balance of payments exemption in the GATT, are all designed by governments to reduce domestic pressures to withdraw from the entire agreement when protectionist pressures grow at home. While these different laws are generally seen as substitutes, they do differ substantially in the costs they impose on the country using them. Usually AD and CVD clauses are seen as less costly to use than are traditional escape clauses. This type of variation is important, as explained below.

Escape clauses are an essential element of trade agreements under conditions of domestic uncertainty. When political leaders cannot foresee the extent of future domestic demands for more protection at home (and/or more open markets abroad), such clauses provide the flexibility that allows them to accept an international agreement liberalizing trade. The greater the uncertainty that political leaders face about their ability to maintain domestic compliance with international agreements in the future, the more likely they are to seek agreements that contain escape clauses. This also suggests that in issue areas where uncertainty about domestic pressures to comply is less, governments are less likely to desire such safeguard measures.

The use of an escape clause, a flexibility-enhancing device, in institutional design can increase institutional effectiveness whenever there is domestic political uncertainty. Flexibility in this context refers to the ability to adapt and respond to unanticipated events within the context of a well-designed institutional system. The system itself is not subject to renewed bargaining. Alternative flexibility-enhancing devices are, of course, available: sunset provisions or anticipated renegotiations are often used. But these mechanisms are even more costly and hence less used than escape clauses.

For escape clauses to be useful they must impose some kind of cost on their use; that is, countries that invoke the escape clause must pay some cost for doing so or else they will invoke them all the time, thus vitiating the agreement. Paying this cost signals their intention to comply in the future. But the different costs of alternative escape clause measures will affect the frequency of their use. Less costly measures will be used more often. If governments understand this, then they should prefer the set of escape clauses that best matches the extent of protectionist pressure they expect to experience from domestic interests. Thus, the architects of international agreements will design such agreements so that the costs of the escape clauses that they most desire are balanced by the benefits of future cooperation. Variation in the nature of the escape clause mechanism – i.e., primarily its cost – is thus an important feature of different agreements. Domestic preferences and institutions will thereby matter in the design of international institutions.

The key factor that renders escape clauses desirable is the presence of uncertainty. Leaders are constantly faced with political pressure for protection at home. The domestic economy is subject to many shocks. Some unanticipated change in the economy or political system produces a surge in imports that triggers a large increase in domestic firms' demands for protection. This shock can be of a very general nature; it is any exogenous and unanticipated change (e.g., price or supply changes; technological change; political change) that affects domestic firms' demand for, or ability to lobby for, protection of their markets. Currency appreciations, downturns in the economy, new competitors aboard, etc. can all produce a sudden, unexpected surge in demands for protection. Leaders who have signed trade agreements then face the quandary of trying to decide how to respond. Saying no to such pressures may have a variety of negative consequences, all of which can endanger the political tenure of leaders. Completely abrogating trade agreements, however, can be costly for leaders, as argued above. So what is a leader to do?

What if countries every now and then face intense pressures to cheat, yet do not want to spark a breakdown in cooperation and certain retaliation by other countries? Can an alternative institutional structure be devised to maintain a cooperative agreement, even in these periods of high political pressure to protect?

In the presence of such unexpected shocks, international institutions may be much better served by allowing countries to make temporary and ad hoc use of escape clauses that allow them to break the rules for a short period and pay a cost to do so. Doing so prevents a spiral of retaliation from occurring. The defection by the country is tolerated, exactly because the other side may wish to use the same instrument in the future. Countries are in a position similar to Rawl's "initial position," where each is behind the veil of ignorance and cannot tell exactly how each will benefit (or lose) in the future from agreements made now. Because shocks can occur in each future period that cannot be predicted beforehand, the leaders do not know with certainty the future distribution of gains and losses from the initial agreement. Hence this is likely to mitigate how hard they bargain in the first place. Including escape clauses may make both enforcement of agreements and distributive bargaining over trade issues easier.

Very little retaliation for treaty violations is actually observed. Under current WTO rules, any punishment can only come after a finding by the dispute settlement procedure at the WTO, and frequently, the dispute is "settled" before punishments are applied. The pre-Uruguay Round rules in fact made findings of allowable retaliation quite rare.[21] Cooperation is deeper, more likely, and international trade institutions are more durable with escape clauses than without them. In the choice, then, between rules versus discretion, rules with costly discretion may be better than no discretion when the future holds unexpected, unpleasant surprises for political leaders.

Domestic political uncertainty may take a number of forms. At the most broad level, there is uncertainty regarding what one might call the future state of the world; i.e., the configuration of political pressures in future periods is not known with certainty by leaders. Uncertainty regarding the preferences of key domestic players is another possibility, one considered elsewhere in an investigation of the effect of elections on the design of international agreements.[22] Another possibility is that the agreement itself is too complex (or time is too valuable) for the domestic policy-makers to understand fully the consequences of its passage and policy-makers therefore rely on the information provided by lobbies and other interested third parties.[23]

Many trade agreements include such escape clauses; indeed, all GATT agreements have at least one type, if not several types, of such escape clauses. Moreover, these alternative escape mechanisms have different costs for their use. In general, a country appealing to an escape clause is allowed, under the rules of the institution, to protect the affected industry for the duration of that period, as long as it (in effect) voluntarily and publicly incurs some penalty. This voluntary penalty is consistent with the reciprocity norm of the GATT, which requires a country that applies a temporary trade barrier to reciprocate by lowering some other barrier elsewhere in order to leave its trading partners unaffected by the action or to face an equivalent trade barrier by its partners.

But this penalty may take any number of forms. For example, in the use of the GATT escape clause, countries must negotiate compensation with

---

[21] B. Peter Rosendorff, *Stability and Rigidity: The Dispute Settlement Procedure of the WTO*, unpublished manuscript (University of Southern California, Los Angeles, CA, 1999).

[22] See Helen V. Milner and B. Peter Rosendorff, "Democratic Politics and International Trade Negotiations: Elections and Divided Government as Constraints on Trade Liberalization" (1997) 41(1) *J. Conflict Resolution* 117.

[23] Milner, *Interests, Institutions, and Information*.

the affected exporter, or face equivalent retaliation from the exporter. For other safeguard-type measures, the cost is often less explicit and smaller. Sometimes there is a presumption that a country invoking the escape clause will be forced to devise and implement a plan of structural adjustment for the affected industry; such plans have costs, both economic and political. Moreover, the costs of filing an escape clause, AD or CVD complaint are also part of the costs that the import-competing firms must face. For many of these, the technical and legal requirements for producing evidence of injury are sufficiently high to merit consideration as a source of costs borne. In any case, each safeguard mechanism entails some costs when it is used, although these costs do differ in important ways.

After invoking the safeguard, in some future period the country returns to the cooperative regime, having preserved its reputation as a cooperator. Moreover, no supranational enforcement agency must force the country to pay this penalty; the country (and everyone else) realizes that paying the penalty is in its best interest in order to preserve its credibility in the future. The institution serves as a verification agency, much as in the Law Merchants institution;[24] it monitors whether defection occurs with a penalty.

The costs that a state must pay for using the escape clause is of great importance. If this penalty is set at an appropriate level, a country may temporarily use the escape clause and then return to the cooperative regime. If the costs are set too high, then countries will abandon the institution and defect when they experience a severe shock. If these costs are set too low, then there is repeated recourse to the escape clause, and the agreement enforces little actual cooperation over time. Escape clauses will thus be used more often when their costs of use are lower. Variations in the costs of different escape clause mechanisms will be an important feature in the design of international trade agreements.

As noted above, most international trade agreements include at least one form of escape clause. Many, such as the GATT, include several. This is due in part to the high levels of domestic uncertainty that surround trade politics. Greater domestic uncertainty, or situations where political leaders are more sensitive to unanticipated changes in political pressures, should be associated with more reliance on escape mechanisms. An interesting

---

[24] Paul R. Milgrom, Douglass C. North and Barry R. Weingast, "The Role of Institutions in the Revival of Trade: The Law Merchant, Private Judges, and the Champagne Fairs" (1990) 2(1) *Economics and Politics* 1.

test of this claim, then, would be to identify those political institutions that magnify the effect of unanticipated shocks and see whether countries with these types of institutions are more likely to devise and use escape clauses in their trade relations. Another test would be to deduce which issue areas are more subject to unanticipated domestic shocks and see if they are more likely to have escape clauses associated with them. Such an exercise, unfortunately, is beyond the scope of this chapter. However, two facts about escape clauses accord with this claim: certain countries which arguably are more sensitive to domestic pressures are the main proponents and users of escape mechanisms, and certain issue areas seem more likely to have escape clauses than others due to their greater levels of uncertainty.

Escape clauses in trade policy exist at both the national and the international level. Interestingly, international usage has often copied domestic laws. Several countries dominate the international use of all forms of escape clauses and these are all countries that have tended to use escape clauses first domestically. The main countries using GATT/ WTO AD, CVD and safeguard clauses are the same ones who earlier developed a battery of domestic laws to use these trade remedies. By and large, the United States, Canada, the EU (or EC) and Australia are the main users of these clauses.[25] These are the same countries that initially built domestic trade laws around such escape mechanisms.

The first instance of an AD law was Canada's 1904 anti-dumping regime.[26] In 1947, the United States instituted the world's first safeguard clause,[27] and the United States and Canada were both the early designers of CVD laws. This suggests that the need for escape clauses may be associated with large democracies with federal structures. It may well be that unanticipated shocks are far more damaging for political leaders in these democracies than in non-democracies. These shocks may be more likely to get them ejected from office in highly competitive elections where negatively affected groups can mobilize against the incumbents, and in federal institutions where such mobilization may be more threatening. If so, this would explain why these types of countries are more likely to have such national escape clause provisions and why they are also more likely to be proponents of these provisions at the international level.

---

[25] Michael Trebilcock and Robert Howse, *The Regulation of International Trade* (2nd ed., Routledge, London, 1995).
[26] *Ibid.* at p. 172.   [27] *Ibid.* at p. 227.

For example, in the realm of safeguard clauses, the United States has the oldest domestic laws and has been their most vocal proponent in international trade negotiations. American trade law puts the escape clause into practice via section 201 of the Trade Act of 1974. Between 1975 and 1990, sixty-two cases under section 201 were initiated, of which thirteen industries received relief, plus seven more who received trade adjustment assistance. High profile cases included color televisions in 1982, which received protection on US$1,543 million of imports that year and non-rubber footwear (US$2,480 million in 1981).[28] Following a petition, which can be lodged by the industry, or by government (including the President, the US Trade Representative or Congress, among others), the US International Trade Commission (ITC) conducts an investigation to evaluate whether imports have been a substantial cause of or threat of injury to the domestic industry. After an affirmative finding by the ITC, the President may grant protection for up to five years, with the possibility of extending it for another three years. This practice has been followed closely in the GATT, largely at the Americans' insistence. Article XIX of the GATT permits a member to escape from its obligations not to raise trade barriers when one of its industries is suffering an economic downturn, and is experiencing "serious injury."

In the realm of AD and CVDs, the same association is apparent. American and Canadian laws have preceded international ones and set the pattern for them. Article VI of the GATT, and the Second Antidumping Code of the Tokyo Round, which define practice in AD and CVD law, allow member states to apply duties when imports are sold at "less than fair value," following American practice describe the American anti-dumping laws (and those of other countries) as "miniature escape clauses," in that the AD Code extends protection to smaller cases on which agreement would be impossible *ex ante*.[29] Between 1994 and 1996 alone, seventy-seven AD petitions were filed in the United States, and worldwide, the AD clause has been invoked over 2,000 times since 1970. Similarly, the American CVD Code (which is consistent with the GATT's Article VI) allows member states to apply a countervailing duty when a subsidy is being provided to the foreign industry. Other forms of the escape clause appear throughout the GATT. Balance of payments exceptions (Articles XVIII and XII), infant industry protection (Article XVIII) and

---

[28] Gary Hufbauer and H. F. Rosen, *Trade Policy for Troubled Industries* (Institute for International Economics, Washington, DC, 1986).

[29] Ronald A. Cass, Richard D. Boltuck, Seth T. Kaplan and Michael Knoll, *Antidumping*, USC Law School Working Paper Series 97–15 (1997), p. 24.

tariff renegotiation (Article XXVII) allow temporary escape from a member's obligations under the agreement.

Trade is, of course, an area where governments are likely to face strong domestic pressures for import protection from time to time. When imports surge or when economic conditions facing an industry turn downward, pressures for protection may suddenly appear. Unfortunately, governments may not be able to anticipate perfectly the magnitude of such pressures or their origin. Cass *et al.*[30] claim that these safeguard mechanisms allow "protectionist sentiment to hold sway" when political pressures are great. Democratic leaders may be especially vulnerable to such unexpected changes, and hence may seek escape clause protection more than leaders in other systems. The greater impact of uncertainty in democratic systems may make their leaders particularly desirous of escape clause mechanisms in trade.

The need for escape clauses may also vary by issue area. Trade, it is widely believed, is an area where governments face domestic uncertainty that has significant costs; such international economic exchanges are susceptible to swift changes due to price or supply shocks, technological change and/or foreign government policy changes. The same is true in the macroeconomic area. Fixed exchange rate systems especially may be vulnerable to unanticipated domestic pressures to devalue. High uncertainty over the timing and magnitude of these domestic pressures seems likely. Thus, in fixed exchange rate agreements, leaders might desire escape clause measures. In the Bretton Woods regime, for example, the simple rule was the requirement to maintain fixed exchange rates. But a country could devalue in the event of "fundamental disequilibrium," a vague phrase allowing escape from the simple rule, since even economists were unable to agree on what balance-of-payments equilibrium meant. The regime did not dictate in advance the size of the devaluation. Instead, it required a member state to seek approval from the International Monetary Fund (at least for an exchange-rate realignment of more than 10 percent).

The European Payments Union (EPU), the post-war multilateral trade deficit clearing system, gave signatories the right to suspend liberalization measures as a result of serious economic disturbance or if liberalization was too disruptive.[31] Similarly, Europe's Exchange Rate Mechanism (ERM) required Member States to maintain bilateral exchange rates

---

[30] *Ibid.*
[31] Thomas Oatley, "Multilateralizing Trade and Payments in Postwar Europe" (2001) *International Organization* 949.

within clearly demarcated target zones, but did allow for realignments of the parity. While the ERM's architects recognized the need for occasional parity realignments, they did not specify exactly when such realignments should take place. Instead, the ERM required that realignments be negotiated among all Members.[32] In all three cases, escape clause mechanisms were included in the design of these institutions to deal with situations where policy-makers face high levels of domestic uncertainty over the pressures that will arise for them to abrogate any international agreement they sign.

Notice that under all three regimes (Bretton Woods, EPU, ERM), devaluation (the use of an escape clause) was not without its costs. Devaluation was permitted only in concert with other measures designed to bring core macroeconomic aggregates back to "acceptable" parameters. Devaluation was therefore frequently associated with fiscal and monetary contraction, policy liberalization and reform, all of which come at a domestic political price.

But in other areas, domestic uncertainty is less pervasive and consequential. In an area like arms control, the public and interest groups tend to be less organized and involved. The most important constituency for these agreements is often the military, which may take part in the negotiations and hence shape them directly. The impact of unexpected changes in this area may be less for political leaders than in areas like trade. Notably, arms control agreements have frequently not included escape clauses. The Anti-Ballistic Missile (ABM) treaty, most of the Strategic Arms Limitation Talks (SALT) treaties and the Intermediate Nuclear Forces (INF) treaties do not contain escape mechanisms; some of these allow countries to withdraw with certain notification provisions and some have definite time limits, but none seem to contain clauses that allow temporary abrogation of the agreements. Arms control may be an area where domestic uncertainty is less important for leaders. Unexpected shocks that greatly increase pressures for leaders to cheat on the agreement (or pay substantial domestic costs) are less common in this area.[33] Hence, one would not expect states

---

[32] Christopher Canavan and B. Peter Rosendorff, *How the EMU Killed the ERM: International Regimes with Temporary Relief Clauses*, unpublished manuscript (University of Southern California, Los Angeles, CA, 1997).

[33] It is interesting to speculate on the causes of the United States' abandonment of the ABM Treaty in order to develop a national missile defense. These pressures for change do not seem to arise from domestic uncertainty, but rather from technological change. Having an escape clause would not resolve the problems posed by the National Missile Defense (NMD).

to be as concerned about including escape clauses in these agreements, as they are in trade and the monetary area. Where domestic uncertainty is less consequential for leaders, escape clauses will be less important and hence less used.

If it is correct that governments choose escape clause mechanisms, then one should see that variations in their cost lead to variations in their usage. Low cost escape mechanisms should have much appeal; high cost ones should not. A good deal of evidence seems to suggest that this argument is valid. For instance, in American trade law, the escape clause (section 201) has been used far less often than have various other safeguard mechanisms. Hanson and Prusa[34] show that the average number of escape clause cases filed has never gone above eleven per year, while for AD and CVD cases the average reached a peak of ninety-two per year in the early 1980s. Moreover, escape clause complaints have been decreasing steadily, with less than one a year filed in the early 1990s. In contrast, AD and CVD cases have been growing over time. What accounts for this difference in usage?

It is the greater cost of invoking escape clauses that makes firms less likely to do so. Hanson and Prusa claim that the lower probability of success makes firms choose to file AD and CVD instead. But the claim here is that the lower probability of success results from the fact that escape clause actions when implemented cost the importing country more and thus make policy-makers less likely to accept petitions for it. Thus firms see it is as less successful and choose other means. The main reasons they cost more is that exporters have a right to demand compensation for escape clause relief and, if it is not forthcoming, to retaliate. Compensation and retaliation create large domestic costs for governments who therefore try to avoid such measures.

The GATT also provides evidence that greater costs mean less use. Under GATT rules, exporters had a right to compensation or retaliatory action if Article XIX, which involved the escape clause, was invoked. Moreover, the standards of proof for "serious injury" caused by imports needed to invoke the escape clause have been the highest of all. Among all the various safeguard means in the GATT, Article XIX was among the least used. It was invoked only 150 times between 1950 and 1994. It has also seen declining use over time: it was used 3.6 times per year from 1950 to 1984 and 3.2 times per year from 1985 to 1994. In contrast, the

---

[34] Hanson and Prusa, "The Road Most Taken," at 296, table 1.

AD clause is much more frequently invoked: over 2,000 times since 1970 alone.[35]

In addition, scholars have noted that costliness of escape clause actions has led to the proliferation of so-called voluntary export restraints (VERs). As Schott[36] states, "Most major trading countries, however, have been deterred from invoking Article XIX less by its requirements than by the availability of less onerous and more flexible channels of protection. These have included coercing trading partners to accept VERs and other so-called gray area measures, as well as frequent recourse to unilateral relief actions under Article VI (i.e., antidumping and countervailing duties)." VERs are less costly to use than the escape clause since they do not assume compensation or allow retaliation from the affected exporter.

But VERs do impose a cost on the importing country. Unlike a tariff or quota which provides rents for the importing country, a VER transfers those rents to the exporter. As Hoekman and Kostecki[37] maintain, "affected exporters tended to accept VERs because they were better than the alternative – often an AD duty – as they allowed them to capture part of the rent that was created. Instead of being confronted with a tariff, the revenue of which is captured by the levying government, a VER involves voluntary cutbacks by exporters in their supplies to a market. This reduction in supply will raise prices – assuming that others do not take up the slack. Exporters therefore get more per unit sold than they would under an equivalent tariff. . . . The key point to remember about VERs is that they imply some direct compensation of affected exporters and selectively target exporters. Thus they practically meet GATT-1947's compensation requirement, while allowing for circumvention of its nondiscrimination requirement." Hence VERs were preferred to escape clause actions because they were less expensive to employ, but even they imposed costs on the importing country.

Interestingly, the GATT recognized that the costliness of using the escape clause was hurting the system and pushing states to develop other means – such as VERs – to deal with domestic pressures. Many GATT officials found other safeguard remedies, such as AD, VER and CVD, very undesirable. They preferred that countries use the escape clause mechanism. But they also realized that this process was too costly and thus

---

[35] Hoekman and Kostecki, *Political Economy*.
[36] Jeffrey, Schott, *The Uruguay Round: An Assessment* (Institute for International Economics, Washington, DC, 1994), p. 94.
[37] Hoekman and Kostecki, *Political Economy*, pp. 168–69.

under-used. In the Uruguay Round, they made several changes to reduce the costs of the escape clause relative to other safeguards. First, they banned the use of VERs in the agreement on safeguards.[38] This in effect raised the costs of such measures.

Second, they decided that it was necessary to reduce the costs of the escape clause option. So they proposed, and countries agreed, that one way to do this was to eliminate the right of retaliation. Hence in the WTO, countries that use the escape clause no longer have to pay compensation and the injured exporters can no longer legally retaliate for the first three years of its use.[39] As Hoekman and Kostecki note,[40] "(b)y the time of the Uruguay Round the major objective of target countries was to constrain the use of AD and VERs and assert the dominance of Article XIX in safeguard cases. Two options were available: either to tighten the discipline on the use of AD, or to reduce the disincentives to use Article XIX. Both approaches were pursued." Lowering the costs of using the escape clause then was seen as a key way to shift countries away from using alternative safeguards like AD and CVD, and toward using more escape clause actions. This seems to provide some evidence that leaders do indeed design international agreements with domestic pressures in mind.

In the international monetary arena, the costs of exercising relief have varied both across institutions and within institutions over time. Again one could argue that these variations are the rational responses of political leaders to the problems associated in part with domestic uncertainty. The Bretton Woods system's vagueness as to the conditions under which a devaluation could occur meant that it was frequently appealed to, and effective cooperation was limited. Both the EPU and the ERM were more specific about the terms of realignments; moreover, the ERM became increasingly more restrictive about the conditions under which escape was possible as the system moved towards monetary union, and accordingly less tolerant of realignments. As a result, the system became somewhat more rigid and less flexible, leading to more periods of instability and exit, as happened in Britain and Italy in 1992.[41]

Including escape clauses may also make initial agreements easier to reach. Their flexibility allows states to be reassured about the division of the long-term gains from the agreement. Indeed it is possible that without

---

[38] Schott, *The Uruguay Round*, p. 94.
[39] Ernest Preeg, *Traders in a Brave New World* (University of Chicago Press, Chicago, 1995), pp. 100–1; Schott, *The Uruguay Round*, pp. 94–97.
[40] Hoekman and Kostecki, *Political Economy*, p. 169.
[41] Canavan and Rosendorff, *How the EMU Killed the ERM*.

escape clauses of some sort many trade agreements would never be politically viable for countries. Increased flexibility necessary to deal with the uncertainty about the future lessens the problems of distribution that may plague an initial agreement. The escape clause adds flexibility to an agreement that might be difficult to sustain in the presence of uncertainty. Hence bargainers are not stuck in a commitment to a distributional outcome for the infinite horizon, thereby making initial bargains easier to strike.

As many have noted about the GATT, it would have been impossible for many countries to sign without various safeguards. Ruggie,[42] for example, has argued that all of the international economic agreements, or regimes, negotiated after World War II had to embody the norm of "embedded liberalism," by which he meant that they had to combine multilateralism with the requirements of domestic stability. Domestic safeguards that allowed countries to protect their economies were thus essential parts of this norm in both the trade and monetary areas. Without such safeguards, countries would have never signed the trade and monetary agreements.

Moreover, Hoekman and Kostecki[43] claim that "(p)olitical realities often dictate that there be a mechanism allowing for the temporary reimposition of protection in instances where competition from imports proves to be too fierce to allow the restructuring process to be socially sustainable. Indeed, a safeguard mechanism is likely to be a pre-condition for far-reaching liberalization to be politically feasible." Or as Sykes[44] has shown, "when self-interested political officials must decide whether to make trade concessions under conditions of uncertainty about their political consequences, the knowledge that those concessions are in fact 'escapable' facilitates initial trade concessions." Following Dam,[45] Sykes[46] maintains that "unanticipated changes in economic conditions may create circumstances in which the political rewards to an increase in protection (or the political costs of an irrevocable commitment to reduce protection) are great. Consequently, in the absence of an escape clause,

---

[42] John Gerard Ruggie, "International Regimes, Transactions and Change: Embedded Liberalism in the Postwar Economic Order" (1982) 36(2) *International Organization* 379 (Spring).
[43] Hoekman and Kostecki, *Poltical Economy*, p. 191.
[44] Alan Sykes, "Protectionism as a Safeguard" (1991) 58 *U. Chicago L. Rev.* 255, 259.
[45] Kenneth Dam, *The GATT: Law and International Economic Organization* (University of Chicago Press, Chicago, IL, 1970), p. 99.
[46] Sykes, "Protectionism as a Safeguard," 279.

trade negotiators may decline to make certain reciprocal concessions for fear of adverse political consequences in the future. But, with an escape clause in place, the negotiators will agree on a greater number of reciprocal concessions, knowing that those concessions can be avoided later if political conditions so dictate." Our claim is that the inclusion of escape clauses should make reaching an initial agreement easier.

This argument shares much with the theory of efficient breach used in legal theory. This theory advances the idea that "there are circumstances where breach of contract is more efficient than performance and that the law ought to facilitate breach in such circumstances."[47] In order to do so, there must be mechanisms that can determine and compel payment of the appropriate levels of damages for such breach. Dunoff and Trachtman[48] also note that "entry into contract may be facilitated by the understanding of parties that breach may be permitted under certain circumstances." They point out that the WTO's safeguard system and its notion of compensation or retaliation provides just such a mechanism for efficient breach.

An alternative flexibility-enhancing device is to build into any agreement the opportunity for regular renegotiation, as in the GATT. It seems likely, however, as Sykes[49] claims, that renegotiation of an entire agreement is probably by far the most costly means of ensuring flexibility and is likely to have a lower probability of success than will the inclusion of escape clauses in the original agreement.

The inclusion of escape clauses in international agreements can be an important response of political leaders to their domestic problems, especially to unanticipated domestic political pressures for protection. These escape mechanisms help political leaders maintain international cooperation without sacrificing their domestic political positions; they thus reduce the costly, contradictory pressures that can emanate from domestic and international politics, helping to make international cooperation more compatible with domestic political success. As we have argued elsewhere,[50] such solutions to the two-level game faced by political leaders are essential for successful international cooperation. Designing flexibility into international agreements thus is important for political leaders

---

[47] Jeffrey L. Dunoff and Joel P. Trachtman, "Economic Analysis of International Law" (1999) *Yale J. Int'l L.* 24 (Winter).
[48] *Ibid.* at 26. [49] Sykes, "Protectionism as a Safeguard," 280.
[50] Helen V. Milner and B. Peter Rosendorff, "Trade Negotiations, Information and Domestic Politics: The Role of Domestic Groups" (1996) 8 *Economics and Politics* 145; Milner, *Interests, Institutions, and Information.*

when faced with domestic uncertainty and international distributional problems. The likelihood and the success of international institutions in turn depend on their internal design, as well as other factors.

Conclusion

International trade agreements thus may depend on domestic politics in a variety of ways. Motivations for leaders to make such agreements can come not just from economic factors or international pressures, but also from domestic political needs. Such agreements can help domestic leaders solve their internal problems. When pressed between concerns over political survival and special interest pressures, leaders may find that international trade agreements are ideal for allowing them to commit credibly to both a lower level of protection and to a signaling mechanism that helps them retain office. All groups, expect perhaps special interests, can gain from this agreement, and the more democratic the country, the more they gain. The international institution provides a credible commitment mechanism and a source of information to domestic society. Its importance is less for punishing cheaters than for informing others that they have cheated.

Agreements may also be shaped the way they are because of domestic concerns. Why do virtually all trade agreements have escape clauses, especially when other agreements often do not? Such breach mechanisms are essential for leaders who face domestic uncertainty. They fear being caught in an inflexible agreement when sudden, unexpected pressures for protection arise domestically that they dearly need to respond to. Having to abrogate the agreement can be very costly, but not being able to respond temporarily to such domestic pressures may also be very costly. Having escape clauses may reduce this dilemma and make agreements more likely and more durable. This dynamic may be especially true in democracies where political uncertainty may be very high for leaders.

Are these two claims contradictory? Does inclusion of escape clauses vitiate the constraining and informative nature of trade agreements for domestic groups? We argue rather that the two work together to make agreements more stable and useful. Leaders enter into such agreements to resist the temptation to erect more protection than is ideal, but they also need some flexibility to temporarily and selectively give protection in the future if sizable domestic pressures arise. The escape clause allows this, while also keeping domestic groups informed about the overall compliance of political leaders with the agreement. Constraint with flexibility is the best option for political leaders facing very unstable domestic conditions. They can bind themselves through the agreement, but they can also respond selectively to domestic interests. In an ideal world, neither international agreements nor escape clauses would be necessary, as leaders would choose the optimal policies for the world economy. But with domestic protectionist pressures and uncertainty about future conditions facing them, leaders most desire a system where they can commit not to give too much protection but where they can also temporarily give selective protection without abandoning the whole agreement.

For these reasons, more attention needs to be addressed to the domestic political incentives for both international agreements in general and their specific internal design in particular. Political leaders face pressures from both domestic and international environments, but in most countries, and especially in democracies, leaders are most attuned to their domestic constituents. This means that international cooperation may only be feasible if it solves domestic political problems for leaders.

10

Human rights, developing countries and the WTO constraint: the very thing that makes you rich makes me poor?

PETROS C. MAVROIDIS

The issue

This chapter focuses on the question whether and, if yes, to what extent, participation in the WTO imposes on its members, and in particular, members with a status of developing country, a certain level of human rights protection.

First, I aim to show that the WTO, with one notable exception (the Agreement on the Protection of Intellectual Property Rights (TRIPS)), is essentially an instrument of negative integration that does not prejudge the level of human rights protection. Indeed, one could go so far and state that the WTO contract per se does not prejudge regulatory intervention in the field of human rights at all: the only element of positive integration in the field of human rights protection is in fact provided by general public international law which makes it clear (Articles 53 and 64 of the Vienna Convention on the Law of Treaties) that states cannot, through conventional means, undo their obligation to respect *jus cogens erga omnes*.

Hence, the question has to be reformulated in the following manner: does participation in the WTO, an agreement which aims, in principle at least, at compensating the most efficient source of production, amount to a race-to-the-bottom when it comes to protection of human rights? My response is that one can construct theoretical examples that respond either positively or negatively to the stated questions. In-built safeguards in the WTO (Article XX GATT, Article XIV GATS), will give an incentive to developing countries dependent on exports to wealthy markets (where human rights are effectively protected) to raise their standard. However, absent an empirical study to this effect, a conclusive response is premature.

Finally, for most developing countries, members of the WTO, the WTO contract is simply policy-irrelevant at the domestic level and hence, their incentive for a race-to-the-bottom is not WTO-related.

The final section contains my concluding remarks. The whole discussion kicks in with semantics: in the next section, I discuss a seemingly "banal" issue: what is a developing country? In the same section, I reproduce thoughts expressed elsewhere (to which, of course, I adhere) as to whether or not the group of developing countries is homogeneous. This discussion seems particularly relevant, because lack of homogeneity in the group of developing countries is a necessary first step in reaching a reasonable prognosis regarding the issues in the rest of this chapter.

A developing country is?

It is widely accepted in international relations that the principle of sovereignty includes the right of states to proclaim that they are developing countries and the ensuing obligation of the international community to respect such a unilateral declaration. This is essentially what the so-called "self-election" principle (itself an expression of the sovereignty principle) amounts to: if country A decides to opt for developing country status, so be it.

Beyond the legal rule described above, a certain *modus vivendi* has developed in international relations that delineates between developed and developing countries. One should not equate the *modus vivendi* established with an intellectually coherent benchmark: for example, state members of the OECD are considered to be developed economies. However, if one were to apply strict criteria to quantify (and qualify) the development of individual OECD members, it would be hard to justify inclusion of certain members in the OECD club: under which criteria, for example, can one justify the membership of Turkey in the OECD and the non-membership of Chile or Slovenia? Political motivations have often been more important than precise criteria.

The same picture can be found in the GATT/WTO. Members choose clubs (developed or developing) according to the self-election principle. In the GATT/WTO system, such election is not void of legal consequences since there are provisions designed especially for developing countries.[1] Yet, unilateral declarations (self-election principle) have largely defined

---

[1] See, e.g., Article XVIII GATT or Part IV GATT or even the provisions in the WTO Subsidies and Countervailing Measures (SCM) Agreement designed only for developing countries.

whether particular GATT/WTO members participate as developing or developed countries.

Unilateral declarations can be challenged and should be, especially if important advantages stem from invoking a developing country status.[2] There are no such challenges, however, in GATT practice.

An illustrative example is offered by the 1989 *Beef Dispute* between Korea and the United States. Korea took protective measures which were prima facie inconsistent with its GATT obligations.[3] To justify these measures, Korea invoked balance of payments (BOP) difficulties.

The GATT contract contains two provisions available to its members which justify trade protection measures through recourse to the BOP exception: Article XII and Article XVIII. The latter can only be invoked by developing countries and reflects a more deferential approach towards the state invoking BOP problems. As a result, GATT members will *ceteris paribus* have a better chance of avoiding condemnation by a GATT Panel if they can invoke Article XVIII rather than Article XII.

To justify import-restricting measures on beef, Korea invoked Article XVIII GATT. Australia and the United States (the plaintiffs in this dispute) did not disagree with Korea's invocation of Article XVIII GATT, its membership in the OECD notwithstanding; they simply argued before the Panel that Korea did not meet the criteria laid down in Article XVIII GATT without, however, formally questioning Korea's right to invoke Article XVIII GATT.

Unilateral invocations of developing country status have not been challenged because most WTO provisions referring to developing countries are usually "best-endeavour" clauses not accompanied by concrete legal obligations/privileges.[4] In terms of market access, the most important privilege for developing countries, inscription in a national Generalized System of Preferences (GSP) list, which guarantees their products access to developed countries' markets on preferential terms, is a unilateral concession which is not justiciable before WTO adjudicating bodies.[5]

---

[2] For an excellent overview of all WTO provisions relating to developing countries, see Michael J. Trebilcock, and Robert Lloyd Howse, *The Regulation of International Trade* (2nd ed., Routledge, London and New York, 1999), pp. 367–94.

[3] See *Republic of Korea, Restrictions on Imports of Beef: Complaint by Australia*, Panel Report adopted on November 7, 1989, GATT Doc. DISD 36S, pp. 202 *et seq.*

[4] The BOP provisions are quite exceptional in this respect.

[5] Actually, it is debatable whether GSP concessions are justiciable or not. The argument could be made that they violate MFN, at least on occasion. Practice reveals that donor countries have excluded some developing countries from inscription in their list based solely on political motivation. Both the Decision of 1971 on the GSP (see GATT Doc.

The picture changed slightly with the advent of the WTO Agreement. Important new Agreements were signed which provided a longer implementation period for developing countries. The WTO Agreement on Intellectual Property Rights (TRIPS) is a prime example. During discussions on the implementation of the TRIPS Agreement, the United States and the European Community voiced their wish that WTO members like Singapore, Korea and Hong Kong (China) be considered as developed nations at least for the purposes of complying with TRIPS.

The discussions in the WTO TRIPS Council show that, although a mutually satisfactory solution for implementation was agreed upon by the three WTO members, the principle of self-election as such was not questioned.[6]

The Agreement on Agriculture is another example of a WTO Agreement which provides for a more "lenient" treatment with respect to implementation of obligations for developing countries. In the second *Korea Beef* case, following the Appellate Body's report condemning Korea's practices, the European Community, during the discussions at the Dispute Settlement Body (DSB), "noted with surprise that Korea had been treated as a developing country for the purposes of the Agreement on Agriculture. Although this issue did not seem to have been in dispute, the EC was compelled to underline its disagreement with Korea's self- characterization as a developing country."[7]

The European Community, however, was not a complaining party to this dispute and WTO Panels (in application of the *non ultra petita* maxim) do not have the legal capacity to decide *motu proprio* on an issue which the complaining party did not raise.

BISD 18S/24) and the 1979 Decision on the Enabling Clause (GATT Doc. BISD 26S/203) clarify that donor countries should not expect reciprocity, but avoid clarifying that GSP privileges must be extended to all developing countries, however defined. The occasional arbitrariness demonstrated by some donor countries in enlisting developing countries to their GSP has never been challenged by disfavoured countries before a GATT/WTO Adjudicating Body. Arguably, non-listed countries have little incentive to do so, for legal challenge could amount to permanent non-inscription. Brazil, for the first time, threatened legal action against EC practices arguably inconsistent with the Enabling Clause. Had Brazil persisted, this would be the first time that a WTO Adjudicating Body would have had the opportunity to consider these issues. Brazil's request for consultations addressed to the European Community, however, was not followed by a request for establishment of a Panel (see WTO Doc. WT/DS209/1 and G/L/399, October 19, 2000). Thus far there has not been notification of any solution between the parties (Article 3.6 DSU), and one can only speculate as to what actually persuaded Brazil to discontinue its original request.

[6] See WTO Doc. IP/C/M/8, August 14, 1996, ss. 58 *et seq.*
[7] See WTO Doc. WT/DSB/M/96, February 22, 2001, s. 14.

The only WTO multilateral scheme that moves towards providing an analytical framework within which the development status of a WTO member can be assessed is the Trade Policy Review Mechanism (TPRM); there the principle of "graduation" has been agreed upon. According to this principle, commercial policies of developed countries will be reviewed more frequently than those of developing countries. WTO members do not have a permanent place under either the developed or the developing countries' group. Depending on their performance, which is evaluated under agreed-upon criteria, WTO members might see their commercial policies reviewed in the future more frequently than in the past ("graduation").

Annex 3 of the WTO Agreement relevantly reads:

> The impact of individual Members on the functioning of the multilateral trading system, *defined in terms of their share of world trade in a recent representative period, will be the determining factor in deciding on the frequency of reviews*. The first four trading entities so identified (counting the European Communities as one) shall be subject to review every two years. The next 16 shall be reviewed every four years. Other Members shall be reviewed every six years, except that a longer period may be fixed for least-developed country Members (emphasis added).

Based on this legal document, the WTO Secretariat adopted a list which places the European Community, the United States, Japan and Canada in the two-year cycle; Hong Kong (China), Korea, Singapore, Mexico, Switzerland, Malaysia, Australia, Thailand, Brazil, Indonesia, Norway, India, Turkey, Poland, South Africa and the Philippines in the four-year cycle; the rest of the WTO membership has been placed in the six-year cycle and beyond.[8]

Arguably, though, a more-or-less frequent review is a rather innocuous exercise, which in itself might explain the multilateral agreement on the "graduation" principle.[9]

---

[8] Surprisingly, this list does not figure in any official WTO document. It is to be found however in the *WTO Training Manual*. Since the inception of the WTO, no WTO member has been reviewed more or less frequently than as appears in the cited list, arguably because there have been no dramatic changes with respect to world trade shares.

[9] The WTO Agreement on Subsidies and Countervailing Measures also provides differential treatment for developing countries (Article 27.2). Annex VII distinguishes between Least Developed Countries that benefit from differential treatment (by referring to the United Nations for the purposes of drawing such list) and to other developing countries the per capita income of which is less than US$1,000 (a list is provided in the Annex).

We see from the analysis above that WTO practice follows the more general paradigm in international relations and evidences considerable heterogeneity of its membership (ranging from Hong Kong (China) and Singapore to countries like Malawi) which assert (or have asserted) a developing country status before the WTO instances.

The picture seems to be slowly changing. The discussions quoted above in the TRIPS Council and the DSB suggest that (at least) some developed countries are not prepared to accept what they think are abusive invocations of the self-election principle. So far, however, no formal challenge against the self-election principle has been made.

What is the consequence of this observation for the purposes of this chapter? In the next section, I make the point that the WTO contract is essentially an instrument of negative integration (i.e., in which, with few exceptions, no common policies are established). This observation is valid for the totality of the heterogeneous group of developing countries. In the following section, I argue that at least for some developing countries, the WTO contract is to some extent domestic policy irrelevant. There, I refer to the sub-group of Least Developed Countries (LDCs). A certain degree of homogeneity can be established with respect to this group: they are mostly countries with an average per capita income of less than US$500 and the vast majority (if not, the totality) of their international trade is channelled through the GSP (rather than through exchange of concessions). For this group of countries, the WTO contract is to some extent neither an impediment nor an incentive with respect to their level of human rights protection. Developed countries, however, can influence policy-shaping in these countries by linking GSP preferences to human rights protection.

The legal nature of the WTO contract

Essentially negative integration

The principle of non-discrimination is omnipresent in the WTO contract. Whether one talks of GATT (trade in goods) or GATS (trade in services), WTO members are requested not to discriminate on nationality grounds in their treatment of goods and services. The legal expression of the non-discrimination principle in the WTO contract is the Most Favored Nation (MFN) clause (Article I GATT and Article II GATS) and the National Treatment clause (Article III GATT and Article XVII GATS).

What does the non-discrimination principle amount to in practice? WTO members are free to intervene through regulatory means that have an effect on trade. If they decide to intervene, then they must ensure that their regulatory intervention does not result in discrimination between national and foreign goods/services/service-suppliers.[10]

A WTO member is free to decide whether to introduce a consumption tax on cars. If a tax is not introduced, this decision must be observed for both domestic and foreign cars. If a tax is introduced, the same level of consumption tax must be applied to both domestic and foreign cars (assuming that the cars compete with each other).

By the same token, WTO members are free to enact environmental/ health/social policies. Each society's preferences may vary. Some states might decide to enter into contractual arrangements with other states on this issue, while others might not. It is within their margin of appreciation to decide whether they will pursue their goals unilaterally, bilaterally or multilaterally.[11]

Entry into the WTO, in contrast with entry into the European Union, does not include a democracy clause: a country (indeed, a customs territory "possessing full autonomy in the conduct of its external commercial relations," according to Article XII of the Agreement Establishing the WTO) does not have to be a democracy (even loosely defined) in order to accede to the WTO. It must only find an arrangement with the incumbents as to the permissible level of trade protection post-accession. As a result, a number of non-democracies with extremely low protection of human rights (compared to what is commonly accepted as adequate) are WTO members. A recent example is the American State of Massachussets, which refused to accept bids relating to government procurement products and services with Myanmar value-added, allegedly because Myanmar does not (sufficiently) protect human rights. Myanmar is not

---

[10] Horn and Mavroidis argue that non-discrimination, a loosely defined concept in WTO case law, is one way to complete the incomplete contract that is the GATT. Whatever WTO Adjudicating Bodies have understood to mean discrimination, they definitely do not extend this concept to include an obligation to take concrete positive action to ensure that no discrimination results against foreign products/services/service-suppliers: Henrick Horn and Petros C. Mavroidis, "Still Hazy After All These Years: The Interpretation of National Treatment in GATT/WTO Case-Law on Tax Discrimination" (2004) *Eur. J. Int'l L.* (forthcoming).

[11] On this issue, see the excellent analysis in Eyal Benvenisti, "Margin of Appreciation, Consensus, and Universal Standards" (1999) 31 *New York U. J. Int'l L. and Politics* 843.

the only WTO member with a poor record of human rights protection. Regulatory diversity is very much part of the WTO world. Note, however, that regulatory diversity must respect the non-discrimination principle.

WTO case law now accepts this point. First in the notorious *Shrimps–Turtles* litigation, where, for the first time in GATT/WTO jurisprudence and contrary to what was the case before, the Appellate Body accepted the sovereign right of a WTO member to define unilaterally its environmental policies.[12]

The same point was clarified even further in the context of the *FSC* dispute between the United States and the European Community. There, the United States argued, inter alia, that the Appellate Body should not accept the EC argument that its policy was an export subsidy. The United States had decided to forego tax income made abroad that several corporations involved in export transactions owed the American tax authorities. EC corporations do not have to pay taxes for income made abroad in the first place (hence the regulatory diversity between the United States and the European Community). The United States claimed that the regulatory diversity in this respect resulted in conferring an advantage to EC corporations. Foregoing the tax income was in the American view the necessary means to restore the balance between American and EC corporations in the world markets. Hence, the United States requested the WTO adjudicating bodies not to find that their practice should qualify as subsidy. The Appellate Body rejected this argument. It relevantly noted:

> To accept the argument of the United States that the comparator in determining what is "otherwise due" should be something other than the prevailing domestic standard of the Member in question would be to imply that WTO obligations somehow compel Members to choose a particular kind of tax system; this is not so. A Member, in principle, has the sovereign authority to tax any particular categories of revenue it wishes. It is also free not to tax any particular categories of revenues. But, in both instances, the Member must respect its WTO obligations. What is "otherwise due," therefore, depends on the rules of taxation that each Member, by its own choice, establishes for itself.[13]

---

[12] See WTO Doc. WT/DS58/AB/R, adopted on November 6, 1998.
[13] See WTO Doc. WT/DS108/AB/R, February 24, 2000, s. 90, emphasis in the original.

The observation that the WTO contract is essentially about negative integration is not even questioned by proponents of a "constitutionalization" of WTO law.[14]

There is, however, a small caveat: once WTO members have revealed their preferences and entered into trade concessions (consolidation of their tariff bindings), they are not completely free to change their policies; to the extent that such a change of their policies might negatively affect the value of their concessions, a non-violation complaint (probably the ultimate WTO particularity) can be raised against them.

A non-violation complaint has to do with the effort to mitigate the reduction of the value of a tariff concession. The institutional argument is as follows: unless the value of concessions is somehow protected, no state will have to engage in exchange of concessions.[15] The legal explanation for this instrument has to be found (although GATT/WTO Panels have never gone into great details about it) in the *pacta sunt servanda* principle which, in this context, is interpreted as prohibiting actions which (at least directly) might have a negative influence on what has been agreed (exchange of concessions). Could then one make the argument that non-violation complaints can serve as an instrument to block regulatory reform? Hardly so: first, the remedy of a successful non-violation complaint is in most cases far from being a credible threat against regulatory change. As Article 26.1b of the Dispute Settlement Understanding (DSU) elucidates, the contested measure does not have to be withdrawn and only a mutually satisfactory adjustment is available. GATT/WTO practice so far shows no case of withdrawal of a measure as a result of a successful non-violation complaint.[16]

---

[14] See, e.g., Ernst-Ulrich Petersmann, "How to Constitutionalize International Law and Foreign Policy for the Benefit of Civil Society?" (1998) 20 *Michigan J. Int'l L.* 1, who essentially focuses his comments on a future-oriented course of action.

[15] The economics of this argument are doubtful. For an insightful and comprehensive analysis of the rationale and the potential use of non-violation complaints, see Kyle Bagwell and Robert W. Staiger, "An Economic Theory of the GATT" (1999) 89 *Am. Economic Rev.* 89, at 215–48; Kyle Bagwell, Petros C. Mavroidis and Robert W. Staiger, "It's a Question of Market Access" (2002) 96 *Am. J. Int'l L.* 56.

[16] Hudec has argued to me that the references in the body of Article 26.1b DSU to Article 22 DSU must be significant. He thinks that such references must be interpreted to include the possibility for a WTO member winning a non-violation complaint to request authorization to impose countermeasures. So far, there is no relevant practice. But even if Hudec's argument is condoned by Panels, one would reasonably expect that the amount to be countermeasured would be less than for a violation complaint (which according to Article 22.4 DSU, is equivalent to the damage suffered).

Second, the enactment during the Uruguay Round of a detailed Agreement on Subsidies is probably the basic reason explaining the reduction in recent years of non-violation complaints. All but one of the non-violation complaints raised during the GATT years followed an identical pattern: first, a concession was concluded, then, the effects of the subsidy granted reduced the value of the concession. Since the "disciplining" of subsidies beginning January 1, 1995, there have been no non-violation complaints whereby a WTO member argued that its benefits under the Agreement had been nullified as a result of a subsidy granted by a WTO member on a commodity on which a concession had been negotiated.

Two non-violation complaints have been raised since 1995: the *Kodak–Fuji* case dealt with the loss of market access as a result of a regulatory (and not a pecuniary) subsidy (lax enforcement of competition laws); and the *Asbestos*[17] case: Canada's argument was that a health-based trade-obstructing measure can form the subject matter of a non-violation complaint – surprisingly, the Appellate Body accepted this argument.[18]

Third, the *Kodak–Fuji* Panel Report[19] made it clear for the first time that the non-violation complaint is a legal remedy that can only be used in exceptional cases. It set the tone for the WTO Adjudicating Bodies' attitude with respect to non-violation complaints.[20]

It is hence reasonable to assume that non-violation complaints do not put into question the above conclusion, that WTO members are largely unconstrained by the WTO contract when deciding their regulatory intervention in various fields.

It follows that incumbent or aspiring WTO members do not *as a matter of WTO constraint* have to ensure a particular level of human rights

---

[17] See WTO Doc. WT/DS135/AB/R, March 12, 2001.

[18] I am surprised as one of the conditions for a non-violation complaint to succeed is the "reasonable expectations" requirement: the complaining party must show that it did not reasonably expect the (legal) measure in issue. It would be quite a burden of proof to show that a WTO member did not expect another WTO member to enforce its health policies in the presence of a health risk. If, of course, there is no health risk, in all likelihood a violation complaint could be launched.

[19] See WTO Doc. WT/DS44/R, March 31, 1998.

[20] The Appellate Body, in its very recent *Asbestos* Report, adhered to the exceptional character of non-violation complaints as expressed in *Kodak–Fuji*. Surprisingly, however, the Appellate Body accepted that a non-violation complaint can be raised even if the value of a concession has been reduced as a result of the enactment of a health policy (see WTO Doc. WT/DS135/R, March 12, 2001, s. 182 *et seq.*). The impact of this statement is hard to quantify at the present time. To my mind, the lack of an effective remedy associated with non-violation complaints will hopefully close the door that the Appellate Body opened through this case law.

protection. This does not mean, however, that developing countries might not be compelled to observe a certain human rights protection for other legal reasons. It could very well be that the origin of their legal obligation lies in sources beyond the WTO contract (see the discussion below). As a matter of WTO law, the only possible route to challenge human rights-related practices is, as discussed above, the one offered by the non-violation complaint. However, zealots will be well advised to be aware of (one of) the condition(s) for a successful mounting of a non-violation complaint: that the *value of concessions* has *deteriorated* as a result of a *change* in the (unilaterally defined) regulatory regime. This condition will be hard to prove for most human rights-related concerns: how can one establish, for example, that the advent of an oppressive regime which restricts freedom of speech has caused a reduction in the volume of foreign goods consumed?

Many (if not most) human rights are largely unrelated to trade flows. A change is necessary for a non-violation complaint to succeed. Hence, an undemocratic regime which accedes to the WTO and which does not change its human rights policy post-accession to the WTO does not risk any legal challenge as to the consistency of its practices with its WTO obligations.

But some . . . to do???

The WTO contract is not, however, a pure "negative integration" instrument. There are WTO provisions that impose positive integration-type obligations on members. Scattered obligations of this type can be found in various Agreements (the Subsidies Agreement, the Agreement on Pre-Shipment Inspection, etc.). They are, however, of minor importance. The only meaningful positive integration-type obligations are contained in the TRIPS Agreement, which obliges WTO members to ensure within their territory a certain level of protection for intellectual property rights.

There are, however, provisions in the WTO contract which allow WTO members to enforce their own standards when they disagree with production methods used elsewhere. Article XX GATT, Article XIV GATS, the Agreements on Technical Barriers to Trade (TBT) and Sanitary and Phyto-sanitary Measures (SPS) contain such provisions. These provisions do not impose a uniform approach: they simply make it possible for those WTO members that want to avail themselves of the possibility of blocking trade for health/environmental and other non-pecuniary concerns, to do so.[21]

Finally, all WTO members have to respect a certain code of conduct (*jus cogens*) imposed on them as members of the international community. Accession to the WTO does not alter this obligation. Moreover, some WTO members might have to ensure a certain level of protection of human rights, either because their own national constitution compels them, or because they have adhered to international treaties requesting respect of specific behavioural regularities in this respect, or because they are bound by norms of customary international law.

To do: so says the WTO

Below I provide a brief overview of the positive integration elements imposed on WTO members upon membership in the WTO.

To do As stated above, one can find scattered positive integration-type obligations throughout the WTO contract. This is the case not only for the Agreement on Pre-shipment Inspection and on Subsidies mentioned above but also with respect to the GATS (Article VI.4 and VI.5), the Agreement on Import Licensing (Article 1.4), the Agreement on Customs Valuation (Article 1 and 2) etc.

I do not mean to provide an exhaustive list of all similar provisions in the WTO contract. Suffice it to state for the purposes of this chapter that such provisions are of a "peripheral" nature.

The only meaningful positive integration-type obligation in the WTO contract is the TRIPS Agreement. Its subject matter, however, is limited to protection of intellectual property rights. Hence, nowhere does the WTO contract prescribe a certain human rights policy to be followed by its members.

To be in a position to The WTO contract explicitly acknowledges the right of its members to enforce their human rights policy. Article XIV

---

[21] Depending on how one defines positive integration, elements of positive integration are to be found in the new generation WTO Agreements, such as the TBT and the SPS: the first imposes an in-principle obligation to use international standards; the second imposes an in-principle obligation to base health-motivated regulatory interventions on scientific results. Hence, although the decision to enact health policies remains a sovereign choice for WTO members, the exercise of these policies must observe a predefined regulatory framework.

GATS allows WTO members to deviate from their obligations under GATS if such deviation is justified on public order grounds. The notion of public order as explained in the footnote to Article XIV GATS is wide enough to cover human rights concerns.

The corresponding provision in the GATT (Article XXa) seems to cover less, in comparison with Article XIV GATS: it only refers to public morals, whereas the GATS provision refers to both public morals and public order. In the absence of jurisprudence in this respect, Charnovitz[22] has already proposed a reading of Article XXa GATT which de facto is coextensive to the *ratione materiae* coverage of Article XIV GATS.

This reading of Article XXa GATT is quite attractive. It would be odd to construe the GATT as allowing its members to deviate from their obligations by invoking health or environmental concerns (Article XXb GATT) and not by invoking human rights concerns. It would be equally odd to construe the WTO contract as allowing deviations from the services-related obligations but not from the goods-related obligations on human rights grounds.

To do: so says public international law

Articles 53 and 64 of the Vienna Convention on the Law of Treaties clarify that states cannot, by entering into contractual arrangements, ignore their obligation to observe *jus cogens*. The exact definition of *jus cogens* is debatable. Ever since the notorious *obiter dictum* in the *Barcelona Traction* jurisprudence, a number of authors have extended or reduced the list provided by the International Court of Justice and some have cast doubt on the concept as such.[23]

The notion has, however, survived through the various drafts of the International Law Commission on State Responsibility.[24] WTO members cannot, consequently, invoke the absence of a mention of human rights in order to excuse themselves from their obligation to observe at least the hard core of human rights (prohibition of genocide, absence of discrimination on racial etc. grounds, prohibition of aggression).[25]

---

[22] Steve Charnovitz, "The Moral Exception in Trade" (1998) 38 *Virginia J. Int'l L.* 689.

[23] For a critical evaluation of the normative graduation in public international law, see Prosper Weil, "International Law?" (1983) 77 *Am. J. Int'l L.* 413.

[24] See UN GA Doc. A/CN.4/600.

[25] Trachtman, who construes the terms of reference of WTO Adjudicating Bodies too strictly to my mind, still acknowledges that "while present WTO law seems clearly to exclude direct application of non-WTO international law, this position seems unsustainable as increasing conflicts between trade values and non-trade values arise": Joel Trachtman, "The Domain of WTO Dispute Resolution" (1999) 40 *Harvard Int'l L. J.* 333.

Moreover, customary international law (assuming it is binding upon some WTO members) obliges its addressees to observe a particular conduct. It could be argued that at least as far as original membership is concerned, the European Convention on Human Rights codifies customary international law binding upon them.

Domestic constitutional constraints

WTO members might have to observe a certain threshold protection of human rights for domestic legal reasons (i.e., because their domestic constitution establishes such a threshold protection).

A partial conclusion with respect to human rights' protection

From the above analysis, we can conclude:

(1) the WTO contract does not impose a human rights policy on its members;
(2) WTO members are free to choose the manner in which to protect human rights;
(3) their freedom in this respect is constrained by reasons unrelated to their WTO membership.

Such reasons extend beyond their obligation to observe the minimum inscribed *in jus cogens*, to the binding (upon them) norms of customary international law and to domestic constitutional reasons.

Participation in the WTO: a race-to-the-bottom?

The argument is sometimes voiced that participation in the WTO gives rise to a race-to-the-bottom in various policy instruments. This argument has been voiced with respect to labor standards, and albeit less frequently, to human rights. There is an overlap. Some labor standards can indeed be classified as human rights.

Let me start with an extreme example. It seems plausible to argue that attempts to maintain lower standards (by this I mean not a lowering of standards per se, but a too-low standard relative to income) than what is motivated by income levels may be met with objection. In a dictatorial state, where no freedom of expression is protected, such opposition may not be voiced. Hence, an argument might perhaps be made according to which WTO members interested in low labor standards are also interested in having low (or no) protection of freedom of expression.

Is this a plausible argument? Even dictatorial regimes need a power base, which could consist of workers. Yes, it is plausible that democratic states will have higher labor standards, but no one should draw conclusions without empirical evidence. On the other hand, the link to human rights protection, such as freedom of expression to productivity of sectors, is quite weak. A country with limited freedom of expression could for whatever reasons be prepared to pay high wages to workers.

Intuitively, the likelihood of a race-to-the-bottom seems higher when it comes to labor rights-related human rights. There is little empirical evidence to suggest that trade liberalization, whether through unilateral or multilateral liberalization, has had negative impact on labor standards. Existing theoretical models on endogenous setting of labor standards show few convincing links through which a trade agreement should lead to sub-optimal labor standards.[26]

I do not mean that it is impossible to construct models in which countries use labor standards to attract, for example, foreign direct investment (FDI). But it could normally be expected that interested countries use other instruments (than lowering of standards) at their disposal to attract FDI: instruments that are less distortionary and probably more efficient. For instance, why choose a sub-optimal labor standard to attract FDI rather than offer lower profit taxes to the potential investors?

The point is not that a race-to-the-bottom is unlikely. The point is that so far we have no proof that this is indeed the case even when it comes to policies (like labor standards) with a more direct impact on productivity and hence on trade flows.[27]

Finally, for many developing countries, participation in the WTO does not mean much. In fact, for many it means nothing at all. There are a series of LDCs which channel a substantial proportion of their trade through

---

[26] See Drusilla K. Brown, Alan V. Deardorff and Robert M. Stern, "International Labor Standards and Trade: A Theoretical Analysis" in Jagdish Bhagwati and Robert E. Hudec, *Fair Trade and Harmonization* (MIT Press, Cambridge, MA, 1996), pp. 227–80. On the other hand, it is at least questionable, as Bagwell, Mavroidis and Staiger point out, to what extent the discussion on labor standards should move from the domestic to the WTO level so as to avoid existing regulatory diversity. Bagwell, Mavroidis and Staiger, "It's a Question of Market Access," 56–76.

[27] This is not to say that I do not subscribe to the distinction between "culmination" and "comprehensive outcomes" as operated in Amartya Sen, *Development as Freedom* (Anchor Books, New York, 2000). On the other hand, keep in mind that a lowering of standards could in principle be condemned by WTO Adjudicating Bodies where a non-violation complaint is raised to this effect; on this issue see the analysis of Bagwell, Mavroidis and Staiger, "It's a Question of Market Access".

GSP.[28] Hence, as far as their export trade is concerned they have less (if any) incentive to lower their standards.

Note, however, that the importance of GSP trade, as it currently stands, should not be exaggerated. In a recent comprehensive study, Inama[29] shows that roughly one-third of the total volume of exports of LDCs benefits from preferential rates. For the rest, MFN rates are relevant for their exports. Inama's conclusions concern the existing shaping of national GSP lists which are flexible and can be modified.

Some concluding remarks

The WTO has been called many names. It is indeed quite remarkable how a simple trade liberalization instrument managed to provoke so many negative reactions in so many different corners. This is in part due to increased dissemination of the unluckiest moments of its dispute settlement function (*Tuna–Dolphin*). A lot is due to pure misinformation. The trade and human rights debate, in the absence of any WTO-dictated policy and consequently any jurisprudence, belongs to the latter category.

Participation in the WTO and protection of human rights is not an either/or-type of dilemma: WTO members (with the caveat of *jus cogens*) are free to choose their human rights policy. There is no evidence that it either directly or indirectly prejudges such choices.

A different question is whether, from a moral point of view, it is desirable that human rights protection not be prejudged through participation in any world integration process.[30] In fact, if the world's rich markets, the champions of human rights, are indeed serious about promoting such policies, they should construct the necessary trade legal instruments (GSP) so as to compensate those developing countries which are willing constantly to raise their policies.

To my knowledge, however, this has not been done systematically. For example, the GSP list of the European Community[31] contains special

---

[28] On this issue, see Bernard Hoekman and Petros C. Mavroidis, "WTO Dispute Settlement, Transparency and Surveillance" (2000) 23 *The World Economy* 527; Joseph E. Stiglitz, "Two Principles for the Next Round or, How to Bring Developing Countries in from the Cold" (2000) 23 *The World Economy* 437.

[29] Stefano Inama, "Improving Market Access for Least Developed Countries," unpublished paper (2001).

[30] See on this issue the views expressed in Joost Pauwelyn, "The Role of Public International Law in the WTO: How Far Can We Go?" (2001) 95 *Am. J. Int'l L.* 535.

[31] National GSP lists are to be found in the website of UNCTAD (www.unctad.org).

incentive arrangements which operate on the basis of an additional preferential margin which is granted to beneficiary countries that comply with certain requirements related to labor standards and environmental protection only. The labor standards, adherence to which is compensated by the European Community, are those reflected in the International Labor Organization (ILO) Conventions No. 87, 98 and 138, i.e. the right to organize and bargain collectively, and child labor. Similar conditions are imposed by the United States for accession to their GSP list. It would be difficult to find good arguments in favor of such prioritizing with respect to human rights protection.

In short, participation in the WTO does not seem to prejudge the level of human rights protection among developing countries. Those that proffer the "carrots" to induce a raising of standards could certainly do a better job in this respect.

11

Back to court after *Shrimp–Turtle*: India's challenge to labor and environmental linkages in the EC generalized system of preferences

ROBERT HOWSE

Introduction

The Appellate Body rulings[1] in the *Shrimp–Turtle* case created a new baseline for the trade and environment debate at the WTO. The Appellate Body held that Article XX GATT can be invoked to justify measures that condition market access on policies adopted by the exporting country, contrary to the approach taken by the unadopted GATT-era *Tuna–Dolphin* panels. Further, the Appellate Body explicitly noted that this holding applied not only to the environmental provision at issue in the case (Article XX(g)), but to most of the paragraphs of Article XX, including, significantly, XX(a) (inter alia), the "protection of public morals"(para. 121) – a rubric often claimed to encompass fundamental labor rights.

Before *Shrimp–Turtle*, it was conventional wisdom[2] that trade measures targeted at other countries' environmental (or for that matter, labor) policies could not be accommodated within the Article XX framework. But, equally, it was conventional wisdom that since preferences to developing countries granted under the Generalized System of Preferences (GSP) were voluntary and non-binding, they could be withdrawn or circumscribed on the basis of matters such as labor rights compliance, without running afoul of WTO law. In general, GSP preferences have been exempted

---

[1] *United States, Import Prohibition of Certain Shrimp and Shrimp Products*, WT/DS58/AB/R, October 12, 1998; *United States, Import Prohibition of Certain Shrimp and Shrimp Products*, Recourse to Article 21.5 of the DSU by Malaysia, WT/DS58/AB/RW, October 22, 2001; for commentary, see R. Howse, "The Appellate Body Rulings in the Shrimp/Turtle Case: A New Legal Baseline for the Trade and Environment Debate" (2002) 27(2) *Columbia J. Environmental L.* 491.

[2] Conventional wisdom that was, to be sure, challenged by some scholars vigorously; Chang, Charnovitz, Howse, Trebilcock, for instance.

261

from the Most Favored Nation (MFN) requirement in Article I of the GATT, first by a waiver,[3] and then by a Tokyo Round Decision, called the "Enabling Clause."[4] But what India now puts in question is how broad or narrow this exemption is and to what extent it is subject to legal scrutiny against criteria that are implicitly or explicitly contained in the Enabling Clause.

After *Shrimp–Turtle*, one would have thought the focus on the environmental and social agenda would shift to political and diplomatic negotiations within the WTO and other international organizations. However, India has now decided to launch a major challenge in WTO dispute settlement to conditionality in the voluntary preference scheme of the European Community, pursuant to the GSP – testing the conventional wisdom that such measures fall outside legal scrutiny at the WTO.[5] The outcome of this case will have, potentially, as profound an impact on the legal baseline for

---

[3] Decision on Generalized System of Preferences, June 25, 1971, L/1845, BISD 18S/24.
[4] Decision of the Contracting Parties on Differential and More Favourable Treatment, Reciprocity and Fuller Participation of Developing Countries ("Enabling Clause"), November 28, 1979, BISD 26S/203.
[5] *European Communities, Conditions for Granting of Tariff Preferences to India*, Request for the Establishment of a Panel by India, WT/DS246/4, December 9, 2002. India also complained about preferences conditioned on drug enforcement. After the present volume went to press, India decided not to move forward with its claims on environmental and labor preferences, the subject of this chapter, but only those concerning the drug preferences. In early January a Dispute Panel, now on appeal, found that the drug preferences did in fact violate both the MFN obligation in Article I of GATT and the terms of the Enabling Clause. In finding that the Enabling Clause incorporated a strict obligation of "non-discrimination," which meant that all developing countries must be offered identical preferences (with only some very narrow exceptions), the Panel established a precedent that would allow India to go ahead and now challenge the environmental and labor preferences that are the focus of this chapter. The Appellate Body, while also finding that there was a hard law obligation of non-discrimination in the Enabling Clause, adopted very different legal reasoning than the panel. The Appellate Body held that the obligation of non-discrimination was consistent with providing different levels of preference to different developing countries, where positively related to the development needs of the beneficiary countries, and where based on objective and transparent criteria. Assuming that the legal analysis of the Panel is not reversed by the WTO Appellate Body, it is the Article XX exceptions that will be of crucial importance in any subsequent case on environmental and labor preferences. The state of play of the dispute after India dropped its environmental and labor claims is discussed in a different version of this chapter, which appears in (2003) 18(6) *Am. U. Int'l L. Rev.* 1333. The claim about drug preferences is addressed in a different article by the author, "India's WTO Challenge to Drug Enforcement Conditions in the European Community's Generalized System of Preferences: A Little Known Case with Major Repercussions for 'Political' Conditionality in US Trade Policy" (2003) 4(2) *Chicago J.Int'l L.* 385. The Panel's ruling on the drug claim is briefly analyzed by the author in the January issues of BRIDGES, www.ictsd.org. A roundtable of WTO scholars, including the present author, considers the implications of the Appellate Body's ruling in the summer 2004 issue of *World Trade Review*, including the implications if India were to revive its claim on labor and environmental preferences in the future.

the trade and environment debate and the trade and labor debate as the *Shrimp–Turtle* ruling itself. Once again, these sensitive and controversial matters have been put squarely in the hands of the judges.

This chapter examines India's legal claim, and its strengths and weaknesses under WTO law. In the final section, I speculate on the possible broader systemic consequences of various possible outcomes of the dispute.

The EC measures[6] being challenged by India, it should at the outset be noted, are atypical of the kind of conditionality imposed in GSP schemes generally (both EC and especially American) with respect to labor rights, in particular.[7] Thus, what is *not* directly challenged by India is the possibility of withdrawal of GSP status altogether, in response to egregious violations of labor rights. Instead, the EC measures that India has named provide an *additional* margin of preference or incentive to countries that implement, through legislation and effective monitoring and enforcement, particular ILO Conventions that are recognized, by virtue of the ILO Declaration on Fundamental Labor Rights, as promulgating core or fundamental rights.[8]

Similarly, the environmental conditionality applies with respect to granting an additional margin of preference beyond what is generally accorded under the GSP scheme of the EC for the products in question. This margin of preference is accorded to tropical timber products from

---

[6] The measures in question are to be found in Council Regulation (EC) 2501/2001, December 10, 2001 applying a scheme of generalised tariff preferences for the period from January 1, 2002 to December 31, 2004 [2001] OJ L346/1. I have found very helpful the exposition of the scheme for special preferential treatment that is challenged by India that is contained in the UNCTAD Handbook on the EC GSP program, which can be downloaded from the digital library on the UNCTAD website, www.unctad.org. *Handbook on the Scheme of the European Community*, UNCTAD/ITCD/TSB/MISC.25/Rev.2, December 2002.

[7] See, for a general discussion current up to the late 1980s, S. Dufour, *Accords commerciaux et droits des travailleurs* (Les Editions Revue de Droit/Universite de Sherbrooke, Sherbrooke, Que, 1998), pp. 42–86. For a more recent discussion of the American GSP scheme in these regards, see K. A. Elliot, *Preferences for Workers? Worker's Rights and the US Generalized System of Preferences* (Institute for International Economics, Washington, DC, May 2000). Elliot concludes: "The US experience in applying worker rights conditionality to trade benefits under the GSP suggests that external pressure can be helpful in improving treatment of workers in developing countries and that linkage of trade and worker rights need not devolve into simple protectionism" (unpaginated).

[8] International Labour Organization Declaration on Fundamental Principles and Rights at Work (1998). The Conventions that constitute the "core" are: Conventions 29 and 105 on forced labor, Conventions 87 and 98 concerning the application of the principles of the right to organize and bargain collectively, Conventions 100 and 111 on non-discrimination in respect of employment and occupation and Conventions 138 and 18 concerning the minimum age for admission to employment (child labor).

countries that implement, through legislation and effective monitoring and enforcement, internationally acknowledged standards and guidelines for sustainable forest management (in large measure, the various standards and guidelines promulgated by the International Tropical Timber Organization (ITTO)).[9]

The Enabling Clause and its relationship to Article I.1 of the GATT (MFN)

India claims that labor and environmental conditionality in the EU GSP scheme violates the MFN clause of Article I.1 GATT. However, a Decision of the contracting parties that emerged from the Tokyo Round negotiations, the so-called Enabling Clause, limits the applicability of Article I.1 to GSP preferences. Thus, paragraph 1 of the Enabling Clause states that: "Notwithstanding the provisions of Article I of the General Agreement, contracting parties may accord differential and more favourable treatment to developing countries, without according such treatment to other contracting parties." By virtue of paragraph 2(a), this override of Article I applies to "Preferential tariff treatment accorded by developed contracting parties to products originating in developing countries in accordance with the Generalized System of Preferences."

In its request for a panel, India claims that the EC scheme is not consistent with several "requirements" of the Enabling Clause.

The first "requirement" mentioned by India is paragraph 2(a), which has been quoted above. While paragraph 2(a) is not worded in the language of a requirement, it is clear that preferences must fall within one of the sub-paragraphs of paragraph 2 in order to benefit from the Article I GATT override in paragraph 1 of the Enabling Clause. Since the EC preferences at issue are a matter of preferential tariff treatment, in stating that paragraph 1 *applies* to preferences in *accordance with* the Generalized System of Preferences, paragraph 2(a) arguably makes it a "requirement" that preferential tariff treatment be consistent with the GSP. This is an issue that will be discussed in depth later in this chapter.

The other two supposed requirements of the Enabling Clause that India claims are not met by the EC, due to the labor and environmental conditionality of its preferences, are that preferences "shall be designed to

---

[9] The standards and guidelines in question are listed, and can be viewed, on the website of the ITTO, www.itto.or.jp/. However, there are many other norms and instruments related to sustainable forest management that may be applicable, including those of relevant United Nations organs.

facilitate and promote the trade of developing countries in the context of any general or specific measures in favour of developing countries and not to raise barriers to or create undue difficulties for the trade of any other contracting parties" (para. 3(a)) and that the preferences be designed, and if necessary, modified, "to respond positively to the development, financial and trade needs of developing countries" (para. 3(c)).

The justiciability of the Enabling Clause and its alleged "requirements"

A common, if not prevalent, interpretation of the GSP framework in WTO law is that it is not subject to dispute settlement under the Dispute Settlement Understanding (DSU).[10] "Based on the permissive rather than mandatory language of the [Enabling Clause] preference givers usually consider that they may also unilaterally modify, extend or withdraw such preferences, including coverage of beneficiaries."[11] Yet, as the outcome of the *Shrimp–Turtle* dispute illustrates, conventional wisdom with respect to GATT/WTO law may well turn out to be erroneous; "conventional wisdom" is not binding legal precedent or authority.[12]

The Appellate Body of the WTO has been very reluctant to interpret WTO legal instruments as outside the jurisdiction of the dispute settlement organs, even where (as was the case for Article XXIV GATT on Customs Unions and Free Trade Areas) the conventional wisdom was that the monitoring of such provisions is left to other political or diplomatic organs of the WTO.[13] This expansive view by the Appellate Body concerning the ambit of dispute settlement has been sharply criticized by commentators such as Frieder Roessler[14] who argue that judicial restraint, or deference, to the political and diplomatic organs is the appropriate posture, even if

---

[10] See, e.g., S. Laird and R. Safadi, *The WTO and Development* (October 2001), p. 7: the "unilateral, non-contractual basis" of GSP schemes has led to lack of enforceability of the principles of GSP, such as non-discrimination.
[11] *Ibid.* at p. 6.
[12] See my response to critics of the *Shrimp–Turtle* ruling, who have complained that the Appellate Body's interpretation of Article XX to permit trade measures to protect the global environmental commons was contrary to the "practice" of the GATT, as reflected in the *Tuna–Dolphin* Panels and the purported wide support among the WTO membership for the narrower approach in those reports. Howse, "Appellate Body Rulings."
[13] *Turkey, Restrictions on Imports of Textiles and Clothing*, Report of the Appellate Body, WT/DS34/AB/R, paras 58, 60. See also, *India, Quantitative Restrictions on Imports of Agricultural, Textile and Industrial Products*, WT/DS90/AB/R, especially para. 83.
[14] F. Roeesler, "The Institutional Balance between the Judicial and the Political Organs of the WTO" in M. Brockers and R. Quick (eds.), *New Directions in International Economic Law: Essays in Honour of John H. Jackson* (Kluwer Law International, The Hague, 2000), pp. 325–46.

in fact there is no formal bar to the dispute settlement organs adjudicating disputes concerning provisions such as Article XXIV. I have argued elsewhere, against these critics, that the Appellate Body acted correctly in such cases; judicial restraint, or as I prefer to call it, institutional sensitivity, should not go so far as to *pre-empt* a right as fundamental as the right to dispute settlement in the DSU, merely because other organs of the WTO are seized with the monitoring or review of compliance with the legal instruments in question.[15] At the same time, where other organs of the WTO do have a role with respect to a particular legal instrument, or indeed where other international institutions are involved (in the case of GSP and the Enabling Clause, UNCTAD), it certainly behooves the Appellate Body of the WTO to take into account the practice of those organs or other institutions.

If the Enabling Clause were simply unjusticiable, this could lead to an absurd result: a WTO member could avoid a fundamental legal obligation of the WTO system, MFN with respect to trade in goods, merely by *asserting* the Enabling Clause applies, no matter how implausible that the member's measures fit within its ambit. Thus, adopted GATT Panels have, rightly, not hesitated to adjudicate the issue of whether the Article I override in the Enabling Clause, paragraph 1, *applies* to a given scheme of trade preferences. In the 1992 case, *Denial of Most Favored Nation Treatment as to Non-Rubber Footwear from Brazil,* a GATT Panel examined whether the Enabling Clause would render GATT-legal preferential treatment in respect of countervailing duties, otherwise in violation of Article I. The Panel held: "It was clear that the Enabling Clause expressly limits the preferential treatment accorded by developed contracting parties in favour of developing contracting parties under the Generalized System of Preferences to tariff preferences only."[16] The Panel noted *dicta* in a somewhat earlier adopted report, *United States–Customs User Fee,*[17] which considered that a non-tariff measure in violation of Article I GATT was not "authorized" by the Enabling Clause.

In sum, the Enabling Clause is justiciable. However, the nature and extent of the *legal effect* of individual provisions within the Enabling Clause is a different matter. That question has to be answered as a matter of interpretation, following the rules in the Vienna Convention on the

[15] "The Least Dangerous Branch? The Extent and Limits of the Judicial Power in WTO Appellate Body Jurisprudence" in Cottier and Mavroidis (eds.), *The Role of the Judge in the WTO* (University of Michigan Press, 2003).
[16] DS18/R, adopted on June 19, 1992, BISD 39S/128, para. 6.14.
[17] Adopted February 2, 1988, BISD 35S/245, *EC Measures Concerning Meat and Meat Products Hormones* 122, para. 122.

Law of Treaties; the ordinary meaning of the words in question must be considered in light of their object, purpose and context.

Some provisions in WTO legal instruments have been held to have a largely aspirational character. In the *Beef Hormones*[18] case, for instance, the Appellate Body found certain provisions of the Agreement on Sanitary and Phyto-Sanitary Measures (SPS) to be in the nature of "best efforts" obligations, where members were being exhorted progressively to achieve a certain goal, but without a binding legal commitment to reach the goal to a particular extent or degree at a particular future point in time (Article 3.1 SPS). The Appellate Body based that interpretation of the legal force or effect of Article 3.1 on a contextual analysis, pointing to wording in the Preamble of the SPS Agreement, as well as to impracticality and unreasonableness of an interpretation that would impose an immediate, absolute obligation on members to base all of their regulations on international standards.

It is to be noted that the language "shall" appeared in Article 3.1 SPS; the Appellate Body's ruling in *Hormones* illustrates that even the presence of wording that suggests a "hard" legal obligation is not itself conclusive in regard to the legal effect of a given provision, which must also be considered contextually.[19]

More recently, in the *Corn Syrup*[20] case, the Appellate Body considered the legal effect of certain provisions of the DSU, including Article 3.7, which provides, in part, that: "Before bringing a case, a Member shall exercise its judgment as to whether action under these procedures would be fruitful." The Appellate Body interpreted the legal effect of this provision, and the role of the dispute settlement organs in policing it, in the following terms:

> We recall that, when we examined the language of Article 3.7 of the DSU in our Report in *European Communities–Bananas*, we stated that:
>
>> a Member has broad discretion in deciding whether to bring a case against another Member under the DSU. The language of Article XXIII:1 of the GATT 1994 and of Article 3.7 of the DSU suggests, furthermore, that a Member is expected to be *largely self-regulating* in deciding whether any such action would be "fruitful". (footnote omitted, emphasis added)

---

[18] AB-1997–4, Report of the Appellate Body, WT/DS26, 48/AB/R, January 16, 1998.
[19] See a similar analysis by a Panel under the Canada–United States Free Trade Agreement, *UHT Milk*.
[20] *Mexico, Anti-Dumping Investigation of High Fructose Corn Syrup (HFCS) from the United States*, Recourse to Article 21.5 of the DSU by the United States, WT AB-2001–5, Report of the Appellate Body.

Given the "largely self-regulating" nature of the requirement in the first sentence of Article 3.7, Panels and the Appellate Body must presume, whenever a member submits a request for establishment of a Panel, that such Member does so in good faith, having duly exercised its judgment as to whether recourse to that Panel would be "'fruitful' . . . Article 3.7 neither requires nor authorizes a panel to look behind that Member's decision and to question its exercise of judgment." (paras 73–74).

In evaluating the legal effect of the individual provisions of the Enabling Clause, and the role of the dispute settlement organs in policing them, a number of general considerations about the nature of this instrument, its status within the GATT/WTO framework, and its context, need to be taken into account.

First of all, there is a tendency in WTO law to regard the provisions of waivers from WTO obligations as strict conditions; a member may only deviate from WTO obligations in reliance on a waiver if and to the extent that it meets such conditions. Thus, if the Enabling Clause is to be considered a waiver, there might be something of a presumption that the "requirements" to which India averts in its complaint are indeed strict conditions, the adhesion to which is subject to close judicial scrutiny. Although usually called a waiver in general and non-technical discussions of GSP, the Enabling Clause is not a "waiver" within the special meaning of Article XXV GATT or Article IX WTO Agreement.[21] Article XXV GATT refers to waivers of an obligation "imposed on *a* contracting party"(emphasis added) in "exceptional circumstances." The Enabling Clause does not refer to any exceptional circumstances, nor does it name any particular contracting party. The Clause is not described on its face as a waiver. It is not temporary, which would be logically the case where exceptional circumstances are concerned. It is not listed among the list of Article XXV waivers in the relevant GATT/WTO instruments.

Thus, the idea of the Enabling Clause is not simply forbearance by the contracting parties in respect of a particular member state's compliance with the existing law of the GATT; the Enabling Clause instead "*enables*" what is to become a basic tenet of the international economic legal order, namely special and differential treatment of developing countries. It modifies the existing law of the GATT to enable the conception already announced in Part IV, and reflected in numerous declarations and other instruments of UNCTAD and the United Nations Social and

---

[21] See J. H. Jackson, *The World Trading System: Law and Policy of International Economic Relations* (2nd ed., MIT Press, Cambridge, MA/London, 1999), p. 164.

Economic Council. Rather than an exception to the GATT, the Enabling Clause is an integral part of the GATT legal system.

For these reasons, it would be inappropriate to apply to the interpretation of the Enabling Clause, the idea of narrow or strict reading of waivers that the Appellate Body promulgates in *Bananas*. This relates as well to the actual language in paragraph 1 of the Enabling Clause. Unlike, for example, the Lomé waiver at issue in *Bananas*, paragraph 1 does not use language such as "to the extent necessary" – rather the formula employed is "Notwithstanding the provisions of Article I." A developed country WTO member does not have to prove that each aspect of its deviation from the strictures of Article I is necessary in order to grant differential and more favorable treatment to developing countries. Rather, provided that the preferential treatment falls under one of the heads of paragraph 2, it operates "notwithstanding" Article I, i.e., Article I does not apply at all.

This is also different from Article XXIV GATT, the MFN exception for Customs Unions and Free Trade Areas. Article XXIV does not contain language that renders Article I GATT inapplicable to measures taken in the operation of Customs Unions and Free Trade Areas; rather, Article XXIV, as the Appellate Body held in *Turkey–Textiles*, provides only that Article I shall not be applied in such a manner as to prevent the formation of Customs Unions and Free Trade Areas. It does not authorize the operation of Customs Unions and Free Trade Areas *notwithstanding* Article I. Instead, unlike GSP, the Article I framework still applies in the case of Customs Unions and Free Trade Areas, to the extent consistent with their formation or existence. The Enabling Clause does not explicitly provide for enforcement or policing of its provisions through dispute settlement. Nor need it, of course, as a formal matter; as a Decision pursuant to the GATT 1947 the Clause is part of the GATT 1994 and therefore, an integral part of one of the Covered Agreements to which the DSU applies. But it *is* relevant to the question of *to what extent* the Clause is self-policing; that the drafters apparently did not consider the nature of its provisions to be such that it was important to stress or emphasize the availability of dispute settlement. Rather than a reference to dispute settlement in the Enabling Clause one finds the formula that the "contracting parties will collaborate in arrangements for the review of the operation of these provisions."

This approach contrasts significantly with that of the predecessor instrument to the Enabling Clause, the GSP Decision of 1971. The GSP Decision contained detailed and explicit language concerning the availability of dispute settlement under the Decision (para. E). This may be related to the fact that, unlike the Enabling Clause, the GSP Decision of 1971 is, in legal structure, a waiver. The operative provision of the Decision states: "the provisions of Article I shall be waived for a period of ten years *to the extent necessary* . . . [to permit developed countries to provide to developing countries generalized, non-discriminatory, non-reciprocal preferential tariff treatment]" (emphasis added). Since in 1971 the legal instrument was a "waiver," the expectation might well have been that the provisions on the waiver would be strictly policed in dispute settlement.

In both *India–Balance of Payments* and *Turkey–Textiles*, the Appellate Body rejected arguments that it should approach adjudication of the legal provisions in question in light of concerns about "institutional balance." The practice of dealing with such issues through avenues other than dispute settlement did not incline the Appellate Body to a less intrusive or less strict scrutiny of the defendant's measures. However, in both cases, the Appellate Body relied in part on an explicit affirmation in Uruguay Round legal instruments concerning the role of dispute settlement in the implementation of the rights and obligations in question (footnote 1 of the Balance of Payments Understanding and paragraphs 12 and 14 of the Understanding on the Interpretation of Article XXIV of the GATT 1994).

Similarly, there is a Uruguay Round instrument that affirms explicitly the availability of dispute settlement in the case of "the failure of the Member to whom a waiver was granted to observe the terms and conditions of the waiver" (Understanding in Respect of Waivers of Obligations under the GATT 1994, para. 3(a)). Again, the issue is not justiciability as such, but rather the fact that this instrument suggests that provisions of a waiver may well be "terms and conditions" to be applied strictly by the dispute settlement organs. In contrast to these three Uruguay Round legal instruments, the Doha instrument that addresses the Enabling Clause,[22] makes no mention or affirmation concerning the availability of dispute settlement to address violations of supposed terms and conditions of the Enabling Clause. Instead, it merely reaffirms that preferences granted to developing countries under the Enabling Clause "*should* be generalized,

---

[22] WTO Ministerial Conference, Implementation-related Issues and Concerns, Decision of November 14, 2001. Within the meaning of the Vienna Convention rules on treaty interpretation, this instrument would be relevant either as a subsequent agreement or subsequent practice of the parties regarding the interpretation of the Treaty.

non-reciprocal, and non-discriminatory" (emphasis added). This formulation, especially the use of "should" rather than stronger obligatory language, makes it clear that these elements of the GSP are *desiderata*, or objectives, and not legally binding preconditions for the applicability of the Enabling Clause. Not only does the Decision not refer to the enforceability of "terms" or "conditions" of the Enabling Clause in dispute settlement, it does not require that non-conforming preferences be phased out or modified within any kind of time period. I will return to this point below, where I address India's contention that EC preferential treatment conditioned on environmental and labor rights performance does not fall within the scope of paragraph 2(a) of the Enabling Clause.

Another consideration to be borne in mind in determining the legal effect of the Enabling Clause is that, as the Appellate Body noted in *Hormones*, the general international law principle of *in dubio mitius* requires that where the extent of a legal obligation is unclear, a treaty interpreter adopt the reading that least restricts the sovereignty of the state that is bound: "We cannot lightly assume that sovereign states intended to impose upon themselves the more onerous, rather than the less burdensome, obligation by mandating conformity or compliance with such standards, guidelines and recommendations. To sustain such an assumption and to warrant such a far-reaching interpretation, treaty language far more specific and compelling . . . would be necessary" (para. 165). Here, the Appellate Body was interpreting the expression "based on" in the SPS Agreement; the wording in paragraph 2(a) of the Enabling Clause, namely that preferential treatment be *in accordance with* the notion of a mutually acceptable system of generalized, non-reciprocal and non-discriminatory preferences, certainly does not amount to "specific and compelling" language that suggests every aspect of a member's scheme of preferential treatment must *conform to* non-discrimination or non-discrimination as juridical norms or conditions.

One final general consideration is the role of UNCTAD in the implementation of the Generalized System of Preferences; this forms part of the "context" of the Enabling Clause and its provisions, within the meaning of Article 31 of the Vienna Convention. By virtue of Trade and Development Board Resolution 75(S-IV), October 12, 1970, a Special Committee within UNCTAD was established to review annually the implementation of the GSP, with more in-depth studies to be conducted on a less frequent basis. By the time the Enabling Clause was negotiated, this Committee had issued numerous detailed reports on the functioning of the GSP, often with detailed recommendations. These reports and various resolutions and other UNCTAD instruments suggest that UNCTAD conceived itself as having a lead role in the oversight of the GSP, and may account in some measure for the lack of more explicit or detailed institutional arrangements in the text of the Enabling Clause itself.

India's claim that EC preferential treatment is contrary to paragraph 2(a)

As noted above, paragraph 2(a) states that preferential tariff treatment for developing countries must be "in accordance" with the Generalized System of Preferences, as "described" in the 1971 GSP Decision, in order for the override of Article I GATT to apply. If we turn to the 1971 Decision, the description of the preferential tariff treatment under the rubric of GSP is, as the 1971 Decision itself tells us (para. (a)), contained in the Preamble to the 1971 Decision. That description is as follows: "a mutually acceptable system of generalized, non-reciprocal and non-discriminatory preferences beneficial to the developing countries in order to increase the export earnings, to promote the industrialization, and to accelerate the rates of economic growth of these countries."

An initial interpretive issue is just what the Enabling Clause means in stating that "*preferential treatment*" must be *in accordance* with this description. Is the requirement that a member's system of trade preferences for developing countries as a whole reflect this description, or must every element in a member's system of trade preferences fully or perfectly realize this description? The Preamble refers to "*mutually acceptable* arrangements . . . drawn up in the UNCTAD concerning the establishment of generalized, non-discriminatory, non-reciprocal preferential tariff treatment in the markets of developed countries for the products originating in developing countries" (emphasis added). It is clear from the relevant UNCTAD instruments, which form part of the "context" for the interpretation of the Enabling Clause within the meaning of Article 31 of the Vienna Convention, that the notion of a generalized, non-discriminatory, non-reciprocal system of preferences refers to an objective to be progressively realized on the basis of arrangements that are *mutually acceptable* to both developed and developing countries.

From the outset, developed countries were not willing to provide preferential treatment that applied to all countries and all products; if one viewed the notion of preferences having to be "generalized" and "non-discriminatory" as requiring that every element of a member's scheme of preferences fully conform to that description in order to take advantage of waiver treatment under the 1971 Decision or the override of the Enabling Clause, then the GSP would never have got off the ground. Developed countries would have been prevented from offering preferences on terms that were acceptable to them. In this respect, the language "mutually acceptable" informs and conditions the entire description of the Generalized System of Preferences in the Preamble to the 1971 GSP Decision. The aspirational character of the notion of preferences being generalized, non-discriminatory and non-reciprocal is reflected as recently as the Doha Decision on Implementation in 2001 which, as noted above, "reaffirms" that preferences granted under the Enabling Clause "should" have these characteristics, but without any defined timetable for the achievement of this goal, or any clear guidelines as to how fully it must be achieved at a given future point in time.

There is little question but that, among developing countries particularly, conditionality with respect to labor rights and (less obviously or uncontroversially) environmental performance has been viewed as detracting from the extent to which preference schemes, including that of the EC, realize the goal of, most notably, a "non-discriminatory" system of preferences. The same goes for limitations on the range of countries or products to which GSP schemes apply. For example, the Comprehensive Review of the Generalized System of Preferences by the UNCTAD Secretariat, issued April 9, 1979, noted that:

> For various reasons, some preference-giving countries have not recognized as beneficiaries all those developing countries which claim developing status. Furthermore, in the administration of their schemes, certain preference-giving countries differentiate among beneficiaries with regard to the product coverage, the depth of tariff cut and/or the level of preferential imports admitted. Strictly speaking, such differentiation and selectivity contravenes the principle of non-discrimination. Also, certain preference-giving countries specify conditions for eligibility for preferences which indirectly imply a certain degree of reciprocity of concessions or a certain pattern of behavior. These conditions would thus seem to be incompatible with the principle of non-reciprocity embodied in the GSP. The principles on which generalized, non-reciprocal and non-discriminatory preferences should be based need to be reaffirmed, and the preference-giving countries should agree to take appropriate measures for the full observance of these principles. To this effect, they should extend generalized tariff preferences to all developing countries without discrimination, reciprocity or other conditions. (paras 153 and 154).

Here, the language "should" and "should *agree*"(emphasis added) displays the understanding that developed countries are not, strictly speaking, *bound* to take the action in question; non-discrimination and non-reciprocity are "principles" as to which developed countries need to agree *in the future* to take measures that will result in "full observance"; i.e. they are not yet bound by any agreement to such full observance.

But the UNCTAD membership has not been prepared to go even this far; the relevant language in the Declaration at UNCTAD IX, in 1980 (the year following this comprehensive review) merely states: "There is concern among the beneficiaries that the enlargement of the scope of the GSP by linking eligibility to non-trade considerations may detract value from its original principles, namely non-discrimination, universality, burden sharing and non-reciprocity." (para. 27). This language is obviously a far cry from a condemnation of such linkage as placing the preferences in question outside the ambit of the relevant description of the GSP, i.e., as a *mutually acceptable* generalized, non-reciprocal and non-discriminatory system of preferences. And the reference to "beneficiaries" in this declaration is a reminder that the entire description of GSP in these terms is informed by the notion that the system is to be "mutually acceptable", i.e., to both developed and developing countries; developed countries have *never* accepted that they should be able to operate a GSP scheme only where the scheme is completely unconditional and non-selective.

Just prior to the coming into force of the Uruguay Round Agreements, and the incorporation of the Enabling Clause into the GATT 1994, the 1994 Joint Declaration of the EC and ASEAN showed that concerns about labor conditionality in the EC's new GSP scheme were not understood to involve a claim of WTO illegality. The language of the Declaration is as follows:

> 10.The Ministers recognized that the General System of Preferences (GSP) has contributed to the growth in exports from ASEAN to the EU. More than one third of ASEAN's exports to the EU enjoy tariff concessions under the GSP. The Ministers noted that the EU envisages a revision and updating of the GSP for the next decade. In this context, the Ministers recognized that the Cumulative Rules of Origin (CRO) provision has contributed to ASEAN's regional integration and would further assist ASEAN in achieving its objectives of an ASEAN Free Trade Area. The

ASEAN Ministers stressed their concerns about certain elements such as 'Social Incentives' in the Commission proposals on the review of the GSP.[23]

It is clear that although the ASEAN Ministers had "concerns" about social incentives, these concerns did not lead to the least hint of questioning the legality of the EC GSP scheme under the GATT Enabling Clause. Moreover, it is clear that there was no agreement between the EC and the ASEAN Ministers that such incentives were disciplined in any legal sense by WTO rules.

In sum, the subsequent practice of the parties within the meaning of Article 31 of the Vienna Convention strongly points to an interpretation of the notion of a "non-discriminatory" and "non-reciprocal" system of preferences as aspirational. Despite persistent concern by developing countries about conditionality and selectivity in GSP schemes over a period of almost thirty years, no legal instrument has ever been promulgated that elevates the elements of non-discrimination or non-reciprocity to a legal condition precedent for the granting of preferences that would otherwise be inconsistent with Article I. The policy basis for continuing to treat these elements as, at most, "basic principles" which developed countries are exhorted to reflect in their GSP schemes, is expressed in the judgment of a 1998 Report to ECOSOC by the Secretariats of UNCTAD and the WTO:[24] "[Despite, inter alia, selectivity and conditionality in some GSP schemes] Nonetheless the GSP remains a valuable tool for promoting developing-country exports" (paras 39, 40). When balanced against various "improvements" in GSP treatment, including "a substantial extension of product coverage for all GSP recipients," the remaining or new elements of selectivity and conditionality did not justify moving to a stricter approach, enforcing the elements of non-discrimination and non-reciprocity as legal conditions precedent. Leaving aside whether it could ever be part of "mutually acceptable" GSP arrangements, such a stricter approach might lead to waning enthusiasm on the part of developed countries to further extend and improve their GSP schemes to the

---

[23] Joint Declaration at Eleventh ASEAN-EU Ministerial Meeting Karlsruhe, September 22–23, 1994.

[24] Secretariats of UNCTAD and the World Trade Organization, *Report on Market Access: Developments since the Uruguay Round, Implications, Opportunities and Challenges, in Particular for the Developing Countries and the Least Developed Among Them, in the Context of Globalization and Liberalization*, E/1998/55, May 22, 1998.

benefit of developing countries. Thus, the repeated reaffirmations of non-discrimination and non-reciprocity as principles of the GSP, up to and including the Doha Decision on Implementation, have never been accompanied by requirements that aspects of WTO members' GSP schemes that detract from those principles be removed or modified within a definite time frame, or completely.[25]

All of these considerations lead to the conclusion that India is wrong to assert that the special preferential treatment accorded by the EC based on labor rights and environmental conditionality falls outside the description of the GSP as a "mutually acceptable system of generalized, non-reciprocal and non-discriminatory preferences beneficial to the developing countries." This is consistent with the approach of the adopted GATT Panel in the *Brazil Rubber Footwear* case, in determining whether preferences fall within paragraph 2(a). The Panel noted that: "the GSP programme of the United States, both in its nature and its design, accords duty-free status to only certain products originating in only certain developing countries" (para. 6.14). The Panel further noted that this entailed *both* a tariff and a non-tariff advantage to the selected beneficiaries. The Panel made it very clear that selective duty-free treatment under the American GSP scheme was excluded from the Article I override in the Enabling Clause, *only* to the extent that such duty-free treatment results in the conferral of an additional, *non*-tariff preference on the beneficiary (para. 6.15); while tariff preferences that are provided on a selective basis, both in respect of products and countries, are protected by the Enabling Clause paragraph 2(a), non-tariff preferences are not.

The wisdom of this interpretive approach is strongly confirmed if we consider the jurisprudential challenge for the dispute settlement organs if, under paragraph 2(a), non-discrimination or non-reciprocity were considered to be legal conditions that determined whether the Article I GATT override was applicable to a given case of preferential treatment.

It is one thing for political and diplomatic bodies and actors to make general assertions that selectivity and conditionality of preferences are inconsistent with, or detract from, the spirit or principle of non-discrimination or non-reciprocity. It is quite another matter for a judicial body to examine the individual features of a preference scheme,

---

[25] Contrast this with the Uruguay Round Balance of Payments Understanding, which reaffirms the commitment "to announce publicly, as soon as possible, time-schedules for the removal of restrictive import measures taken for balance-of-payments purposes" (para. 1).

to determine whether each of them meets a legal condition of non-discrimination. In the GATT/WTO legal framework, non-discrimination is a complex and varied concept. One need only contrast, to use a single example, the notion of discrimination in Article I GATT, which involves a comparison of the treatment of *like products*, with the concept in the *chapeau* of Article XX, which entails a comparison of the treatment of countries "where the same conditions prevail. The concept of non-discrimination in Article III of the GATT is different yet again, informed as it is by the objective of avoiding protection of domestic production."[26]

To even begin an analysis of whether EC preferential treatment based on labor and environmental conditionality violates a purported legal condition of non-discrimination in the Enabling Clause, the Panel and the Appellate Body would have to cut from whole cloth, as it were, an appropriate juridical concept of non-discrimination. Since the issue here is whether an *override* to Article I applies, the dispute settlement organs could not simply appropriate the MFN concept of non-discrimination, without the risk that the Clause would be rendered, in important respects, inutile.

In the case of special preferences based upon labor conditionality, the conditions in question are based on the core labor standards in the ILO Declaration on Fundamental Principles and Rights at Work. All ILO members are committed to these standards, as indeed are all WTO members, indirectly, through the Singapore Declaration. As such all developing countries are similarly situated with respect to the conditions for special preferential treatment by the EC: does the condition therefore result in any "discrimination"?

A different kind of issue about the concept and meaning of non-discrimination would arise with respect to the preferences with environmental conditionality. These preferences apply only to products from certain forests, where the country of origin "effectively applies national legislation incorporating the substance of internationally acknowledged standards and guidelines concerning sustainable management of forests"

---

[26] See *European Communities – Measures Affecting Asbestos and Asbestos – Containing Products*, Report of the Appellate Body, WT/DS135/AB/R (March 12, 2001). As discussed below, however, there is one relatively uncontroversial meaning to non-discrimination as a characteristic of GSP schemes – preferential schemes restricted permanently to an exclusive regional grouping of countries do not fall within the GSP rubric. But this meaning, while sufficient to allow the WTO adjudicator to play its proper role under Enabling Clause paragraph 2(a), would be entirely insufficient if the adjudicator were called upon to evaluate all the individual distinctions and differentiations drawn within a GSP scheme against "non-discrimination" as a legal condition.

(Article 21.2 EC Regulation 2501/2001). What if a potential recipient country were to argue that, despite absence of national legislation, products from its tropical forests do not create environmental externalities of the kind addressed by internationally acknowledged standards and guidelines? It is not obvious that the EC Regulation *prohibits* the European Commission from granting preferences where there is such equivalence. Thus, the EC Regulation could be interpreted as not mandating discrimination of the kind based on country of origin, as opposed to differential treatment of products that are "unlike" in respect of the environmental externalities that they create – which may or may not be discriminatory, depending (again) upon the concept of discrimination in question, and the legally required comparator. Neither the Enabling Clause or the GSP Decision of 1971, to which the Clause refers, provides the dispute settlement organs of the WTO with a textual anchor in articulating an appropriate concept of discrimination to apply to these complex legal and administrative facts. Not even an appropriate comparator is specified.

Here, it should be recalled that the 1971 GSP Decision describes GSP as a *mutually acceptable* system of generalized, non-reciprocal and non-discriminatory preferences. Developed countries have never accepted the notion of non-discrimination invoked by those developing countries who claim that conditioning preferences on criteria related to environmental and labor rights performance is discriminatory; instead the developed countries in question have maintained that such conditionality is non-discriminatory because all developing countries are judged equally against the same neutral or objective criteria.[27]

If they were to regard each element of a member's GSP scheme as reviewable against independent (but undefined) legal norms of non-discrimination and non-reciprocity, the dispute settlement organs would be throwing into profound uncertainty the operation of the GSP as it now stands; all of these schemes contain elements of selectivity and conditionality that could, on some conception or other of discrimination, be viewed as discriminatory; this uncertainty would in the short term make the preferences in question even more precarious and uncertain, from the perspective of developing countries, and in the longer term perhaps erode the viability of any "*mutually acceptable*" system of preferences.[28] These consequentialist concerns would not matter if

---

[27] Here I draw on research in progress by Mr. Lorand Bartels on this issue.
[28] On the difficulties of drawing a line between permissible and impermissible differential treatment *within* a preferential, and thus inherently discriminatory scheme, see R. Hudec, "The Structure of South-South Trade Preferences in the 1988 GSTP Agreement: Learning to Say MFMFN" in John Whalley (ed.), *Developing Countries and the Global Trading System*,

the dispute settlement organs were *explicitly* directed to adjudicate non-discrimination as a *legal condition* of the Enabling Clause (as *was* the case with Article XXIV GATT in *Turkey–Textiles*), but they do certainly go to whether such a directive or mandate should be inferred *in the absence of* explicit language.[29]

The above analysis obviously points to the conclusion that, as a general matter, the reference to a non-discriminatory and non-reciprocal system of preferences, as incorporated in the Enabling Clause, is of an aspirational nature, and not in the manner of a binding condition. But just as subsequent practice sustains this conclusion as a *general* matter, subsequent practice, including adopted GATT Panel Reports and the existence of waivers such as the Lomé waiver, *also* suggests that there are *some* kinds of discriminatory preferential trading relations clearly understood to fall outside the ambit of the Enabling Clause altogether, in particular preference schemes confined to regional or other specific and exclusive groupings of countries.

As was held by the Panel in the *Brazil Rubber Footwear* case, preferential treatment *must* fall in the categories described in one of the heads of paragraph 2 in order to benefit from the MFN override in the Enabling Clause. The WTO adjudicator must consider whether, overall or generally, the preferential treatment at issue is in "accordance" with the description imported from the 1971 GSP Decision. This is the very limited extent, in fact, to which one can say that there is *some* discernable mutually acceptable meaning to the idea of non-discrimination in relation to GSP: there are certain kinds of discriminatory preferential schemes that are agreed to fall outside the idea or concept of GSP. But, whatever criticisms have been made of elements of policy conditionality in developed countries' GSP programs, for instance in UNCTAD, these criticisms have never been couched in terms that suggest in any way that the programs, by virtue of those elements of conditionality, fall outside the GSP rubric altogether.

vol. I, *Thematic Studies from a Ford Foundation Supported Project* (Macmillan, London, 1989), pp. 210–37.

[29] It is true that paragraph 2(d) of the Enabling Clause, in *explicitly* allowing additional margins of preferences to be granted to least-developed countries, could be interpreted as *implicitly* prohibiting the granting of additional margins of preferences to any select group of countries within a GSP scheme except on grounds that they are "least developed." In this sense, it could be argued that there is one permitted comparator for differential treatment within GSP schemes, whether a country is "least developed," with all other comparators prohibited. But given the enormous consequences described above in the text, it would seem judicial overreaching to derive a prohibition on other distinctions within GSP schemes by implication alone of what is *permitted* in paragraph 2(d).

Paragraph 3(a) of the Enabling Clause

Paragraph 3(a) of the Enabling Clause states that "[any differential and more favourable treatment provided under this clause] shall be designed to facilitate and promote the trade of developing countries and not to raise barriers to or create undue difficulties for the trade of any other contracting parties." This language, unlike that in paragraph 2(a) does appear to establish something like a legal condition for the operation of the MFN override in the Enabling Clause. Paragraph 3 makes stipulations not concerning the *overall* description of a member's GSP scheme but rather applies to "*Any* differential and more favourable treatment provided" (emphasis added). Thus, *all* particular instances or aspects of preferential treatment must be consistent with the strictures of paragraph 3(a). At the same time, the language in question also suggests that these provisions, even if conditions of a sort, may be largely self-policing (see the discussion of the *Corn Syrup* ruling, above), or more appropriately policed by other institutions than the dispute settlement organs of the WTO. The question of whether a given preference scheme is designed to facilitate and promote the trade of developing countries seems to be, in essence, an economic and policy question, and has been treated as such in, for example, the numerous UNCTAD studies of the GSP.

With respect to the second clause of paragraph 3(a), India would appear to be ill-situated to complain concerning negative trade effects of GSP preferences on *developed* countries. As for the first clause, "designed to facilitate and promote the trade of developing countries," this language must now (since the incorporation of the Enabling Clause in the GATT 1994) be read in light of the Preamble to the WTO Agreement, which deals with the objective of facilitating and promoting developing country trade in light of the general purposes of the WTO.

The Preamble refers to the principle that trade relations should be conducted with a view to "raising standards of living, ensuring full employment and a large and steadily growing volume of real income and ... expanding ... trade in goods and services, while allowing for the optimal use of the world's resources in accordance with the objective of sustainable development, seeking both to protect and preserve the environment and to enhance the means for doing so in a manner consistent with ... [the] respective needs and concerns [of WTO Members] at different levels of economic development."

Are the EC's labor preferences designed to facilitate and promote the trade of developing countries, when those words are understood in the context of the Preamble to the WTO Agreement? Essentially, these preferences provide lower rates of tariff applicable to imports from developing countries that can certify that they are complying with core labor standards: If the preferences were not designed to facilitate and promote trade, it is difficult to see how they could operate as an incentive to developing countries to comply with core labor standards: if a developing country's trade were not promoted or facilitated by a scheme of this design, it is very difficult to imagine why that country would bother electing to participate in it. But there is more: to the extent that, at the margin, these principles actually induce or sustain higher levels of fulfillment of core labor standards, they may positively contribute to enabling the kind of growth and income-enhancing effects of liberal trade that are described in the Preamble to the WTO Agreement. Studies by the OECD and more recently by independent academic economists suggest a positive correlation between compliance with core labor standards and higher levels of economic growth and development.[30]

With respect to the environmental preferences, again, in addition to the obvious trade promotion effect of a reduced level of tariff, the environmental conditionality in these preferences may, exogenously, contribute to the objective of increased trade consistent with sustainable development, as stated in the Preamble to the WTO Agreement. To the extent that adherence to international guidelines on sustainable forest management results in better internalization of environmental externalities, it will contribute to "optimal use of the world's resources," and more efficient trade based upon the relative environmental costs of different sources of tropical timber. Moreover, the conditionality in the EC scheme requires only that the "substance" of such guidelines be implemented and enforced. The European Commission therefore has the discretion to decide that a developing country qualifies for the special preferences even if that country, for example, decides not to incorporate aspects of the guidelines that appear to be inappropriate to its needs. India's position here is not that of a developing country that has applied for the special preferences but been refused because its domestic legislation or the application of that legislation does not assure the "substance" of international standards and guidelines. Given the experience with the European Commission's

---

[30] See, e.g., OECD, *Trade, Employment and Labour Standards: A Study of Core Workers' Rights and International Trade* (OECD, Paris, 1996) and Peter Morici (with Evan Schultz), *Labor Standards in the Global Trading System* (Economic Strategy Institute, Washington, DC, 2001).

administration of the special preferences so far, a claim that the conditionality in question is not sufficiently accommodating or supportive of the different needs of different developing countries would clearly be premature.

Paragraph 3(c) of the Enabling Clause

Paragraph 3(c) states that preferences provided under the Enabling Clause "shall... be designed and, if necessary, modified, to respond positively to the development, financial and trade needs of developing countries." With respect to labor conditionality, the labor rights at issue have been declared as "fundamental" by the International Labor Organization, with the support of its developing as well as developed country membership. In respect of environmental conditionality, the internationally acknowledged standards and guidelines to which the EC scheme is indexed are essentially those developed in the International Tropical Timber Organization, an entity where both (developing country) producers and (predominately developed country) consumers have equal voting rights and full membership. The WTO adjudicator is not institutionally competent to make its own judgments about whether the design of the preferences in question responds positively to the development and related needs of developing countries; this involves complex policy and economic judgments. Thus, assuming that paragraph 3(c) is not entirely self-policing, the full and active involvement of developing countries themselves in the elaboration of the standards in question should provide the appropriate assurance that the EC scheme is consistent with paragraph 3(c) of the Enabling Clause.[31]

Moreover, as noted with respect to paragraph 3(a), the conditionality in the EC scheme entails only that the recipient of the special preferences

---

[31] This should not be understood as an "estoppel" argument against the possibility of developing countries complaining about the standards in question being a basis for trade conditionality – after all, not all the instruments in question are binding, and there was no consent to these instruments being enforced or applied through trade conditionality. It is only an argument that the *standards themselves* could not easily be considered to be at odds with paragraph 3(c). As I go on to suggest, the way that trade conditionality is *applied* on the basis of such standards may indeed raise separate issues under paragraph 3(c). So far, however, as is noted in the text below, there does not seem to be any evidence that the application of the conditionality in the EC scheme has taken place in a manner contrary to the norm in paragraph 3(c). Of course, if India is able to muster such evidence it would have to be taken seriously, and the claim would be in no way undermined by the fact that the standards themselves represent broad agreement between developed and developing countries.

implement and enforce "the substance" of the international standards and guidelines in question. On its face, this allows the European Commission to apply the special preference conditionality in such a manner as to permit recipients to maintain and adapt forest management legislation and regulation so as to "respond positively to their development, financial and trade needs."

The consistency of EC labor and environmental preferences with Article I GATT

Article I.1 GATT, the so-called Most Favored Nation clause, requires that, with respect to customs duties, inter alia, "any advantage, favour, privilege or immunity granted by any contracting party to any product originating in or destined for any other country shall be accorded immediately and unconditionally to the like product originating in or destined for the territories of all other contracting parties." Obviously, the extra margin of preference accorded under the EC scheme to products from developing countries that meet the relevant labor and environmental criteria is an advantage or favor with respect to customs duties. Since the preferential treatment in question is only authorized in the context of the EC's GSP scheme, such treatment is simply unavailable to WTO members who are not developing countries, even if they happen to be fully compliant with the criteria in question. There seems to be therefore no question that this preferential treatment violates Article I GATT.

At the same time, the EC scheme does not mandate the exclusion of *India* from such preferential treatment. The EC Regulation merely authorizes the European Commission to grant an additional margin of preference to developing countries that ask for it and that the Commission deems to meet certain (non-country-specific) criteria. There has been no decision of the Commission denying to India the special preferential treatment in question, and indeed India has apparently not asked for such treatment.

It is a long-established GATT doctrine, reaffirmed by the Appellate Body in recent cases, that only legislation that mandates a violation of WTO rules can be effectively challenged in dispute settlement; it is not enough that the legislation authorize or permit the exercise of a discretion that may in a particular instance be used to violate WTO rules. In the case of discretionary legislation, a complainant's case must be based on an actual instance of application of the law that violates WTO rules. There is a third, or hybrid case, where the granting of discretion in legislation creates the kind of threat to legal security of specific rights under the WTO Agreements that leads to a deprivation of the normal enjoyment of those rights even before an actual instance of application, for example, through a "chill" effect on market activity.[32] This third or hybrid case does not, however, apply here, as an uncertainty about India's rights could be eliminated simply through India applying to the European Commission, which would make a decision as to whether or not to extend the preferential treatment in question to India. More generally, even if preferential treatment were granted *without* labor or environmental conditionality, India and its partners in the marketplace could not, in any event, expect to depend on the legal security of such a grant, since the preferential treatment is not binding under the WTO but rather is voluntary and could legally be removed altogether.

With respect, however, to developed countries, there is little question but that the EC legislation is mandatory: the European Commission is effectively excluded from granting the preferential treatment in question to developed country WTO members, regardless of their labor and environmental rights performance. The question is whether the WTO adjudicator could find a violation of this nature, in a case where the violation does not apply to the complainant, in this case a developing country.

The answer would appear to be "yes." In the *Havana Club* ruling, the Appellate Body found that the United States had violated the National Treatment obligation in the TRIPS Agreement, by treating Cuban nationals more favorably than American nationals;[33] however, the complainant in that case was the EC, not Cuba. There may be some rights and obligations in the WTO that are not *erga omnes partes*, and which therefore, arguably, could only be enforceable by the party whose rights are directly affected, but certainly Article I GATT is no less an obligation *erga omnes partes* than National Treatment in TRIPS; MFN in Article I is a foundational or structural norm of the multilateral trading system as a whole, in respect of trade in goods.[34]

In sum, India has a clear and persuasive case that the EC special preferential treatment violates Article I of the GATT.

---

[32] *United States, Sections 301–310 of the Trade Act of 1974*, Report of the Panel, WT/DS152/R, February 24, 2000, paras 7.72–7.94.

[33] *United States, Section 211 Omnibus Appropriations Act of 1998*, Report of the Appellate Body, WT/DS176/AB/R, January 2, 2002, para. 281.

[34] But see, on the issue of whether and which WTO obligations are *erga omnes partes*, J. Pauwelyn, "The Nature of WTO Obligations," Jean Monnet Working Paper (2002).

Article XX GATT

It was settled in the *Shrimp–Turtle* case that Article XX can be used to justify measures that condition market access on the policies adopted by the exporting WTO member; indeed, the Appellate Body made the strong statement that many if not all the heads of justification in Article XX would be inutile, if that were not the case. Thus, even though the EC special preferential treatment violates Article I GATT, it may nevertheless be justified, and therefore GATT-legal, under one of the heads of Article XX, the general exceptions provision. In such a case, the EC would not need to depend on the Enabling Clause to maintain its special preferential treatment. Labor rights and environmental conditionality raise rather different sets of issues with respect to Article XX justification, and thus need to be considered separately.

Labor rights conditionality

The first step in considering an Article XX justification is to determine whether the defending member's measures fall into any of the individual heads or paragraphs of Article XX.[35] There are three possible heads in Article XX that may apply to measures concerned with the enforcement of labor rights. Article XX(a) refers to measures that are necessary to protect public morals; Artcle XX(b) refers to measures necessary to protect human, animal or plant life or health; Article XX(e) refers to measures "relating to the products of prison labor."

Article XX(a): "public morals"

The meaning and scope of "public morals" has never been adjudicated in the GATT or WTO.[36] I and others have argued that internationally recognized human rights articulate elements of international public morality and therefore come within the ordinary meaning of "public morals."[37] In the Singapore Declaration, WTO members renewed their commitment

---

[35] *Shrimp–Turtle, EC – Asbestos.*
[36] The most comprehensive study of Article XX(a) of which I am aware is C. T. Feddersen, *Der ordre public in der WTO: Auslegung und Bedeutung des Art. XX lit. a) GATT im Rahmen der WTO-Streitbeilegung* (Duncker und Humblot, Berlin, 2002).
[37] R. Howse, "The World Trade Organization and the Protection of Worker's Rights" (1999) 3(1) *J. Small and Emerging Business* 131; S. Charnovitz, "The Moral Exception in Trade Policy" (1998) 38 *Virginia J. Int'l L.* 689; G. Marceau, "WTO Dispute Settlement and Human Rights" (2002) 13(4) *European J. Int'l L.* 753; Werner Meng, paper presented to the World Trade Forum, Berne, Switzerland, 2001.

to internationally recognized core labor standards, and to the role of the ILO in articulating and dealing with these standards. The ILO in turn has declared these core labor standards to be "Fundamental Principles and Rights"; it would seem implausible to *exclude* those rights, and the commitment to observance of them in the Singapore Declaration, as a source for interpreting the content of public morality under Article XX(a).

In the modern world, the very idea of public morality has become inseparable from the concern for human personhood, dignity and capacity reflected in fundamental rights.[38] A conception of public morals or morality that excluded notions of fundamental rights would simply be contrary to the ordinary contemporary meaning of the concept.[39] One kind of argument that is sometimes made for the exclusion of labor rights trade measures from Article XX(a), is that "public morals" in Article XX(a) refers only to public morals within the territory of the defending member; this should not be confused with arguments concerning whether certain kinds of *means* of achieving the objective in question are excluded from Article XX(a) because they have inappropriate extra-territorial *effects*; as the Appellate Body indicated in *Shrimp–Turtle*, the question of whether a member's objective falls within one of the heads of Article XX is a separate and prior question to the question of whether, under the wording of a particular head, the means the member adopts is appropriate to the achievement of that objective within the WTO legal framework.

---

[38] See Charter of the United Nations, Preamble, which refers to "faith in fundamental human rights, the dignity and worth of the human person, in the equal rights of men and women."

[39] It might be argued that the meaning of "public morals" should be frozen to reflect the ordinary meaning of the expression at the time the GATT 1947 came into effect. However, with the endorsement by the Appellate Body of a dynamic interpretation of the meaning of "exhaustible natural resources" in Article XX(g) GATT in *Shrimp–Turtle*, the notion that Article XX(a) should be interpreted on the basis of the ordinary meaning of public morals in 1947 seems highly implausible. Admittedly, the Appellate Body, in *Shrimp–Turtle,* related its dynamic interpretation to the mention of "sustainable development" in the Preamble to the WTO Agreement. However, in the case of Article XX(a) it simply defies common sense to interpret the provision as allowing governments to respond only to the moral imperatives that existed over fifty years ago: responsible and representative governments clearly have to be accountable to the values and interests of the citizens of today – and tomorrow – not those of yesteryear. In any case, in reaffirming their commitment to observance of core labor standards in the Singapore Declaration, as well as the role of the ILO, the membership have now explicitly acknowledged the importance and legitimacy of the protection of fundamental labor standards as a goal of national and international policy. See also Feddersen, *Der ordre public*, p. 301, noting, "Die textuelle Auslegung der Vorschrift des Art. XX lit. a) GATT erweist, dass es sich bei dem Begriff der *pubic morals* um einen Relationbegriff handelt, der auch einer dynamischen Entwicklung zugaenglich ist."

The text of Article XX(a) contains no territorial limitation on a member's *objective* in protecting public morals. In the *Shrimp–Turtle* case, the Appellate Body of the WTO raised, in *obiter dicta*, the question of whether there needed to be a territorial nexus between the exhaustible natural resources that the defending member is seeking to conserve and the territory of that member. The Appellate Body decided that it did not have to answer that question to dispose of the appeal, because even if a territorial nexus were required, this requirement would be met by the fact that the resource in question is migratory and could sometimes be found in American waters.[40]

The very existence of international human rights and international labor rights law and institutions reflects acceptance by the international community that legitimate concern by states concerning the morality of the treatment of individuals is not limited to their own nationals (denial of justice, for instance); this marks the fundamental dividing line between the traditional law on the protection of aliens, where a state's legally recognized concern with the treatment of individuals extended beyond its own territory *only* where its own nationals were subject to that treatment, and the modern international law of human rights, where in fact states have gone so far as to make binding obligations to *one another* to protect the human rights of their own citizens on their own territory.

An issue sometimes confused with that of whether the concept of "public morals" in Article XX(a) is territorially limited, is whether a provision such as Article XX(a) could be used to justify actions that violate general public international law norms concerning extra-territorial regulation; this goes to the appropriateness of the means, not the scope of the objective, under Article XX(a).[41] The default rule in international law with respect to extra-territorial regulation is stated in the *Lotus* case: "Far from laying down a general prohibition to the effect that States may not extend the application of their laws and the jurisdiction of their courts to persons, property, and acts outside their territory, [international law] leaves them in this respect a wide measure of discretion which is only limited in certain cases by prohibitive rules."[42] Many such prohibitive rules have arisen with respect to particular subject matter in individual treaties and

---

[40] Report of the Appellate Body, para. 133.
[41] On this second issue, see L. Bartels, "Article XX of GATT and the Problem of Extraterritorial Jurisdiction: The Case of Trade Measures for the Protection of Human Rights" (2002) 36(2) J. World Trade 353.
[42] SS. Lotus (France–Turkey) [1927] PCIJ (Ser. A.) No. 10.

conventions; however, attempts[43] to create a more restrictive general or default rule concerning extra-territorial jurisdiction have not succeeded in attracting sufficient state practice and *opinio juris* to dislodge or modify the *Lotus* default rule.[44]

In any case, the controversies in this area of international law are irrelevant to the case of EC preferential treatment based on environmental and labor conditionality. EC Regulation 2501/2001 purports only to provide the European Commission with powers to make a determination of whether certain products can enter the Community at particular rates of duty. It does not purport to regulate the conduct of, or give any jurisdiction to the Commission over, any persons, property or transactions outside the EC. The only legal effect, if a developing country is determined not to comply with the conditionality in question, is a change in the rate of duty at which its products are admitted to the EC; neither the government, nor the nationals, nor the property and territory of that country, is subject to any legal penalty or sanction, or other form of control. Indeed, countries must apply, and declare themselves eligible, in order to be subject to the scheme at all.

This being said, the WTO 1996 Singapore Declaration does appear to establish some kind of limit to the sort of trade measures that WTO members deem consistent with the WTO legal framework. The Declaration states: "We reject the use of labour standards for protectionist purposes, and agree that the comparative advantage of countries, particularly low-wage developing countries, must in no way be put into question." Given its nature as an *extension* of trade preferences, one could hardly attribute "protectionist purposes" to the EC scheme; at least with respect to core labor rights, evidence from the OECD and other sources suggests that observance of these does not threaten the comparative advantage of low-wage developing countries, but may actually enhance it.[45]

---

[43] Many of these attempts, especially by publicists, have been described in Bartels, "Article XX of GATT." One prohibitive rule recognized in the *Lotus* case itself is that a state may not exercise power "in" the territory of another state, e.g., attempting to arrest, try or punish foreign nationals on their own territory.

[44] Thus, the International Court of Justice has held there is no general or customary rule of international law that prohibits as such the use of economic pressure such as trade sanctions. See *Military and Paramilitary Activities (Nicaragua v. United States)*. [1986] ICJ Reports 14, 125–26.

[45] See Morici, *Labor Standards*, p. 76, concluding: "empirical evidence does not support the notion that lax enforcement of [core labor standards] aids long-term development. Effective enforcement within the WTO could be expected to improve the circumstances of workers and the development prospects of countries that played by the rules."

In sum, there do not exist good reasons for *excluding* fundamental labor rights from the ambit of the concept of "public morals." Thus, the remaining issue under Article XX(a) is whether the EC measures are "necessary" for the "protection" of public morals. It would be difficult for the EC to make the case that its measures are necessary in the sense of indispensable; countries that can be effectively encouraged to improve labor rights compliance in response to this kind of incentive would probably be equally or more encouraged to do so by other kinds of incentives, such as subsidies and technical assistance. We are not dealing here with a situation like Myanmar, where the EC has withdrawn GSP treatment altogether; i.e., a country that is simply unwilling to engage in serious dialogue about its labor rights commitments, where trade measures are used as a last resort.

This being said, in the *Korea Beef* case, the Appellate Body has held that in some cases measures may be justifiable under Article XX even if they are not strictly speaking "indispensable" to the objective in question (here the paragraph at issue is Article XX(d), but there is nothing in the Appellate Body's reasoning that suggests it cannot be applied *mutatis mutandis* to other paragraphs of XX):

> It seems to us that a treaty interpreter assessing a measure claimed to be necessary to secure compliance of a WTO-consistent law or regulation may, in appropriate cases, take into account the relative importance of the common interests or values that the law or regulation to be enforced is intended to protect. The more vital or important those common interests or values are, the easier it would be to accept as "necessary" a measure designed as an enforcement instrument. There are other aspects of the enforcement measure to be considered in evaluating that measure as "necessary." One is the extent to which the measure contributes to the realization of the end pursued, the securing of compliance with the law or regulation at issue. The greater the contribution, the more easily a measure might be considered to be "necessary." Another aspect is the extent to which the compliance measure produces restrictive effects on international commerce.[46]

The importance of the common values or interests that the EC measures are intended to protect is obvious from the fact that they are the subject of a multilateral declaration in the ILO that describes these in terms of "fundamental" rights and principles; the WTO Singapore Declaration uses

---

[46] *Korea, Measures Affecting Imports of Fresh, Frozen and Chilled Beef*, Report of the Appellate Body, WT/DS161/AB/R, December 11, 2000, paras 162–63.

the expression "core."[47] Moreover, in this case, the restriction of commerce produced by the measure is minimal. It is true that if the EC were to provide the special preferential tariff rate to all developing countries, regardless of labor or environmental conditionality, commerce would be less restricted, albeit not to a very great extent because all developing countries already benefit from significant margins of preference under the EC scheme. But in considering the trade-restrictiveness of the EC measure, it must also be taken into account that the EC would be entirely within its rights in withdrawing the special preferential treatment altogether, and offering it to *no* developing country.[48]

While the preferences in question are not indispensable, neither is there reason to believe they make a merely trivial contribution to the achievement of compliance with the rights in question, relative to other available instruments.[49] The design and structure seem well-suited to making a significant contribution to the protection of the interests in question: it provides a meaningful incentive to developing countries to improve and maintain compliance with fundamental labor rights.

Article XX(b): protection of human life and health

At least two of the fundamental labor rights indexed to the EC scheme clearly relate to the protection of human life and health: the elimination of all forms of forced and compulsory labor, and the effective abolition of child labor. Such labor practices notoriously endanger human life and health. A relationship between the other rights, freedom of association

---

[47] I do not mean to suggest here that *only* those values or interests widely recognized in international instruments or by the international community can be a basis for action under Article XX(a). However, the analysis is easier in a case like this where the values or interests are not simply idiosyncratic or parochial to a given political community. In the latter case, controversy may exist about the bona fide nature of the objectives which could entail a more complex inquiry to resolve.

[48] I do not mean to introduce here the simplistic notion that the EC measure is merely a "carrot" not a "stick," or to suggest that under some competitive conditions a significant trade restrictive or distorting effect could not be achieved through the selective granting of preferences of this kind. But the inquiry here is one that concerns the *degree* and *nature* of trade-restrictiveness, and this feature of the EC measure is pertinent to making such a *relative* assessment. In its effects, on the behavior of individual market actors, the granting of additional selective preferences cannot be considered equivalent to the withdrawal or suspension of binding concessions, on the legal security of which market actors may have been expected to rely in their economic decision-making.

[49] While the structures are admittedly not the same as the preferences challenged by India, see the conclusions about the positive impact of GSP labor conditionality in the American GSP by Elliott, based on a comprehensive empirical study: Elliott, *Preferences for Workers*.

and the effective recognition of the right to collective bargaining, and the elimination of discrimination in respect of employment and occupation could also be plausibly connected to health, understood broadly as physical and psychological well-being.[50]

The other issues concerning whether the EC measures fit under Article XX(b) are quite similar to those that exist for Article XX(a).

Article XX(e): prison labor

It has been suggested that a teleological interpretation of Article XX(e) might extend that provision to include measures that address the right against forced labor generally. However, the Appellate Body of the WTO has held repeatedly that teleological interpretations non-supported by, or at odds with the ordinary meaning, of treaty provisions are unsustainable under the Vienna Convention on the Law of Treaties.[51] The ordinary meaning of the word "prison" does not encompass other, non-penal settings, even if they entail coercion; such a use of the word prison would be metaphorical or rhetorical and not "ordinary."[52]

Article XX *chapeau*

Once the EC labor rights measures are found to fall into one of the heads of Article XX, the remaining issue, under the *chapeau* of Article XX, is whether these measures are applied in a manner that gives rise to unjustified or arbitrary discrimination between countries where the same conditions prevail, or a disguised restriction on international trade. The *Shrimp–Turtle* Appellate Body rulings illuminate the meaning of unjustified and arbitrary discrimination where Article XX measures condition market access on the exporting member's policies. The requirement to avoid unjustified discrimination implies that the way conditionality in the measure is applied should be sufficiently flexible as to permit the exporting member to satisfy the conditionality in a manner appropriate to its own conditions and circumstances. The exporting country is required only to adopt in domestic legislation and apply the *substance* of the labor rights in the ILO Conventions in question, which are fundamental or core labor rights within the meaning of the ILO Declaration. The EC Regulation thus provides the exporting country with flexibility

---

[50] See, e.g., World Health Organization, *Health for All-Policy* (World Health Declaration, May 1989).
[51] See, e.g., *EC–Hormones*, note 17, para. 103.
[52] And see F. J. Garcia, "Trading Away the Human Rights Principle" (1999) 25(1) *Brooklyn J. Int'l L.* 51, at 79–80.

with respect to the legal and regulatory modalities by which it implements this substance. Moreover, the Regulation provides the European Commission with discretion to grant the special preferential treatment with respect to products from certain particular sectors or areas of the country, in cases where the legislation is applied only in those sectors and not throughout the country. Finally, while the exporting country must report to the Commission the measures taken to implement and monitor these provisions effectively, the EC leaves it up to the exporting country to devise implementation and monitoring measures, as long as these are effective. In sum, the EC scheme, on its face, does not contain features that would result in it being applied in a manner that gives rise to "unjustified discrimination," within the meaning of that expression determined by the Appellate Body in the *Shrimp–Turtle* rulings. Thus, the EC should be able to make a prima facie case that its scheme conforms to this condition of the *chapeau*; it would then be up to India to allege specific instances where, *in fact*, the European Commission and its officials have applied the scheme in a manner that gives rise to unjustified discrimination. In this respect, it is recalled that India has not applied to participate in the scheme, and therefore has not been itself subject to any specific instances of Commission administrative action in respect thereof.

As for the "arbitrary discrimination" within the meaning of the *chapeau*, the EC scheme provides transparent criteria which a developing country application for the special preferences must meet, specifies a decision-maker (the European Commission), requires that a decision be made in a fixed period of time (one year), and that reasons be provided for a negative decision, if requested. The relevant authorities of the applicant developing country "are invited to cooperate" in the Commission's investigation of whether the country meets the criteria for the granting of the special preferences. These "due process" features on the face of the EC scheme should be sufficient to discharge the burden of proof to make a prima facie case that the *scheme itself* conforms with the *chapeau* prohibition on "arbitrary discrimination." It would then be up to India to allege any instances where, in fact, in applying the scheme, the European Commission has engaged in "arbitrary discrimination."

Environmental conditionality

Based upon the Appellate Body's reading of "exhaustible natural resources" in the *Shrimp–Turtle* case, which includes living resources and is based on the international law and policy of sustainable development, it would seem fairly certain that measures to conserve tropical forests and their ecosystems would come within Article XX(g) GATT, which concerns measures "in relation to exhaustible natural resources." That the sustainability of tropical forests and their ecosystems is a legitimate and important policy goal, and indeed a pressing environmental priority, is confirmed by a wide variety of international activities in this regard, including the various policy statements and guidelines of the International Tropical Timber Organization (ITTO), as already noted, a multilateral organization whose members include both countries with tropical forest and those that are consumers of tropical forest products.[53]

Providing a tangible incentive for developing countries to implement internationally acknowledged standards and guidelines concerning sustainable management of tropical forests seems to have a real and close connection with the policy objective of conserving these exhaustible natural resources.

Article XX(g), however, also includes the condition that the measures in question be "made effective in conjunction with restrictions on domestic production or consumption." Since there are no tropical forests within the EC itself (with the extremely limited exception, perhaps, of some offshore territories of EC members) the focus here would naturally be on restrictions on domestic consumption. In this regard it should be noted that the EC is progressively taking steps effectively to halt the importation of "illegal" tropical timber, i.e., timber harvested in violation of the laws of the exporting country. These restrictions on consumption of tropical timber within the EC clearly relate to the effectiveness of the EC trade preferences. To the extent that illegally harvested timber can find a market in the EC, a major consumer, the incentives for compliance with domestic legislation, including the legislation that developing countries are encouraged to provide and enforce by the EC preferences, will be undermined, with consequent negative affects on the conservation of forests.

---

[53] It is irrelevant here that the material in question is in the form of voluntary non-binding guidelines that states are to implement in their own domestic systems. Action under Article XX(g), as the Appellate Body emphasized in the *Shrimp–Turtle* implementation ruling, does not require the existence of a multilateral treaty at all (para. 123). The international policy material in question is here being invoked only as evidence that sustainable forest management is widely viewed in the international community as an important and legitimate goal of public policy, and as a matter that transcends the particular interests of consumer and producer countries taken individually, but rather concerns the tropical forests as a global commons.

Finally, the issue of territorial nexus may arise, one on which (as noted) the Appellate Body did not pronounce as a matter of law in *Shrimp–Turtle*. As the various policy statements of the ITTO and the international community more generally on the issue of sustainable forestry show, understood as an exhaustible natural resource, tropical forests and their ecosystems have a global "commons" or public good dimension; this is reflected in the fact that both producer and consumer countries are fully represented, and indeed on terms of equal voting rights, in the ITTO. This "commons" dimension creates an appropriate nexus with the interests of the EC.[54]

Article XX *chapeau*[55]

With respect to "unjustified discrimination," EC preferences are based on implementation of guidelines and standards that have been agreed internationally, which are principally those developed through the ITTO. Because such guidelines and standards are agreed among a wide variety of both producer and consumer countries, they reflect flexibility and sensitivity with respect to conditions in different countries, and do not seek to impose or copy the regulatory approach of any single jurisdiction. Moreover, the EC preference scheme requires only that developing countries implement "the substance" of such standards and guidelines, thereby providing a further margin of flexibility to adapt them to distinctive local conditions and priorities.

As for "arbitrary discrimination," in referring to international standards and guidelines generally, rather than to a defined set of rights in fixed legal instruments (as is the case with the labor preferences), the EC scheme clearly confers a large measure of discretion on the European Commission in determining whether the legislation, monitoring and enforcement activities of a particular developing country meet the conditionality. This discretion is disciplined, however, by the right to request reasons, where a country is denied preferential status. WTO doctrine is want to find a violation of WTO legal requirements merely on

---

[54] By "commons" here is not implied a legal state of affairs where individual states have ceded jurisdiction to control forests within their territory; rather, that, conceptually, the way that one state exercises, or fails to exercise, that jurisdiction may have significant effects on other states and the international community in general, thus leading other states and the international community to have a legitimate interest in how domestic jurisdiction is exercised.

[55] I have not considered whether the EC measures are a "disguised restriction on international trade" within the meaning of the *chapeau*, because issues of possible hidden protectionism simply do not seem to arise on the facts.

the basis of the scope of *discretion* afforded to a decision-maker under a statute; in the case of statutes that do not *mandate* violations of WTO treaty obligations state responsibility is normally engaged when WTO law is violated through the exercise of discretionary powers granted by the statute.[56] This view of state responsibility is especially applicable to the conditions of the *chapeau* of Article XX, since as the Appellate Body has held in the *Shrimp–Turtle* case, the conditions in the *chapeau* govern how a legislative or regulatory scheme is applied, rather than its general structural features or characteristics.

Absent evidence of specific instances where the Commission has acted arbitrarily, for example, giving vague or inconsistent reasons for denial of preferential status, or interpreting the "substance" of international standards and guidelines in an inconsistent or discriminatory manner with respect to different applicants for preferential treatment, it would seem at the very least premature to conclude that the nature of the criteria or conditions in and of itself results in "arbitrary discrimination."

Conclusion: the policy and economic stakes in the outcome of India's challenge

In this concluding section, I wish to speculate on the political and economic consequences that would flow from various possible outcomes[57] of this dispute, assuming that it is fully litigated in the WTO.

Scenario 1: the EC preferences are upheld under the Enabling Clause

Were the Panel and/or the Appellate Body to find that the EC preferences are consistent with the Enabling Clause, especially on the general jurisprudential ground that the clause, at least in respect of Article 2(a), does not import strict legal conditions on the nature of GSP preferences, the policy status quo with respect to GSP and related issues of environmental and labor conditionality would be largely preserved. WTO members would be confirmed, more or less, in the intuition that they can operate voluntary GSP preference schemes outside the (strict) scrutiny of the WTO adjudicator. A ruling on general jurisprudential grounds would say little,

---

[56] See *United States, Sections 301–310*, note 32.
[57] I have selected only some of the possible outcomes, and not considered others that I view as remote or largely insignificant variations, i.e., that the Appellate Body would go one way on labor preferences and the opposite way on the environmental preferences.

or need not say much, about the legitimacy of trade action for labor and environmental purposes as such, and would leave the current state of play in that debate essentially intact. On the other hand, it is possible (though I believe unlikely, based on the analysis above), that, for example, the WTO Panel or Appellate Body could find that "non-discrimination" is a strict legal condition of the Enabling Clause, but that labor and environmental preferences are not discriminatory, because they are based on general and objective criteria applied equally to all developed countries. Such a statement would enhance in a general way the legitimacy of linkage between trade and labor and environmental issues, and would undermine the strong (if often not well-reasoned) intuition of the traditional trade policy elite (including many WTO heads of delegation) that labor and environmental conditionality is somehow inherently at odds with the idea of non-discriminatory liberal trade. Such a ruling would reinforce the developments in the *Shrimp–Turtle* Appellate Body decisions, and take them further, for the first time legitimizing linkage with labor rights.

The consequences of a positive signal on labor and environmental conditionality are likely to be complex. On the one hand, such a signal would reinforce the position of "moderate" activists and civil society groups that the WTO is not hopelessly hostile to environmental and labor interests; on the other hand, it would undermine, with respect to labor issues, the legitimacy of the current leadership or elite at the WTO, which has sought to keep such questions "out" of the trading system.

Scenario 2: EC preferences upheld under the Enabling Clause and under Article XX

The Appellate Body could hold that the EC preferences are legal, despite Article I GATT, on two separate grounds: the Enabling Clause and Article XX. Such a departure from strict judicial economy would create a signal that labor and environmental linkage are legitimate and appropriate within the WTO system, especially if the Enabling Clause analysis is based on general jurisprudential grounds, such that if it wanted to, the Appellate Body could have stopped there, and not waded into the labor and environmental questions.

Scenario 3: EC preferences upheld under Article XX alone

A ruling upholding the EC preferences under Article XX alone would not introduce any new instability into the GSP and its operation, but would send a positive signal about the legitimacy of labor and environmental linkages.

Scenario 4: EC preferences fail Enabling Clause but are upheld under Article XX

Of all the outcomes where the EC measures are upheld, this one would have the most dynamic effect on current debates and negotiations within the WTO. If the EC preferences fail the Enabling Clause, then this will send, at a minimum, a signal that the individual elements of members' GSP schemes will be subject to meaningful or even strict scrutiny of the WTO dispute settlement organs. This would make GSP preferences less attractive, from a political economy perspective, as the room to maneuver in balancing the interests of different constituencies would be constrained; most of the selective or possibly discriminatory features of GSP schemes have nothing to do with labor and environmental concerns (or indeed any legitimate non-commercial policies) but everything to do with the standard political economy of commercial policy. Thus, this outcome would signal the vulnerability of current GSP schemes to a challenge under the Enabling Clause, but without the possibility of justification under Article XX GATT. At the same time, because of the Article XX justification, there would be, as well, a positive signal concerning the legitimacy of labor and environmental linkage.

The GSP is already subject to much criticism, including sophisticated economic and political economy analysis that suggests developing countries would be better off with deeper, bargained MFN tariff cuts.[58] The outcome of striking down the EC preferences based on the Enabling Clause might well give greater emphasis to proposals in the current Round for significant bound tariff cuts that would benefit developing countries. On the other hand, it could further intensify the trend towards regionalism, as preference-granting countries look for other mechanisms where they can operate selective and conditional preferential trade policies. Obviously, offering concessions on an MFN basis in multilateral negotiations might reduce the value or extent of any preferential treatment one may be able to offer to regional trading partners, so the ultimate impact could be to

---

[58] C. Ozden and E. Reinhardt, "The Perversity of Preferences: GSP and Developing Country Trade Policies 1976–2000," April 9, 2002, available on the World Bank website, www.worldbank.org/wbi/B-SPAN/sub_perversity.htm.

undermine the extent to which the current Round generates tariff cuts on an MFN basis.

Scenario 5: EC preferences fail both the Enabling Clause and Article XX

This scenario, with the EC preferences failing both the Enabling Clause and Article XX, would have a very significant impact on the trading system. The result on the Enabling Clause would have the effects discussed under Scenario 4. However, the fact that labor and environmental conditionality in preferences can be justified neither under the Enabling Clause nor under Article XX would be very likely to undermine the political equilibrium on the labor issue in the United States, in Congress in particular. The assumption that conditional preferences are WTO-legal, and the possibility that other kinds of trade action related to labor rights might be justifiable under Article XX GATT, has served to counter pressures to make the negotiation of a "social clause" in the WTO a condition of the President's fast-track authority and of the ultimate approval by Congress of a new multilateral trade deal. Especially if the partisan balance changes in Congress after the next congressional elections (in 2004), a ruling by the WTO Appellate Body that narrowed or eliminated the possibility for labor conditionality under GSP and more generally through Article XX justification, could well lead to, and provide a principled pretext for, a reconsideration of the basis on which the President has been granted fast-track authority. And this would occur in what is supposed to be the final year or so of the Doha Round negotiations.

At the same time, a ruling of this nature, with its negative signal on labor and environmental linkage, would be likely to (re)unite more moderate activists, who are critical but also hopeful for change at the WTO, with diehard anti-WTO people. A united front of "civil society" against the Doha Round itself is a possible outcome.

INDEX

Aegean Continental Shelf case 108n. 75
Agriculture Agreement (WTO) (1994), developing country status and 247
Angola, human rights, compliance 119
Antarctic Treaty (1959) as supplemented by subsequent agreement 57n. 18
APEC 75, 76, 82
The Arantzazu Mendi case 115
arbitration awards relating to territorial disputes, compliance: *see also* Beagle Channel dispute; *Eritrea-Yemen Arbitration* (Phase II); Oriente/Marañón dispute
  binding effect 197
  comparisons 202–203
  factors affecting 199, 204, 205, 211, 212–213, 214–215
  Latin American record 11–12, 194, 201, 202–205: *see also* Latin America
  legalization 197, 205
arbitration, reasons for recourse to: *see* Latin America, arbitration, reasons for resort to
Argentina: *see also* Beagle Channel dispute
  dispute settlement, commitment to 204
arms control agreements, compliance 10, 161–163, 228, 236–237: *see also* Chemical Weapons Convention (1993); landmines; Limitation of Anti-Ballistic Missile Systems Treaty (1972), compliance; Non-Proliferation of Nuclear Weapons Treaty (1968), compliance
Asbestos case 253
ASEAN 76, 82
ASEAN-EU Joint Declaration (1994) 274–275

Balance of Payments Understanding case 270, 276n. 25
  India – Balance of Payments case 270
Bananas case 267, 269
Barcelona Traction case 256
Beagle Channel dispute 209–213
  UK Arbitration Award (1977) 210, 211–213
Beef Hormones case 267, 271, 291
Beijing Conference on Women (1995) 72, 73
Beijing Declaration on the Rights of Women (1995), non-binding nature, relevance 52
Biological Diversity Convention (1992) 57n. 18, 147–148
boundary delimitation
  equity and
    land boundaries 106–107
    maritime boundaries
    international rivers
      equity and 109: Beagle Channel dispute 109; *Oder* River case 109
  land boundaries 106–107
  maritime boundaries
    relevant circumstances 108–109, 109n. 79
Brazil, compliance record 118–119

299

Brazil – Rubber Footwear case 266, 276, 279
Bretton Woods 235, 239

Cameroon, compliance record 118–119
Canada, AD laws 233
Chemical Weapons Convention (1993), incentives to improve capacity 161–163
China
  compliance record 118–119
  human rights undertakings in relation to WTO 67n. 37, 128
CITES (1973), compliance 118–119, 134–136, 140, 141, 148–149
civil society, role 9, 139, 147, 150, 164, 165
civil war, human rights and 119
climate change 63
Climate Change, Framework Convention (1992), compliance 6, 147–148, 149–150
collective action: *see* international cooperation
compliance: *see also individual agreements*
  arbitration awards: *see* arbitration awards relating to territorial disputes, compliance
  definition 140–141, 171n. 20
  developing states and 8–9, 11, 40–41, 117, 118n. 1, 118–119, 120–121, 130–131, 132–133, 153, 190–192
    see also reputation, role *and* strategies for ensuring compliance *below*
  factors affecting 40–41, 171–182, 183
    acceptance and internalization of evolving norms 5, 11, 36, 38n. 68, 65, 179, 181, 183, 214: unachievable norms 192
    agreement on common rules 177
    alienation from norm-setting group 11, 182–183
    ambiguity of treaty language/norm 11, 120, 182, 231

battle fatigue 208–209
capacity to implement 9–10, 120, 137, 143, 144–146, 150–151, 156, 164, 198: *see also* strategies for ensuring, incentives to improve capacity *below*
common interests 9, 24, 27–28, 208–209
conflict of national and international norms 11, 182, 188–190
domestic politics 46–48, 137, 144–146, 231
external shocks 120, 230, 235–237, 241–242
face-saving possibilities 208–209
globalization: *see also* globalization
incorporation of obligations into national law 60, 197, 214
information about likely behavior 10–11, 27, 175–176, 178, 188, 192–193, 231
international expectation of compliance 121, 122, 143, 197
international Secretariat monitoring and compliance-related support 143
iteration of actions 175–176, 177, 178: globalization and 10–11, 184, 185, 192–193
justification for derogation 214–215, 225–226
large country leadership 144
large country participation 144
market demand 143
negative externalities 67, 175: rebound, risk of 11, 192–193
NGO involvement 143
normative consensus 199, 204, 214
number of participating countries/firms 141
political system (and size) of country concerned 143, 197, 205, 214
Prisoner's Dilemma (PD) 175–176
rationalism 173–174

reciprocity 27, 197, 204, 214
record of performance in relevant area 143
retaliation, scope for 10–11, 175–176, 178, 184–185, 192–193
social, economic and political changes/crises 120, 141, 143, 144–146, 198
stochastic costs of compliance varying applicability 138, 144–146, 150: over time 124–125, 138, 144–146, 150, 164–165
varying content of obligation 138
varying value of agreement to signatories 40–41, 125–126, 144–146, 197: discount factor 10–11, 175–176, 178
vital interests 212–213
vulnerability of developing countries: *see* developing countries and *above*
willingness/intention to comply 134–136, 141, 144, 145–146, 150–151
human rights agreements 119, 134–136
Latin America 11–12, 194, 198–215
as non-issue 54
as norm 9, 53–54, 134–136, 141, 166, 181–182, 194–195, 196, 197: post-1988; reliability of evidence 118n. 1
penalties for non-compliance/varying level of compliance balance 125, 175–176
 GATT 125
reputation, role 7–9, 40–41, 117–118, 197: *see also* Constructivism
 arbitration awards 204, 214
 Assurance Game 176
 Constructivism and 180–183
 determination of attractiveness as treaty partner 121–123, 132

developing state/developing state relationships 8–9, 131
dispute settlement mechanisms compared 117
encouragement to comply 146
erosion of general compliance expectations/multilateral cooperation 121, 122
inefficiency of according poor reputation 123–124
institutionalism and 27
iteration of actions, relevance 175–176, 177, 178, 184, 185, 192–193
linkage penalties distinguished 128–129
multilateral agreements regulating private goods 8–9, 131–132
multilateral agreements regulating public goods 8–9, 132
multiple reputations/selective assessment 118, 123–129, 132–133: cross-impact between organizations 127–128; developed states as beneficiaries 7–9, 118, 131–132, 133; developing states as beneficiaries 40–41, 118, 129–130; developing states as losers 8–9, 130–132; US, UN and NATO compliance 127
reputation as a non-reality 123, 126–127, 128–129
sanctions compared 117
strategies for ensuring: *see also* factors affecting *above*
 incentives to improve capacity 9–10, 147–148, 150, 164
 institutional arrangements 149–150, 163, 191–192
 peer group pressure 181
 penalties 125, 128–129, 148, 184–185
 political incentives 163

INDEX

compliance (*cont.*)
  sanctions 9–10, 117, 139, 148–149, 150–151: arms control agreements 10, 163; public goods/free-rider issues 149; WTO 151–155
  screening 65–66
  transparency/empowerment of non-state actors ('sunshine' strategies) 9–10, 139, 146–148, 150–151: *see also* incentives to improve capacity *above*
    advantages/disadvantages 150
    arms control agreements 10
    civil society pressure 9, 46–48, 139, 147, 150, 164, 165
    experts, role 147
    human rights/labor agreements 9–10, 158–161
    informal persuasion by signatories and Secretariats 146, 158
    information technology 139, 146
    institutionalism and 27
    monitoring 146, 147, 161, 225
    naming and shaming 146, 148, 150: *see also* reputation, role *above*
    national reporting obligation 146, 147, 157–158, 161
    on-site consultancy 146
    public access to information 146, 242
    scrutiny of reports 146
    Trade Policy Review Mechanism (TPRM) 155, 156–157, 225
    WTO 153, 155–158
  variation and targeting, need for 150
Constructivism: *see also* calculation/socialization; institutionalism; Liberalism; norm-setting process; Rationalism; Realism
  calculation, role 5, 36–37, 38n. 68
  compliance and 179–183: *see also* compliance
  factors affecting 5, 11, 36–37, 38n. 68, 179, 181–183, 188–190, 191

  as evolutionary process 37, 180
  globalization, effect 11
  international law and 5, 37
  Liberalism and 39
  as ontology 34–35
  pacta sunt servanda 196
  Realism, shared presumptions 35
  reputation, role 180–183
  social structure as basis of individual choice/norm-setting 36, 179
Continental Shelf (Libya/Malta) case 96, 108–109
Continental Shelf (Tunisia/Libya) case 107–108
Continental Shelf (Tunisia/Libya) (Application for Revision) case 107
Corn Syrup case 267
Council of Europe
  as combination of FC and PL Pathways 81
  Program of Assistance with the Development and Consolidation of Democratic Stability (ADACS) 159–161
Croatia, human rights, compliance 119
customary international law: *see also* state practice
  burden of proof 93–94
  conflict between norms and practice 102–104
  conflicting conceptions of rules 92–93
  efficiency principle, as proxy for 7, 87, 88–104: *see also* efficient distribution of natural resources
    as justification for unilateral modification of international law 102–104
    objectivity/subjectivity conflict, resolution 103–104
    as replacement for state consent requirement 104
  state practice, effectiveness 88–90
  in national courts 115
  reciprocity as governing force 88–89
    diplomatic relations
    war, laws of

requirements 20–21, 85–87, 87n. 9, 104: *see also* state practice
as strategy for legalization of soft law
sui generis norm 100–101

delimitation: *see* boundary delimitation
demonstration, role 58–59, 60, 67, 69
developing countries: *see also* compliance, developing states and; globalization
definition as 245–249
least developed countries (LDCs) 249, 258–259
OECD membership, relevance 245
Trade Policy Review Mechanism (TPRM) 247–248
WTO/GATT and: *see also* Generalized System of Preferences (GSP); human rights, WTO/GATT and; Subsidies and Countervailing Measures Agreement (SCM); TRIPS (1994) 246, 249, 258–259
dispute settlement 117, 198–199, 200, 204, 208–209, 214–215: *see also* arbitration awards relating to territorial disputes, compliance; co-existence with undemocratic domestic regimes 11–12, 200–201
WTO system 60, 74–79, 83–84
dispute settlement agreements (Latin America) 198–199, 201

East Timor, human rights, compliance 119
EC – Asbestos case 277
EC – Conditions for Granting of Tariff Preferences to India case
Ecuador: *see* Oriente/Marañón dispute
efficient breach theory 220, 241
efficient distribution of natural resources: *see also* equity; transboundary resources
boundary delimitation 106–107
constraints 88, 90, 92–98, 113–114
customary international law as proxy: *see* customary international law, efficiency principle, as proxy for
efficiency/fairness equilibrium 104–105, 106: *see also* equity
'efficient norm' 88
environment: *see also* efficient distribution of natural resources; environment agreements; GATT XX justification; Generalized System of Preferences (GSP), conditionality as alleged breach of requirements; transboundary pollution
customary international norms, inadequacy 102–103
economic growth and 281–282
as global commons/public good 293–294
Global Environmental Facility (GEF) 147–148
WTO/GATT 250, 251, 280–282
environmental agreements 57: *see also* Biological Diversity Convention (1992); CITES (1972), compliance; Climate Change, Framework Convention (1992), compliance; compliance; London Convention on Marine Dumping (1972), compliance; Montreal Supplementary Protocol on the Protection of the Ozone Layer (1987); Tropical Timber Agreement (1983/1994), compliance; Vienna Convention for the Protection of the Ozone Layer (1985); Watercourses Convention (1997); World Heritage Convention (1972), compliance
compliance 10, 132, 148–149, 165
FC Pathway 57
epistemic communities: *see* experts, role

equity
  as discretion 106
    as ad hoc solution 106
    boundary delimitation 106–107:
      see also boundary delimitation
    efficiency/fairness equilibrium
      104–106
    equity ex aequo et bono distinguished
      106
    as equity of needs 109–113
    as incentive to international
      cooperation/negotiation
      111–113
    as fairness 104–106
    fairness distinguished 106, 107–109
    as incentive to efficiency 106,
      109–110, 111, 113
Eritrea-Yemen Arbitration (Phase II)
escape clauses: see safeguard clauses
EU
  anti-bribery treaties 76
  as combination of FC and PL
    Pathways 81
  compliance 118–119, 153, 225
  PL Pathway 6, 58–59, 65–66
EU Regulations
  2501/2001 (generalized tariff
    preferences) 263, 277–278,
    280–282: see also Generalized
    System of Preferences (GSP),
    conditionality
    consistency with GATT I:1
      281–284, 285–290, 291–292,
      294–295
  2641/84 (EEC) (strengthening of
    CCP against illicit commercial
    practices) 153
European Convention on Human
  Rights (1950) 81, 256
European Payments Union (EPU),
  safeguard clause 235, 239
exchange rate agreements, safeguard
  clauses 235–236, 239
Exchange Rate Mechanism (ERM),
  safeguard clause 235–236, 239
experts, role 64, 72, 99–102, 147
extra-territorial jurisdiction 286–288,
  288n. 44

fairness: see equity
FAO Code of Conduct on Pesticides
  (1985) 59
Filartiga 73
Financial Action Task Force 60n. 26,
  76–77
fisheries jurisdiction 95–96, 97, 102
Framework Convention Pathway 6,
  55–57: see also Soft Law
  Pathway, in combination with
  FC Pathway
  administrative support, need for 74,
    77
  binding effect 55–56
    advantages of legally binding
      agreement 63, 64–65
    in combination with PL Pathway
      81–82
  compliance, as norm 53–54
  definition 55–57, 60–61, 64–65
  NGOs and 74
  norm-setting process 56n. 16, 56–58,
    58n. 22, 64–65
  Rationalism 60, 64–65: see also
    Plurilateral Pathway
  states' preference for 72
  uncertainty and 62–65, 72
  Vienna Convention for the
    Protection of the Ozone Layer
    (1985) 6, 57
freedom of navigation, efficiency 90,
  93–94

Gabcikovo-Nagymaros 85–87, 94,
  99–100
game theory 174–176, 177–178: see also
  norm-setting process;
  Rationalism
Generalized System of Preferences
  (GSP) 14–15, 261–262,
  263–264, 270n. 22, 269–271,
  272, 273–277, 277n. 26, 279,
  280–283, 295–296, 298
  Enabling Clause 14–15, 246,
    258–259, 261–262, 264–267,
    268–269, 270, 271–272, 273,
    274–279, 280–284, 295–298:
    see also conditionality as alleged

breach of requirements *above*;
requirements *below*
Geneva Convention on Conventional Weapons with Excessively Injurious or Indiscriminate Effect (1980), optional protocol approach 82
Global Environmental Facility (GEF) 147–148
globalization 10–11, 168–169, 184–186, 188–193
  Constructivism and 11, 168–169
  inequality and 169–170
  linkages 184–185
  multifaceted nature 168
  negative externalities, effect on 11, 185–188
  non-state actors, role 10–11, 169, 185–188: *see also* multinational corporations; NGOs
  territorial/relational communities, effect on 189–190
  as transformational process 167–168
Grotius, H. 89, 90, 103
Gulf of Maine case 109

Havana Club case 284
Helsinki Final Act, non-binding effect, relevance 54
human rights 10, 88, 113–114, 119, 134–136, 158–161, 255: *see also* labor rights

ICJ, legislative role: *see* judicial legislation
ILC Draft Articles on State Responsibility, *ius cogens* 256
ILO 159, 263, 277, 285–286, 289–290
incorporation: *see* international law, incorporation into national law
India 119, 121
India – Balance of Payments case 270
India – Quantitative Restrictions on Imports of Agricultural, Textile and Industrial Products case

information, role 176, 185
  compliance 175–176, 178, 185, 188, 192–193, 224–225, 242
  globalization and 10–11, 188, 192–193
  trade barriers, effect 224–225
information technology (IT)
  compliance, role in promoting 139, 146, 185, 189, 192–193
  'digital divide' 169–170
institutional setting, effect on international cooperation 45–46, 51, 74–79: *see also* institutionalism
  administrative support, need for 74, 76–78
  exclusion of 75–76
  forum, choice: *see* forum; forum shopping
  strengthening the weak element, inadequacy of processes 76
  PL Pathway 76
  SL Pathway 76
institutionalism 25–28: *see also* institutional setting, effect on international cooperation
  assumptions 26–27
  common interest, need for/absence 27–28, 38
  compliance, factors affecting and 27: *see also* compliance, factors affecting
  international law and 25, 28
  linkages and 38
  negotiation and 27
  public goods/free-rider issues 38n. 68
  reciprocity and 27
  as reflection of prevailing state power 21, 40–41
  regime theory 25–26, 38
  reputation, role 27
  transaction costs and 27, 38
  UN Charter and 5, 28
interest-based policies: *see* Rationalism
international agreement: *see also* legalization; Soft Law Pathway

international agreement (*cont*).
  binding effect, relevance 52, 54: *see also* Framework Convention pathway, binding effect
  effectiveness, criteria 51–52
international cooperation 10–11, 51, 83–84, 111–113, 173–174, 216–219: *see also* game theory; institutional setting, effect on international cooperation; institutionalism; negotiation; trade agreements
  incremental approach 50n. 1, 50–51, 54, 64–65, 69–70, 71, 83n. 55, 221–227: *see also* Constructivism
  interests of protagonists, role 51
  Liberalism and 31
  opposition tactics 61, 63–64, 139n. 17
  pathways: *see also* Framework Convention Pathway; Plurilateral Pathway; Soft Law Pathway
    blending and sequencing 79–84
    choice 7, 40–41, 54–55, 60–61, 68n. 38, 62–76, 83: *see also* identity of protagonists, effect on choice of pathway; institutional setting, effect on international cooperation; uncertainty, effect on choice of pathway/as constraint on international cooperation
  transaction costs 86–87, 90–91, 99
  institutionalism and 27, 38
  transboundary resources: *see* transboundary resources
  variation, reasons for 216–217
International Covenant on Civil and Political Rights (1966) 6
International Covenant on Economic, Social and Cultural Rights (1966) 6
International Criminal Court 60
international law: *see also* compliance; positivism; Soft Law Pathway; sovereignty
  consent as basis 20–21, 137, 138
  Constructivism and 5, 37
  dualism 137
  enforceability 122: *see also* compliance
  general principles of: *see also* Latin America, general principles of international law attributable to/applied by
  in dubio mitis 271
  hierarchical nature 137
    networking alternative 137–138
  incorporation into national law
    compliance and 60, 197, 214
    Liberalism and 31–32
  institutionalism and 25, 28
  as instrument of change 3
  liberalism and 5, 31–32
    incorporation of obligations into national law 31–32
  norm-setting process as basis 52–53
  public/private international law as part of 138
  Realism and 23–25, 40–41
  regional law (Latin America) 200–201
  sources
    as bottom up process 47–48
    decisions of national courts 115
  subjects: *see also* globalization; multinational corporations; NGOs
    entities other than states 137–138
    individual as sovereign unit 138–139
    states: *see* state, as principal subject of international law
  theory, role 17–20
    trade conflicts 18–19
    war, prevention 18
international rivers 85–87, 93–95, 99–100, 109–113: *see also* Watercourses Convention (1997)
  equity and 109
  human rights and 113–114
  as shared resource 94
  interpretation of legislation, as strategy for legalization of soft law 73

INDEX 307

ius cogens
  Barcelona Traction case 256
  ILC Draft Articles on State
    Responsibility 256
  Vienna Convention on the Law of
    Treaties (1969) 256
  WTO/GATT and 14, 255, 256–257

Jan Mayen case 109n. 79
Japan, compliance record 118–119
judicial legislation
  Continental Shelf (Libya/Malta) case
    96
  customary international law
    application as a guise for 7, 97–98
    sui generis norm 100–101
  disincentives to litigation 90–91
  efficient distribution of natural
    resources 7, 43, 90–91, 92,
    93–97, 98, 99–101, 102
  Eritrea-Yemen Arbitration (Phase II)
    100–101
  Fisheries Jurisdiction cases 95–97, 102
  Gabcikovo-Nagymaros case 85–87,
    94, 99–100
  implicit 90
  justification 7, 94, 95, 98, 99–102,
    115–116
  Lac Lanoux Arbitration 94–95
  legalized agreements, limitation to
    43
  as legitimate function under
    international law 7, 86–87, 98,
    115–116
  negotiation as [preferred] alternative
    96–97: *see also* negotiation;
    advantages of judicial
    legislation 115–116
  Oder case 93–94
  as residual function 86–87, 90,
    96–97
  Trail Smelter Arbitration 94
judicial restraint, WTO dispute
  settlement (DSU) 265–266,
  270, 296

Kodak – Fuji case 253
Korea – Restrictions on Imports of Beef
  case 246

Korea – Restrictions on Imports of
  Beef II case 247
Kyoto Protocol 57, 63–64

labor agreements 9–10, 158–161
labor rights: *see also* GATT XX
    justification, labor rights
    conditionality; Generalized
    System of Preferences (GSP),
    conditionality as alleged breach
    of requirements
  economic growth and 280–281, 288
  ILO Declaration on Fundamental
    Principles and Rights at Work
    (1998) 14, 186–187, 257–259,
    261, 263, 277, 285–286,
    289–290
  Singapore Declaration (1996) 277,
    288, 289–290
Lac Lanoux Arbitration 79, 94–95
Latin America
  arbitration, reasons for recourse to
    202, 214
  compliance record 11–12, 194, 201,
    202–205: *see also* arbitration
    awards relating to territorial
    disputes, compliance;
    arbitration awards relating to
    territorial disputes, compliance
    204
  dispute settlement 11–12, 198–199,
    201, 204, 205, 214
  dispute settlement agreements
    198–199, 201
  general principles of international
    law attributable to/applied by
    199, 200–201
  legalization 41–43, 52–54: *see also*
    Framework Convention
    Pathway, binding effect
  advantages 60
  definition 41–42, 54n. 13
  elements 41–42, 51–54, 60
  SL Pathway 43–44, 60, 73
  states' power to control 57n. 17
  territorial dispute 205
legitimacy
  judicial legislation 7, 86–87, 98,
    115–116

legitimacy (cont.)
    norm-setting process 56–57, 60, 65, 70–71, 182–183, 191
Liberalism 29–32: see also Constructivism; institutionalism; Rationalism; Realism
    assumptions 29–30
    Constructivism and 39
    definition 29
    international law and 5, 31–32
    social identity and 39
    state as representative/reflection of society 5, 29–32, 39
        implications for conflict resolution/cooperation 31
Limitation of Anti-Ballistic Missile Systems Treaty (1972), compliance 163
    US withdrawal, reasons 236n. 33
linkages, role 38, 128–129, 184–185
London Convention on Marine Dumping (1972), compliance
    Protocol (1996), compliance, institutional arrangements 149–150
    Russian military dumping of radioactive wastes in the Arctic 140–141
Long-Range Transboundary Air Pollution Convention (LRTPA) (1979) 6, 57n. 18
Lotus- case 85n. 2, 93–94, 137n. 11, 287–288

maritime delimitation: see boundary delimitation
MARPOL 67n. 36
Mercosur, PL Pathway 58–59
MFN treatment (GATT I/GATS II) 249
Military and Paramilitary Activities case 288n. 44
Montreal Supplementary Protocol on the Protection of the Ozone Layer (1987) 57, 67n. 6: see also Vienna Convention for the Protection of the Ozone Layer (1985)
compliance
    incentives to improve capacity 147–148
    institutional arrangements 149–150
    sanctions 148–149
multinational corporations 169

NAFTA, PL Pathway 58–59, 66
national treatment (GATT III/GATS XVII) 249
NATO, PL Pathway 65–66
natural resources: see efficient distribution of natural resources; international rivers; Watercourses Convention (1997)
negative externalities 11, 67, 175, 186–187, 192–193
negotiation
    incentives 111–113
    institutionalism and 27
    judicial legislation as preferred alternative 115–116
    as [preferred] alternative 96–97
    UNLOSC III 96–97
NGOs
    Beijing Conference on Women (1995) 73
    compliance, role in promoting/obstructing 143, 147
    FC Pathway 74
    globalization and 169
    PL Pathway 74
    Rio Conference on Environment and Development (1992) 73
    SL Pathway, advantages 73–74
non-discrimination principle, WTO/GATT 249–250
non-intervention as general principle of international law 199
Non-Navigational Uses of International Watercourses Convention (1997): see Watercourses Convention (1997)

Non-Proliferation of Nuclear Weapons
    Treaty (1968), compliance
    121
  political incentives 163
  transparency/empowerment of
    non-state actors ('sunshine'
    strategies) 163
norm-setting process: *see also*
    Constructivism;
    demonstration, role;
    legalization; rationalism
  forum for, UNEP 70–71
  FC Pathway: *see* Framework
    Convention Pathway,
    norm-setting process
  international law, dependence for
    authority on 52–53
  legitimacy 56–57, 60, 65, 70–71,
    182–183, 191
  PL Pathway 67–69: *see also*
    Plurilateral Pathway
  SL Pathway 70–71
North Sea Continental Shelf cases 85,
    107, 108

Oder River case 93–94, 109
OECD
  developing country status and
    245
  effectiveness as plurilateral
    organization
  SL Pathway 75n. 47
  strengthening the weak element,
    inadequacy of processes 76
OECD Anti-Bribery Convention
    (1997) 75n. 47
  SL leading to FC Pathway 80
  SL/FC leading to PL Pathway
    82–83
  optional protocol approach 81–82
    Geneva Convention on
      Conventional Weapons with
      Excessively Injurious or
      Indiscriminate Effect (1980) 82
Oriente/Marañón dispute 195, 206,
    208–209
  Rio Protocol (1942) 206–209
    terms 206

Ottawa Convention on the
    Prohibition of Anti-Personnel
    Landmines (1997) 50n. 1, 69,
    161–163
ozone depletion, difficulty in achieving
    consensus 63: *see also* Vienna
    Convention for the Protection
    of the Ozone Layer

pacta sunt servanda 195–197
  WTO non-violation complaint and
    252
Pakistan, human rights, compliance
    119
pathways: *see* international
    cooperation, pathways;
    Framework Convention
    Pathway; Plurilateral Pathway;
    Soft Law Pathway
Peru: *see* Oriente/Marañón dispute
Pesticides Convention 59
Plurilateral Pathway 6, 58, 59, 60–61,
    65, 66, 67–68, 74, 75, 77–78,
    82–83
  FC Pathway compared: *see also*
    Framework Convention
    Pathway, in combination with
    PL Pathway
  free-rider issues 66–67
  negative externalities 67, 175
  NGOs and 74
  norm-setting process 67–69
  non-members and 69
  parallel systems 67
  Rationalism 58–59, 60, 67–68
  screening 65–66, 69n. 39
  states' preference for 72
  strengthening the weak element,
    inadequacy of processes 76
  third party institutions 66
  UN 75–76
  uncertainty and 62–63, 65–69:
    see also screening *above*
positivism 16n. 1, 24–25, 104, 137
  see also Realism
pressure group influence 46–48,
    222–227
protectionism: *see* trade barriers

310 INDEX

public morals
    labor rights and 261, 285–290
    Shrimp/Turtle 261
    territorial nexus, relevance 286–288
public order, human rights and 255

Rationalism: *see also* calculation/
        socialization; Constructivism;
        game theory; institutionalism;
        Liberalism; norm-setting
        process; Realism
    compliance and 173–174
    definition
    FC Pathway 60, 64–65
    globalization, effect 10–11
    pacta sunt servanda 196
    PL Pathway 58–59, 60, 67–68
    as privileged theory 5, 37
        Constructivist alternative 38
    Realism, Liberalism and
        institutionalism, relation to 173
    SL Pathway 70
Realism: *see also* Constructivism; game
        theory; institutionalism;
        Liberalism; norm-setting
        process; positivism;
        Rationalism
    assumptions 5, 20–21, 22, 23, 24
    Constructivism, shared
        presumptions 35
    as descriptive process 23
    international law, applicability to
        23–25, 40–41
    positivism and 24–25
regime design: *see* institutional setting,
        effect on international
        cooperation
regime theory 25–26, 38: *see also*
        institutionalism
regional economic integration 59n. 24,
        66; *see also* EU; Latin America;
        NAFTA
renegotiation clauses 62n. 30
reputation: *see* compliance, reputation,
        role; Constructivism
Rio Conference on Environment and
        Development (1992), NGOs 73

Rio Declaration on Environment and
        Development (1992),
        non-binding nature, relevance
        52, 54
rivers: *see* international rivers

safeguard clauses 219–221, 227–243
    arms control agreements 228,
        236–237
    cost of invoking, relevance 13, 220,
        229–230, 231–232, 237–239
    definition 219, 228
    domestic pressure and: *see*
        uncertainty and *below*
    efficiency principle 220
    exchange rate agreements 235–236,
        239
    flexibility 13, 219–221, 227–229,
        239–243
    reciprocity and 231–232
    as reflection of national practice
        233–235
        Canadian AD laws 233
        US AD laws 233–235
    renegotiation provision as
        alternative 241
    uncertainty and 12, 219–221, 229,
        230–233, 239–243
        democracies and 235, 242–243
        domestic shocks 231, 239–243
        exchange rate agreements and
            235–236
        external shocks 230, 235–237,
            241–242
    varying forms 228–229
    WTO/GATT: *see* WTO/GATT,
        safeguard clauses
sanctions as means of ensuring
        compliance 9–10, 117, 139,
        148–149
    environmental agreements 10,
        148–149
Sanitary and Phytosanitary Measures
        Agreement (SPS)
    'best efforts' nature of obligations
        267
    notification obligations 157–158

INDEX

separation of powers, judicial respect for executive as impediment to effective use of customary international law 115
Shrimp/Turtle case 251, 261–264, 286–287, 292–294
Sierra Leone, human rights, compliance 119
Singapore Declaration (1996) 277, 288, 289–290
Soft Law Pathway 6, 43–45, 59: *see also* Plurilateral Pathway, in combination with SL Pathway
  administrative support, need for 76–77
  advantages 42–43, 44, 50n. 2
    see also NGOs, Soft Law Pathway, advantages 44, 69–70, 72
  as alternative to PL Pathway 67–68
  in combination with FC Pathway 75n. 47, 80–81
  definition 6, 43–44, 54n. 11, 59, 60–61, 70–71
  government ministries' and officials' preference
    avoidance of domestic negotiating and approval processes
    flexibility
  international law, whether 43–44, 138
  international officials' preference 72
  judicial legislation and 43
  legalization 43–44, 60, 73
  methods of limiting legal obligation 54
  NGOs' preference 73–74: *see also* NGOs, Soft Law Pathway, advantages
  norm-setting process 70–71
  OECD 75n. 47
  Rationalism 70
  states' preference for 44, 72: *see also* advantages *above*
  strengthening the weak element, inadequacy of processes 76
  uncertainty and 62–63, 69–70, 71, 72
  WTO 75

sovereignty: *see also* state
  as basis of international law 20–21, 137
  developing country status, right to claim 245
  instrument for distribution of powers, limitation to 104
  limitations on, presumption against 271, 287–288
  maritime delimitation and 107–108, 108n. 75
  natural resources and
  territorial nature 5, 24
state
  demise/declining relevance 138–139, 169, 190: *see also* globalization
  equality 199
  'government' as alternative 30
  interdependence and 30–31
  Liberalism and 29–32, 39
  as principal subject of international law 20–21, 23, 137, 190
    institutionalism and 26–27
    Realism and 20–21, 22
  as representative/reflection of society 5, 29–32, 39
    implications for conflict resolution/cooperation 31
  territory as basis 5, 24
state practice
  conflict with norms 102–104
  customary law, as requirement for 85–87
    objectivity/subjectivity conflict 103–104
  as rule of the strong 88–89, 93
  efficiency principle and 88–90, 115–116
  efficient breach of treaty 220, 241
  Grotius and 89–90
  judicial legislation as response to failure to implement 7, 115–116: *see also* judicial legislation
  market failures as constraint 92–98
    changing practice/technology 95–97

state practice (*cont.*)
    conflict of state interests 92–93
    domestic pressure group influence 46–48, 217–218
    transnational pressure group influence 92, 93
    modification of rule as response to inefficiency 88–89
Subsidies and Countervailing Measures Agreement (SCM)
    developing country status and 245, 248n. 9
    non-violation complaint/bindings and 252–253
'sunshine' strategies: *see* compliance, strategies for ensuring, transparency/empowerment of non-state actors ('sunshine' strategies)
sustainable development principle 54n. 12, 95–96, 99–100
    human right 114
    Johannesburg World Summit (2002), civil society, role 165
    Preamble to WTO Agreement 281–282
    Tropical Timber Agreement (1983/1994) 119, 263–264, 292–294: *see also* GATT XX justification, environmental conditionality (tropical timber products); Generalized System of Preferences (GSP), conditionality

taxation, right to define own policies, WTO/GATT 251
technical experts: *see* experts, role
technical uncertainty: *see* uncertainty, effect on choice of pathway/as constraint on international cooperation, technical uncertainty
territorial disputes: *see* Oriente/Marañón dispute; arbitration awards relating to territorial disputes, compliance; Beagle Channel dispute

third party institutions: *see also* arbitration awards relating to territorial disputes, compliance; dispute settlement; legalization
    Financial Action Task Force 60n. 26
    legalization and 41–42, 53–54, 60
    WTO dispute settlement (DSU) 60
trade agreements: *see also* EU; WTO/GATT
    domestic politics 12–13, 216–226, 227–243: *see also* safeguard clauses
    reasons for concluding 221: *see also* domestic politics *above*
    gains equal to or greater than those from unilateral policy setting 224–227
    pressure group influence, as means of reconciling 12–13, 222–227, 242
    safeguard clauses: *see* safeguard clauses
trade barriers
    disadvantages to economy 222–223
    negative externalities 186–187
    public attitudes towards 222–224
trade conflicts, prevention, theory, role 18–19
Trade Policy Review Mechanism (TPRM)
    developing country status, relevance 247–248
    transparency/empowerment of non-state actors ('sunshine' strategies) 155, 156–157, 225
Trail Smelter Arbitration 94, 99
transboundary pollution 6, 57n. 18, 94, 103n. 61
transboundary resources 100–101, 113–114, 186: *see also* efficient allocation of natural resources; international rivers; judicial legislation; transboundary pollution; Watercourses Convention (1997)
treaty interpretation
    in absence of guidance from text or state practice 93–94

INDEX 313

ambiguity as cause of non-compliance 120, 124–126, 198, 231
Doha Decision on Implementation of GSP (2001), role 270n. 22
ordinary meaning in light of object, purpose and context 266–267
as at time of implementation 286, 291
subsequent practice/agreement as aid 57n. 18, 270n. 22, 275–276, 279, 280–282
treaty obligations: *see also* compliance
incorporation into domestic law 60, 197, 214
TRIPS (1994)
developing country status 246–247
incremental approach 50n. 1
positive integration and 255
Tropical Timber Agreement (1983/1994): *see also* GATT XX justification, environmental conditionality (tropical timber products); Generalized System of Preferences (GSP), conditionality
compliance 118–119
incentives to improve capacity 147–148
global commons/public good considerations 293–294
sustainable development principle 119, 263–264, 292–294
Truman Proclamation (1945) 97
Turkey–Restrictions on Imports of Textiles and Clothing case 265–266
Turkey–Textiles case 265–266, 269, 270

Uganda, human rights, compliance 119
UN, PL Pathway, exclusion 75–76
UN Charter, as institutionalist instrument 5, 28
UN General Assembly
FC Pathway, exclusion 75
PL Pathway, exclusion 75
strengthening the weak element, inadequacy of processes 76

UN Secretariat, support services 76–77
UN Secretary-General's Office, Global Compact 79
UNAIDS, creation 79
uncertainty, effect on choice of pathway/as constraint on international cooperation 62–71
examples 62, 231
FC Pathway and 62–63: *see also* Framework Convention Pathway
technical uncertainty 63–65
incremental approach, advantages 51, 54
institutional need to address issues raised by 62n. 29
institutionalism and 27
PL Pathway and 62–63
actor uncertainty 65–69: *see also* Plurilateral Pathway
political uncertainty
actor uncertainty 65–70
domestic considerations 69–71
safeguard clauses and 12, 219–221, 229, 230–233, 239–243
SL Pathway and 62–63, 69–71, 72: *see also* Soft Law Pathway
technical uncertainty 63–65
changing values 64–65
examples 63
FC Pathway and 63–65, 72
opposition tactics 63–64
UNCTAD, Generalized System of Preferences (GSP) and: *see* Generalized System of Preferences (GSP)
UNEP
Chemicals Guidelines (1989) 59
as forum for norm-setting process 70–71
Guidelines on Compliance with and Enforcement of Multilateral Environmental Agreements (2002) 165
support services 76–77
UNHCHR human rights training 159

United States
  AD laws 153, 233–235
  compliance 118–119
  UN/NATO 127
  Vienna Convention on Consular Relations (1963) 134
  WTO, unilateral measures to enforce 153
  labor rights/environment conditionality 263
  political effect of determination of inconsistency with WTO/GATT 298
  Limitation of Anti-Ballistic Missile Systems Treaty (1972), withdrawal 236n. 33
Universal Declaration of Human Rights (1948) 6
  non-binding nature, relevance 52
US – Customs User Fee case 266
US – Section 211 Omnibus Appropriations Act of 1998 (Havana Club) case 284
US – Sections 301–310 of the Trade Act of 1974 case 283–284
uti possidetis 106–107, 199

Vienna Convention on Consular Relations (1963), compliance 134–136
Vienna Convention on the Law of Treaties (1969): *see also* treaty interpretation
  GATT Enabling Clause, applicability to 266–267, 270n. 22, 272
  ius cogens 256
Vienna Convention for the Protection of the Ozone Layer (1985): *see also* Montreal Supplementary Protocol on the Protection of the Ozone Layer (1987): FC Pathway 6, 57
vital interests 212–213

war
  laws of, reciprocity as governing force 88–89
  prevention, role of theory 18

Watercourses Convention (1997)
  as customary international law 85–87
  equity as incentive to efficiency 109–110, 111
  opposition to 86
  shortcomings 99
WHO Tobacco-Free Initiative, SL leading to FC Pathway 80
World Bank Trade and Development Centre 156
World Heritage Convention (1972), compliance 118–119, 147–149
WTO 2000 156
WTO dispute settlement (DSU) 60, 74–79, 83–84
  applicable law 256n. 24, 265–266, 267–268
  judicial restraint 265–266, 270, 296
  jurisdiction: *see also* Generalized System of Preferences (GSP), justiciability
    India – Balance of Payments case 270
    India – Quantitative Restrictions on Imports of Agricultural, Textile and Industrial Products case 265–266
    non ultra petita 247
    non-mandatory legislation 281–284: in case of threat to security of specific rights 283–284; *US – Sections 301-310 of the Trade Act of 1974* case 283–284
    Turkey – Restrictions on Imports of Textiles and Clothing case 265–266
    Turkey – Textiles case 265–266, 270
  non-violation complaint/bindings 252–253
    Asbestos case 253
    burden of proof 253n. 18
    effectiveness 252
    human rights and 253–254
    Kodak – Fuji case 253

pacta sunt servanda 252
SCM agreement and 252–253
Panel Reports
  binding effect 153–155
  compliance prior to DSU 153
  compliance subsequent to DSU 153–155
  retaliatory/coercive measures by state bringing complaint 153–155, 230–231
  standing
    party not directly affected 284
    US – Section 211 Omnibus Appropriations Act of 1998 (*Havana Club*) case 284
  transparency/confidentiality of proceedings
    amicus curiae briefs 157
WTO enlargement, human rights 67n. 37, 128
WTO Integrated Framework for Trade-Related Technical Assistance to Less-Developed Countries 156
WTO Training Institute 155–156
WTO/GATT: *see also* Agriculture Agreement (WTO) (1994); Sanitary and Phytosanitary Measures Agreement (SPS); Subsidies and Countervailing Measures Agreement (SCM); Trade Policy Review Mechanism (TPRM); TRIPS (1994)
  Balance of Payments Understanding case 270, 276n. 25
  binding nature of agreements 75
  bindings: *see* WTO dispute settlement (DSU), non-violation complaint/bindings
  competence, strict approach to 79
  complexity of evolutionary process 83–84
  compliance 134–136, 151–158
    developing states and, differential obligations 153
    incentives to improve capacity: GATT/WTO trade policy courses 155; World Bank Trade and Development Centre 156; WTO 2000 156; WTO Integrated Framework for Trade-Related Technical Assistance to Less-Developed Countries 156
    sanctions, preference for 10, 151–155
    transparency/empowerment of non-state actors ('sunshine' strategies) 153, 155–158, 225: informal persuasion by signatories and Secretariats 158; national reporting/notification obligation 157–158; Trade Policy Review Mechanism (TPRM) 155, 156–157, 225
    unilateral measures 153
  customs unions and free trade areas (GATT XXIV) 269
  developing countries and: *see* developing countries, WTO/GATT and
  environment policies and 250: *see also* Generalized System of Preferences (GSP)
    Shrimp/Turtle case 251
  erga omnes obligations 284
  FC Pathway, exclusion 75
  GATT enforcement/varying compliance 125
  human rights: *see* human rights, WTO/GATT and
  interpretation of WTO instruments, applicable rules
    Beef Hormones case 267, 291
    Corn Syrup case 267
    ordinary meaning as at time of implementation 286
    Korea – Beef case 289
  as negative integration 14, 249–254
    exceptions: *see* as positive integration *below*

WTO/GATT (*cont.*)
  right to define own policies: environment 14, 251; international standards, obligation to apply 14, 255n. 21; scientific basis, need for 255n. 21; taxation 251
  non-discrimination principle 249–250: *see also* Generalized System of Preferences (GSP)
    MFN treatment (GATT I/GATS II) 249
    national treatment (GATT III/GATS XVII) 249
  PL Pathway, exclusion 75–76
  as positive integration 254
    ius cogens obligations 14, 255, 256–257
    right to impose own policies 254–255
    TRIPS 255
    WTO agreements promoting 254–255
  safeguard clauses 219, 228–229
    GATT VI 234
    GATT XII 246
    GATT XVIII 234, 246
    GATT XIX 234, 237–238, 239
    GATT XX 14–15, 256, 285–287, 288–295, 298: *see also* Generalized System of Preferences (GSP)
    GATT XXVII 234
    reciprocity and 231–232
    renegotiation provision as alternative 241
  SL Pathway, exclusion 75
  taxation, right to define own policies 251
  TBT Agreement, notification obligations 157–158
  waiver (GATT XXV/WTO IX)
    Decision on Generalized System of Preferences (1971) 261–262, 269–270
    Enabling Clause, whether 268–269, 279
    strict reading, need for 268–269: *Bananas* case 267, 269

Yugoslavia, human rights, compliance 119